INJUSTICE
GODS AMONG US

WRITTEN BY:
SAM BISHOP, CARL WHITE,
EMMANUEL BRITO, AND BILL MENOUTIS

PRIMA GAMES • 3000 LAVA RIDGE ROAD • SUITE 100 • ROSEVILLE, CA • 95661 • PRIMAGAMES.COM

CONTENTS

INTRODUCTION

GODS AMONG US

Living in a world with super heroes is a charmed life. Sure, there are villains to deal with, but they're always countered by the forces of good and order. It's a situation that might become commonplace for those living in it: a bad guy causes trouble, and the good guys swoop in, flashing their pearly whites while rattling off a witty catchphrase or striking a stoic pose, all while putting an end to any evildoing. The day is saved, the world keeps spinning (at least until some villain decides to stop it), and all is well. There's a flip side to any sense of safety afforded by beings with super-human abilities, though. What if those who have chosen to uphold order and justice caused the same mayhem and destruction as their enemies, even through no fault of their own? Those same abilities, untethered from the control and restraint normally keeping them in check, could be the most terrifying destructive force on the planet.

Hero. Villain. What really separates the two? And what happens when the barrier between them is completely destroyed?

Injustice: Gods Among Us presents this scenario as a grim reality. Birthed from the minds at NetherRealm Studios in Chicago and supported by a series of DC comics prior to launch, *Injustice* takes the fundamentals of the developer's *Mortal Kombat* series and injects them directly into the DC Comics universe. Though the two were married in the past with *Mortal Kombat vs. DC Universe*, *Injustice* focuses solely on some of DC's most memorable characters, pitting them against one another in a battle that will rend the very fabric of reality. Along the way, the best DC has to offer will encounter a world at once familiar yet dangerously changed by events that could come to pass in their own universe.

INJUSTICE FOR ALL

Designed to be both accessible to new players and deep enough for high-level tournament play, *Injustice* lets you take the reins of some of the DC universe's most memorable characters. Battles take place in arenas littered with interactive objects that can provide speedy escapes or brutal attacks—and many of these battlegrounds offer the chance to launch an enemy into a completely new section of the environment where the battle continues. Though we'll cover exactly how a set of normally mortal characters can go toe-to-toe with those brimming with power in later chapters, know that just because a character isn't normally the type to take a bus to the face, that doesn't necessarily mean they aren't a match for those that can fly and *do* normally take buses to the face.

A NOTE FROM THE AUTHORS

Though we have taken every available precaution to ensure the data presented in this guide are accurate from the moment you fire up the game for the first time, fighting games are by their nature living, ever-changing products. As new insights are discovered by the community, characters' moves and properties, including speed, damage, and combo potential can and often will change in the weeks and months after the game is released. Injustice is an incredibly complex game, and as such will be tinkered with regularly. To that end, we've tried to stick with character strategies that aren't likely to change. In this guide, you should expect to learn the ins and outs of each character in the roster. If something does change though, we'll post the tweaks on www.primagames.com/InjusticeUpdates. While raw numbers are important, timing and learning how to best use your favorites are far more valuable. That's where we've put the bulk of our focus.

TRAINING STARTS HERE

Learning the basics of *Injustice* doesn't take long, but mastering a character won't come easy. Upon first entering the Single Player Menu, you'll be prompted to run through the tutorial. There's no better way to learn things like timing and movement than to actually work with the fighters directly, so we recommend following along. If for some reason you happen to accidentally cancel the tutorial pop-up, all the lessons can be run through again using the Tutorial option in the Practice Menu. If you're the type to just jump in, we'll cover the basics here, but know there's no substitute for hands-on practice.

MOVEMENT

Though *Injustice* operates on a 2D plane, meaning combatants only move left and right in the environment rather than in and out of the foreground or background, movement is still one of the most fundamentally crucial ways to control momentum and pacing. Simply tilting toward or backing away from an opponent using the analog stick or directional buttons will walk a character in that direction, while double-tapping institutes a dash, useful for closing distance or making a hasty retreat. Characters can jump (including forward and backward) or crouch by pressing up and down, respectively. Some characters like Superman and Wonder Woman also have the ability to air dash, providing even more opportunities to surprise your opponent.

ATTACKING

Regardless of the game console you're using, the attack button layouts are exactly the same, and include a Light, Medium, and Hard attack. As the attack strength increases, often the time it takes for that impact to land also increases. Attacks can hit Mid (blocked by simply holding back), High (also blocked by holding back, though High attacks will also pass over a ducking player's head), Low (blocked by crouching or by holding down and back), or Overhead (blocked only while standing). Every character is also equipped with unique Special Moves that deal different types of damage and round out a fighter's repertoire. These simple properties are the crux of all brawls in *Injustice*, but are only the start of the available options for dishing out punishment.

DEFENDING

Injustice may share part of its DNA with previous NetherRealm Studios games, but there's one important distinction: blocking is no longer controlled with a dedicated button. Instead, simply holding Back to move away from an enemy will block Mid, High, and Overhead strikes while standing, and holding Down to block against Low and Mid attacks like sweeps takes care of defense automatically. While there are moves that are unblockable, they're never the first regular attack a character can make, but are instead introduced as part of a combo or special ability. Holding Back blocks incoming strikes automatically, but using back dashes can provide a speedier (and thanks to its built-in attack-nullifying properties, safer) escape.

CHARACTER POWERS

Every *Injustice* fighter has a unique ability that is triggered with the Character Power button. These abilities can buff attacks (making them hit harder or pass through normal defenses), can increase speed, can change the properties of projectiles, and can provide many other offerings that have the potential to turn the tide of battle if used properly. Consult each character's section later in this guide to see not just what the abilities are, but when and where they can be most useful. Powers, like their effects, are unique to each character; some refill automatically and can be used multiple times, others must be built up through attacks, some must be charged up during rare down time, and still others are constantly at the ready. In fact, some characters' strategies revolve around near-constant use of their Power.

SUPER MOVES

Like Powers, each character has his or her own unique, high-damage special attack that, while sometimes block-able, can be devastating if it connects. Super Moves can be introduced in the middle of a combo for added effect, but can only be used when a character's Super Meter is full, and will consume that entire Super Meter when the attack is initiated.

ON DAMAGE AND GRAVITY

While some Supers *can* be used as part of a combo, doing so isn't necessarily advantageous. With every subsequent hit of a combo, the damage for that hit is reduced and the character being attacked will hit the ground a little bit faster. This system keeps players from keeping their opponents in a constant state of being pummeled, and reduces the effectiveness of extremely long juggles. The combos we've developed balance impact with length. Just because a combo incorporates a ton of hits, there's no guarantee that it'll do more damage than a few well-timed, well-chosen ones.

METER BURN

Using any Special Move automatically builds energy for a character's Super Meter. By sacrificing a full section of that Meter, characters can augment a Special attack, lengthening or modifying it in ways that are meant to throw an opponent off his or her rhythm. A projectile may become remotely explosive, or could stack into multiple rapid-fire attacks, for instance. Careful use of Meter Burn moves is what separates those still learning a character from those that have the move sets down pat.

THE CLASH

Injustice's wager system, The Clash, lets defending characters spend part or all of their Super Meter to break out of an incoming attack or combo and turn it back on his or her attacker. By wagering up to four quarters of a Meter, the two fighters will race to the middle of the level and literally clash. If the defender's wager is enough to win The Clash, the defender walks away with a measure of regenerated health equal to the difference in how much the defender wagered. If a defender loses The Clash, the defender absorbs damage equal to the difference between the wager of the defender and that of the attacker. Should both players wager the same amount, The Clash will tie, and no health will be gained or lost, but the amount of the Super Meter wagered will be spent. Clashes are rare; only one can be initiated by a given character per match, and only once the character's second life bar is visible. Because the wagers are based on how much Super Meter has been accrued, The Clash is best attempted when your character has more Super Meter than the character pummeling you. Should you find yourself at a deficit or simply don't wish to expend any Meter unnecessarily, a "fake" bet can be wagered that will spend no Meter by double-tapping the Meter Burn button.

YOU SHALL NOT CLASH

Though most moves can be broken with The Clash, there are at least a couple moves that each and every character has that are Unclashable: their Back+Hard and Forward+Hard attacks. These should be your go-to option when putting final pressure on an opponent to keep him or her from recovering health off a successful Clash. If your opponent has more Super Meter than you, be prepared to integrate Unclashable attacks to pour on the damage and end the match as quickly as possible.

GOT THE MOVES

Any starting player can pull up the in-game moves list and start memorizing the various special attacks for a character. It's how a player strings them together along with some more advanced techniques that elevates the player's game. These strategies are explained in detail for each character later in this guide and in the in-game tutorial, but the basics are universal.

EXTRA OOMPH

Overhead strikes (Forward + Hard) and Level Transition attacks (Back + Hard) used away from the edges of levels have the added benefit of popping a character up into the air for additional juggles. Like most Hard attacks, the wind-up can leave you vulnerable to attack, but the benefits if it connects are huge. Additionally, Overhead attacks can *only* be blocked by a character that is standing. If the character is standing, he or she can't block a Low attack. Conversely, learning which attacks are safely blocked without leaving you vulnerable to a counter-attack during recovery time should be one of the first bits of acclimation to a new character. This concept of safe vs. unsafe will be used liberally throughout the rest of this guide.

THROWS

So an opponent has figured out some of your best combos? They're blocking everything you throw at them, and nothing seems to be slipping past their defenses? The solution — Grab 'em with a throw and punish their lack of offense. Throws come in two flavors: a simple Throw button press and a Back + Throw option when you need to create space (or push someone into a corner). Throws allow for breathing room, letting you set up a new set of moves or reset the rhythm of combat, or they can be integrated into an offensive push to keep your opponent guessing.

WAKEUPS AND TECH ROLLS

When a Special Move is unleashed as a character is getting up after being knocked down, it becomes a Wakeup attack. Wakeups are great for ambushing an enemy that might be waiting for your character to make a standard move, and can slip past the enemy's defenses, opening your opponent up to a combo or punishing blow. Learning the timing for Wakeups can take a bit of practice, so use the aptly named Practice Mode to get a feel for the timing. The Tutorials also indicate the Wakeup window on screen if just reacting to animations isn't clear enough. Alternatively, a Tech Roll can get you back into the fight quickly if you press any of the attack or Character Power buttons the moment your character lands. Like Wakeups, Tech Rolls need practice to pull off reliably, so now you have two things to rehearse in Practice Mode.

COMBOS

The lifeblood of any good fighter, combos allow you to pour on damage while minimizing your opponent's options for counter-attacking. While ground-based combos like a simple Light, Medium, Hard attack string can dole out a measure of damage, it's the integration of Special Moves that helps make them more devastating. Start simply, using a couple of Light or Medium attacks to get a sense of the timing necessary to link in a follow-up Special. The best combos are ones that can eject an opponent into the air, juggling the opponent with a series of hits that can't be blocked. Simply throwing out one Special Move after another might build your Super Meter, but it won't have nearly the same impact as a string of hits or combined Specials.

ESCAPES AND CANCELS

When Super Meter juice isn't at a premium, chunks of the Meter can be sacrificed to perform defensive breaks. Tap the Meter Burn button as an incoming hit is blocked to push your opponent back, causing you both to recover at neutral. The space this move, better known in the fighting game community as a Push Block, creates can create breathing room, or can be used to shift momentum back toward your attacks. By quickly double-tapping Forward or Back and pressing the Meter Burn button at the tail end of a combo, two sections of your Super Meter can be burned to turn the final attack into a Bounce Cancel. Not only are these powerful staggering tools, they leave your opponent open to follow-up attacks by juggling the opponent into the air.

ENVIRONMENTAL INTERACTIONS

The various arenas where combatants square off are anything but static. Every one has numerous objects in the background that can be grabbed, used for speedy escapes, or have players knocked into for quick damage. These areas are highlighted in the Stages section in the next chapter, along with the Level Transition areas useful for piling on unblockable damage (not to mention a change of scenery).

USING PRACTICE MODE

MAIN MENU

After entering Practice Mode, pressing the Start Button will bring up the Main Menu. From here, you can scroll through the Practice Mode options. There is also a Quick Reference moves list where a brief rundown of a few of the Special Moves for both characters is displayed (this will not include Meter Burn Specials, Super Moves, or Character Powers).

MOVE LIST

While in the Practice Mode Main Menu, scrolling over to and selecting the Move List option will bring up a complete list of all a character's moves. Once in the Move List you can select from Move List Menu consisting of Basic Attacks, Combo Attacks, Special Moves, and Character Power. You can also choose to sticky certain moves (up to six at a time) to be displayed while in game during Practice Mode.

BASIC ATTACKS
This will display all of a character's single attacks, meaning attacks that are not a combo string. This will also display your character's Air Attacks and Throws.

COMBO ATTACKS
This will display all of a character's attack strings and their Bounce Cancels.

SPECIAL MOVES
This will display all of a character's Special Moves, Meter Burn Special Moves, and their Super Move along with a description of the moves.

CHARACTER POWER
This will display the Character Power(s) along with a description of what each Character Power does.

When scrolling through each move, the Move Data and Frame Data of each attack is displayed. The Move Data will display the Hit Level of the move as well as the Damage the move inflicts. The Frame Data will display the Start-Up Frames, Recover Frames, Hit Advantage, and Block Advantage of each move.

MOVE DATA
This displays the Hit Level of the move:

High	The move can be blocked standing or crouched under (causing the move to miss).
Mid	The move can be blocked high or in a crouch, but cannot be crouched under.
Low	The move must be blocked from a crouch, and will hit a standing blocking opponent.
Overhead	The move must be blocked from standing and will hit a crouching opponent. The Move Data also includes the damage the move inflicts, meaning the percentage of health the move will take from the opponent upon hitting them.

FRAME DATA
The Frame Data displays the actual data of the move:

Start-Up Frames	The speed of the move; how long it takes the move to impact with the opponent once you have executed the command.
Recovery Frames	How long it takes the character to recover after performing the attack.
Hit Advantage	Refers to what the character's recovery is after landing the move. Hit Advantage is based off of how long it takes the character to recover from the move along with how long it takes the opponent to recover from being hit.
Block Advantage	Refers to what the character's recovery is after the opponent blocks the move. Block Advantage is based off of how long it takes the character to recover from the move along with how long it takes the opponent to recover from the block stun/push back (or lack thereof).

AI OPTIONS

While in the Practice Mode Main Menu, scrolling over and selecting AI Options will bring up the AI Options Menu. From here you can use the Left or Right Bumper on your control pad/joystick to select your enemy type. You can choose between Custom, AI, Human, Record, and Playback.

CUSTOM
Custom Mode allows you to set what you would like the AI to do. Custom Mode offers several options:

Block Mode	This sets how you would like the AI to block. Auto has the AI block at the first available chance after being hit, Stance has the AI block in the position they are in (standing or ducking), Always has the AI block all attacks, and Random has the AI block your attacks at random (great for practicing how to hit confirm attacks into Special Move cancels).
Movement Mode	This sets how you would like the AI to stand or move. You can select Stand, Duck, Jump (jumps straight up), Jump Forward, or Jump Back.
Reversal Mode	This sets the Reversal Attack options. You can choose "OFF" to have the mode remain off, "ON" to enable the AI to execute a Reversal Attack every time at the first possible opportunity after blocking any attack, or "Random" to turn the mode on but have the AI Reversal Attack randomly.
Reversal Attack	This sets the Reversal Attack you would like the AI to perform. "Random" will have the AI perform any one of its Special Moves or Super Move as a Reversal Attack at random, or you can scroll through your Special Moves and Super Move and select a specific Reversal Attack for the AI to perform every time.
Wakeup Mode	This sets the Wakeup Attack options. You can choose "OFF" to have the mode remain off, "ON" to enable the AI to perform a Wakeup Attack every time it is getting up after getting knocked down, or "Random" to turn the mode on but have the AI Wakeup Attack randomly.
Wakeup Attack	This sets the Wakeup Attack you would like the AI to perform. "Random" will have the AI perform any one of its Special Moves or Super Move as a Wakeup Attack at random, or you can scroll through your Special Moves and Super Move and select a specific Wakeup Attack for the AI to perform every time.
Roll Mode	This will set the AI to Tech Roll (if possible) after a knockdown. You can select "OFF" to have the mode remain off, or select "ON" to enable the AI to Tech Roll after knockdowns.
Clash	This sets the AI to initiate a Clash after being hit. You can choose "OFF" to have the mode remain off, "ON" to enable the AI to initiate a Clash at the first possible opportunity after being hit, or "Random" to turn the mode on but have the AI randomly Clash after being hit.
Block Escape	This sets the AI to perform a Block Escape after blocking an attack. You can choose "OFF" to have the mode remain off, "ON" to enable the AI to perform a Block Escape every time it blocks an attack, or "Random" to turn the mode on but have the AI randomly Block Escape after blocking an attack.
Throw Break	This sets the AI to break the universal throws of the game. You can choose "OFF" to have the mode remain off, "ON" to enable the AI to break the throw every time, or "Random" to set the AI to randomly break the throw.
Power	This will set the AI to activate their Character Power. You can choose "OFF" to have the mode remain off, or "ON" to have the AI activate their Character Power. When set to "ON" the AI's Character Power will expire as the Character Power Meter is drained, but will re-activate on its own once the Character Power Meter has refilled.
Ai	AI Mode option will set the AI to engage in an actual versus match while in practice mode. You can also set the AI's level of difficulty.
Human	Human Mode option allows another person to control the opposite character.
Record	Record Mode option allows you to record the opposite character and play the recording back.
Playback	Playback Mode option allows you to set your position to be reset after the playback has finished.

PRACTICE OPTIONS

While in the Practice Mode Main Menu, scrolling over and selecting Practice Options will bring up the Practice Options Menu. These options control you characters settings.

Damage Info — Choosing "ON" will keep the damage that each attack and combo inflicts displayed on screen while in practice mode. Choosing "OFF" will no longer display any attack or combo damage.

Super Meter — Choosing "Normal" will require you to build and use your Super Meter under normal conditions. Choosing "Refill" will fill your Super Meter, and refill it after a move that requires Super Meter is used. Choosing "Full" will fill your Super Meter and have it remain full at all times.

Button Log — Choosing "ON" will keep your button and directional inputs displayed in practice mode, and choosing "OFF" will turn off the button and directional input display.

Reset Position — This option allows you to set your starting point on the stage after resetting your position.

Control Player — This option allows you to choose which of the two characters are being controlled.

Game Hud — Choosing "ON" will keep the health bars, Super Meter, and Character Power Meter displayed in game while in practice mode. Choosing "OFF" will remove the health bar, Super Meter, and Character Power Meter display.

Clash — Choosing "OFF" will keep your ability to Clash turned off. Choosing "ON" will turn on your ability to Clash, allowing you to Clash indefinitely.

Collision Region — Choosing "OFF" will keep the ability to see the collision on your physical attacks turned off. Choosing "ON" will cause the area of collision of your physical attacks.

End Of Round Anim — This mode allows you to turn the bubble effect animation that signals the end of a round "ON" or "OFF". If the mode is turned on, the animation will appear after you have taken the AI's first heath bar.

Life Percentage — This allows you to set how much heath both you and the AI have.

Area — This option allows you to select what specific area of the stage you wish to fight on.

Interaction Zones — You can choose "Show" to have an indicator placed on the areas where you can interact with the stage. Choosing "Hide" will keep the indicators hidden.

RECORD PLAYBACK

This allows you to record yourself doing attacks, combos, etc., then save it and play those exact actions back at any time.

CONTROLLER PRESET

This allows you to custom set your buttons to what feels most comfortable. This option also allows you to select your control schemes with Release Check and Alternate Control.

TIP *Many of the screens in this guide were taken from the Xbox 360 version of the game, but the strategies are universal and apply to all console versions. As this is a button-heavy section, your version of the game may look slightly different.*

RELEASE CHECK

More commonly known in the fighting game world as "Negative Edge", setting Release Check to "ON" will cause your button inputs to remain stored for short period of time. This allows you to tap a button, then input a directional input after the fact and still get the Special Move. An example of this would be Green Lantern: With Release Check "ON" you would be able to enter Down + Light then quickly tap Down, Back which will cause you to get a crouching jab into a Lantern's Might Special Move cancel, even though you only tapped the attack button once. Turning this mode "OFF" will not store your attack button inputs.

ALTERNATE CONTROL

Turning Alternate Control "ON" will change the directional inputs on the characters Special Moves, adding more gradual, sweeping motions rather than simple cardinal directions. You can experiment with this mode "ON" or "OFF" and decide which control scheme you are most comfortable with.

GAME INFO

WHO YOU ARE AND WHERE YOU'LL FIGHT

The way of justice or villainy is a battle fought without and within. To help chart your progress through the *Injustice* experience, NetherRealm Studios developed the Hero Card, a way of seeing not just your stats throughout both the Single Player and Multiplayer parts of *Injustice*, but a means of customizing your appearance when you venture online. By completing challenges throughout all the various game modes, you'll earn XP to level up, unlocking rewards that can lead to new Backgrounds, Portraits, and Icons. These customized parts of your Hero Card can be swapped out as you unlock them to act as the face of your online profile. Will other players come to fear the face of Harley Quinn, or will they laugh at the sight of The Dark Knight? Your performance online can determine just how notorious—for good or ill—your Hero Card is.

IT'S ALL ABOUT EXPERIENCE

XP is the beginning and end of your cumulative progress throughout the Story Mode, S.T.A.R. Labs challenges, Battles, and online brawls. Nearly every action in the game, from lengthy combos to environmental destruction to, yes, winning and losing a match accrues XP at the end of the brawl. As your Hero Card profile levels up through all of these modes, you'll unlock additional goodies, including the all-important Access Codes (used to unlock nearly everything in the Archives) and Armory Keys (used to unlock alternate costumes for your favorite characters). We'll reveal all the Armory contents later in this guide, but know that leveling up is the key to actually unlocking them for yourself, and the only way to level up is to grab XP.

BOOSTERS? GOLD!

Though early XP levels will likely come fast and often, as you level up, the XP needed to keep leveling up can happen a little more slowly. To overcome this, Access Cards can be used to buy XP multipliers, but only once you've leveled up enough. The larger a multiplier, the higher the level and the more Cards are needed, but the effect will linger for more matches. The first Match Boost unlocks at Level 5, the next at Level 10, then Level 25, and finally Level 50. Keep this in mind if you're grinding XP for more unlockables. Earning those levels can feel like unreachable slogs or blissfully frequent rewards depending on how those multipliers are managed.

THE WORLD AWAITS

The resurgence of fighting games in recent years has brought with it an update not just to how the games look, but how they play. Though side-by-side duels with another human being is and always will be the preferable way to enjoy a fighter game (and if you can do it in a crowded room with a rapt audience, so much the better), having an always-on connection to the Internet means competition is only a few button presses away. Best of all, your Hero Card keeps a constant tally of your online exploits, with all the same data tracked in offline play accounted for. There's more than just straight 1v1 fights, though; NetherRealm has assembled a hodgepodge of different options for beating down your foes.

365 NEW GOALS

The first time you log in to the online portion of *Injustice*, you'll be prompted with the Daily Challenge, a simple additional objective you can choose to pursue while squaring off against fighters from around the globe. Though these challenges are optional, they often provide a way to get to know the roster better and earn a fairly hefty reward in the process—especially when coupled with an XP multiplier. True to their name, Daily Challenges will only last for 24 hours, start at 6:00 PM Central, and begin counting down in real time. If the ticking clock feels like too much pressure, there are also Challenges that can be voluntarily undertaken on a per-match basis that also reward bonus XP to those that can complete them. These include finishing a match with a specific type of attack, finishing with a certain amount of health remaining, and many more. The more difficult the challenge parameters, the greater the reward.

Daily Challenges are always visible from the Main Menu, tucked into the upper-right corner of the screen with a running tally of the current requirements and how many you've met. In the upper-left corner is your Hero Card, showing your level and just how much XP it'll take to reach the next one. Between the two is a running tally of some of *Injustice*'s best facts, including things like character usage and level destruction tallies. Keep an eye out for your name here if you're on a hot streak. Players that have risen to the top of the Leaderboards will have their records highlighted.

MATCH TYPES

Regardless of the individual style of play, all online *Injustice* matches are divided into a handful of categories. Ranked Matches contribute to your overall global ranking and XP level, Player Matches won't track stats but will still earn you XP, and Private Matches let you determine the battle parameters to play against friends and rivals (including the exclusive online Practice Mode) with user-defined rules, but aren't tracked or rewarded like Ranked and Player Matches.

1v1

The classic showdown: just you and a rival in a match to see who can burn through their opponent's life bars the fastest. Straightforward and easily understandable, 1v1 matches are where scores are settled based on skill alone.

Survivor

KOTH wasn't fancy enough for you? Fine. Try applying the same winner-stays-on rules, but instead of getting a full refill of your life after every match, *health is carried over between matches*. Yeah, we thought that might pique the interest of some of you hardcore players.

King of the Hill

Arcades may have all but vanished these days, but there's still nothing like the winner-stays-on approach of KOTH. Challengers must defeat the reigning champ, who continues fighting newcomers until the champ is dethroned and the process starts all over again. While waiting for their chance to play the champ, other players can wager XP on the results of the current fight. To sweeten the pot, players can also bet on the likelihood of a player winning *and* completing the challenge they picked while waiting for their match to start.

Rooms

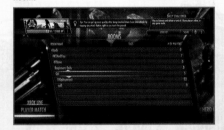

When you just want to play with the same group of people, or attract public players searching for a specific type of game, Rooms are your ticket. Unlike, say, a Party option where your friends move from one match to another, Rooms let players come and go as they please, challenging each other to matches free of the need to move as a group between modes. Rooms are great for letting players square off among each other on a challenge basis. Highlight another player in the Room and issue a challenge to fight to reach the top of the heap, in a 1v1 brawl, or keep a Survivor match going. It's the next best thing to playing a bunch of games with friends and rivals sitting next to you—and possibly more pleasant smelling. Simply choose the Join Room option to jump into another player-created Room, or select Create Room to set up one of your own where you can invite specific players as you see fit.

Leaderboards

When only official stats will do, look no further than the Leaderboards, which track win/loss records, streaks, player popularity, and more. This where the tale of online prowess is told, and where those looking to take down the best can find their names. Be forewarned: many of these top players got there the hard way, so don't underestimate them.

Hero Card

Just as it is during *Injustice*'s Single Player modes, the Hero Card while online keeps track of all your best stats, from combos to damage to wins and losses to character preference and everything in between. You can quickly swap out any unlocked Icons, Portraits, and Backgrounds (or see some of the criteria for unlocking new ones) to refresh your online identity, as well as view two very important long-term new options.

Rivals and Awards

Once you've fought enough matches online, you'll begin to develop rivalries (friendly or otherwise), which are tracked automatically by *Injustice*'s online Hero Card. This is a great way to keep an eye out for players that are either bothersome or especially challenging, indicating their stats and online status so you're never far away from a challenge. Of course, other players may have you added as a rival too, so don't be surprised if you're challenged shortly after getting online.

Awards are honors bestowed for fulfilling specific accomplishments over the course of your online career. These include earning streaks, participating in enough battles with a character, winning without using certain abilities, finishing a match a certain way, and achieving plenty more. There are dozens of Awards, and each can be earned multiple times. That's right, those carrots dangling on sticks aren't going anywhere. Keep reaching.

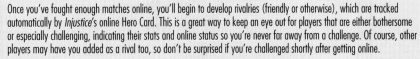

STAGES

The arenas where you'll do battle against some of the most powerful combatants in the DC universe aren't static backdrops—they're teeming with little details. Littering each stage are multiple interactive points that can be utilized while in combat to unleash damaging attacks, incapacitate your foes, or make a hasty retreat far faster than your normal movements could carry you. These Interactive Objects aren't universal, however; characters use them in a way that complements their particular skill sets. We've highlighted these in the character sections to come, and we are also sure to point out any particular characters that might treat things a bit differently from their similar cohorts. Knowledge of how the stages themselves can be used is fundamental to getting the upper hand in battle, so study the pages to come carefully.

Also important to many stages are the various transitional elements. By using a Level Transition attack at certain points, you can smash your opponent through a series of brutal impacts before continuing the fight in a new part of the stage. Level Transitions are a great way to heap additional damage on your enemies, and some can even be worked into combos. Better still, these new parts of a stage are peppered with new Interactive Objects, allowing you to continue beating down your opponent or escape his or her onslaught as the case may be.

HARD BREAK

As you'll no doubt discover while duking it out with other players, the arenas that serve as your battleground are constantly crumbling around you. These background changes are great for showing the level of power these characters have, but there's more to it than just beautiful destruction. By using your Forward + Hard and Back + Hard or Uppercut attacks, the impacts from them can cause some objects closer to the foreground to fall apart, which can yield even more Interactive Objects. Case in point: the upper Crime Lab part of the Batcave. Land enough Hard attacks on your foe and the glass cases holding backup Batsuits will shatter, releasing bombs anyone can pick up by pressing the Interact button when nearby. After picking them up, you'll lose the ability to block or throw your opponent, but you more than make up for it with three ways to unleash your newfound bombs. A Light attack will throw a bomb straight across the level, Medium attacks lob the bomb as an anti-air option, and Hard chucks it near your character's feet.

TYPE-OGRAPHY

As we mentioned before, a character's Interactive Object Type is listed front and center on his or her character page in the next chapter, but certain characters have crossover properties. Batman, for instance, marries the best of nearly all worlds, being able to spring off some surfaces to get to safety like Acrobatic characters, but he can also plant an unblockable explosive as he leaps away like a Gadget character, something normal agility-based fighters can't do. He's also able to turn his normal leaping Interactive Object escapes into a series of unblockable hits when positioned next to waist-high objects. The Flash is also capable of such moves, and he joins Raven and Killer Frost in being able to leap off overhanging objects to attack with an extremely quick flying kick. Of the bunch, only most Power characters fit into a singular (but burly) role, picking up huge objects and using them as bludgeoning tools that the other characters couldn't hope to lift, but even they can differ depending on their Power type, by using a short-range melee strike (Grounded) or throwing their enemies into Interactive Objects. It can be a lot to take in at first, but with a little practice, the patterns of who can use what will become clear.

BURNING AMBITION

Meter Burn isn't just relegated to bolstering special moves or canceling into further attacks. It's also useful for adding un-interruptible armor to an Interactive Object action. Though it doesn't work for every Interactive Object, the added insurance that you won't be stopped while trying to slam an object into someone's forehead or jumping out of range of an attack might just be worth the Meter cost to get the desired results. Not surprisingly, Meter Burn Interactive Objects are activated by pressing the Meter Burn and Interact buttons simultaneously.

CHARACTER TYPES:

[POWER - GROUND]

	Aquaman
	Ares
	Bane
	Cyborg
	Doomsday
	Lex Luthor
	Shazam
	Solomon Grundy

[POWER - FLYING]

	Black Adam
	Hawkgirl
	Green Lantern
	Sinestro
	Superman
	Wonder Woman

[ACROBATIC]

	The Flash
	Killer Frost
	Raven

[GADGET]

	Batman
	Catwoman
	Deathstroke
	Green Arrow
	Harley Quinn
	The Joker
	Nightwing

INJUSTICE
GODS AMONG US

BATCAVE

Levels: Crime Lab | Lagoon

Few have seen Batman's secretive lair, and fewer still know it connects to millionaire playboy Bruce Wayne's palatial abode. From here, The Dark Knight can survey Gotham City and beyond, using a vast network of sensory equipment and a powerful computer to help him with investigations. The World's Greatest Detective has a keen intellect, but even he needs a little help crunching numbers from time to time.

Injustice's Batcave is a multi-level collection of some of Batman's most iconic hardware. The Batplane sits ready in the background, spare suits hide behind glass, and the Batcomputer and Batmobile actually serve as functional objects in the world, allowing for some background-assisted pop-up combos and a pair of powerful missiles that can be unleashed on opponents with the right timing. In the lagoon below, the bobbing Batboat "cushions" a fighter's impact as he or she lands after being blasted with a Level Transition attack from up above, and an elevator can be used to return to the upper Crime Lab (with a few high-impact punches for good measure, of course).

CRIME LAB

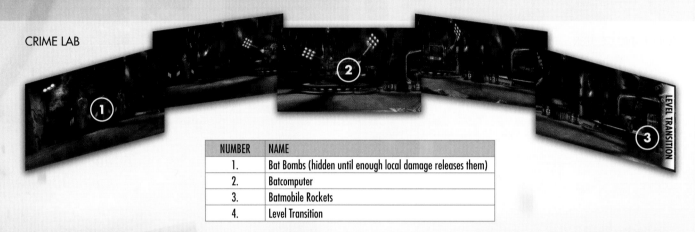

NUMBER	NAME
1.	Bat Bombs (hidden until enough local damage releases them)
2.	Batcomputer
3.	Batmobile Rockets
4.	Level Transition

LAGOON

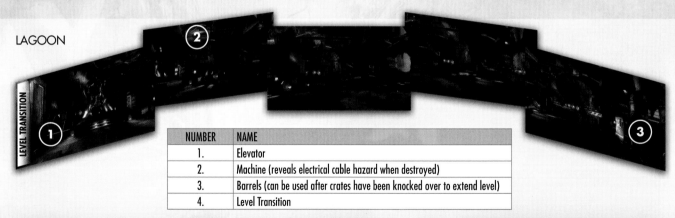

NUMBER	NAME
1.	Elevator
2.	Machine (reveals electrical cable hazard when destroyed)
3.	Barrels (can be used after crates have been knocked over to extend level)
4.	Level Transition

INSURGENCY

Levels: Command Center | Luthor's Lab

The Resistance has a home, and though it may not look like much, this is where the fight against oppressive forces begins. From here, our heroes are able to plot a means to overthrow the oppression that has engulfed the world, and reclaim the freedom they once took for granted. The underground nature of Insurgency belies the true scope of the project. The command center is overflowing with computer terminals and clear signs of self-sufficiency, from the massive tank of fuel at one end to a powerful set of electrical turbines on the other. The monitors overhead are great for quick attacks by all character types, and the steam vent caused by breaking the pipe on the left end can easily halt advances from an opponent. Every character can also channel the energy from the turbines and release an unlimited number of blasts (with a slight recharge period between blasts, of course). The Level Transition is a brutal series of slams through the rock surrounding the Command Center and into a driller that grinds away at your opponent before eventually depositing him or her in Lex Luthor's high-tech lab below. Here, Lex Luthor's automatons and armor are crafted, and once again the Interactive Objects offer plenty of variety depending on your character type. Lasers at the left end can be used multiple times. On the right, all but Power characters have access to a powerful set of twin lasers *and* a quick escape. The assembly line-assisted Level Transition is especially interesting, as it offers a brief peek into Lex Luthor's operation — not to mention plenty of damage.

COMMAND CENTER

NUMBER	NAME
1.	Pipe (in air)
2.	Monitors (in air)
3.	Turbine
4.	Level Transition

LUTHOR'S LAB

NUMBER	NAME
1.	Mechanized Suit of Armor
2.	Laser (in air)
3.	Lights (in air)
4.	Console
5.	Level Transition

FERRIS AIRCRAFT

Before Hal Jordan ever found the power ring that would eventually transform him into the Green Lantern, he made his living as a gutsy test pilot where he met and fell in love with Carol Ferris, daughter of founder Carl Ferris and Vice President of the very Ferris Aircraft that owns this hanger. Always on the cutting edge of aerospace design, Ferris Aircraft is constantly working to develop new technologies that they can sell to world superpowers, and as such the hanger is bustling with top-secret activity.

One of only two stages in *Injustice* that lacks any Level Transition elements, Ferris Aircraft is also a rather tight, cramped level in its own right. Even so, it's packed with Interactive Objects, from a swinging jet engine on the far left that can be reused throughout the fight to a limitless supply of rockets on the far right that can be shot or thrown at opponents. Nearby, a set of pressurized canisters make for a great bat at close range, and can be thrown to injure targets at a distance. Be careful when approaching the edges of the hangar; the options here can put a defending character on offense quickly.

NUMBER	NAME
1.	Jet Engine (in air)
2.	Tool Chest
3.	Missile (in air)
4.	Storage Tanks
5.	Rockets

GOTHAM CITY

Levels:	Rooftop | Alley

It's never been clear how the residents of Gotham City feel at any given time. On the one hand, they have a vigilant caped crusader watching over them, but it sure seems like there are more two-bit crooks per capita than nearly any other city in the U.S. Worse, there's no shortage of proper villains unleashing their latest scheme in between stints at Arkham Asylum. It also seems to be inordinately dark around there. All that nocturnal activity makes for some great steamy alleyways and darkness-cloaked eaves from which friend or foe could pounce.

Both levels of Gotham City are rife with opportunities to pour on a little Batman-themed damage. Not surprisingly The Dark Knight has more options here than any other character, from objects that can be used to jump to safety or detonated, *plus* the Bat-Signal up on the rooftops that he and The Flash can use for some face-smashing antics. The Level Transition down to the rain-soaked alleyway below is one of the most dramatic of the bunch, sending the victim careening through walls and riding the business end of a subway train right off the rails. Down below, an Ace Chemicals tanker truck offers a quick attack, or can be used in conjunction with a Level Transition attack to launch enemies back up to the rooftop. A fire hydrant at the far end can also be reused by Gadget and Acrobatic characters (Power characters just throw the whole thing), and a dumpster can be thrown repeatedly by Acrobatic or Gadget fighters, though it's destroyed upon use by Power characters.

ROOFTOP

LEVEL TRANSITION

NUMBER	NAME
1.	Bat Signal
2.	Air Conditioner
3.	Helicopter
4.	Water Tower
5.	Level Transition

LOOK BEFORE YOU LEAP

Beginning players will likely see Interactive Objects that allow for hasty escapes as a simple either/or option; either they stick around for some pummeling or leap away to restart the conflict on their terms. There's more to it than just a simple press of the Interact button, though. By pressing Left or Right while tapping Interact on Interactive Objects in corners, the jump's distance can be changed. For Gadget-based characters, this offers a chance to mix things up, leaping far away from their attackers one moment, then planting an explosive and landing closer to follow up during their target's momentary daze. Some Interactive Objects, such as the glass orb in Atlantis, are a little different. Instead of changing jump distance by pressing Left or Right, using direction-based inputs actually changes the direction of the jump, allowing for not just escapes, but quick coverage of distance to close in and strike. Play around with the distances and directions achievable with these objects. You never know when a little extra distance could help avoid a follow-up attack.

ALLEY

NUMBER	NAME
1.	Ace Chemicals Tanker
2.	Dumpster
3.	Fire Hydrant
4.	Parking Sign (in air)
5.	Level Transition

INJUSTICE
GODS AMONG US

WATCHTOWER

Levels:	Bridge	Reactor

Justice League HQ is aptly named, with clear views of planet Earth from orbit. From this vantage, the massive space station allows the residents to respond to threats planet side or extra-solar, and serves as a place for some of Earth's most valiant protectors to convene. The Watchtower's construction is a perfect example of the range of alien races that make up the Justice League and their compatriots, integrating technology from (among other places) Mars and Krypton.

Divided into two levels and densely packed with ways to unload damage, The Watchtower also happens to have some of the most outrageous Level Transitions in *Injustice*. Launching a foe through a set of shuttlecraft and then watching one of the craft plunge down into the station's Reactor (taking your opponent with it) is a blast, but the return trip *out into space and back* certainly does its best to one-up the rest of the stages' over-the-top cinematic bridges. The central computer on both levels offers the chance to combo into bounces, and in a rare bit of fortune, the computer console on the Bridge can be used repeatedly, even by Power characters.

BRIDGE

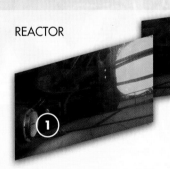

NUMBER	NAME
1.	Shuttlecraft Controls
2.	Flying Robots (in air)
3.	Center Console
4.	Moon
5.	Computer Terminal
6.	Level Transition

REACTOR

NUMBER	NAME
1.	Exhaust Valve
2.	Flying Robots (in air)
3.	Center Console
4.	Laser
5.	Level Transition

FORTRESS OF SOLITUDE

Levels: Laboratory | Menagerie

Superman's place of refuge, research, and introspection is part crystalline domain, part zoo. In it rests massive digital archives containing the last records of his home planet, Krypton. Even the Fortress itself is of Kryptonian origin, and is a constant tether for the Man of Steel to his bygone roots, particularly his parents. With doorways to the Phantom Zone, a penal dimension responsible for holding some of the universe's most dangerous criminals, Superman can keep tabs on the prisoners without fear of their escape.

The Phantom Zone is actually witnessed in the Level Transition from the underground Menagerie section of the stage, which sends the recipient hurtling through the alternate dimension for a few brief but damaging moments. The Fortress itself is also home to a very rare Interactive Object: a Teleporter that will track and attack characters that have been juggled. There's only one other stage in *Injustice* where this is possible, but this is the only stage where that Interactive Object can be comboed into a Level Transition. That Transition sends characters hurtling down through crystal-lined slopes before depositing them in Supes' intergalactic holding cell. The deeper level of the Fortress introduces a portal for teleporting attacks and some interesting alien life that can be used to escape attacks or cause damage.

LABORATORY

NUMBER	NAME
1.	Ship
2.	Doomsday
3.	Crystal (in air)
4.	Teleporter (during juggle)
5.	Level Transition

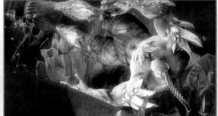

MENAGERIE

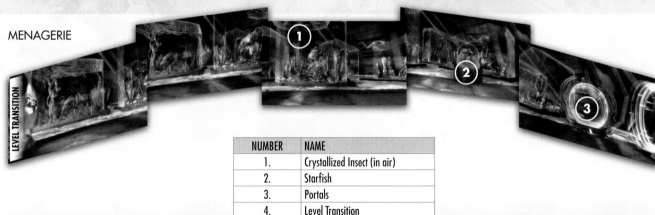

NUMBER	NAME
1.	Crystallized Insect (in air)
2.	Starfish
3.	Portals
4.	Level Transition

INJUSTICE
GODS AMONG US

THEMYSCIRA

Levels:	Temple	Port

The island nation of Themyscira has gone by different names (Paradise Island being the most common), but this verdant, ancient Amazonian home is unchanging in its dutiful training of the all-female inhabitants. Residents of the island are cared for and nurtured by the gods, taught the importance of communion with nature, and hardened into powerful warriors many times more hardy than ordinary men. Themyscira is recognized as a world superpower, often consulting with other city-states like the Vatican and participating in United Nations talks.

Ancient and inviting, the golden hues of *Injustice*'s take on Themyscira presents a set of battlegrounds with a multitude of combat options. The chains on either side can be pulled by Gadget and Acrobatic characters to spit fire from twin lion heads (which can be ripped off and thrown by Power characters), the central statues offer bounce potential, and potent reusable Interactive Objects on either end of the area give all but Power characters options for repeated beatdowns. The Level Transition from the Temple down to the bustling port is the very definition of "beatdown," sending the victim crashing through statue and tree branch alike. The port offers multiple options for firing cannonballs, rolling barrels, and swinging around as needed. The Level Transition trip back up to the Temple is nearly as cringe-inducing as the trip down, assisted in large part by a catapult.

TEMPLE

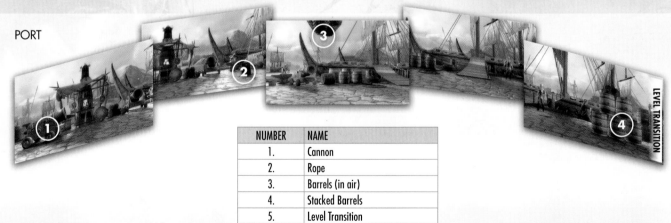

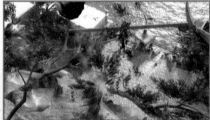

NUMBER	NAME
1.	Brazier
2.	Chains
3.	Lion Heads
4.	Central Statues
5.	Tree
6.	Level Transition

PORT

NUMBER	NAME
1.	Cannon
2.	Rope
3.	Barrels (in air)
4.	Stacked Barrels
5.	Level Transition

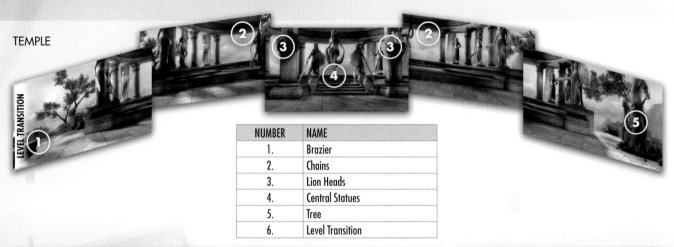

STRYKER'S ISLAND

Levels: Cell Block | Yard

Stryker's Island is to Metropolis what Arkham Asylum is to Gotham City, a collection of some of the worst villains the world has ever known. Super-powered ne'er-do-wells are kept here in great numbers, so expect to see some seriously imposing figures being corralled. Superman has put many a threat away here, but like Arkham Asylum, some villains just don't take well to long-term incarceration, even if they almost inevitably end up back in cryo containment.

During the events of *Injustice*, Stryker's Island is in a state of shifting control, with the prison staff attempting to restore order. This is no small task, considering the appearance of Gorilla Grodd down in the Yard and The Parasite up in the Cell Block, neither of which seem too well-protected. The Cell Block not only offers a Level Transition with some of the most collateral damage, but plenty of automated firepower to the left and a unique opportunity for Gadget characters to freeze other combatants on the right. Aside from Grodd (who happens to be a bounce-ready Interactive Object), the Yard continues to favor Gadget characters with a reusable set of huge weights that can have explosives planted during an escape multiple times. The trip through the processing center of the prison for the Level Transition also ends with a bang—or perhaps more fittingly a slam.

CELL BLOCK

NUMBER	NAME
1.	Robotic Guard
2.	Turret (in air)
3.	Metallo
4.	Cryo Pod
5.	Level Transition

YARD

NUMBER	NAME
1.	Weights
2.	Gorilla Grodd
3.	Explosive Tanks
4.	Generator
5.	Level Transition

INJUSTICE
GODS AMONG US

METROPOLIS

Levels: Street | Rooftops | Museum

Superman's home town has seen better days, but in the wake of terrible tragedy, it's clear that the city has found a way to rebuild. The question, though, is whether or not it can ever truly recover, and what the cost of restoring order and peace in the wake of that tragedy truly is. This is a city ruled by an unflinching police state, and gifted with technology that would have seemed downright futuristic to the residents living here before the events that unfolded those years before.

Metropolis is the only *Injustice* stage that has three separate areas, leading to plenty of Level Transition-assisted damage. Down on the streets, the other juggle-based Interactive Object on the left side can use the firepower of a nearby armored transport for extra damage and air time, while a nearby car lets Batman and The Flash do a little involuntary head banging. After being blasted up to the Rooftops *through* a building via Level Transition, three different security bots can have their munitions turned on opponents by Gadget and Acrobatic characters that leap up to point and fire their different payloads: grey (machine gun), purple (electricity), and red (fire). A smash down back through the building with another Level Transition opens up the rubble-strewn Museum section, which offers a sight not seen since the Batcave: a weapon that can be snatched from the background with enough local damage. The Level Transition nearby affords a brief glimpse of some of Metropolis' hidden pipeworks—a *painful* glimpse, really.

STREET

NUMBER	NAME
1.	Car
2.	Security Truck
3.	Hovercar
4.	Level Transition

ROOFTOPS

NUMBER	NAME
1.	Power Conduit
2.	Security Bots (in air)
3.	Level Transition

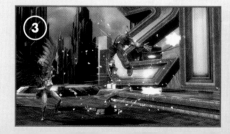

MUSEUM

LEVEL TRANSITION

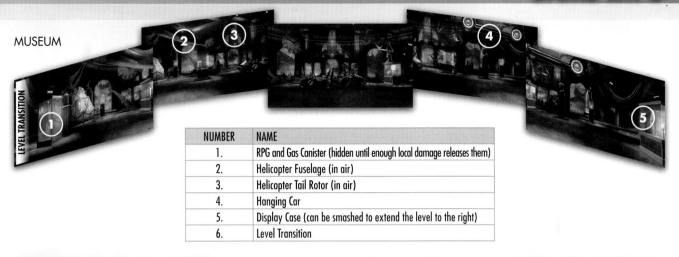

NUMBER	NAME
1.	RPG and Gas Canister (hidden until enough local damage releases them)
2.	Helicopter Fuselage (in air)
3.	Helicopter Tail Rotor (in air)
4.	Hanging Car
5.	Display Case (can be smashed to extend the level to the right)
6.	Level Transition

INJUSTICE
GODS AMONG US

ARKHAM ASYLUM

Levels:	Cell Block | Mess Hall

The Elizabeth Arkham Asylum for the Criminally Insane is nearly as famous for the patients/inmates that reside here as its apparent inability to keep them from escaping back into Gotham City. Only the biggest and baddest actually find a way back out to cause trouble (usually gunning straight for Batman because he put them there), but it's still remarkable how easily they seem to slip through the warden's clutches. The Asylum also seems to have a propensity for attracting crooked crazies among the staff, as dirty guards and a doctor-turned-villain Harleen Quinzel were once just meant to oversee the patients.

The upper Cell Block of Arkham Asylum is fairly straightforward, with a pair of TVs in the center and a few more interesting tidbits at the edges, including a pipe that can freeze for a couple seconds and a rack that offers a few different ways of dispensing pain or escaping from it depending on your character type. The Scarecrow makes an appearance during the Level Transition down to the Mess Hall, and the return trip involves a rogue's gallery of Batman villainy faves. The lower level also has a unique Interactive Object in the form of a pig carcass that can be repeatedly thrown back and forth. All of the character types are given ample room to use their particular talents here, even if the actual number of Interactive Objects isn't incredibly high.

CELL BLOCK

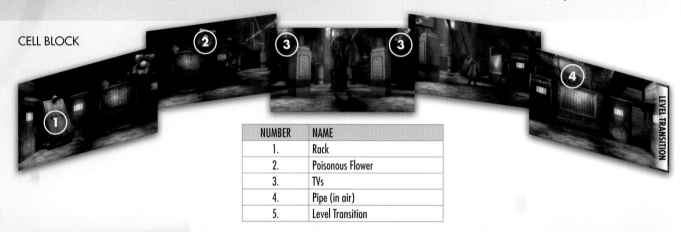

NUMBER	NAME
1.	Rack
2.	Poisonous Flower
3.	TVs
4.	Pipe (in air)
5.	Level Transition

MESS HALL

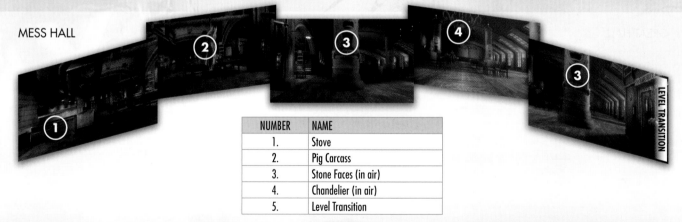

NUMBER	NAME
1.	Stove
2.	Pig Carcass
3.	Stone Faces (in air)
4.	Chandelier (in air)
5.	Level Transition

HALL OF JUSTICE

Levels: Plaza | Great Hall

This iconic Metropolis-based building is still relevant to the ongoing conflict. Housed inside are decades of valuable information, accessible to those who would seek it out. For the New 52 reboot, DC Comics even gave the Hall a few new residents, though they were from... let's call it "out of town," which didn't sit too well with some of the residents of Metropolis.

The Hall as a stage is an interesting mix of a bounce-happy central Plaza with some robotic denizens and a few stone-carved Interactive Objects. The Level Transition actually incorporates the ongoing battle of fisticuffs between Giganta and Atom Smasher, becoming wrapped up in Giganta's fist for a few blows before getting tossed into the Great Hall. Once inside the building proper, a handful of different options become available, though the right side of the stage is actually concerned with attack avoidance Interactive Objects, including what might be the shortest-range teleporter ever seen in a video game. Just past it, though, is the Level Transition that dumps the recipient into Darkseid's inner sanctum on Apokolips for a beating and Omega Beam blast back out to the Plaza.

PLAZA

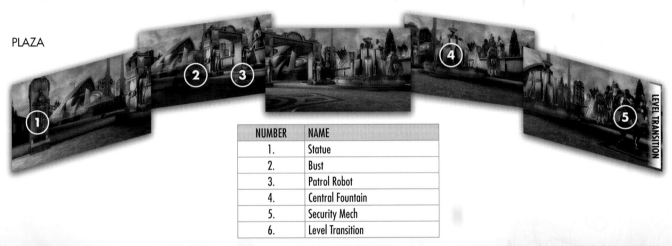

NUMBER	NAME
1.	Statue
2.	Bust
3.	Patrol Robot
4.	Central Fountain
5.	Security Mech
6.	Level Transition

GREAT HALL

NUMBER	NAME
1.	Watchtower Replica
2.	Planet Replica (in air)
3.	Transport Ship
4.	Teleporters
5.	Level Transition

INJUSTICE
GODS AMONG US

WAYNE MANOR

Levels: Entrance | Great Room

When young Bruce Wayne's parents were murdered in front of his eyes on a dark night, they left him an empty mansion with only a dutiful butler to watch over the grieving boy. The years haven't been kind to this once-majestic estate, with a crumbling facade and an overgrown entrance. Even still, the sheer size of the property is impressive in its own right, and a constant reminder that Batman's alter ego came from less than humble beginnings. Thankfully, all that leftover money has gone toward a plethora of high-tech gadgets to help protect the people of Gotham City — a fitting tribute to the people that once called this place home.

Wayne Manor's courtyard has a few of the things you'd expect (a fountain ready for bouncy impact, some gargoyles that for once can't be detonated by Gadget characters, and run-down vehicles that definitely can), but the rev-ready motorcycle proves it's not entirely abandoned, and the Level Transition blow that sends the recipient scraping along the weathered shingles down into the Great Room gives the property more action than it's ever seen. Once inside, the ancient suits of armor, throwable chair and piano, and elaborate chandelier all make for some great means of dishing out punishment before another Level Transition sends the fight back out to the Entrance through the library.

ENTRANCE

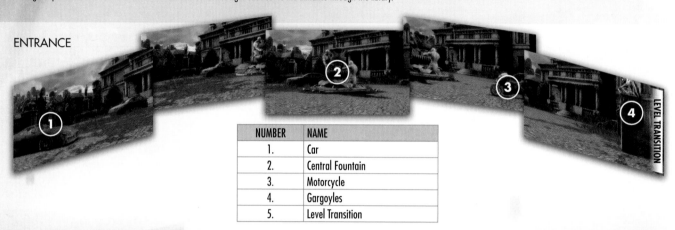

NUMBER	NAME
1.	Car
2.	Central Fountain
3.	Motorcycle
4.	Gargoyles
5.	Level Transition

GREAT ROOM

NUMBER	NAME
1.	Suit of Armor
2.	Chair
3.	Chandelier (in air)
4.	Table
5.	Piano
6.	Samurai Armor
7.	Level Transition

JOKER'S ASYLUM

Levels: Cell Block | Mess Hall

Though the level itself isn't any different from the Arkham Asylum level in terms of functionality, having the inmates run the asylum is clearly bad for upkeep. The Joker has plastered his face all over Quincy Sharp's bronze mug in the Cell Block, the inmates have spray-painted nearly every surface in gaudy greens and reds, and the passage of time hasn't been kind on the porcine carcass down in the Mess Hall. In short, it's Arkham Asylum, but somehow that much worse when there's nobody bothering to check on the crazies.

CELL BLOCK

MESS HALL

> **NOTE** See Arkham Asylum on page 24.

WAYNE MANOR NIGHT

Levels: Entrance | Great Room

Brace yourself for a massive change to the look and feel of the Wayne Manor level, for when night falls, it becomes... slightly hard to see! No, really, that's about the only difference here, but since a part of the story revolves around revisiting this most extravagant of hovels, it was included here too. At least you can enjoy some starlight in the Great Room's ceiling holes while attacking your enemy's fists and feet with your face and body. Maybe stargazing is a bad idea in the middle of combat.

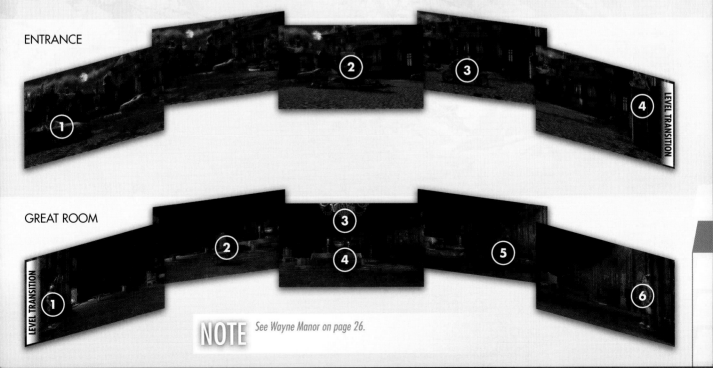

ENTRANCE

GREAT ROOM

> **NOTE** See Wayne Manor on page 26.

INJUSTICE
GODS AMONG US

ATLANTIS

The domain of Aquaman is one few mortals will ever see, but it is intrinsically tied to their actions on land. As these surface dwellers continue to pollute and transform the world above, the repercussions echo down into the depths, siring contempt and increased retraction from the upper world. Despite this, Aquaman's role as one of the founding members of the Justice League and increased desire to secure the future of his home means the autonomy of Atlantis is central to the events that unfold in *Injustice*.

Like Ferris Aircraft, Atlantis has no Level Transitions. As a result, this single underwater room is packed with a host of Interactive Objects. It may well be the most simply structured of the battlegrounds the *Injustice* roster does battle in, but that doesn't mean there aren't interesting things to use. For instance, there are means of scooting quickly around that can't be destroyed like in other stages and twin retaining walls with water all too eager to esc — wait, is that a *whale* in the background?!

THRONE ROOM

NUMBER	NAME
1.	Water Tanks
2.	Glass Sphere
3.	Throne
4.	Water Pipe
5.	Stone Tablet

CHARACTERS

AN EXTRA-DIMENSIONAL BATTLE ROYALE

What happens when two dozen characters ripped from two different dimensions square off? You get one of the most varied and surprising casts ever seen in a fighting game. Sure, there will be some familiar faces here for those that enjoyed NetherRealm Studios' first foray into comic book brawlers with *Mortal Kombat vs. DC Universe*, but *Injustice*'s roster is littered with new moves, new play styles, and most importantly, new Character Powers that complement and augment each character's abilities. In the pages to come you will discover what makes these characters tick and how best to adapt them to your particular play style. The goal of this guide is to give newcomers a leg up on the competition while letting veterans dive deep into advanced techniques.

LINGO LESSONS

The fighting game community is brimming with specialized terminology that may sound foreign to first-time players, and it can be a lot to take in. Some terms aren't as straightforward as one would hope, but these bits of shorthand are perfect for concisely explaining a particular theory, technique, or gameplay opportunity, and the sooner you learn these inside and out, the faster you'll be able to absorb the information in the pages ahead. If you ever get confused, consult this handy cheat sheet for guidance, then get back into the fight.

50/50
Simply put, a 50/50 scenario forces an opponent to commit to one potential attack over another. If your character is capable of attacking low or overhead, an opponent ordinarily can't block both at the same time, so you've got a 50/50 chance of breaking through his or her defenses.

ADVANTAGE/BLOCK STUN
Frame advantage and block stun are tightly interwoven concepts based around the idea of recovering from a blocked attack. Not all strikes are created equal; some may finish faster than others, so even when an opponent blocks your attack, frame advantage lets you attack again before the block stun wears off. If your attack has advantage, that means you'll be able to attack again before your opponent can counter-attack.

ARMOR
Absolutely core to some of the bigger characters in *Injustice*'s gameplay is their ability to essentially coat their attacks in nullifying properties. When an attack has armor, hits or projectiles that would normally interrupt an attack are ignored, allowing the original attack to continue through to damage a player. Characters like Doomsday and Solomon Grundy use armor to slip past attacks and pour on damage.

BUFFERING
Fighting games are speedy by nature. In some instances, an additional input or set of inputs can be entered while another action is taking place, which then activate automatically when that first action completes. Understanding how buffering works can take some time, but we've outlined a few instances for some characters where the process can be more tangibly understood.

CROSS UP
2D fighters are great for keeping the action on one plane, but they create an interesting effect when one character jumps toward another: sometimes the game will place the jumping character *behind* his or her target. Cross-ups aren't just relegated to jumping attacks, but they're the most common instance. Should a character block left or right depending on when an incoming character will attack? By attacking late, some strikes can hit from behind, crossing up the target.

HIT CONFIRMED
Combos can be devastating strings that pile on damage without giving an opponent a way out, but they still have to sneak past those initial defenses to have a chance. By using testing attacks to see if a move has connected, more advanced players can quickly make decisions about what follow-up attacks to use that will continue to slip past an opponent's defense.

POKING
A quick strike used to reliably deliver damage without the risk of a counter-attack, pokes are a fundamental means of testing range and keeping an opponent on his or her toes. Pokes can interrupt slower moves, making them a great tool for negating bigger attacks before countering with some of your own.

PRESSURE
Many of the bigger characters in Injustice revolve around the idea of staying heavily offensive, getting in close to deliver big hits that translate to plenty of damage. Applying pressure keeps an opponent on the defensive, reacting to your attacks rather than pushing back with attacks of his or her own. Pressure is crucial for short-range characters' momentum and moves.

PUNISHED
It's bound to happen; you have a perfect string of attacks you've prepared, but for some reason your opponent saw through the incoming strike and blocked or avoided it. Now, thanks to the recovery from the attack, your opponent is free to punish your whiff without fear of your recovery. Punishing a failed attack is at the crux of any fighting game; mistakes must be taken advantage of wherever possible to get or maintain the upper hand.

SAFE/UNSAFE
The holy grail of information, knowing whether an attack is safe or unsafe is the genesis of any character strategies. If an attack can be blocked without the chance of counter-attack, it is considered safe. Any attack that leaves your opponent ready before you are is unsafe. These two terms are used liberally throughout our guide. Just blocking an attack isn't enough; you have to know that the attack was unsafe to turn the tables and punish that failed attempt.

TECH ROLL
Press any of the attack buttons at the moment your character lands and your character will roll backwards out of the impact to relative safety. Tech Rolls aren't universal, as there are attacks that hit in a way to prevent them, but generally speaking there's no better way to quickly get back into the fight or throw off the rhythm of your opponent than careful use of a Tech Roll. Smart players know that Tech Rolls don't need to be used every time — it's the *possibility* of their use that makes them strategic.

WHIFF
Look at that big, dumb opponent, just waiting for your fist to meet his fa—whoops, he ducked your attack. Or dashed away from it. You just whiffed, and in addition to not even making contact, you're now left open to some serious damage. Whiffs are bad. Whiffs get punished.

ZONING
Projectile-based characters often have their ranged attacks for a reason. Maybe they aren't as damaging up close, or maybe their moves work best at a certain range. Using attacks like projectiles to keep an opponent at bay and control the space between is the simple act of zoning. Characters that can zone have control over what attacks can be used by an enemy on approach, but they also know which of their moves can connect at a particular distance. Many starting players think this is synonymous with repeatedly throwing out those projectiles, but this process of spamming is only one aspect. A character that works best up close can still zone; they're just using their knowledge of their moves (and, just as importantly, their opponent's moves) to create situations where those moves are most effective.

INJUSTICE
GODS AMONG US

AQUAMAN

The ability to control your opponent's movements from anywhere on the screen, great overall damage, and the ability to slip out of ground combos after being hit are what makes Aquaman such a good character. He also makes for the perfect beginner character—basic but extremely effective even without a full grasp of his abilities. He doesn't offer a lot of moves (one of the reasons why he's so great for starting players), but the ones he does use do the job well. His combos are also great for beginners as they're basically made up of the exact same components, regardless of how the combo is started.

INTERACTIVE OBJECT TYPE: POWER

SUPER MOVE

ATLANTEAN RAGE
Hit Level: Overhead
Range: Sweep
Description: Aquaman summons the sea, stabs his opponent with his trident, and then holds the opponent up to be swallowed by a shark. This attack hits overhead so it must be blocked from the standing block position. When this attack is blocked, his opponent can punish it with fast normal attacks and fast special attacks.

CHARACTER POWER

WATER OF LIFE
Command: Press the Power button
Description: When activated, Aquaman can recover while being hit by attack strings, allowing him to block the remainder of his opponent's attacks even after being hit initially. Though he can activate Water of Life while being hit, he will only escape and block if he is grounded.

For character information updates please visit www.primagames.com/InjusticeUpdates

BEST BASIC ATTACKS

SHARK STRIKE
Command: Down + Light
Hit Level: Mid
Range: Sweep
Description: Aquaman quickly pokes his opponent with a crouching trident stab. This attack is only punished by Superman's Super Move when blocked.

URCHIN KICK
Command: Jumping Light
Hit Level: Overhead
Range: Close
Description: Aquaman performs a jumping kick attack, which allows him to chain into other combo attack strings versus a grounded opponent. This attack hits overhead, so it must be blocked from the standing block position.

RISING TRIDENT

Command: Down + Medium
Hit Level: Mid
Range: Close
Description: Aquaman performs an uppercut with his trident that launches his opponent. This attack can be punished with a full combo when blocked.

TRIDENT SLAM

Command: Back + Medium
Hit Level: Overhead
Range: 1/4 Screen
Description: Aquaman bashes his opponent with an overhead launcher using his trident. This attack hits overhead, so it must be blocked from the standing block position. This attack is punished by fast normal attacks and fast Special Moves when blocked at close range. When this attack is blocked near its maximum range, it is only punished by the faster Super Moves of the game.

AIR STAB
Command: Jumping Medium
Hit Level: Overhead
Range: Sweep
Description: Aquaman performs a jumping trident attack, which allows him to chain into other combo attack strings versus a grounded opponent. This attack hits overhead, so it must be blocked from the standing block position.

WHIRL POOL

Command: Back + Hard
Hit Level: Mid
Range: Sweep
Description: Aquaman smashes his opponent with his trident, which bounces him or her off of the corner of the screen and back to him, giving him a juggle combo opportunity. This attack can be charged by holding the Hard attack button and canceled out of with a forward or backward dash while you are charging the attack. Pressing the Meter Burn button during this attack (which burns one bar of meter) will add one hit of armor. Whirl Pool is also Aquaman's Back, Back + Meter Burn Bounce Cancel (bounce cancel burns two bars of meter). This attack leaves Aquaman at advantage when blocked, allowing him to follow up with additional attacks.

FOR NEPTUNE

Command: Forward + Hard
Hit Level: Overhead
Range: Close
Description: Aquaman jumps up and smashes his opponent overhead with his trident, which launches the opponent and gives him a juggle combo opportunity. Like Whirl Pool, this attack hits overhead, so it must be blocked from the standing block position, can be charged by holding the Hard attack button, and can be canceled out of with a forward or backward dash while you are charging the attack. Pressing the Meter Burn button during this attack will add one hit of armor. For Neptune is also Aquaman's Forward, Forward + Meter Burn Bounce Cancel, and leaves Aquaman at advantage when blocked, allowing him to follow up with additional attacks.

TRIDENT JAB

Command: Jumping Hard
Hit Level: Overhead
Range: Close
Description: Aquaman spikes his trident down onto his opponent's head, which results in a small launch. This attack hits overhead, so it must be blocked from the standing block position. This attack is advantage when blocked, allowing Aquaman to follow up with additional attacks.

BEST COMBO ATTACKS

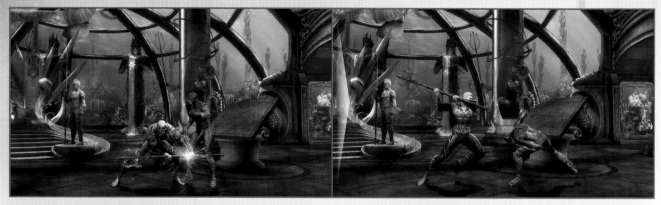

FROM THE DEPTHS

Command: Back + Light, Medium

Hit Level: Low, Mid

Range: Sweep

Description: Aquaman uses his trident and quickly jabs his opponent's legs, and then jabs them in the chest. This attack is only punished by Superman's Super Move.

DEEP SEA

Command: Forward + Medium, Light + Hard

Hit Level: Low

Range: Sweep

Description: Aquaman grabs his opponent by the feet using his trident, tosses the opponent into the air, and then stabs and throws the opponent to the ground. This is Aquaman's staple combo ender—you can end every single combo with this attack. Deep Sea, however, is full combo punished when blocked.

SPECIAL MOVES

TRIDENT RUSH

Command: Down, Forward + Light
Hit Level: Mid
Range: Sweep
Description: Aquaman rapidly strikes his opponent multiple times using his trident. This attack is only punished by the faster Super Moves of the game.

METER BURN TRIDENT RUSH

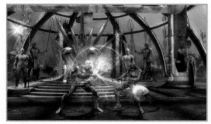

Description: Pressing the Meter Burn button during Trident Rush will add to the number of trident strikes, doing additional damage. Aquaman can dash forward or backward while executing this attack and is very difficult to punish when blocked, providing Aquaman does a forward dash while attacking.

FROM THE DEEP

Command: Down, Back + Medium
Hit Level: Mid
Range: Full Screen
Description: Aquaman summons his trident to appear beneath his opponent. This attack is full combo punished when blocked at close range. When blocked from outside of sweep range or farther, this attack is punished by fast advancing attacks that can reach Aquaman.

METER BURN FROM THE DEEP

Description: Pressing the Meter Burn button after a successful From The Deep will cause a bolt of lightning to come down from above, launching the opponent by bouncing him or her off of the ground. This attack is punished when blocked at close range by advancing attacks that can reach Aquaman. When blocked from up to 1/3 screen distance, this attack is only punished by very fast advancing Special Attacks that can reach Aquaman.

WATER SHIELD

Command: Down, Down + Hard
Description: Aquaman forms a water shield around his entire body. By holding the Hard attack button, Aquaman can keep his shield up and absorb strikes and projectiles. You can cancel Water Shield by dashing forward or backward.

METER BURN WATER SHIELD

Description: Pressing the Meter Burn button during the Water Shield will cause a short-range explosion, sending your opponent flying back across the screen while inflicting damage. This attack leaves Aquaman at advantage when blocked.

TRIDENT SCOOP

Command: Down, Back + Light
Hit Level: Low
Range: Sweep
Description: Aquaman uses his trident to lift an opponent up by the feet and launch the opponent over his head. This attack is punished when blocked by fast advancing attacks that can reach Aquaman.

TRIDENT TOSS

Command: Back, Forward + Medium
Hit Level: High
Range: Full Screen
Description: Aquaman hurls his trident at his opponent. This attack is full combo punished when blocked or crouched at close range.

USING WHIRL POOL (BACK + HARD) AND FOR NEPTUNE (FORWARD + HARD)

There really isn't any benefit to using one attack over the other as both attacks cover the same range, both launch, and both lead to the exact same combos. The only difference is Whirl Pool will activate stage transitions and is easier to juggle after due to the kind of launch it gives.

USING SHARK STRIKE (DOWN + LIGHT)

Shark Strike is one of the best pokes in the *Injustice* roster. It out-ranges most other Down + Light attacks, making this an ideal tool in a poking/counter-poking situation. When this attack hits, Aquaman is at advantage and can follow up with his From The Depths (Back + Light, Medium) attack string, and the opponent cannot interrupt your attack string follow up unless he or she uses a Super Move.

After landing a successful Shark Strike in open space, the opponent can backward dash out of your From The Depths attack string follow up. However, if you follow up the advantage after Shark Strike hits with your From The Deep (Down, Back + Medium) ground trident attack or your Trident Rush Special Move, your opponent will be hit as he or she attempts to backward dash away.

USING RISING TRIDENT (DOWN + MEDIUM)

This is one of the best uppercuts in the game and is Aquaman's staple anti-air. What makes this attack work so well is how far the trident rises into the air. Jumping opponents cannot hit Aquaman out of this attack without connecting with a hit to his body—just hitting his trident isn't enough. When this attack is timed right against a jumping opponent, there is no way to make contact with Aquaman without first going through his trident.

USING FROM THE DEEP (DOWN, BACK + MEDIUM)

From The Deep appears beneath Aquaman's opponent's feet, regardless of his or her position on the screen. You can also use From The Deep to punish an opponent on a decent from a jump anywhere on the screen.

This attack can actually be timed to beat out or trade with some of the quicker projectile attacks in the game. Even in a situation where your From The Deep attack trades with a projectile, most projectiles do not knock down, whereas this attack does. This allows Aquaman to attack with another From the Deep as his opponent is getting up.

> **TIP** Meter Burn From The Deep has the same properties and uses as the normal version of the attack with an added feature: it now launches your opponent, allowing for a juggle anywhere on the screen. When an opponent is even as far away as full screen, your Meter Burn From The Deep allows for a normal From The Deep follow up for a 20% juggle combo.

From The Deep is also a great tool to use in wakeup situations. After knocking your opponent down, a properly timed From The Deep attack can stuff certain wakeup attacks or any other option besides getting up and blocking. This attack is also a great ranged whiff punisher as it allows you to punish your opponent's missed attacks from anywhere on the screen.

USING TRIDENT SLAM (BACK + MEDIUM) AND FROM THE DEPTHS (BACK + LIGHT, MEDIUM)

This attack is an overhead launcher that you can try to use as a mix-up with Aquaman's low starting From The Depths (Back + Light, Medium) attack string, and you will have some success with this mix-up at the lower to middle levels of competition. Higher levels of play is where this mix-up becomes harder to use due to how much slower Trident Slam's start-up is in comparison to the first hit of the From The Depths attack string, making it harder to fool a highly skilled opponent.

From The Depths is your main attack string. It starts with a fast low attack, forcing opponents to constantly be crouch blocking anytime they are reasonably close to Aquaman. It's also safe when blocked, so there is no real consequence for poking with it. When this attack hits, it can be hit confirmed and canceled into Aquaman's Trident Scoop launcher.

This attack string has a range of just outside of sweep range, making this your main whiff-punishing tool from just outside of sweep distance to close range.

USING TRIDENT TOSS (BACK, FORWARD + MEDIUM)

Aquaman's Trident Toss is the perfect complement to his From The Deep attack when it comes to screen control. Trident Toss can be used to catch opponents attempting to jump out of your From The Deep attack, forcing them to time their jumps rather than constantly jump in random anticipation of an attack. Trident Toss also comes in handy as a tool to help Aquaman keep up with some of the more powerful projectile characters in the game.

USING JUMP IN ATTACKS AND CROSS UPS

Jumping Light is used for close-range jump in attempts as well as cross up jump attempts.

Jumping Medium is best suited for jumping in on your opponent from a distance, or in air-to-air combat situations.

Jumping Hard should be used only at very close range. This attack gives more of an ambiguous cross up jump then your jumping Light attack, and while it produces a launcher when it hits, this attack can be hard to juggle off of when it hits a crouching opponent because the opponent is lower to the ground.

AQUAMAN

USING TRIDENT RUSH (DOWN, FORWARD + LIGHT)

This attack is fairly safe on block, only punishable by the Super Moves of Superman and The Flash. Trident Rush quickly hits four times, allowing it to break some armor attacks. When this attack hits, it leaves Aquaman close to his opponent, with both fighters recovering at about the same time. Even when blocked, it still deals a good amount of block damage, inflicting upwards of 6%.

TIP In open space, your Meter Burn Trident Rush will miss towards its later strikes unless you forward dash during the attack. You will need to rapidly and continually forward dash during the Meter Burn Trident Rush in order to prevent any of the trident strikes from whiffing in open space situations. If any part of the Meter Burn Trident Rush whiffs, your opponent has a very small window to backward dash away from the attack or interrupt you with a Super Move.

When your opponent is cornered, do not forward dash during your Meter Burn Trident Rush attack, as there's no need to; the corner will not allow the push back that the attack has in open space, preventing any part of the attack from whiffing. Not using the forward dash during your Meter Burn Trident Rush against a cornered opponent will actually cause the attack to be made safer, only punished by Superman's Super Move.

TIP Meter Burn Trident Rush inflicts over 10% in block damage, making it a great tool on block or hit. You can cancel out of basic attacks and combo attack strings with your Trident Rush or Meter Burn Trident Rush, and inflict a good deal of damage to your opponent, whether the attack is blocked or hits.

USING WATER SHIELD (DOWN, DOWN + HARD)

After putting up the Water Shield, charging the Hard button allows Aquaman to keep the shield up and absorb strikes and projectiles. Note that while Aquaman does not receive damage from absorbing projectiles, he *is* damaged by absorbing physical strikes.

TIP Your Meter Burn Water Shield, on the other hand, can absorb your opponent's up-close physical striking attacks, allowing you to explode your Water Shield as your opponent is attacking, causing damage and knocking the opponent back across the screen.

USING WATER OF LIFE CHARACTER POWER

Aquaman's Character Power allows him to slip out of grounded attacks and block, even after being hit. He can activate at any time, be it before or during his opponent's attacks, and can even activate as he is being hit. However, Aquaman cannot escape juggles by using his Character Power; the ability to escape and block out of combos only applies to grounded situations. When activating as he is being hit by an attack string, Aquaman cannot guard the next immediate attack, and will get hit by the next immediate attack of the combo string. At this point, he can then guard the following attack. If Aquaman has activated his Character Power before he gets hit, he will be able to guard immediately after he is hit (again, provided he is grounded).

INJUSTICE
GODS AMONG US

COMBOS

NO METER BURN:

Down + Medium > Back + Light, Medium ~ Trident Scoop > Forward + Medium, Light + Hard — 19%
Back + Medium > Back + Light, Medium ~ Trident Scoop > Forward + Medium, Light + Hard — 25%
Air-to-Air Jumping Medium > Back + Light, Medium ~ Trident Scoop > Forward + Medium, Light + Hard — 25%
Back + Light, Medium ~ From The Deep > Back + Light, Medium ~ Trident Scoop > Forward + Medium, Light + Hard — 30%
Jumping Hard > Back + Light, Medium ~ Trident Scoop > Forward + Medium, Light + Hard — 29%
Forward + Hard > Jumping Hard > Back + Light, Medium ~ Trident Scoop > Forward + Medium, Light + Hard — 34%

Back + Hard > Jumping Hard > Back + Light, Medium ~ Trident Scoop > Forward + Medium, Light + Hard — 33%

METER BURN:

Down + Medium > Back + Light, Medium ~ Trident Scoop > Medium, Medium ~ Meter Burn From The Deep > Forward + Medium, Light + Hard — 27%
Back + Light, Medium ~ Trident Scoop > Medium, Medium ~ Meter Burn From The Deep > Forward + Medium, Light + Hard — 34%
Back + Medium > Back + Light, Medium ~ Trident Scoop > Medium, Medium ~ Meter Burn From The Deep > Forward + Medium, Light + Hard — 37%
Air-to-Air Jumping Medium > Back + Light, Medium ~ Trident Scoop > Medium, Medium ~ Meter Burn From The Deep > Forward + Medium, Light + Hard — 37%

Back + Light, Medium ~ From The Deep > Back + Light, Medium ~ Trident Scoop > Medium, Medium ~ Meter Burn From The Deep > Forward + Medium, Light + Hard — 39%
Jumping Hard > Back + Light, Medium ~ Trident Scoop > Medium, Medium ~ Meter Burn From The Deep > Forward + Medium, Light + Hard — 41%
Forward + Hard > Jumping Hard > Back + Light, Medium ~ Trident Scoop > Medium, Medium ~ Meter Burn From The Deep > Forward + Medium, Light + Hard — 42%
Back + Hard > Jumping Hard > Back + Light, Medium ~ Trident Scoop > Medium, Medium ~ Meter Burn From The Deep > Forward + Medium, Light + Hard — 42%
Back + Light, Medium ~ Meter Burn From The Deep > Back + Hard > Jumping Hard > Back + Light, Medium ~ Trident Scoop > Forward + Medium, Light + Hard - 41%

SUPER MOVE: ATLANTEAN RAGE

NO METER BURN WITH AQUAMAN'S BACK TO THE CORNER:

Down + Medium > Back + Light, Medium ~ Trident Scoop > Medium, Medium ~ From The Deep — 19%
Back + Light, Medium ~ Trident Scoop > Medium, Medium ~ From The Deep — 22%

Back + Medium > Back + Light, Medium ~ Trident Scoop > Medium, Medium ~ From The Deep — 25%
Jumping Hard > Back + Light, Medium ~ Trident Scoop > Medium, Medium ~ From The Deep — 30%
Back + Hard > Jumping Hard > Back + Light, Medium ~ Trident Scoop > Medium, Medium ~ From The Deep — 33%
Forward + Hard > Jumping Hard > Back + Light, Medium ~ Trident Scoop > Medium, Medium ~ From The Deep — 33%

METER BURN WITH AQUAMAN'S BACK TO THE CORNER:

Down + Medium > Back + Light, Medium ~ Trident Scoop > Medium, Medium ~ Meter Burn From The Deep > Medium, Medium ~ From The Deep — 27%
Back + Light, Medium ~ Trident Scoop > Back + Light, Medium ~ Meter Burn From The Deep > Forward + Medium, Light + Hard — 34%
Back + Light, Medium ~ From The Deep > Back + Light, Medium ~ Meter Burn From The Deep > Forward + Medium, Light + Hard — 39%
Back + Medium > Back + Light, Medium ~ Trident Scoop > Medium, Medium ~ Meter Burn From The Deep > Medium, Medium ~ From The Deep - 37%

Jumping Hard > Back + Light, Medium ~ Trident Scoop > Medium, Medium ~ Meter Burn From The Deep > Medium, Medium ~ From The Deep — 41%
Forward + Hard > Jumping Hard > Back + Light, Medium ~ Trident Scoop > Medium, Medium ~ Meter Burn From The Deep > Medium, Medium ~ From The Deep — 42%
Back + Hard > Jumping Hard > Back + Light, Medium ~ Trident Scoop > Medium, Medium ~ Meter Burn From The Deep > Medium, Medium ~ From The Deep — 42%

INJUSTICE
GODS AMONG US

ARES

Ares is a character that excels at far range, utilizing his projectile-based Special Move and Character Power attacks to control space. He is all about making opponents play into his game and fight in a projectile war so that he can anticipate their next move while using his warp to avoid their attacks, giving him the opportunity to punish their attempts. Up close he is able to defend himself with attacks that will push opponents full screen and use a warp to force whiffs and then punish their recovery.

INTERACTIVE OBJECT TYPE: POWER

SUPER MOVE

ANNIHILATOR
Hit Level: Overhead
Range: 1/3 Screen
Description: Ares summons his sword, and then slashes it down, hitting the opponent overhead. Full combo punishable when blocked.

CHARACTER POWER

WEAPONS OF WAR
Command: Press the Power button
Description: Ares summons either a sword or an axe that he can throw full screen, use as an overhead, or launch the opponent into the air.

For character information updates please visit www.primagames.com/InjusticeUpdates

BEST BASIC ATTACKS

LOW SWEEP
Command: Down + Light
Hit Level: Low
Range: Close
Description: Ares crouches and a delivers a short-range kick that hits low. Safe when blocked.

RAGING FISTS
Command: Forward + Hard
Hit Level: Overhead
Range: Sweep
Description: Ares advances forward, hitting the opponent overhead with a closed double fist attack. Safe when blocked.

DOWNWARD HAMMERFIST
Command: Back + Medium
Hit Level: Overhead, Mid
Range: Close
Description: Ares performs a close-range overhead punch attack. Safe when blocked.

BEST COMBO ATTACKS

OLYMPIAN MIGHT
Command: Back + Light, Hard
Hit Level: Mid, Mid
Range: Sweep
Description: Ares advances forward with an elbow that ends in a punch, which knocks enemies back full screen. Both hits are safe when blocked.

MALEVOLENT VIOLENCE
Command: Hard, Down + Medium
Hit Level: Mid, Overhead
Range: Close
Description: Ares stomps the ground and then performs an overhead attack that launches the opponent. Both hits are safe when blocked.

SUPREME GENERAL
Command: Light, Light, Medium
Hit Level: High, Mid, Mid
Range: Close
Description: Ares performs a three-hit combo that stuns the opponent. Safe when blocked.

SPECIAL MOVES

DARK ENERGY

Command: Down, Forward + Light
Hit Level: High
Range: Full Screen
Description: Ares shoots a fireball made of Dark Energy that staggers the opponent on hit. Safe when blocked.

METER BURN DARK ENERGY

Description: Pressing the Meter Burn button during Dark Energy will increase the blast's size and damage and change it to hit overhead. Safe when blocked.

GOD SMACK

Command: Down, Down + Medium
Hit Level: Overhead
Range: Close, Mid, Far
Description: Ares leaps into the air with a double fist attack that hits unblockable as well as knocks the opponent down.

METER BURN GOD SMACK

Description: Pressing the Meter Burn button with God Smack will give the attack a hit of armor, increase the damage, and make it launch for a combo on hit.

PHASE SHIFTER

Command: Down, Back + Light
Hit Level: N/A
Range: Any
Description: Ares becomes almost invisible when using this Special Move.

METER BURN PHASE SHIFT

Description: Pressing the Meter Burn button with Phase Shifter will make Ares completely invisible.

WARP TRANSMISSION

Command: Down, Forward/Back + Hard
Hit Level: N/A
Range: Any
Description: Ares warps to his opponent. With Down, Forward + Hard, Ares will reappear behind his opponent and with Down, Back + Hard, he will reappear in front.

STRATEGY

USING LOW SWEEP (DOWN + LIGHT)

Low Sweep is Ares' best and fastest attack up close. It hits low, is safe when blocked, and can be canceled into his Specials and Character Power attacks. Low Sweep is reinforced as a big threat because Ares' overhead attacks are quick and lead to the same combo damage. His overheads are all safe when blocked, and are great to use as a retaliation poke up close.

USING DOWNWARD HAMMERFIST (BACK + MEDIUM)

Downward Hammerfist is an overhead attack used in situations where the opponent is crouching. When a jumping attack is blocked, it is best to go for Downward Hammerfist or a Low Sweep to start a combo. Using Downward Hammerfist and Low Sweep as a 50/50 mix-up will keep the opponent guessing defensively. Downward Hammerfist is safe when blocked, so it cannot be punished, and has a follow up by pressing Hard after Downward Hammerfist executes, launching the opponent into the air for a combo. Be careful not to just toss out Invading Force, as it can be interrupted by a backward dash or a Super Move.

USING OLYMPIAN MIGHT (BACK + LIGHT, HARD)

Olympian Might fully covers sweep range and is Ares' fastest attack in this range, perfect as a whiff punisher or to poke an opponent up close, and the full string of this attack will push the opponent full screen. The first hit can be canceled into Specials, Character Power, and Ares' Super Move. Olympian Might is safe when blocked, so it can be used without any risk. The first hit can be used to poke. Since the opponent will be aware of the next hit, he or she may freeze up and block in anticipation of the next hit, which opens up options for a grab, overhead, or Low Sweep attack.

USING SUPREME GENERAL (LIGHT, LIGHT, MEDIUM)

Supreme General is a combo starter best used after landing a jumping attack, when successfully warping behind an opponent, or when punishing a blocked attack that has enough disadvantage to let this starter sneak in. Ares can perform a 40% combo using his Weapons Of War with Supreme General. Supreme General is also safe when blocked.

USING MALEVOLENT VIOLENCE (HARD, DOWN + MEDIUM)

Malevolent Violence is a safe combo starter that cannot be punished or interrupted. It can be used inside of sweep range to either poke or whiff punish the opponent, and it doesn't have to be hit confirmed. Moreover, both hits can be canceled into Weapons Of War or any Special Attack. Malevolent Violence is totally safe when blocked.

USING RAGING FISTS (FORWARD + HARD)

Raging Fists is Ares' longest range normal in close range despite being his generic overhead that every character has. Not just safe when blocked, Raging Fists will pop the opponent up for a juggle on normal hit. Use it with armor to blow through single hit attacks and single hit projectiles.

USING DARK ENERGY (DOWN, FORWARD + LIGHT)

Dark Energy is Ares' primary way of zoning other than his Character Power since he doesn't have to wait for it to recharge. It also travels full screen, and the Meter Burn version not only hits overhead, but increases in size as well. Dark Energy gives his Character Power enough time to recharge so he can unleash Weapons Of War, and it also helps set up his Warp Transmission. Dark Energy is also safe when blocked.

USING GOD SMACK (DOWN, DOWN + MEDIUM)

God Smack is an overhead that can be close, medium, or long range, and when used with Phase Shifter it is very difficult to see coming. You can use the Meter Burn version of this attack as a reversal since it has armor, as well as to punish projectiles, since it will jump full screen or wherever you direct it. The best part about this attack is its unblockable properties, and the Meter Burn version has armor and launches the opponent into the air for a combo. It's great to use when you know an opponent is going to try to counter zone you with his or her own projectiles, or try to get close to stop you from zoning, only to end up getting God Smacked (pun intended). Meter Burn God Smack used against an opponent's wakeup attacks is worth it because it will bypass the invincibility and hit the opponent out of his or her attack. This tactic lets Ares continue pressure on downed opponents.

USING PHASE SHIFTER (DOWN, BACK + LIGHT)

Phase Shifter is a great way to throw off the opponent and make it look like you used Warp Transmission, since they deceptively have the same animation. The Meter Burn version of this Special is even better, allowing Ares to become completely invisible and more difficult to zone. When using Phase Shifter, God Smack becomes even more of a threat, since it is even more difficult to know if Ares is flying through the air towards you, ready to knock you down or launch you. Warp Transmission can also be used while in Phase Shift, making it nearly impossible to detect where he will be.

USING WARP TRANSMISSION (DOWN, FORWARD/BACK + HARD)

Warp Transmission allows Ares to avoid attacks and get behind or in front of the opponent. This tactic lets him set up pressure or go for a combo attempt. When he anticipates an opponent is trying to hit him with a projectile or up close, he can teleport behind the opponent and punish him or her during recovery. It's probably best to use the behind teleport over the front version since you may get caught by a follow up attack and are a bit safer when warping behind. After a successful warp, follow up with a combo starter that is quick enough such as Light, Medium, Heavy, Back + Light, Hard or Down + Light.

USING WEAPONS OF WAR CHARACTER POWER

Ares' Weapons Of War are mainly used to follow up normals for combos, used in projectiles, and used to zone the opponent.

WEAPONS OF WAR: STRAIGHT AXE, SWORD

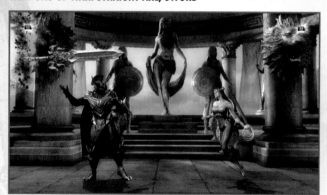

These Character Power projectiles travel the full distance of the screen, and are used to push the opponent a distance away from Ares when blocked and on hit. This will annoy the opponent into wanting to shoot his or her own projectiles, advancing forward, or beginning to crouch since Straight Sword/Axe can be ducked. When the opponent begins to crouch, Ares can perform a Meter Burn Dark Energy, God Smack, or Downward Sword/Axe, all of which hit overhead. Be careful, though; if Ares is hit before Straight Sword/Axe reaches the opponent, it will disappear. You can anticipate the opponent using a projectile trying to stop your Weapons Of War and punish your foe accordingly with either God Smack or a knockdown. If you use the Meter Burn version, you will get a launcher into a combo, or use Warp Transmission to teleport behind your opponent as he or she is recovering and pull off a full combo punish. Straight Sword and Axe can be dash canceled out of, which is great to mess with the opponent trying to duck in anticipation, and will let Ares either advance to get in for a combo or retreat to set up more zoning. Straight Axe is also the best combo ender for Ares at mid screen.

WEAPONS OF WAR: DOWNWARD AXE, SWORD

Downward Sword/Axe both hit overhead. Axe hits for a knockdown that can't be Tech Rolled out of, while Sword will stagger the opponent. The reason to use Downward Sword, Axe is whenever the opponent is ducking against Ares to avoid his Straight Sword/Axe and Dark Energy because they all can be crouched under. Downward Sword and Axe can be dash canceled out of, which can throw off the opponent trying to duck in anticipation and will let Ares either advance to try to get in for a combo or retreat to set up more zoning.

WEAPONS OF WAR: RISING AXE, SWORD

Rising Sword is a key combo starter for Ares that launches the opponent into the air and can be used as anti-air defense. It's best to use when canceled from a Down + Light, Back + Medium or Light, Light, Medium attack. Rising Axe is better used as anti-air since it has a bigger area of effect.

USING ANNIHILATOR

Annihilator is a Super Move that dominates at mid range. It has armor and hits overhead, but is combo punishable when blocked. It can also be used for anti-air, catching opponents rising into the air who try to jump away or those falling out of the air, and can be used after a Warp Transmission for players who try to immediately attack and punish Ares after he warps.

USING JUMP IN ATTACKS AND CROSS UPS

Ares' jumping Light attack is the most effective for jumping in from a distance and clearing projectiles since it has a long range. Use jumping Light when leaping over a projectile that has a lot of recovery time, since it will reach and can give Ares a successful combo opportunity. Use jumping Medium for crossing the opponent up. In the corner, jumping Medium becomes very tricky to determine if it will hit on the left or right.

USING AIR-TO-AIR

Ares' best air-to-air is jumping Light because of the range it covers and the area of effect it has. Use jumping Light when trying to retreat away from an opponent trying to pressure you with jumps in. Not only will you retreat from the opponent but you will hit the opponent out of the air and put Ares a distance away from his opponent.

INJUSTICE
GODS AMONG US

COMBOS

Light, Light, Medium ~ Rising Sword > Jumping Medium > Forward + Medium, Hard ~ Straight Axe - 37%

Back + Medium ~ Rising Sword > Jumping Medium > Forward + Medium, Hard ~ Straight Axe - 33%
Down + Light ~ Rising Sword > Jumping Medium > Forward + Medium, Hard ~ Straight Axe - 30%
Hard, Down + Medium ~ Straight Sword Dash Cancel Forward > Forward + Medium, Hard ~ Straight Axe — 35%

TIP *Where combos end in Straight Axe they can be ended with Dark Energy for additional damage.*

SUPER MOVE: ANNIHILATOR

ONE METER BURN:

Meter Burn God Smack > Forward + Medium, Hard ~ Straight Axe — 29%

TIP In the corner instead of ending with Straight Axe, end the combo with Back + Light, Hard.

TIP Where combos end in Straight Axe they can be ended with Dark Energy for additional damage.

INJUSTICE
GODS AMONG US

BANE

Bane is a grapple character that works best up close and can increase his damage output with Venom Boost. Most opponents will try to keep Bane at a distance so they can't be thrown, but using Venom Boost will give his Special Attacks a hit of armor, allowing him to attack and advance forward at the same time. The downside to this strategy is that when his Venom Boost runs out, he will deal less damage and take more damage when he is hit for a limited time until he recovers Venom Boost.

INTERACTIVE OBJECT TYPE: POWER

SUPER MOVE

BREAK THE BAT
Hit Level: Throw
Range: 1/2 Screen
Description: Bane jumps half screen and grabs his opponent. Cannot be blocked, you must jump out. It has a hit of armor so it will bypass any single-hit attacks.

CHARACTER POWER

VENOM BOOST
Command: Press the Power button
Description: Venom Boost powers up Bane, giving him armor properties on his Special Moves as well as making all of his normal moves, combos, Specials, Meter Burn specials, and Super Moves more damaging when they hit. There are three levels of Venom Boost: Level 1 lasts the longest, Level 2 is shorter but still fairly lengthy, and Level 3 is very short. The more Venom you use, the longer the recovery is until Bane can use Venom Boost again. To offset this boost in damage during Bane's Character Power, while he is recovering he takes additional damage when hit or blocking, and deals a weaker amount of his normal damage.

For character information updates please visit www.primagames.com/InjusticeUpdates

BEST BASIC ATTACKS

CRUSHING

Command: Jumping Medium
Hit Level: Overhead
Range: Sweep
Description: Bane lands with a kick angled downwards that gives enough advantage on hit for a combo attack attempt.

BODY SPLASH

Command: Jumping, Down + Hard
Hit Level: Overhead
Range: Close
Description: A jumping belly splash attack that is primarily used for crossing up the opponent.

QUICK KICK

Command: Down + Light
Hit Level: Low
Range: Sweep
Description: Bane performs a far-reaching crouching low kick.

LUCHO POWER PUNCH

Command: Forward + Medium
Hit Level: Mid
Range: 1/2 Screen
Description: Long-range punch that can be charged and dash canceled. Gains armor when Bane uses a level 3 Venom Boost.

FIST SLAM

Command: Forward + Medium, Down
Hit Level: Overhead
Range: Sweep
Description: An overhead that covers sweep distance and can be canceled into a Special Attack, Fist Slam gains armor when Bane uses a level 3 Venom Boost and is also safe when blocked.

BEST COMBO ATTACKS

FEEL THE PAIN

Command: Light, Light, Hard

Hit Level: High, Mid, Overhead

Range: Close

Description: Feel The Pain is a three-hit combo attack that is safe when blocked, but the last hit can be interrupted or avoided by backward dashing. Fortunately, connecting with a successful hit produces a bounce for a combo.

MASTER OF DISGUISE

Command: Back + Medium, Hard

Hit Level: Low, Mid

Range: Sweep

Description: Master Of Disguise is a combo starter that begins low and ends mid. The attack launches the opponent into the air for a juggle and is safe when blocked.

KNIGHTFALL

Command: Back + Medium, Light

Hit Level: Low, Overhead

Range: Close

Description: Knightfall is a short-ranged low kick that ends in a knockdown that can't be Tech Rolled out of and is safe when blocked.

SPECIAL MOVES

BODY PRESS

Command: Down, Back, Forward + Hard
Hit Level: Throw
Range: Sweep
Description: Body Press grabs the opponent whether he or she is standing, crouching, or jumping.

METER BURN BODY PRESS

Description: By pressing the Meter Burn button after landing Body Press, Bane will slam his opponent down onto his knee for more damage instead of slamming the opponent to the ground.

VENOM UPPERCUT

Command: Down, Back + Medium
Hit Level: Mid
Range: Sweep
Description: Bane performs a jumping Double Fist uppercut, launching both him and his opponent into the air.

METER BURN VENOM UPPERCUT

Description: Pressing the Meter Burn button after landing Venom Uppercut causes Bane to follow up with extra hits for additional damage.

RAGING CHARGE

Command: Back, Forward + Light
Hit Level: Mid
Range: Full Screen
Description: Bane runs full screen until he hits the opponent or gets to the opposite side of the screen.

METER BURN RAGING CHARGE

Description: Pressing the Meter Burn button after landing Raging Charge has Bane follow up with an elbow drop after knocking the opponent down.

RING SLAM

Command: Down, Back + Light
Hit Level: Throw
Range: Close
Description: Ring Slam plucks any airborne opponent out of the air and slams him or her to the ground.

DOUBLE PUNCH

Command: Back, Forward + Medium
Hit Level: Overhead
Range: Sweep
Description: Double Punch grabs the opponent whether he or she is standing, crouching, or jumping, but is combo punishable when blocked only by the fastest combo starters.

METER BURN DOUBLE PUNCH

Description: When pressing the Meter Burn button after landing Double Punch, Bane will follow up with extra hits for additional damage.

USING QUICK KICK (DOWN + LIGHT)

A fast low normal attack that covers sweep range, use Quick Kick to poke the opponent and get him or her to begin blocking. This sets up Bane to hit the opponent with Body Press since the opponent will start crouch blocking or follow up with his or her own attack. This would be a great time to use a Venom Boost Body Press or Lucho Power Punch. You can also cancel Quick Kick into a Double Punch to make the opponent block overhead, however this tactic can be back dashed to avoid the Double Punch. If you think the opponent will back dash then you can perform a Raging Charge to catch the opponent in back dash.

USING LUCHO POWER PUNCH (FORWARD + MEDIUM)

Lucho Power Punch is a long-range normal that can be charged and dash canceled out of. Unlike most of his normal attacks, it can gain a hit of armor only under the conditions that a level 3 Venom Boost is active. It can be used as a long-range whiff punish attack, and it's a reliable way for Bane to get through projectile attacks. Once it hits, it knocks the opponent backward, but is very unsafe when blocked. For this reason, Lucho Power Punch must be used with caution, and only when you're sure an opponent won't have time to recover.

USING FIST SLAM (FORWARD + MEDIUM, DOWN)

This is the overhead version of Lucho Power Punch. It has all of the same properties as Lucho Power Punch, but Fist Slam is very safe when guarded, hits overhead, and can be special/super canceled. Fist Slam covers sweep range, and is faster, so it is better used for up close.

USING FEEL THE PAIN (LIGHT, LIGHT, HARD)

Feel The Pain is a combo starter that can be used up close as a poke since it is safe. The last hit can be back dashed away or interrupted, however the first two hits are safe against everything but Superman's Kryptonian Crush Super, so other than that you can use it to bait interrupts and punish the opponent with a Venom Boost Body Press to absorb the hit. Also to punish backward dashing opponents, you can use Raging Charge to hit them while they are mid-dash. Since it advances forward and with Venom Boost, Raging Charge will absorb a hit due to the armor the Character Power gives to all special attacks. When the last hit of Feel The Pain connects, you can cancel it into Body Press or Break The Bat for a combo.

USING MASTER OF DISGUISE (BACK + MEDIUM, HARD)

A combo attack that begins low and ends mid. When the last hit connects, it will launch the opponent into the air for a juggle attempt. When used with Fist Slam and Double Fist, it creates a 50/50 chance of an overhead or low mixup. This attack is best used up close after Bane gains advantage by landing a blocked jump in, after landing a quick kick in a counter-poke war, and on wakeup where the opponent is expecting a Venom Boost Fist Slam or Double Fist. Master Of Disguise is totally safe when blocked, but can be interrupted by Armor and Super Moves.

USING KNIGHTFALL (BACK + MEDIUM, LIGHT)

A low to overhead combo attack that leads to a knockdown that can't be Tech Rolled, Knightfall is best to use if you want to get a knockdown on the opponent—especially in the corner where you can pressure the opponent with cross ups as well as a Venom Boost Body Press grab. If your opponent expects the grab and tries to jump, then you can go for a Master Of Disguise combo attack or a Ring Slam. Knightfall is totally safe when blocked, but can be interrupted by parries and Super Moves.

USING DOUBLE PUNCH (BACK, FORWARD + MEDIUM)

Double Punch is an overhead attack that knocks the opponent down that, with Venom Boost, gains a hit of armor. The best way to use Double Punch is when trying to quickly advance forward and attack at the same time up close. Because of Venom Boost, Double Punch can be used recklessly in situations up close, such as a poke war or on the opponent's wakeup where he or she may try to repel Bane's offense.

USING VENOM UPPERCUT (DOWN, BACK + MEDIUM)

Venom Uppercut, an attack that rises into the air and, with Venom Boost, gains a hit of armor. When Meter Burn is applied with Venom Uppercut, Bane will land an extra drop kick hit for additional damage and push the opponent into the corner. Use Venom Uppercut in situations where the opponent is airborne or as a wakeup attack.

USING RING SLAM (DOWN, BACK + LIGHT)

Ring Slam is best used as an anti-air and to end combos where Body Press won't land. Whenever the opponent is close to Bane and airborne, Ring Slam will snatch the opponent out of the air and throw him or her to the ground. Use Ring Slam whenever you feel an opponent will try to jump away from Bane's Body Press, since jumping is the only way to escape Body Press.

USING BODY PRESS (DOWN, BACK, FORWARD + HEAVY)

This is a command throw—a throw that requires more inputs than just a press of the Throw button—that will hit the opponent whether he or she is standing, ducking, or being juggled. It will not hit a regular airborne opponent unless he or she is in a juggle state, so the only ways to escape it are to be airborne or out of its range. This strategy reinforces Ring Slam, which is the air version of this Special Move. Since it too is a Special Move, it gains a hit of armor with Venom Boost, which makes it a primary attack to use in close while Venom Boost is still active.

USING RAGING CHARGE (BACK, FORWARD + LIGHT)

Raging Charge is best used in anticipation of another character's projectile or normal attack so Bane can close the distance to his opponent. Being a special attack, Venom Boost gains a hit of armor, making this his best tool from far range to get closer to a defensive opponent—especially projectile-heavy opponents. Raging Charge is safe when blocked, but if the opponent jumps over Bane, he is left vulnerable.

USING JUMP IN ATTACKS AND CROSS UPS

Bane has a very slow and floaty jump, and the only time you will be jumping at the opponent is when trying to clear an attack with a lot of recovery, or in situations where the opponent is knocked down or in the corner. You have three jumping attacks: Light has the widest potential as far as consistently hitting the opponent; jump in Medium has the most range and can be used as a cross up if precisely timed, but against lower crouching characters it will miss; and jump in Hard is much slower than both, so it must be done earlier while jumping, making it harder to use, but stronger and causing a juggle if it lands. His Body Splash is best for up-close situations for crossing the opponent up as they attempt a wake up in open space, and in the corner. It's best to use jumping Medium for punishing failed projectile attempts when you don't want to use Venom Boost and a special attack to get in, while jumping Body Splash is best for close situations where you don't have that much space to cover, for wakeup situations, and in the corner.

USING AIR-TO-AIR

Bane's jumping Light is his fastest attack to use in the air, and using it to combat the opponent in the air, he has a better chance to win out. After landing a jumping Light, he doesn't get any combos, however he does get a knockdown that will let him set up pressure against his opponent with Venom Boost.

USING VENOM BOOST CHARACTER POWER

Bane's Venom Boost is his whole game; it gives him Special Moves and two normal attacks armor, and increases his damage when he hits his opponent. Venom Boost must be used precisely or Bane will be at a big disadvantage when in down time while he recovers. Level 1 Venom Boost is really all Bane needs so that he can have armor on his attacks, plus it recovers the fastest. The up side is that even while the match is transitioning to the next round, his Venom Boost is recovering. You can also wait until Venom Boost is almost finished and then add on another Boost to keep it going, but at Level 3 it lasts the shortest and the recovery-weakened state is the longest, so you'll have to make sure it counts. The best time to go into Level 3 is when the opponent is knocked down and Bane is right next to them, since it will make Bane's next attack deal that much more damage. Level 1 is best to use just to get in and Level 2 is a great medium in between 1 and 3. Level 3 is also best for when going for the kill and you know your next attack will hit.

USING BREAK THE BAT

Break The Bat is Bane's Super Move. It is a throw that has armor when executed, so it will blow through attacks. Break The Bat is best used in anticipation of an opponent's offense or it can be used in situations where the opponent is in a juggle state. Because of Venom Boost, Bane rarely ever has to spend his super meter for his Meter Burn Special Moves, but with that said, he can save all of his meter for Break The Bat so he can unleash a devastating combo that will take up to 70% of the opponent's life bar with a Level 3 Venom Boost.

INJUSTICE
GODS AMONG US

COMBOS

Back + Medium, Hard > Light, Light, Hard ~ Body Press — 29%

Forward + Medium, Down ~ Body Press — 21%
Light, Light, Hard ~ Body Press — 25%

SUPER MOVE: BREAK THE BAT

ONE METER BURN:

Back + Medium, Hard > Light, Light, Hard ~ Meter Burn Body Press — 32%

Forward + Medium, Down ~ Meter Burn Body Press — 26%
Light, Light, Hard ~ Meter Burn Body Press — 29%

BREAK THE BAT COMBOS:

Back + Medium, Hard > Light, Light, Hard ~ Break The Bat — 41%

Forward + Medium, Down ~ Break The Bat — 39%
Light, Light, Hard ~ Break The Bat — 41%

INJUSTICE
GODS AMONG US

BATMAN

Batman is arguably the most versatile jack-of-all-trades character available, able to do everything without overly excelling at any one area. When at a distance, he is all about keeping his opponent on his or her toes with his projectiles, but even when the opponent decides to get into close range, Batman can use attacks up close to retreat and deflect characters who give him a hard time. His only downside is that he isn't the best at anything, so against characters who have better projectiles, he has to get up close. Against characters who are stronger in close, he has to play a distance game. Fortunately, Batman has the tools for every situation.

INTERACTIVE OBJECT TYPE: GADGET/ACROBATIC

SUPER MOVE

THE DARK KNIGHT
Hit Level: Mid
Range: Full Screen
Description: Batman throws a smoke bomb at his opponent's feet and follows up with a series of brutal hits. The start up has one hit of armor and is safe when blocked, but tracks the opponent's position anywhere on the screen. The Dark Knight is unsafe the closer you are to an opponent that blocks until about a half screen away, at which point it becomes totally safe even when blocked.

CHARACTER POWER

Command: Press the Power button
Description: Batman calls down Mechanical Bats that hover around him, assisting his offense or defense to create a variety of strategic uses.

For character information updates please visit www.primagames.com/InjusticeUpdates

BEST BASIC ATTACKS

STRAIGHT KICK

Command: Jumping Medium
Hit Level: Overhead
Range: Close

Description: Batman attacks with a downward-angled kick that allows him to chain into other combo attack strings against a grounded opponent. This attack hits overhead, so it must be blocked from the standing block position.

LOW JAB

Command: Down + Light
Hit Level: Mid

Description: A low jab attack that is built for gaining advantage in close quarters so Batman can put himself in an advantageous situation as well as make the opponent guard. Gives enough advantage on hit to be canceled into a special. Safe when blocked.

FLYING KICK

Command: Back + Hard
Hit Level: Mid
Range: 1/2 Screen

Description: Flying Kick is a long-range attack that will bounce his opponent off of the corner of the screen and back to him, giving Batman a juggle combo opportunity. This attack can be charged by holding the Hard attack button and can be canceled out of with a forward or backward dash while you are charging the attack. Pressing the Meter Burn button during this attack (which burns one bar of meter) will add one hit of armor. Flying Kick is also Batman's Back, Back + Meter Burn Bounce Cancel (bounce cancel burns two bars of meter). This attack is safe when blocked.

WHEEL KICKS

Command: Forward + Hard
Hit Level: Overhead
Range: Sweep

Description: A no-handed cartwheel kick that launches the opponent and gives Batman a juggle combo opportunity, this attack hits overhead, so it must be blocked from the standing block position. This attack can be charged by holding the Hard attack button and canceled out of with a forward or backward dash while you are charging the attack. Like the Flying Kick, pressing the Meter Burn button during this attack will add one hit of armor. Wheel Kicks is also Batman's Forward, Forward + Meter Burn Bounce Cancel. This attack is safe when blocked.

FLIP KICK

Command: Jumping Hard
Hit Level: Overhead
Range: Close

Description: A flipping kick that, if it connects, juggles the opponent. When this attack is blocked, Batman is left at advantage, allowing him to follow up with additional attacks. This attack hits overhead, so it must be blocked from the standing block position.

INJUSTICE
GODS AMONG US
BEST COMBO ATTACKS

TRICKY BAT
Command: Light, Medium, Medium
Hit Level: High, Mid, Mid
Range: Close
Description: Tricky Bat is an attack string that begins high and ends overhead. This combo attack knocks the opponent backwards, and when blocked is punishable by fast Special Moves. For example Batman himself can punish Tricky Bat with his Slide Kick.

MIND GAMES
Command: Light, Medium, Hard
Hit Level: Mid, High, Low
Range: Close
Description: Mind Games begins the same way as Tricky Bat, but instead of ending with an overhead attack, it finishes low and is a combo starter. Unlike Tricky Bat, Mind Games can only be punished by the fastest basic attacks in the game at point blank range, as well as Kryptonian Crush, Superman's Super Move.

STAY DOWN
Command: Back + Medium, Hard
Hit Level: High, Overhead, High
Range: Close
Description: Batman swipes at his opponent, lays a bomb, and then quickly rolls away as it explodes, resulting in a knockdown. Opponents can jump or back dash as Batman is planting the Batarang Bomb on the ground. This attack is punished by any Super Move that advances fast enough and far enough to reach Batman.

DARKNESS
Command: Back + Light, Light, Hard
Hit Level: Low, Mid, Mid
Range: Close
Description: Darkness is a string that begins low and ends mid, and gives a combo opportunity when it hits.

HIGH TECH
Command: Back + Light, Light, Medium
Hit Level: Low, Mid, Overhead
Range: Close
Description: High Tech is similar to Darkness, but starts low and ends overhead. When it hits the opponent, High Tech causes an knockdown that cannot be Tech Rolled out of.

CAPED CRUSADER
Command: Medium, Medium, Hard
Hit Level: Mid, High, High
Range: Low
Description: A combo attack that leads to a launcher at the end. The second hit of the combo can be ducked and the last hit can be interrupted with a fast normal attack after crouching. All hits are safe when guarded.

SPECIAL MOVES

STRAIGHT GRAPPLE

Command: Down, Forward + Light
Hit Level: High
Range: Full Screen
Description: Batman fires a grappling hook towards the opponent. Straight Grapple travels full screen until it hits, is blocked, or travels off screen. If it hits, Batman reels himself in toward the opponent and lands an airborne kick. This attack can be punished with counter attacks if the grapple either misses or is blocked while Batman is still recovering. This attack hits high so it can be crouched under by most characters.

METER BURN STRAIGHT GRAPPLE

Description: By pressing the Meter Burn button during Straight Grapple, Batman will stop just short of the opponent instead of executing his normal kick, leaving him or her open to more attacks like a Flying Kick or Wheel Kicks. If landed on an airborne opponent, it will bring him or her back down to a standing position on the ground, allowing for follow-up attacks.

SKY GRAPPLE

Command: Down, Back + Light
Hit Level: Mid
Range: Vertical 1/3 Screen
Description: Batman deploys his Grappling Hook skyward, hitting any airborne opponents. Upon connecting, Batman will slam his opponent into the ground far behind himself.

METER BURN SKY GRAPPLE

Description: Pressing the Meter Burn button during Sky Grapple will cause Batman to slam his opponent down, dealing additional damage, and will bounce the opponent for a juggle opportunity.

UP BATARANG

Command: Down, Back + Medium
Hit Level: Mid
Range: Vertical 1/3 Screen
Description: Batman throws a batarang at an upward angle that will hit any airborne opponents.

METER BURN UP BATARANG

Description: Pressing the Meter Burn button during Up Batarang will detonate the batarang and bounce the opponent into the air, allowing you to follow up with a juggle combo.

BATARANG

Command: Back, Forward + Medium
Hit Level: Mid
Range: Full Screen
Description: Batman pulls out two batarangs and throws them towards his opponent horizontally. This attack cannot be crouched; it must be blocked.

METER BURN BATARANG

Description: Pressing the Meter Burn button at any point during Batarang will detonate the projectiles, causing additional damage as well as a knock back. Even when blocked, the explosion will push the opponent backwards.

SLIDE KICK

Command: Back, Forward + Hard
Hit Level: Low
Range: 1/2 Screen
Description: Batman quickly slides across the ground with a kick that will knock the opponent down. Very punishable when blocked.

METER BURN SLIDE KICK

Description: Pressing the Meter Burn button during Slide Kick after it hits will shoot an exploding batarang that deals additional damage. When this attack is blocked, it is still very punishable.

(AIR) SCATTER BOMBS

Command: Down, Back + Medium
Hit Level: Mid
Range: Sweep
Description: Batman scatters bombs in front of him that cover sweep distance. Versus standing opponents, it staggers them enough for him to apply pressure, while in air-to-air situations it knocks the opponent clear out of the air.

CAPE PARRY

Command: Down, Back + Hard while in the air
Hit Level: N/A
Range: Close
Description: Batman pulls his cape over his torso and deflects any high or overhead attacks. If an opponent falls for Cape Parry, Batman unleashes a series of strikes that eventually leaves him or her on the ground.

STRATEGY

USING FLYING KICK (BACK + HARD) AND WHEEL KICKS (FORWARD + HARD)

When using either of these attacks without Meter Burn to add armor, there are a few things to take into account: If you are outside of point-blank range, you will obviously need an attack that will reach your opponent, and if you are close to your opponent you will want a faster attack as well as an attack that can beat out some of your opponent's faster pokes.

TIP *Flying Kick is a bit slower than Wheel Kicks, but it travels half screen, making it more useful from outside of point-blank range.*

TIP *Wheel Kicks is faster, but covers only up to sweep range. This makes it a better option up close over Flying Kick, but when timed right this attack can jump over and hit your opponent's faster generic pokes, such as Down + Light attacks or even sweeps.*

NOTE When using the Meter Burn versions of these attacks for armor, the move you choose can also vary based on the situation. If your opponent is pressuring you with ranged attacks, you will need an attack that will connect with your opponent from the distance he or she is attacking. This is where you would use the Flying Kick Meter Burn. At very close range you will need an attack that is fast enough to go through your opponent's attack while still connecting before he or she is able to recover and block. This is where you use the Wheel Kicks Meter Burn.

You can also use the Meter Burn versions of these attacks offensively. In situations where your opponent blocks one of your attacks that doesn't have advantage, but still leaves you at low negative frames (meaning you recover quickly after your attack is blocked), you can follow up with the Meter Burn Flying Kick or Wheel Kicks. With the Meter Burn versions, you can punish opponents eager to go back on the offensive by using the armor in these attacks to absorb your opponent's blow while you go through his or her attack, hitting the opponent and getting awarded with a juggle combo starter. This can open up a mind game where the opponent may become hesitant to attack after blocking some of your safer attacks and can allow you to continuously attack even at slight disadvantage because your opponent is now aware of your option to armor through his or her attack.

You can use the charging version of Flying Kick or Wheel Kicks as a baiting tool. You can begin to charge these attacks from close to its maximum range, then cancel with a backward dash. This acts as a lure to see if you can get your opponent to hit you out of the attack. After back dashing the attack successfully, you can now whiff punish your opponent with your Straight Grapple special attack or Character Power if the bats have already been called down.

Batman doesn't need to make practical use out of his combo cancel attacks. His need for meter for his special attacks to control the match with his zoning is far more important than the small damage a combo cancel offers at the cost of two bars of meter. His Meter Burn Straight Grapple and Sky Grapple also set up situations for him to use his Flying Kick/Wheel Kicks as part of a combo, which only costs him one bar of meter as opposed to two.

USING STAY DOWN (BACK + MEDIUM, HARD)

Stay Down offers a staggering number of possibilities. Whether it hits or is blocked, it will move Batman a half screen away from his opponent. This string starts with a fast upwards swipe that begins mid to overhead and ends mid. On hit or guard, Batman flips backward extremely quickly and puts him in a range where he is safe to start using projectiles. Use this to retreat away from a close-range opponent, as well as an anti-air to stop the opponent from jumping in. After the opponent blocks or is hit, Batman is free to move; he can dash in for pressure after it hits or stay at his current distance and throw projectiles. Stay Down can be used along with his projectile strategy to maintain distance on opponents, thus zoning them out. It can also be Special Canceled at the end, which makes approaching Batman even more difficult after blocking this attack because the opponent now has to worry about a Straight Grapple, Slide Kick, Batarang, or Mechanical Bats. Mechanical Bats will allow you to dash or jump in safely after releasing them whether the opponent has blocked or been hit, and either option is advantageous for Batman.

After Stay Down lands, Batman can either dash in for pressure or choose to maintain his space. In the corner, this can be canceled into a Straight Grapple for a combo or Batman can dash forward and perform a Double Jump Dive Kick for a cross up, or attempt a cross up Jumping Medium. Stay Down is also Batman's combo ender of choice; if Stay Down hits in open space and you have Mechanical Bats, you can use Release Bats late after Stay Down hits to combo into a Straight Grapple. The first hit of Stay Down can be Special Canceled — preferably into a Meter Burn Straight Grapple — to further add to Batman's damage. Batman can be interrupted by a Super Move that is fast enough to reach him as he rolls back from planting the Batarang Bomb. In order to interrupt this attack, your opponent must activate their Super Move as Batman is planting his Batarang Bomb on the ground. The Batarang Bomb finish to the string can also be avoided by a forward, backwards, or neutral jump as well as a back dash.

USING MIND GAMES (LIGHT, MEDIUM, HARD)

Mind Games is a combo attack that begins the exact same way as Tricky Bat, but ends with a very safe low attack that is only punishable at point blank range by attacks like Batman's Palm Strike and by Superman's Kryptonian Crush. Being a safe combo starter, you can use it whenever Batman is in close or to punish unsafe attacks that have been blocked up close. If you want to mix up the opponent with a 50/50, you can go for an overhead in place of the last hit, but you will need to spend two bars of Meter Bounce Cancel into Wheel Kicks, which hits overhead.

The first two hits of Mind Games and Tricky Bat are totally safe when blocked and cannot be interrupted by any other move. Moreover, the full combo attack of Tricky Bat and Mind Games cannot be interrupted by any attack in the game.

USING CAPED CRUSADER (MEDIUM, MEDIUM, HARD)

Caped Crusader is Batman's most damaging combo attack starter. It can be used as an up close whiff punish, as a poke, as well as after landing a Jumping Attack to begin a combo. The only issue you will run into using Caped Crusader lies in the fact that the second hit of the string is high, so it can be ducked and the last hit will get interrupted. The up side is that the opponent has to be very fast to duck to interrupt the string. If the opponent chooses to interrupt, you can use Cape Parry to punish his or her interrupt attempt, but if your opponent reads your attempt properly, Batman is open for punishment. You can also use a Bounce Cancel Flying Kick to punish the opponent's interrupt for max damage, but it will cost you two bars of meter. The best way to cover the holes of Caped Crusader is having Mechanical Bats active to release if you feel the opponent will try to interrupt. Caped Crusader, when blocked, cannot be punished and is totally safe.

USING DARKNESS (BACK + LIGHT, LIGHT, HARD)

Darkness is Batman's go-to combo starter, however it must only be used when it is guaranteed to hit the opponent or you have your Mechanical Bats deployed to cover your recovery, as this attack is unsafe when blocked. Batman can combo into Darkness after the Mechanical Bats hit an opponent, when landing a jump in attack, and when the opponent isn't crouched (because the first hit starts low). Darkness is safe against most characters in the game, though Superman's Super Move can punish Darkness (just as it can many attacks) when blocked. Be careful when attempting that in a classic Batman/Superman brawl.

USING HIGH TECH (BACK + LIGHT, LIGHT, MEDIUM)

High Tech is a good attack string to use when you want to score a knockdown that can't be Tech Rolled. The low hit is quick to execute and, when blocked, the last hit pushes the opponent away. If you have Mechanical Bats deployed, you can use Release Bats while the opponent is being pushed away and Batman is recovering. This gives Batman the opportunity to maintain pressure and go for a cross up attempt for big damage. High Tech cannot be punished by most of the cast, however Superman can (of course) punish it with Kryptonian Crush.

USING STRAIGHT GRAPPLE (DOWN, FORWARD + LIGHT)

Straight Grapple is used to counter projectiles in a projectile war as well as to add damage to Batman's combos. Straight Grapple is unsafe — very easily punishable up close, but at far range it offers a bit more security. Use this in anticipation of an opponent who tries backward dash, forward dash, or jump, or who you think will try to toss a projectile of his or her own. Straight Grapple isn't fast enough to stop an opponent's projectile on reaction, but with anticipation it can. With the Meter Burn version, Batman will just pull himself to the opponent and the opponent will be staggered long enough for Batman to perform a standing jump Medium, Flying Kick, or Wheel Kicks, all of which lead into a damaging combo. The Meter Burn version of Straight Grapple is Batman's most important Meter Burn Special Attack, as it is his best combo extender.

USING BATARANG (BACK, FORWARD + MEDIUM)

Batarang is Batman's primary projectile. It builds meter, travels full screen, and if it catches an airborne opponent, it will hit them out of the air, though it is unsafe when blocked up close. For that reason, it's best to use Batarang when your opponent is at such a distance away that he or she can't punish it. If the opponent is able to punish and you have Mechanical Bats, you can Release Bats to cover the recovery of a Batarang throw. The Meter Burn version of Batarang will detonate, causing a knockdown on hit, and even on block will push your opponent back. Better still, if an opponent jumps, thinking he or she has avoided the Batarang, the Meter Burn detonation is big enough to catch your opponent in the air.

USING CAPE PARRY (DOWN, BACK + HARD)

Cape Parry is one of Batman's key tools to use as defense against strong opponents up close. Use the Cape Parry when you know an opponent will do a High or Overhead attack. Cape Parry can also be used to interrupt opponents out of combo attacks that have big enough gaps, and can parry linked Special Moves as long as there is a big enough window for the move to execute.

USING JUMP IN ATTACKS AND CROSS UPS

As Batman, you have three jumping attacks to choose from: Light, Medium, or Heavy attacks. A jumping Medium attack is the most effective option for a chance for a combo attack chain, as that jumping Medium has a chance to cross up depending on the timing and range in which you have jumped in on the opponent.

Overall, jumping Medium is your absolute best jumping tool when it comes to jumping in on a grounded opponent as well. It has advantage when it's blocked, and can cause ambiguous cross ups. Some ways to set up your jumping Medium are after ending juggles with a Stay Down combo attack in the corner, or after using High Tech or Diving Elbow, as your opponent has to deal with your cross up attempt. If it hits, you get a combo, and if it's blocked, you get pressure.

Batman can also use Scatter Bombs when he is jumping in to punish opponents for trying to anti-air his jump ins. Scatter Bombs also keep Batman in the air, making it more difficult to determine when he will land.

USING MECHANICAL BATS

Release Bats can be used to extend Batman's combos or anti-air, aid his projectiles, and enhance his offense. Summoning Mechanical Bats is usually what Batman will want to do whenever he starts a match. It will allow him to pressure the opponent and go for cross ups as well as throws, overheads, and low attacks. Best of all, Batman is able to release Mechanical Bats even while he is locked in any animation other than block stun, stopping the opponent from retaliating. When he's under assault from zoning attacks, Batman can use Release Bats to stop them from throwing projectiles and advance forward safely, or confirm that the opponent has been hit by the Mechanical Bats and then use Straight Grapple to combo after landing Mechanical Bats from anywhere on the screen. Up close, it would be best to use Batman's Back + Hard Flying Kick to combo, since the bats offer enough hit stun to combo into a Flying Kick for massive damage.

Batman can make situations where he is unsafe and at risk for punishment safe with the use of Mechanical Bats. If Slide Kick is blocked, Batman can Release Bats to protect him from getting punished while he recovers. Batman can also use Cape Parry the same way. If you use Cape Parry and the opponent doesn't respond with attacks, you can Release Bats to protect him from getting punished as well as being able to hit the opponent or go for pressure, depending on if the opponent was hit or blocked.

Bat Swarm is primarily used as a combo starter or combo extender. It can be used for anti-air if the opponent jumps into the Bat Swarm vertically, but if opponents jump on top of Batman's head they will land a hit. When Bat Swarm is blocked or hits, all bats will disappear, and Bat Swarm can only be used when all three Mechanical Bats are available.

USING DOUBLE JUMP

Double Jump can be used either forward or backward. When going backward, Batman performs another flip that will propel him higher into the air while retreating. Double jumping forward, he will begin to glide through the air at a slow pace. When pressing Medium during a Double Jump, Batman will fall out of the air with a Dive Kick that behaves like a jump in combo starter and can also be used to cross up the opponent. When pressing Hard, he will perform a Diving Elbow that will knock the opponent down and cause a knockdown without Tech Roll escape, allowing Batman to follow up with enough pressure to go for a cross up attempt.

The best time to use Double Jump forward is when trying to get next to an opponent who has better projectile attacks than Batman, since he won't be able to do much from a distance. The Double Jump forward will also help Batman avoid most anti-air attempts when he jumps. Double Jump backward is best for retreating away from strong offensive characters up close, which puts him in range to use projectiles. The Double Jump Dive Kick can be used for cross ups on a knocked down opponent as well as after avoiding a projectile moving forward, allowing Batman to punish the opponent while he or she is recovering if close enough. Batman's Double Jump Diving Elbow can be used as an opening attack. He can also use Scatter Bombs during Double Jump to further change and delay his time in the air.

USING THE DARK KNIGHT CHARACTER POWER

The Dark Knight is a fast Super Move that is best used as a reversal. If you anticipate an opponent will throw out a Normal, Special, or Super attack of his or her own, you can wait for the opponent's start-up animation, then release your Super Move against your foe. It is best not to use The Dark Knight with Batman's combos, as the damage won't be as high as any of his regular single Meter Burn combos.

INJUSTICE
GODS AMONG US

COMBOS

NO METER BURN:

Back + Light, Light, Hard > Back + Medium, Hard — 21%
Light, Medium, Hard > Back + Medium Hard — 22%
Medium, Medium, Hard > Back + Hard > Jumping Hard > Back + Medium, Hard — 33%
Back + Hard > Jumping Hard > Back + Medium, Hard — 30%
Forward + Hard > Jumping Hard > Back + Medium, Hard — 30%

CHARACTER POWER:

Release Bats > Back + Hard > Jumping Hard > Back + Medium, Hard — 32%
Release Bats > Jumping Medium > Medium, Medium, Hard > Back + Hard > Jumping Hard > Back + Medium, Hard — 37%
Bat Swarm > Back + Hard > Jumping Hard > Back + Medium, Hard — 31%
Back + Medium, Heavy > Release Bats > Straight Grapple — 27%

SUPER MOVE: THE DARK KNIGHT

CORNER NO METER BURN:

Back + Light, Light, Hard > Medium, Medium, Hard > Back + Medium, Hard — 26%
Light, Medium, Hard > Medium, Medium, Hard > Back + Medium, Hard — 28%
Medium, Medium, Hard > Medium, Medium, Hard > Back + Medium, Hard — 28%

TIP After landing Back + Medium, Hard you can Release Bats while Batman is rolling backward to keep the opponent juggled, which allows you to combo into a Straight Grapple at the end.

ONE METER BURN:

Meter Burn Straight Grapple > Back + Hard > Jumping Hard > Back + Medium, Hard — 28%
Meter Burn Sky Grapple > Back + Hard > Jumping Hard > Back + Medium, Hard — 32%
Meter Burn Up Batarang > Back + Hard > Jumping Hard > Back + Medium, Hard — 32%

CORNER METER BURN:

Back + Light, Light, Hard > Hard~Meter Burn Straight Grapple > Jumping Hard > Back + Medium, Hard — 31%
Light, Medium, Hard > Hard~Meter Burn Straight Grapple > Jumping Hard > Back + Medium, Hard — 34%
(With Batman's back to the corner) Medium, Medium, Hard > Forward + Hard > Meter Burn Sky Grapple > Neutral Jumping Hard > Back + Medium, Hard — 34%
Back + Hard (let the opponent pass over your head) > Meter Burn Sky Grapple > Jumping Hard > Back + Medium, Hard — 32%
Back + Medium, Hard~Meter Burn Straight Grapple > Jumping Hard > Back + Medium, Hard — 36%

BLACK ADAM

Black Adam can fight from any range; he has tools for both up-close and ranged fighting. He is also one of the best characters when it comes to options after he gets airborne, as he has attacks that can hit his opponents and juggle them from anywhere on the screen. As a Black Adam player, you will find no problems getting close to your opponent, as you have one of the fastest moving and fastest recovering forward dashes in the game. Black Adam's only downside is his anti-air game; lacking a good and reliable anti-air forces him to fight any airborne assault with one of his own.

INTERACTIVE OBJECT TYPE: POWER

SUPER MOVE

TETH-ADAM
Range: 1/2 Screen
Hit Level: Mid
Description: Black Adam calls upon the powers of SHAZAM! and gives his opponent a god-like beating. This move travels very quickly and is good for punishing projectiles, but is not safe when blocked.

CHARACTER POWER

ORBS OF SETH
Command: Press the Power button
Description: Black Adam summons three orbs that revolve around his body for a decent amount of time. These orbs cause no hit stun, so you can't combo after they hit, but each orb does decent damage on both hit and block. When the orbs fade away they take about five seconds to charge, making Black Adam's offense really good (not to mention cheap).

For character information updates please visit www.primagames.com/InjusticeUpdates

BEST BASIC ATTACKS

KNEE STRIKE

Command: Back + Light
Hit Level: Mid
Range: Sweep
Description: The Knee Strike is a fast advancing mid attack. This move is safe when blocked, and can be canceled into any Special Move.

THUNDERING AXE KICK

Command: Jumping Medium
Hit Level: Overhead
Range: Sweep
Description: This move is a jumping kick attack that allows Black Adam to chain into attack strings against a grounded opponent, and is safe when blocked.

REVOLVING CONTACT

Command: Forward + Hard
Hit Level: Overhead
Range: Sweep
Description: This move is a ground bounce attack that leaves the opponent in a juggle state. This move can be Meter Burn canceled to have one hit of armor and is safe when blocked.

MIGHTY ADAM

Command: Back + Hard
Hit Level: Mid
Range: Close
Description: This move causes a wall bounce leaving your opponent in a juggle state, is safe when blocked, and can be Meter Burned for one hit of armor.

BEST COMBO ATTACKS

NINE BOWS

Command: Back + Medium, Hard
Hit Level: Overhead, Mid
Range: 1/4 Screen
Description: This combo attack is a fast-advancing overhead that ends with a launcher leaving the opponent in a juggle state.

CORRUPTION

Command: Light, Light, Medium
Hit Level: High, Mid, Overhead
Range: Close
Description: A combo attack that ends with an overhead and is safe when blocked, this combo can also be canceled into any Special Move.

SPECIAL MOVES

LIGHTNING STORM

METER BURN LIGHTNING STORM

Description: The Meter Burn version of Lightning Storm does more damage and sends the opponent flying across the screen. This move is a good way to end combos when you want to keep your opponent away.

Command: Down, Forward + Light
Hit Level: Mid
Range: 1/4 Screen
Description: Black Adam electrocutes his opponent with currents of electricity. This move is safe when blocked and does a decent amount of damage. Lightning Storm is also very good for keeping opponents away that try to rush you down when you've got the health lead.

BLACK MAGIC

Command: Down, Back + Light
Hit Level: Mid
Range: Full Screen
Description: Black Adam summons a black cloud near his opponent that triggers bolts of lightning, stunning the opponent and allowing a follow up with an attack or combo of choice. This move is very unsafe on block, and should only be used in combos or if you are sure the move won't be blocked.

METER BURN BLACK MAGIC

Description: The Meter Burn version of Black Magic adds an additional lightning strike that will bounce the opponent off the ground, allowing you to follow up with a combo of choice.

LIGHTNING CAGE

Command: Down, Back + Hard
Hit Level: Mid
Range: Close
Description: Black Adam slaps the ground with both of his hands and creates a cage of lightning around him. This move is safe when blocked.

METER BURN LIGHTNING CAGE

Description: Pressing the Meter Burn button after the move hits or is blocked will summon a huge bolt of lightning that will pop up the opponent, allowing for a follow-up combo.

LIGHTNING STRIKE

Command: Down, Forward + Medium
Hit Level: Low
Range: Full Screen
Description: Black Adam summons a dark cloud above his head that sends out a fast bolt of lightning, hitting his opponent low. This move is safe when blocked, and is good for keeping opponents out.

(AIR) CLOSE/FAR BOOT STOMP

Command: Down, Back + Hard/Down, Forward + Hard
Hit Level: Overhead
Range: Close or 1/2 Screen
Description: The Boot Stomp is one of the best air attacks in the game because it's quick and safe when blocked. The Far Boot Stomp is best used to punish projectiles from a distance, while the Close Stomp is good for crossing opponents up.

LIGHTNING BOMB

Command: Down, Back + Medium
Hit Level: Low
Range: Varies
Description: The Lightning Bomb is a projectile that attaches to the ground and explodes in about two seconds after touching the ground. You can change the trajectory of the Lightning Bomb by holding forward or back after performing the move.

METER BURN LIGHTNING STRIKE

Description: The Meter Burn version of Lightning Strike adds two more bolts of lightning and does more damage.

METER BURN BOOT STOMP

Description: The Meter Burn version of Boot Stomp bounces the opponent off the ground, allowing for follow-up attacks.

USING MIGHTY ADAM (BACK+ HARD) AND REVOLVING CONTACT (FORWARD + HARD)

Mighty Adam leads to a more damaging juggle, but is slightly slower than Revolving Contact and doesn't advance forward. This makes Revolving Contact the better choice of the two attacks, as it's faster than Mighty Adam and has more range. When either of these attacks is blocked, Black Adam is left at advantage. After landing a successful Mighty Adam or Revolving Contact, the opponent is launched, allowing Back Adam to follow up with a juggle combo.

USING CORRUPTION (LIGHT, LIGHT, MEDIUM)

Corruption is your main up-close punishing tool. The initial jab attack of the string is very fast, allowing Black Adam to punish many unsafe attacks up close. Corruption is also the attack string used to extend combos. After most launching attacks, you can follow up with Corruption, then cancel into your Black Magic or Meter Burn Black Magic and continue your combo.

USING NINE BOWS (BACK + MEDIUM, HARD)

This is your best attack string. This attack will launch the opponent when it hits, and leave Black Adam at advantage when it's blocked. This attack has great range, covering 1/4 screen, and allows you to use it as both a whiff punishing tool and a way to approach your opponent as you get within the 1/4 range. Nine Bows is also your main way to end juggle combos. After this attack hits, Black Adam can finish it by holding Up and then pressing Light + Hard to finish the string.

USING LIGHTNING STORM (DOWN, FORWARD + LIGHT)

Lightning Storm is completely safe when blocked, which allows Black Adam to cancel into this attack from any unsafe normal attack or attack string, effectively making the attack safe. By doing this, you can actually catch your opponent as he or she attempts to punish your unsafe attack. This can make certain unsafe attacks safer as opponents will be hesitant to attempt to punish those attacks. This guessing game now allows you to continue to attack rather than cancel into Lightning Storm.

USING BLACK MAGIC (DOWN, BACK + LIGHT)

Black Magic and Meter Burn Black Magic are mainly used inside of combos as a way to extend the combo's length—both attacks will home in on the opponent and hit the opponent where he or she stands. Black Magic will stun when it hits a grounded opponent and allows Black Adam to follow up with a combo from anywhere on the screen. This will cause a low re-launch inside of combos on a juggled opponent. Meter Burn Black Magic will launch the opponent from anywhere on the screen, as well as re-launch the opponent inside of juggle combos. This attack appears where the opponent is standing, so it cannot be seen and avoided on reaction, forcing opponents to move with caution.

USING LIGHTNING STRIKE (DOWN, FORWARD + MEDIUM)

This attack should mainly be used from a distance to keep a degree of safety. Lightning Strike will not only catch opponents standing but can also catch opponents jumping as there is some collision on the entire Lightning Strike projectile. The Meter Burn Version of this attack hits three times for increased damage, and can catch opponents off guard, as it can appear to only be the normal Lightning Strike attack. This attack is great for a full screen juggle ender after the Meter Burn Black Magic Special Move launches the opponent from a range too far for you to dash in and combo. While Lightning Storm is very unsafe and not recommend to be abused up close, it can be used as a 50/50 mix-up with your Nine Bows attack string. Nine Blows is the safe and most damaging option, so opponents will usually block while standing and defend against that option first, allowing you to connect with a Lightning Strike or Meter Burn Lightning Strike.

USING LIGHTNING CAGE (DOWN, BACK + HARD)

Your Lightning Cage Special Move is your best wakeup attack option; this allows Black Adam to get out of knockdown pressure with a safe attack. Using the Meter Burn Lightning Cage will launch the opponent for a juggle combo, which will force opponents to become hesitant on their follow ups after knocking Black Adam down. When this happens, you can take advantage of your opponent, allowing you to get up in an attempt to bait your Lightning Cage by not using the move as a wakeup attack. Instead you can get up and attack your opponent or use the space your opponent gave you to retreat to safety.

USING AIR BOOT STOMP (DOWN, BACK + HARD/DOWN FORWARD + HARD)

Your Air Boot Stomp allows you to force your way close to your opponent from anywhere on the screen. When Air Boot Kick connects, Black Adam is left at advantage, allowing him to follow up with additional attacks. The Meter Burn Air Boot Stomp will launch the opponent when it connects, giving Black Adam a juggle combo opportunity from anywhere on the screen. You can also use your Boot Stomp to jump over, and then punish, all projectile attacks.

Black Adam's anti-air game leaves much to be desired. Your Air Boot Stomp allows Black Adam to play more of an airborne style and use the move as an anti-air when you see the opponent jump.

USING LIGHTNING BOMB (DOWN, BACK + MEDIUM)

This attack is used in corner combos to set up an unblockable situation. By ending corner juggles with a cancel into your Lightning Bomb, you can immediately follow up with a jumping Medium, close Air Boot Stomp, or your Nine Bows attack string. All of those attacks hit overhead, and, if timed right, will cause the opponent to try to block both the overhead attack and low Lightning Bomb at the same time, which is impossible, causing an unblockable situation.   You can also throw the Lightning Bomb down in front of you while in open space, preventing the opponent from advancing.

USING THUNDERING AXE KICK (JUMPING MEDIUM)

This is Black Adam's best jumping attack. Thundering Axe Kick has good range and excellent collision in front and in back of Black Adam. The collision on this attack is so big that Black Adam can easily use this attack for a cross up jump in without having to use any real kind of strict timing on when you need to execute the attack. Besides using this attack as a cross up, Black Adam can actually use this attack as he is on the way down from his jump, after jumping over the opponent. Doing this will allow him to mix up a late cross over jumping Medium with an empty jump, and then land and throw.

USING ORBS OF SETH CHARACTER POWER

Black Adam's orbs allow him to do 4% per orb of unblockable damage to his opponent. Any time Black Adam comes into contact with his opponent, the orbs will damage him or her even if his opponent is hitting him. Black Adam can also cancel out of certain normal and combo attacks with his orbs, causing him to be left at major advantage and follow up with more attacks. If Black Adam is hit while his orbs are summoned, the orbs will disappear and he will have to wait the full five-second cool-down period before he can summon them again.

USING FORWARD DASH

Black Adam has one of the best forward dash speeds and recovery in the game. He will close space at a ridiculous speed, and is one of the only characters in the game who can use his dash inside of juggle combos to extend the juggle.

INJUSTICE
GODS AMONG US

COMBOS

(Far) Black Magic, (Quick Forward Jump) Far Air Boot Stomp — 12%
(Mid-range) Black Magic > Jump In Medium, Back + Medium, Hard, Up, Light + Hard — 25%

Back + Medium, Hard > Light, Light, Medium ~ Black Magic > (Quick Forward Jump) Far Air Boot Stomp — 27%
Light, Light, Medium ~ Black Magic > (Quick Forward Dash) Back + Medium, Hard, Up, Light + Hard — 27%
Forward + Medium > Back + Medium, Hard, Up, Light + Hard — 26%

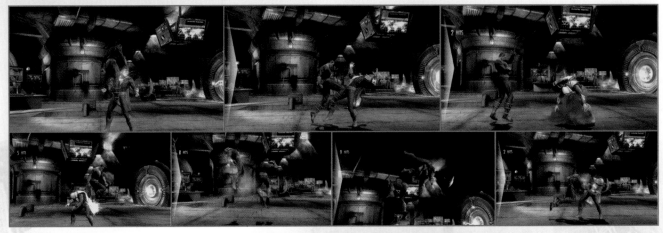

Jumping Medium, Back + Light ~ Black Magic > Cross Up Jumping Medium, Back + Medium, Hard, Up, Light + Hard — 30%
Back + Hard > Jumping Hard > Back + Medium, Hard, Up, Light + Hard — 33%
Back + Medium ~ Power ~ Light, Light, Medium ~ Black Magic > (Quick Forward Dash) Back + Medium, Hard, Up, Light + Hard — 39%
(Corner) Close Lightning Bomb > Neutral Jump Hard (Timed to connect as or close to Lightning Bomb explosion) > Neutral Jump Hard > Back + Medium, Hard, Up, Light + Hard — 39%

SUPER MOVE: TETH-ADAM

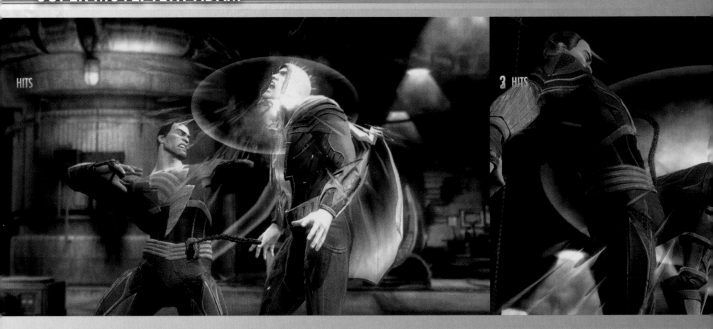

METER BURN:

(Far) Black Magic, (Quick Forward Jump) Meter Burn Far Air Boot Stomp > (Quick Dash Forward) Light, Light, Medium ~ Lightning Storm — 22%

Meter Burn Air Boot Stomp, (Quick Forward Dash) Light, Light, Medium ~ Black Magic > (Quick Forward Jump) Far Air Boot Stomp — 27%

Light, Light, Medium ~ Meter Burn Black Magic > (Quick Forward Dash) Jumping Hard > Back + Medium, Hard, Up, Light + Hard — 34%

Back + Medium, Hard > Light, Light, Medium ~ Meter Burn Black Magic > (Quick Forward Dash) Back + Medium, Hard , Up, Light + Hard — 36%

Meter Burn Lightning Cage > Neutral Jump Medium > Back + Medium, Hard, Up, Light + Hard — 36%

Back + Medium ~ Power ~ Light, Light, Medium ~ Meter Burn Black Magic > (Quick Forward Dash) Jumping Hard > Back + Medium, Hard, Up, Light + Hard - 47%

INJUSTICE
GODS AMONG US

CATWOMAN

Catwoman is a character who works best from half screen to close range. At half screen she can use her whips to stop the opponent from trying to zone her with projectiles, and use her evades to build her Cat Scratch Character Power so she can hit the opponent with a safe five-hit combo. Up close, Catwoman can be overwhelming to block with her fast 50/50 mix-ups and her Cat Stance, which applies pressure on the opponent from a distance as well as being evasive, forcing the opponent into mistakes for big damage. Catwoman's special attacks are very unsafe, so you will have to poke with Cat Scratch to accrue damage safely, or hit confirm into her special attacks from her combo attacks for big damage.

INTERACTIVE OBJECT TYPE: ACROBATIC

SUPER MOVE

NINE LIVES
Hit Level: Mid
Range: Close
Description: Nine Lives is a Super attack that is best used within sweep distance, and has one hit of armor. Nine Lives is unsafe when blocked, and can be punished by a full combo.

CHARACTER POWER

CAT SCRATCH
Command: Press the Power button
Description: Cat Scratch is a unique Character Power that is built up by simply hitting the opponent; each hit has a chance of adding a tick to her overall Scratch count, up to five. The number of Scratches accrued determines how many hits will be performed on the opponent when she uses her Cat Scratch Character Power. Once she has at least one Scratch stored, anytime she uses the Power to hit an opponent, she will perform a combo equal to the number of stored Scratches. Once used, the Scratch count is reset to zero.

For character information updates please visit www.primagames.com/InjusticeUpdates

BEST BASIC ATTACKS

KITTY KICKER
Command: Jumping Light
Hit Level: Overhead
Range: Close
Description: Catwoman jumps in with a kick that has a chance to cross up with precise timing.

AIR WHIP
Command: Jumping Medium
Hit Level: Overhead
Range: 1/4 Screen
Description: Catwoman cracks her whip forward, hitting an opponent from long range.

BALINESE BOOT

Command: Back + Medium
Hit Level: Overhead
Range: Sweep
Description: Catwoman jumps into the air and strikes with an overhead kick attack to bounce the opponent. This attack is safe when blocked.

SIAMESE SLAM

Command: Forward + Hard
Hit Level: Overhead, Mid
Range: Sweep
Description: Catwoman crouches and then rises up with an attack that launches and bounces the opponent. This attack is safe when blocked and hits overhead.

TAIL SPIN

Command: Back + Hard
Hit Level: Mid
Range: 1/2 Screen
Description: Catwoman leaps forward with a long-range legs extension. If Tail Spin connects, it bounces the opponent off the edge of the screen for a combo, and is safe when blocked.

PERSIAN POUNCE

Command: Down + Hard
Hit Level: Low
Range: Sweep
Description: Catwoman crouches low and sticks out her leg to knock the opponent down. Unsafe when guarded.

WHIP TRIP

Command: Down + Forward + Hard
Hit Level: Low
Range: 1/2 Screen
Description: Catwoman uses her whip to knock the opponent down from a long range. Unsafe when blocked, but not full combo punishable, Whip Trip can be punished by fast, far-reaching attacks.

PURRFECT

Command: Back + Light, Medium, Down + Hard
Hit Level: Low, Mid, Low
Range: Close
Description: Catwoman performs a low kick attack that ends in another low attack that staggers. While unsafe, it has a fast recovery, so opponents must be quick to punish. This combo string cannot be interrupted.

KITTY KITTY

Command: Forward + Light, Light, Medium, Hard
Hit Level: Mid, Mid, Mid, Overhead
Range: Sweep
Description: Catwoman leans forward with her claws to perform a combo that knocks the opponent down for a knockdown that can't be Tech Rolled. This string is safe against most of the cast, but the second and third hits can be interrupted by Superman, who can also punish with Kryptonian Crush after blocking. The first and last hits are safe.

HELL CAT

Command: Back + Medium, Hard
Hit Level: Overhead, Mid
Range: Sweep
Description: Catwoman hits the opponent with a double palm strike that knocks the opponent full screen. Hell Cat is safe when blocked.

SPECIAL MOVES

CAT CLAWS

Command: Back, Forward + Light
Hit Level: Mid, Mid, Mid
Range: Sweep
Description: Catwoman extends herself and her claws forward, swiping at the opponent. If it connects, she launches the opponent into the air for a combo attempt. Cat Claws is full combo punishable when blocked.

METER BURN CAT CLAWS

Description: Pressing the Meter Burn button after landing Cat Claws adds two additional hits and bounces the opponent.

CAT DASH

Command: Back, Forward + Medium
Hit Level: Mid
Range: 1/3 Screen
Description: Catwoman dashes forward through the opponent and stuns him or her long enough for a combo follow up. Combo punishable when blocked so it is very unsafe.

METER BURN CAT DASH

Description: Pressing the Meter Burn button during Cat Dash will give Catwoman a hit of armor on the dash and will dash through the opponent a second time for additional damage, stunning the opponent long enough for a combo attempt.

STRAIGHT WHIP

Command: Down, Forward + Light
Hit Level: High
Range: 1/3 Screen
Description: Catwoman cracks her whip in front of her, knocking the opponent down on hit. If it connects, the knockdown cannot be Tech Rolled out of, and is unsafe when blocked up close only against Superman's Super Move.

UP WHIP

Command: Down, Back + Light
Hit Level: High
Range: 1/3 Screen
Description: Catwoman cracks her whip vertically and hits any airborne opponent backwards out of the air.

HIGH FELINE EVADE

Command: Down, Back + Medium
Hit Level: N/A
Range: Any
Description: Catwoman bends backwards and avoids all high attacks and projectiles. Every successful attack evaded will add a Scratch to her Character Power.

LOW FELINE EVADE

Command: Down, Back + Medium, Up
Hit Level: N/A
Range: Any
Description: Catwoman hops into the air avoiding all low attacks and projectiles. Every successful attack evaded will add a Scratch to her Character Power.

CAT STANCE

Command: Down, Down + Hard, Light for Cartwheel/ Medium for Up Whip/Hard for Pounce
Hit Level: N/A
Range: Varies
Description: Catwoman crouches low and performs either a cartwheel that knocks the opponent into the air for a combo attempt, a whip attack that strikes upward and hits airborne and grounded opponents, or a pounce attack that travels 1/2 screen and knocks the opponent down. The cartwheel is the safest of attacks up close because it is only punishable by Superman's Super. With Up Whip, the farther away, the safer it becomes. Cat Pounce is unsafe, but the opponent has to be very quick to punish it with a combo.

STRATEGY

USING BALINESE BOOT (BACK + MEDIUM)

Balinese Boot is a safe overhead attack that launches if it connects. When blocked, it has a follow up that carries advantage properties, allowing Catwoman to continue pressure. This move is best used when opponents are trying to poke Catwoman with low attacks, since it will hop over them. It can also be used in a poke war when you block an opponent's attack, after you successfully land a hit that gives you enough time for a quick follow up, or after a blocked jump in. Balinese Boot goes hand in hand with Purrfect because the latter is a low attack combo starter, which gives Catwoman an effective 50/50 mix-up. The follow up to Balinese Boot, Hell Cat, is safe and can only be interrupted by the fastest attacks in the game or Supers. Hell Cat can be used whenever the opponent tries to punish Balinese Boot with a slower attack.

USING TAIL SPIN (BACK + HARD)

Tail Spin is best used as a whiff punish, long-range poke, combo extender, or with meter use to absorb a hit with armor or travel through projectiles and attacks. Tail Spin has a lot of range and is one of the longest range Level Transition attacks in the game. Using this along with her other long-range normals and Special Moves definitely allows her to control the middle range.

USING SIAMESE SLAM (FORWARD + HARD)

Siamese Slam is an overhead bounce attack, and is best used when the opponent is crouch blocking. Though it doesn't have a lot of range, Siamese Slam executes quickly, making it harder to see on reaction. It also crouches under high attacks in its opening animation.

USING PURRFECT (BACK + LIGHT, MEDIUM, DOWN + HARD)

Purrfect is a low combo starter that can be hit confirmed into any of her Special Moves. It is safe against every attack in the game except Superman's Kryptonian Smash, and is a big part of her 50/50 mix up; Balinese Boot is the overhead that works with Purrfect being low to be a mix up. When Catwoman recovers faster than her opponent after landing a poke, when her jump in attack is blocked, or if she blocks a slower poke from her opponent, it is the best time to perform the mix up. Both options lead to big damage and are a core part of her close-range game.

USING PERSIAN POUNCE (DOWN + HARD)

Persian Pounce is Catwoman's up-close low sweep attack, and a quick whiff punish attack. This forces the opponent to have to use a wake up attack because, like every character, after a sweep knockdown you get a free throw.

USING WHIP TRIP (DOWN/FORWARD + HARD)

Whip Trip is a long-range sweeping attack that works as though it were a low projectile for the range that it has. It's great to use against opponents who try to dash in, and it also helps Catwoman keep a bigger screen presence so the opponent will always be on his or her toes. Whip Trip also causes Catwoman to crouch, which comes in handy against high traveling projectile attacks.

USING KITTY KITTY (FORWARD LIGHT, LIGHT, MEDIUM, HARD)

Kitty Kitty is a great whiff punisher from sweep distance. It can also be used as a hit confirming combo starter that can lead to a knockdown that can't be Tech Rolled to set up a cross up attempt. The first three hits of the combo attack can be canceled into Special Moves, and because there are three hits, it gives Catwoman enough time to hit confirm into a Special Move for more damage.

USING CAT CLAWS (BACK, FORWARD + LIGHT)

Cat Claws is a safe Special Move that covers sweep distance range. On hit, it launches opponents into the air for a full combo and can be hit confirmed into from Catwoman's strings like Purrfect. The Meter Burn version of this attack deals more damage and causes a ground bounce for even better juggle opportunities.

USING CAT DASH (BACK, FORWARD + MEDIUM)

Cat Dash works just like Cat Claws except that it is unsafe when blocked, but travels a much longer range. The Meter Burn version of this attack has armor to go through a projectile or any single-hit attacks. When successfully landed, it will stun the opponent, even out of the air, allowing Catwoman to follow up for a combo where she normally wouldn't be able to.

USING STRAIGHT WHIP (DOWN, FORWARD + LIGHT)

Straight Whip can be used along with Whip Trip to give Catwoman some semblance of zoning. Straight Whip hits high while Whip Trip hits low and Up Whip hits in the air. These are good ways to counter zoning characters that try to keep Catwoman at bay with projectiles. After either one of these hit, she can advanced forward to put pressure on her opponent.

USING UP WHIP (DOWN, BACK + LIGHT)

Up Whip is the anti-air version of Straight Whip. This is to be used whenever the opponent jumps into the air, which he or she often will when Whip Trip and Straight Whip are used constantly. It cannot be used on reaction, as it executes too slowly, so it must be used in anticipation of a jump in.

USING HIGH FELINE EVADE (DOWN, BACK + MEDIUM)

High Feline Evade is Catwoman's parry attack that evades all high attacks and projectiles. While it's great to use at any range, note that you have to have precise timing. As mentioned before, any time she evades an attack or projectile, it will add a Scratch to her Character Power, making it a good way to avoid attacks and consistently build Scratches.

USING LOW FELINE EVADE (DOWN, BACK + MEDIUM, UP)

Low Feline Evade is Catwoman's second evasion option, helping her to avoid all low attacks and projectiles. Just like High Feline Evade, it adds a Scratch to her Character Power.

USING CAT STANCE (DOWN, DOWN + HARD)

Cat Stance is a very versatile maneuver that allows Catwoman to back or forward dash to cancel out of it as needed. Her Cartwheel flips backward, evading high attacks, and launches the opponent into the air for a juggle opportunity. The Up Whip attack covers most of the range in front of Catwoman, and will hit airborne as well as grounded opponents, knocking them down. Up Whip also covers a lot of bases as a whiff punisher, anti-air, and regular poke attack in sweep distance. Catwoman's Pounce attack leaps forward and knocks the opponent down, covering plenty of range, and can be used as a long-range whiff punisher as well as a way to close in on the opponent. When blocked it is safe, just like the other options.

USING CAT SCRATCH CHARACTER POWER

Catwoman's Cat Scratch Character Power is a series of attacks that are unleashed whenever she has a Scratch available, and needs to be built up by hitting the opponent multiple times. Every time you hit an opponent, Catwoman has a random chance of gaining another Scratch. Cat Scratch is safe when blocked and can be used as a poke or a combo ender.

USING NINE LIVES

Nine Lives is safe when blocked and covers sweep distance, but doesn't deal a whole lot of damage, so it is best used to end a round as a means to get unclashable damage. Other than that, it is better to save your meter for her Meter Burn combos.

USING JUMP IN ATTACKS AND CROSS UPS

Catwoman's jumping Light is quick, fast executing, and hard to see which side it will land on when over the opponent's head for a cross up. Use this whenever the opponent is knocked down on the ground and you are next to him or her, or when your opponent is knocked down in the corner.

USING AIR-TO-AIR

Catwoman's best air-to-air is her jumping Medium. When she unleashes her jumping Medium, she uses her whip and cracks it in front of her, which allows her to out-range a lot of other characters' attacks. Use Catwoman's jumping Medium to poke opponents safely from the air, as well as to keep them at a distance, or use it when jumping backward to retreat from an aggressive opponent who is trying to pressure you with jump ins.

COMBOS

NO METER BURN:

Back + Light, Medium, Down + Hard ~ Cat Dash > Back + Hard > Jumping Medium > Hard ~ Cat Stance Pounce — 34%
Back + Medium ~ Cat Stance Pounce — 21%
Back + Hard > Jumping Medium > Hard ~ Cat Stance Pounce — 28%
Forward + Hard > Back + Medium, Hard — 26%
Cat Stance Cartwheel > Back + Hard > Jumping Medium > Hard ~ Cat Stance Pounce — 28%
Cat Claws > Back + Hard > Jumping Medium > Hard ~ Cat Stance Pounce — 29%
Forward + Light, Light, Medium ~ Cat Dash > Back + Hard > Jumping Medium > Hard ~ Cat Stance Pounce — 31%

SUPER MOVE: NINE LIVES

ONE METER BURN:

Meter Burn Cat Claws > Back + Hard > Jumping Medium > Light ~ Straight Whip — 30%
Meter Burn Cat Dash > Back + Hard > Jumping Medium > Hard~ Cat Stance Pounce — 27%

CHARACTER POWER CAT SCRATCH:

Five Scratches — 23%

TIP *Every combo can be ended with Cat Scratch for additional hits and damage.*

CYBORG

Cyborg is a character that has a lot of tools to keep opponents away. He can be very annoying from full screen with his projectile, the Nova Blaster, and his Target Acquired projectile, which are launched from his back and can be placed anywhere on the screen. Cyborg might not have a lot of combos in open space, but he has a lot of mix-ups in the corner that are very hard for an opponent to block. His offense is decent—not too good but not too bad—as he has a command grab that reaches 1/4 of the screen. Cyborg can also escape any situation by using his Grappling Hook, which takes him the full screen away from his opponent, or he can use it to get close to his opponents when he is far from them. Cyborg is a complicated character, but when mastered he becomes a deadly machine.

INTERACTIVE OBJECT TYPE: POWER

SUPER MOVE

TARGET LOCK
Range: 3/4 Screen
Hit Level: Mid
Description: Cyborg's arm turns into a huge bionic pile driver as he launches himself towards his opponent. If the move connects, his upper body turns into the ultimate weapon and unloads a powerful beam at his opponent.

CHARACTER POWER

REPAIR CIRCUIT
Command: Press the Power button
Range: N/A
Hit Level: N/A
Description: By holding the Power button, Cyborg regenerates lost health for a period of time, but leaves himself open for attacks since he can't block while in this mode. This move can be cancelled by dashing backward or forward.

For character information updates please visit www.primagames.com/InjusticeUpdates

BEST BASIC ATTACKS

POWER KNEE

Command:	Medium
Hit Level:	Mid
Range:	Close

Description: Power Knee is a fast kick to the lower body, good for counter-poking and can be canceled into any Special Move.

LEFT FIELD

Command:	Back + Hard
Hit Level:	Mid
Range:	Outside Sweep

Description: Cyborg hits his opponent with a powerful punch that causes a wall bounce. Cyborg moves forward when doing this move, so you can use it to get close to your opponent.

TOUCHDOWN

Command:	Forward + Hard
Hit Level:	Overhead
Range:	Outside Sweep

Description: Cyborg leaps forward and performs an overhead attack that opens up combo opportunities.

BEST COMBO ATTACKS

ANDROID

Command:	Light, Light
Hit Level:	High, Mid
Range:	Close

Description: Android issues two quick jabs that are good for punishing combo attack strings or Special Moves that are slightly unsafe on block when close to the opponent.

HUMANITY

Command:	Light, Light, Medium
Hit Level:	High, Mid, Overhead
Range:	Close

Description: This combo attack is very good for pressure because the last hit is an overhead strike and, when blocked, Cyborg is in advantage because the opponent is still stuck in block stun.

LOST FAITH

Command: Back + Medium, Hard, Light
Hit Level: Low, Mid, Mid
Range: Sweep
Description: Lost Faith is a fast, low starter that ends with two mid punches, knocking your opponent away. Unfortunately, you can't continue with a combo, but you can set a mix-up with the Target Acquired projectile afterward.

SIDELINE

Command: Forward + Medium, Medium
Hit Level: Mid, Mid
Range: Sweep
Description: Cyborg kicks his opponent twice in the stomach, knocking him or her 1/2 screen away. This move leaves Cyborg in advantage when it's blocked, so he can continue his pressure game.

SPECIAL MOVES

NOVA BLASTER

Command: Back, Forward + Light
Hit Level: Mid
Range: Full Screen
Description: Cyborg fires a fast projectile that travels full screen. You can hold the Light button to delay the Nova Blaster, or cancel it by dashing backward or forward.

AIR NOVA BLASTER

Command: Back, Forward + Light (in air)
Hit Level: Mid
Range: Full Screen
Description: Same as the ground Nova Blaster, but in the air, and Cyborg recovers a little faster after performing the move.

POWER FIST

Command: Down, Back + Light
Hit Level: Mid
Range: Outside Sweep
Description: This is an anti-air Special Move good for punishing opponents who like to jump a lot.

METER BURN NOVA BLASTER

Description: Cyborg releases a second projectile that travels upward when the Meter Burn button is pressed.

METER BURN AIR NOVA BLASTER

Description: Cyborg releases a second projectile that travels downward and can be delayed after the first one is fired.

METER BURN POWER FIST

Description: Cyborg fires an upward Sonic Disruptor by pressing the Meter Burn button after the Power Fist connects.

TECHNO TACKLE

Command:	Down, Back, Forward + Hard
Hit Level:	High
Range:	1/4 Screen

Description: This is an unblockable grab that can be ducked and punished hard on whiff, but you can also cancel some strings into this command grab, which makes it a deadly mix-up.

METER BURN TECHNO TACKLE

Description: Pressing the Meter Burn button after the command grab connects adds an additional hit that knocks the opponent away.

SONIC DISRUPTOR

Command:	Down, Forward + Medium
Hit Level:	Mid
Range:	Outside Sweep

Description: A burst of energy that knocks the opponent away from you, Sonic Disruptor can be held or dashed out of either backward or forward. You can also cancel Sonic Disruptor into Up Sonic Disruptor by pressing Up twice.

UP SONIC DISRUPTOR

Command:	Down, Back + Medium
Hit Level:	Mid
Range:	Above Body

Description: The up variant of the Sonic Disruptor is identical in properties to its horizontal version, but this one hits airborne opponents.

TARGET ACQUIRED

Command:	Down, Down + Hard
Hit Level:	Overhead
Range:	Full Screen

Description: Cyborg launches two slow rockets from his back that can be placed anywhere on the screen. Pressing the Back button after doing the move places the projectiles close to Cyborg, the Forward button places them full screen, and neutral drops them in the middle of the screen.

FORWARD/BACK GRAPPLE

Command:	Down, Up + Back/ Down, Up + Forward
Hit Level:	N/A
Range:	N/A

Description: The Forward and Back Grapple can be used to close in or get away from your opponent. This move has armor on start up.

STRATEGY

USING HUMANITY (LIGHT, LIGHT, MEDIUM)

Humanity is Cyborg's go-to move to punish close attacks that are not safe on block, because the first jab of the move is quite fast. This combo attack is only punishable by the fastest attack in the game (Superman's Super Move), but you can always cancel the last hit of the move into Sonic Disruptor to make the string completely safe when blocked. Cyborg can also combo and create some really good mix-ups from this move using the Target Acquired and Grapple Special Moves. After hitting your opponent with this string, you can follow up with Nova Blaster for a decent amount of damage, or you can go into Target Acquired and make your opponent guess where on screen you are going to place the projectiles. Another option is to simply cancel Humanity into a Grapple to follow your opponent and continue to pressure them. Always remember to cancel this string into Sonic Disruptor if the opponent you are fighting against can punish the string.

USING BLOWOUT

This combo attack is good for keeping pressure because the move is safe on block and can be canceled into any Special Move. This move is good to start Cyborg's mind game with his Target Acquired move; if you think your opponent will not Tech Roll after he or she gets hit by this move, you have enough time to cancel into Target Acquired, then dash forward and apply pressure. If you think your opponent will jump back or forward, execute Back + Hard and it will hit him or her out of the air cleanly. If the opponent wakeup attacks with a move that is a single hit, Meter Burn Back + Hard or Forward + Hard to absorb the hit and punish. If your opponent Tech Rolls, use the far version of Target Acquired and either dash up twice and apply pressure, or start your keep-away game with Nova Blast.

USING SIDELINE

This is Cyborg's best combo attack for applying pressure. This move leaves Cyborg in enough advantage when blocked to throw out another attack before your opponent can counter-attack. One attack that you can use after having your opponent block, this string is a standing Medium that is fast and will beat out your opponent's next attack unless it is a Super. Though Supers have armor and activate extremely fast, if you think your opponent will activate a Super, you can just pause, block the Super, and then punish. If your opponent continues to block after blocking this string, expecting you to go for standing Medium, you can just use Sideline again and put them back in the same situation, or just go for a grab attempt. The only way the opponent can get away from this situation is to either push block or get hit on purpose.

USING NOVA BLASTER

The Nova Blaster is a good projectile that hits mid and is only punishable by the fastest attacks in the game on block. The Nova Projectile plays a big role in Cyborg's keep-away game; the fact that he can charge his Nova Blaster offers a way to create mind games against your opponent. By holding the release of Nova Blaster, you have a significant leg up if you are 1/2 screen away from an opponent that does not have a move that can reach that far to punish you. Since your opponent does not know when you will release the projectile, he or she might try to jump and you can just wait and let it rip when your opponent is about to land. The Air Nova Blaster leaves Cyborg in advantage, as your opponent can't block in mid-air. There is, however, a trick to make the Air Nova Blast hit lower to the ground: instant Air Nova Blast. The way to perform this move is by releasing an Air Nova Blast as soon as you are about to land. Hold Up right before landing so you can buffer the jump, enter the inputs of the move, and it will come out right after you leave the ground—you can do this repeatedly. Even though you can crouch the instant Air Nova Blast, it is good for keeping your opponent out because he or she is forced to walk and crouch to get close. If your opponent jumps or dashes, he or she will be caught in the Nova Blast.

USING TARGET ACQUIRED

Target Acquired is another move that is central to Cyborg's play style. It's hard to get in on Cyborg when he has those two projectiles on the screen. When you are far from your opponent (about 1/2 screen away) and the opponent doesn't have fast advancing moves, you can use Target Acquired to space them out, and, as soon as you release the projectiles, start using instant Air Nova Blasts to stop all of your opponent's movement. Cyborg basically creates a wall in front of him when he does this, because if the opponent jumps, he or she gets hit by the blast, and if he or she stays on the ground, the opponent has to block both the Nova Blast and the other projectiles because they hit overhead. When you are a full screen away from your opponent, always use this strategy to frustrate your opponent and keep him or her from getting too close. When your opponent gets close, just use Cyborg's Grappling Hook to get away to start this keep-away game again.

CYBORG

USING FORWARD AND BACK GRAPPLE

The Grappling Hook is one of the best run-away moves in the entire game; no other character has the ability to travel an entire screen away in seconds. The good thing about this move is that it has armor on start up, which means that if your opponent is pressuring you, you can simply use the Grappling Hook to get away. Even if the opponent hits you, you absorb the attack because of the armor. The Grappling Hook also changes Cyborg's corner game completely; Cyborg has plenty of really good mix-ups and ambiguous cross-ups in the corner using the Grappling Hook in combination with his Target Acquired Special Move. You can cancel his Back + Light, Medium, Hard string into Target Acquired when you have your opponent in the corner, then go into Forward Grappling Hook. Depending on how early or late you perform an air normal after using Forward Grapple, you will cross up your opponent or stay in front of him or her, creating a complete 50/50 situation.

Light, Light, Hard ~ Nova Blast — 15%
Back + Light, Medium, Hard ~ Nova Blast — 18%
Back + Light, Medium, Hard ~ Power Fist — 22%

Back + Light, Medium, Hard ~ Meter Burn Power Fist — 27%
Back + Hard > Jumping Hard > Back + Light, Medium, Hard ~ Nova Blast — 31%

Back + Light, Medium, Hard ~Meter Burn Power Fist > Back + Light, Medium, Hard ~ Power Fist — 41% (Corner Only)

SUPER MOVE: TARGET LOCK

Back + Hard > Jumping + Hard > Back + Light, Medium, Hard ~ Target Lock — 47%

INJUSTICE
GODS AMONG US

DEATHSTROKE

Deathstroke is effective both at close range and from afar thanks to his sword and guns, and his Character Power, Enhanced Reflexes, gives him the ability to make his projectiles unblockable. Deathstroke is a hassle from any range. At close distance, he has his sword normal and Special attacks to knock the opponent down, as well as poke from a safe distance up close while going for combos. At range, Deathstroke can wear the opponent down with his gunshot projectiles. Deathstroke has combo attacks that have built-in gunshots, and with Enhanced Reflexes activated they become unblockable.

INTERACTIVE OBJECT TYPE: GADGET

SUPER MOVE

EYE FOR AN EYE
Hit Level: Mid
Range: Full Screen
Description: In the blink of an eye, Deathstroke attacks the opponent from full screen with a sword slash that has one hit of armor.

CHARACTER POWER

ENHANCED REFLEXES
Command: Press the Power button
Description: With Enhanced Reflexes activated, all of Deathstroke's gunshots become unblockable for a limited time. When the Character Power runs out, all of Deathstroke's gunshots will miss until it recovers.

For character information updates please visit www.primagames.com/InjusticeUpdates

BEST BASIC ATTACKS

RAZOR'S EDGE

Command:	Jumping Hard
Hit Level:	Overhead
Range:	Close
Description:	Deathstroke slashes his sword downwards, juggling the opponent.

NON-LETHAL

Command:	Light
Hit Level:	Overhead
Range:	Close
Description:	Deathstroke performs a fast jab attack.

SLICING MOON

Command:	Hard
Hit Level:	Mid
Range:	Sweep
Description:	Deathstroke lets loose with a sword swipe that covers sweep distance.

SWEEP KICK

Command:	Down + Hard
Hit Level:	Low
Range:	Inside Sweep Distance
Description:	A crouching attack that hits low into a knockdown that can't be Tech Rolled.

SPINNING HOOK

Command:	Down + Medium
Hit Level:	Mid
Range:	Inside Sweep Distance
Description:	A crouching attack that hits mid and launches his opponent into the air. Safe when blocked.

PIERCING SUN

Command:	Back + Hard
Hit Level:	Mid
Range:	Sweep
Description:	A standard Level Transition attack that covers sweep range and bounces his opponent off the edge of the screen.

FLYING AXE

Command:	Forward + Hard
Hit Level:	Mid
Range:	Sweep
Description:	An overhead bounce attack that is quick to start up and jumps over low attacks.

BEST COMBO ATTACKS

CONTRACT KILLER

Command: Back + Light, Medium + Up
Hit Level: Low, Overhead
Range: Close
Description: A low kick that leads to a launching overhead flip attack, Contract Killer can be interrupted by fast normals or Supers and can be back dashed. The second attack is safe when blocked.

NEVER SAW IT

Command: Back + Light, Hard + Down
Hit Level: Low, Low
Range: Close
Description: Never Saw It starts as a low kick that leads to a sword swipe attack that sweeps and knocks the opponent down. Though this combo is unsafe when blocked, it can only be interrupted by fast attacks with armor or Super Moves.

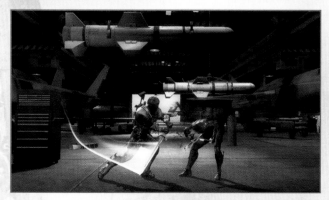

COLD STEEL

Command: Hard, Medium
Hit Level: Mid, Mid
Range: Sweep
Description: Cold Steel is a two-hit sword swipe combo attack that is safe when blocked against most of the cast at a distance. It is a fast attack, but punishable—most consistently by Superman's Kryptonian Crush.

SPECIAL MOVES

QUICK FIRE

Command: Down, Forward + Light
Hit Level: High
Range: Full Screen
Description: Deathstroke fires off two high shots that travel full screen and can be avoided by crouching. Quick Fire can be used on the ground or in mid-air, is unsafe when blocked up close, and can be punished by fast advancing attacks. At full screen it is totally safe when blocked.

METER BURN QUICK FIRE

Description: Pressing the Meter Burn button during Quick Fire allows Deathstroke to fire an additional four shots for a total of six.

LOW SHOTS

Command: Back, Down + Light
Hit Level: Low
Range: Full Screen
Description: Low Shots behaves the same as Quick Fire, except Deathstroke crouches and fires two shots that hit low. Low Shots is unsafe up close, but at half screen it is totally safe when blocked.

METER BURN LOW SHOTS

Description: By pressing the Meter Burn button during Low Shots, Deathstroke will fire an additional four shots for a total of six.

MACHINE GUN

Command: Down, Forward + Medium
Hit Level: Mid
Range: Full Screen
Description: Deathstroke uses his machine guns to fire off five shots that travel full screen. Though unsafe up close and full screen, at a distance Machine Gun must be punished by faster advancing attacks.

METER BURN MACHINE GUN

Description: Pressing the Meter Burn button during Machine Gun will shoot a grenade that knocks his opponent down.

UPWARD MACHINE GUN

Command: Down, Back + Medium
Hit Level: Mid
Range: Vertical 1/3 Screen
Description: Deathstroke fires his machine gun in an upward arc, hitting any airborne opponent.

METER BURN UPWARD MACHINE GUN

Description: Pressing the Meter Burn button during Upward Machine Gun will shoot a grenade that knocks his opponent down.

SWORD SPIN

Command: Down, Back + Hard
Hit Level: Mid
Range: Close
Description: Deathstroke spins and slashes his opponent twice. Unsafe up close, but if blocked at tip range, it is only punishable by Superman's Kryptonian Crush.

METER BURN SWORD SPIN

Description: Pressing the Meter Burn button when Sword Spin is hit or blocked will add an additional hit to the Sword Spin that is an overhead. Pressing the Meter Burn button and Down will stop the Sword Spin early and perform a low attack that hits the opponent for a knockdown that can't be Tech Rolled out of. Both options are unsafe and combo punishable when blocked.

SWORD FLIP

Command: Down, Forward + Hard
Hit Level: Mid
Range: Sweep
Description: Deathstroke slices his opponent with three leaping sword slashes ending in a knockdown. Totally safe when blocked except against Superman's Kryptonian Crush.

INJUSTICE
GODS AMONG US
STRATEGY

USING NON-LETHAL (LIGHT)

Non-Lethal is Deathstroke's fastest normal attack, but it is only effective at close range. Non-Lethal branches off into strings that leave Deathstroke at advantage, such as Carbine (Light, Medium) and Human Hunting (Light, Hard, Medium), so that he can pressure with his Forward + Hard, Back + Light variation and his throw.

Deathstroke can also slip into one of his combo attacks that includes a gunshot like Human Hunting. This is important because while his Character Power activated, the opponent won't be able to block the gunshot, guaranteeing another attack that is part of the string. If Deathstroke hits with Human Hunting in the corner, he can get a whopping 38% combo. Even if he only lands the second hit due to the opponent either not blocking or getting hit with an unblockable Enhanced Reflexes-assisted gunshot, the last part of the combo attack will still cause damage. Make sure to use Non-Lethal and its string follow-ups up close in counter-poke wars, after blocking a disadvantageous attack attempted by the opponent, or as a poke in general. The middle of Human Hunting can be interrupted by Supers or fast attacks that have armor, so watch your opponent's Super Meter to make sure it is used in situations where Deathstroke cannot be interrupted.

On the other hand, Carbine can transition into an overhead attack called Terminator (Light, Medium, Hard) that knocks down, and with Low Shots can be used as a 50/50 overhead or low mix-up.

USING SLICING MOON (HARD)

Slicing Moon is a sword swing that covers sweep range and has a follow-up that leads into a launcher. The second hit is safe, so it is ideal to use to poke in sweep range. Slicing Moon can also be used as a whiff punisher or to annoy opponents at sweep distance by just poking with the first hit, and then performing the second hit at random to throw the opponent off.

USING SWEEP KICK (DOWN + HARD)

Sweep Kick is a low attack that knocks down and cannot be Tech Rolled, and is best used up close as a quick whiff punisher. Sweep Kick creates a knockdown and leaves the opponent laying next to Deathstroke. This is perfect for a throw attempt, but it is unsafe when blocked and is combo punishable.

USING SPINNING KICK (BACK + LIGHT)

Spinning Kick is a low attack that goes into an overhead called Never Saw It, which launches for a combo when it hits. It can be interrupted by fast normal attacks and Supers and can be back dashed away from. If the opponent always tries to interrupt your Never Saw It or back dash, you can do the Contract Killer low attack variation, which will stop all but Super attacks or very fast attacks with armor. The only downside to this using Contract Killer is that it is full combo punishable when blocked. Never Saw It is a launcher and Contract Killer is a low knockdown that cannot be Tech Rolled. Great to use in counter-poke situations where Deathstroke has advantage or after Deathstroke has created an advantageous situation. For example, use it when landing a jump in when blocked or after an opponent blocks a advantageous poke.

USING COLD STEEL (HARD, MEDIUM)

Cold Steel is used as a poke from sweep range that goes into a canned combo attack. It is ideal for poking, combo extending, and whiff punishment in sweep or close range. Cold Steel will out-range most attacks at this distance and keep Deathstroke a distance away from most opponents. Cold Steel can also be Special canceled into Sword Spin or Sword Flip to make it a safer poke to use when blocked.

USING PIERCING SUN (BACK + HARD)

Piercing Sun is a standard wall bounce transition attack that is also a combo starter. Best used in sweep distance, it also has the ability to be meter burned with armor so that it can blow through attacks. Because of the range, it makes Deathstroke's up-close game very powerful.

USING FLYING AXE (FORWARD + HARD)

Flying Axe is a generic ground bounce attack that everyone has. This attack hits overhead like the rest of the generic ground bounce attacks in the game. What separates this from the others is the speed and the range. It also jumps over low attacks and can be used when Deathstroke has the advantage, such as after a blocked jumping attack with Spinning Kick to provide an overhead and low mix-up.

USING QUICK FIRE (DOWN, FORWARD + LIGHT)

Quick Fire is to be used as Deathstroke's primary Special attack. Great from a distance and only in close when he has his Character Power activated (otherwise it is unsafe to use in close range), but it can be performed in the air as well. The ground version can be meter burned to throw the opponent off from trying to advance, since the opponent will think the attack is over and then get pushed back. With Character Power this is unblockable. Quick Fire can be crouched under, so it's best used to counter zone other projectiles. When the opponent starts crouching, you can use Low Shots or Machine Gun to hit him or her while crouching. Quick Fire can also be performed in the air, but the air version cannot be meter burned.

USING LOW SHOTS (BACK, DOWN + LIGHT)

Low Shots is the low version of Quick Fire and behaves the exact same way. Its main purpose is to catch an opponent who tries to crouch under Quick Fire and force him or her to jump. Low Shots can also be used in Deathstroke's attack strings to hit the opponent low in situations where he or she can only hit overhead, creating a overhead or low mix-up.

USING MACHINE GUN (DOWN, FORWARD + MEDIUM)

Machine Gun, unlike Quick Fire, hits mid and so it cannot be crouched. It is also unblockable with Character Power and does the most damage out of all of the gunshot attacks. The meter burn version of this attack launches a grenade that pushes back when blocked and, on hit, knocks the opponent down. It's ideal to use this to keep the opponent out if you want to continue to annoy your foe. Machine Gun is also great to end rounds when Character Power is activated.

USING UPWARD MACHINE GUN (DOWN, BACK + MEDIUM)

Upward Machine Gun is the upward vertical anti-air version of Machine Gun and behaves the same, except its main purpose is to hit players out of the air when you anticipate their jump from a distance to avoid Deathstroke's other gunshot Special attacks. It is too slow to perform as an anti-air on reaction, but it's good enough for anticipated anti-air.

USING SWORD SPIN (DOWN, BACK + HARD)

Sword Spin is best used as a reversal attack when the opponent is trying to overwhelm Deathstroke in close distance. Sword Spin is unsafe when guarded, so you can't just throw it out. It must be used when you know the opponent is going to attack Deathstroke up close or at tip range. Pressing the Meter Burn button and Meter Burn + Down, Sword Spin becomes a 50/50 overhead bounce or low sweep mix-up that cannot be Tech Rolled. In the corner, this becomes a strong mix-up. Since the low cannot be Tech Rolled, it gives a cross up opportunity and the overhead lets Deathstroke pull off a combo that isn't possible midscreen, since it knocks the opponent too far away.

USING SWORD FLIP (DOWN, FORWARD + HARD)

Sword Flip is best used in sweep distance and up close when canceled from normal attacks. It knocks down on hit and is at advantage when blocked, so it is Deathstroke's primary special attack to use in close and at sweep distance. It also jumps over low attacks.

USING ENHANCED REFLEXES CHARACTER POWER

When Enhanced Reflexes is activated, Deathstroke's guns begin to glow red. This signals that all of Deathstroke's gunshots will become unblockable since he will never miss his target. This makes his zoning and his up-close pressure more difficult to deal with because the opponent will have to deal with unblockables from anywhere on the screen and making strings normally blockable to be unblockable. It also makes it so if canceling normals or strings into gunshots Deathstroke will score free hits. Enhanced Reflexes is very good for helping close out rounds and whittling down defensive opponents. With Enhanced Reflexes activated, it makes the opponent second guess whether he or she should fight Deathstroke up close or at a range since he is effective in both.

USING EYE FOR AN EYE

Eye For An Eye is a Super Move that goes full screen in a flash, making it optimal for punishing whiffed attacks or going through any attacks in their active phase. When it connects, it does a huge amount of damage, but when blocked it is very unsafe, so it must be used with precision.

USING JUMP IN ATTACKS AND CROSS UPS

The best jumping attack for Deathstroke is jumping Hard. It has the best hit box, goes the longest distance, and is the best cross up. Jumping Hard will put the opponent in juggle state so that when Deathstroke lands he is able to follow up with a combo.

USING AIR-TO-AIR

Jumping Hard is the best air-to-air for Deathstroke. Deathstroke can either advance forward or retreat backwards, and because of the hit box on the sword he is protected and will beat out most attacks the opponent tries to use to compete with it. Deathstroke can also use his Air Quick Fire to out-range other air attacks done by the opponent, making it very difficult to fight Deathstroke in the air.

NO METER BURN:

Back + Light, Up + Medium > Hard, Medium, Hard, Light ~ Air Quick Fire — 24%
Hard, Medium, Hard, Light ~ Air Quick Fire — 20%
Forward + Hard > Hard, Medium, Hard, Light ~ Air Quick Fire — 26%
Back + Hard > Jumping Hard > Hard, Medium, Hard, Light ~ Air Quick Fire — 33%
Down + Medium > Forward + Hard > Hard, Medium, Hard, Light ~ Air Quick Fire — 22%

SUPER MOVE: EYE FOR AN EYE

NO METER CORNER:

Light, Hard, Medium > Hard, Medium, Hard, Light ~ Air Quick Fire — 25%

CORNER METER BURN:

Meter Burn Sword Spin > Hard, Medium, Hard, Light ~ Air Quick Fire — 28%
Light, Hard, Medium > Meter Burn Sword Spin > Hard, Medium, Hard, Light ~ Air Quick Fire — 31%

INJUSTICE
GODS AMONG US

DOOMSDAY

Doomsday is a close offensive character. He wants to do nothing but destroy and maul his opponent. Doomsday has lows, overheads, and safe Special Moves that all reinforce his game plan: a strong corner and wakeup game that will pick apart most opponents. No one wants to fight Doomsday up close, so opponents will try to keep him at a distance. This allows Doomsday to make easier reads on his opponent as he or she tries to keep him away while using his Meter Burn Special Moves and his Doom To All Character Power to shrug off attacks that normally would knock him down. For all of the reasons above, Doomsday is a great beginner character.

INTERACTIVE OBJECT TYPE: POWER

SUPER MOVE

MASS DESTRUCTION
Hit Level: Mid
Range: Full Screen
Description: Mass Destruction is a high-hitting attack that travels the full range of sweep attacks. It is safe when blocked from close range and is only punishable by the fastest advancing forward attacks in the game.

CHARACTER POWER

DOOM TO ALL
Command: Press the Power button
Description: When Doom To All is activated, Doomsday gains the ability to shrug off hits that normally would knock down or juggle.

For character information updates please visit www.primagames.com/InjusticeUpdates

BEST BASIC ATTACKS

EARTH SHATTERING

Command: Jumping Hard
Hit Level: Overhead
Range: Sweep
Description: Doomsday swings his arm downward, hitting his opponent to put him or her in a juggle state.

FALLING BRIMSTONE

Command: Jumping Down + Hard
Hit Level: Overhead
Range: Close
Description: Doomsday performs a body splash that, when landing on the opponent, gives him a combo attempt.

LOW FIST

Command: Down + Light
Hit Level: Mid
Range: Sweep
Description: Doomsday swings his arm, swiping at the opponent. Low Fist is safe when blocked against the whole cast but is unsafe against Superman's Kryptonian Crush.

GEYSER LIFT

Command: Hard
Hit Level: Mid
Range: Inside Sweep
Description: Geyser Lift is an attack that launches the opponent into the air when it hits.

SWEEPING HOOK

Command: Down + Hard
Hit Level: Low
Range: Sweep
Description: A crouching attack that hits low and knocks down with that cannot be Tech Rolled. Sweeping Hook is safe at a distance, but combo punishable up close.

UPWARD STRIKE

Command: Down + Medium
Hit Level: Mid
Range: Sweep
Description: Doomsday performs a rising headbutt that launches an opponent into the air. Upward Strike is punishable at point-blank range by the fastest basic and combo attacks in the game, but at longer range, it is totally safe when blocked.

CRUSHING STRIKE

Command: Back + Hard
Hit Level: Mid
Range: Sweep
Description: A standard Transition attack available to every character in the game, Crushing Strike will bounce enemies off the edge of the screen if not near a transition area, and gives Doomsday a juggle attempt. This move is safe when blocked, and with Meter Burn it gains a hit of armor.

MEGATON

Command: Forward + Hard
Hit Level: Overhead
Range: Sweep
Description: An overhead bounce attack that is safe when guarded and can lead to big combos.

INJUSTICE
GODS AMONG US

BEST COMBO ATTACKS

REIGN SUPREME

Command: Light, Medium, Hard
Hit Level: Overhead
Range: Close
Description: Doomsday's primary combo starter, the first two hits of Reign Supreme can be ducked and the last hit is overhead. The second hit can be interrupted by fast-armored and Super attacks, but the last hit is totally safe.

PREHISTORIC KRYPTONIAN

Command: Back + Light, Hard
Hit Level: Overhead
Range: Sweep
Description: Prehistoric Kryptonian is an overhead string that ends with a mid knock back, hits inside of sweep distance, and is totally safe when blocked.

SPECIAL MOVES

AIR SNATCH

Command: Down, Forward + Light
Hit Level: Throw
Range: Close
Description: Doomsday grabs the opponent out of the air and slams him or her to the ground.

METER BURN AIR SNATCH

Description: When the Meter Burn button is pressed after landing Air Snatch, Doomsday relaunches the opponent into the air, catches the opponent on his back, and bounces him or her again before then landing on the ground for additional damage.

VENOM

Command: Down, Forward + Hard
Hit Level: Mid
Range: 1/2 Screen
Description: Using Venom will cause Doomsday to rush in from half screen with a shoulder attack that is safe when blocked, and knocks the opponent back closer to the corner. This move is full combo punishable when blocked.

METER BURN VENOM

Description: Pressing the Meter Burn button during Venom will cause Doomsday to do an additional shoulder attack, grants him a hit of armor, and gives him advantage when blocked.

UPWARD VENOM

Command: Down, Back + Hard
Hit Level: Mid
Range: Close
Description: This is the airborne version of the Venom attack. Instead of moving along the ground, it moves into the air vertically by leaping into the air, launching the opponent. Combo punishable when blocked.

METER BURN UPWARD VENOM

Description: Pressing the Meter Burn button after landing Upward Venom will cause Doomsday to follow up with a double drop kick that sends the opponent back down to the ground and causes additional damage. If it hits, the second part of Meter Burn Upward Venom will ground bounce the opponent on hit, but it is unsafe when blocked.

EARTH SHAKE

Command: Down, Forward + Medium
Hit Level: Overhead, Low
Range: Close
Description: Doomsday slams his fist into the ground, causing a shockwave that knocks his opponent down. It must be blocked overhead and then low and is safe when blocked.

METER BURN EARTH SHAKE

Description: Pressing the Meter Burn button during Earth Shake will turn the attack into a single low hit that launches the opponent into the air for a combo attempt. It cannot be punished when blocked.

SUPERNOVA

Command: Down, Back + Medium
Hit Level: Mid, Unblockable
Range: Close
Description: Doomsday jumps high into the air with a mid strike, then slams down onto his opponent with an unblockable attack. Both hits cause a knockdown.

METER BURN SUPERNOVA

Description: Pressing the Meter Burn button during Supernova will make the downward attack track the opponent wherever he or she is on the screen, causing a guaranteed knockdown.

USING LOW FIST (DOWN + LIGHT)

Low Fist is Doomsday's fastest poke, and the most useful of his normal attacks. It will interrupt a lot of pressure, and since it cancels into Special attacks for a combo and is safe when blocked, it is an important all-around tool. Low Fist is also the same range as Doomsday's grab range so it can be used along with his grab for pressure. Because of Doomsday's walk speed, he can walk back and forth in grab and Low Fist range. In this range he can use Supernova, well as his overhead attacks to break the opponent's defense. Low Fist to Earth Shake, when blocked, can be interrupted with a fast normal attack if an opponent is close enough to Doomsday, and it can be back dashed away from. Low Fist canceled into Venom is fast enough to beat any fast normal and punish back dash, though it can be interrupted by a Super Move.

USING CRUSHING STRIKE (BACK + HARD)

Crushing Strike is Doomsday's standard Transition attack available to the rest of the cast, though it has a plenty of range thanks to Doomsday taking a big step forward before delivering the blow. Crushing Strike can be used as a mid-range poke outside of sweep distance, as well as Meter Burned for armor to get through projectiles or any of an opponent's single-hitting attacks, or used as a combo starter.

USING MEGATON (FORWARD + HARD)

Megaton is Doomsday's bounce attack best used for hitting the opponent when he or she is crouching. Megaton can be used with Meter Burn to absorb attacks that have only one hit, and can also be used as a sweep-ranged poke to score damage.

USING THE DESTROYER (HARD, HARD)

A launching combo attack that is safe when blocked, the first hit of The Destroyer can be used as an anti-air and as a good cross up defense, since it will hit near the top of Doomsday's head. It can also be used as a poke or whiff punisher. When the opponent is hit, he or she is launched high enough to get a Low Fist canceled into a Venom Special Attack for a combo. The Destroyer is a safe way to put the opponent into the corner whether he or she is blocking or hit.

USING UPWARD STRIKE (DOWN + MEDIUM)

Upward Strike is a ranged safe uppercut attack when blocked. It's only consistently punishable when blocked by Superman's Super, Kryptonian Crush. Against the rest of the cast, it is extremely difficult to punish. Upward Strike can be used as an anti-air as well as a poke attack from inside sweep range.

USING SWEEPING HOOK (DOWN + HARD)

Sweeping Hook is a standard sweeping attack that is safe when blocked against most of the cast and causes a knockdown on hit. Knockdowns are very important for Doomsday because, with his Character Power, he can doesn't have to worry about wakeup attacks interrupting his offense. Causing the opponent to block will open room up for Doomsday's overheads, lows, and grabs.

USING PREHISTORIC KRYPTONIAN (BACK + LIGHT, HARD)

Another overhead attack that Doomsday possesses, Prehistoric Kryptonian recovers fast enough when blocked for Doomsday to follow up with pressure. The first hit can be used as a poke, and instead of finishing the string you can go for a grab when you know the opponent is blocking, afraid of the follow up. This move can be Special canceled when blocked and hit, so players who try to interrupt your pressure attempts can be checked with your Special Move to discourage them from trying to interrupt. After a blocked Prehistoric Kryptonian, you can follow up with a ranged normal attack or dash in and unleash a grab, Low Fist, Reign Supreme, Sweeping Hook, or another Prehistoric Kryptonian to reset the situation. In the corner, the opponent is at a big disadvantage and will have to spend a bar of meter to push block to get out of the situation, or get hit and take a chance to escape the corner with a wakeup attack. This is where Doomsday shines the most: while the opponent is in the corner knocked down.

USING REIGN SUPREME (LIGHT, MEDIUM, HARD)

Reign Supreme is a combo-starting string and is great to use once you have Doom To All activated near an opponent. The first two hits can be crouched and interrupted, but with Doom To All activated, that won't matter, and since the opponent is crouching it opens up Doomsday's overhead attacks to break the opponent's defense. The last hit is safe when blocked, but can be back dashed away from. When the opponent begins to back dash to escape, you can cancel the second hit of Reign Supreme into Venom or Earth Shake instead of finishing the last hit to push the opponent into the corner. The last hit of Reign Supreme also can be interrupted by Super Moves.

USING AIR SNATCH (DOWN, FORWARD + LIGHT)

Air Snatch is used to quickly grab an opponent out of the air, of course, but it can be used as a late anti-air since Air Snatch executes very fast. The Meter Burn version of this attack costs one bar of meter, but instead of throwing the opponent to the ground, the enemy will be launched back into the air, fall onto and bounce off of Doomsday's back, and *then* finally fall to the ground, picking up additional damage. Use Air Snatch whenever an opponent tries to jump away from Doomsday's pressure.

USING VENOM (DOWN, FORWARD + HARD)

Doomsday bulldozes his way forward with a shoulder that knocks his opponent close to the corner. Venom is combo punishable when blocked, but the Meter Burned version of this attack has advantage when blocked and allows Doomsday to follow up with additional pressure. In addition to that, it becomes a mix-up when guarding against the regular Venom because he can delay and use the Meter Burn version as a second hit, which gains armor. When the opponent tries to retaliate, thinking it's the regular version, he or she will get hit and knocked backward onto the floor. The armor properties can also be obtained from a distance to allow Doomsday to blow through projectile attacks. However, if the opponent anticipates this, he or she can use an armor attack of his or her own to punish the Meter Burn version of Venom. If the opponent crouch blocks the Meter Burn version of Juggernaut, it lessens the advantage.

USING UPWARD VENOM (DOWN, BACK + HARD)

Using Upward Venom is another way for Doomsday to attack enemies who try to attack him from the air. There's nothing different here from Venom, except that it rushes into the air and the Meter Burn version of this attack causes Doomsday to perform a drop kick that sends the opponent to the ground for additional damage. If the Meter Burn version is done without hitting the opponent during the initial rising attack, the drop kick is a ground bounce against grounded opponents, allowing Doomsday to follow up with a juggle. Another great way to utilize Upward Venom is by jumping over projectiles, since it works like an advancing forward jump. Upward Venom is faster and travels farther than Doomsday's normal jump, making it very useful to use for advancing. Both versions of this attack are punishable when blocked, however.

USING EARTH SHAKE (DOWN, FORWARD + MEDIUM)

Earth Shake is a safe attack that quickly transitions from overhead to low. From across the screen, Doomsday can perform Earth Shake so that he can use it for a Meter Burned Venom to advance or when he is close. This, of course, will tempt players to try to prevent Doomsday from building meter, so they will either begin to throw projectiles at him or get next to him and attack. If they choose to get close, this is exactly what he wants. The Meter Burn version of this attack hits low and launches the opponent into the air for a combo attempt. The Meter Burn version can also be used in situations to hit the opponent low where the opponent may be expecting an overhead, thus creating a mix-up.

USING SUPERNOVA (DOWN, BACK + MEDIUM)

Supernova is a two-part attack: the first hit is mid, but the second hit is unblockable. Doomsday leaps into the air and rains down on his opponent head-first, knocking him or her down. The only way to avoid the second hit is to dash away or use armor. The Meter Burn version of this attack lets Doomsday home in on wherever the opponent is instead of just leaping up and falling straight down right next to where he leapt. Doomsday doesn't really need meter for his damage, so it is best to spend most of his meter on trying to get in on the opponent, because a smart opponent will try to keep Doomsday as far away as possible. Supernova is a great way to get in on even the best projectile zoning characters.

USING DOOM TO ALL CHARACTER MOVE

Doom To All allows Doomsday to absorb hits and avoid getting knocked down for a limited time. This makes it very scary to fight Doomsday up close or try to zone him out with projectiles because no matter what, he will close in on you. Consider using Doom To All after scoring a knockdown with Doomsday with a sweep, grab, overhead, or a Special Move. Remember, while Doom To All is activated, it doesn't matter if the opponent does a wakeup attack because Doomsday can continue to attack him or her until his Character Power meter runs out. This makes Doomsday a monster for pressure, and helps his already scary up-close game as well as his wakeup game. The opponent may not be able to get up when Doomsday knocks him or her down, and before the opponent knows it, he or she has already lost a lot of health or been defeated. Doom To All is great to use in the corner to aid Doomsday's jump in Down + Heavy cross up attack to score even more damage, though it can run into problems against multi-hitting projectiles, which can stop Doomsday in his tracks. When Doom To All is active, Doomsday loses his priority on all armor attacks including his Super Move. This means that opponents can knock you out of these attacks even though the attacks have armor.

USING MASS DESTRUCTION

Mass Destruction is a mid-hitting attack that travels the full range of sweep distance and is safe when blocked to most characters, especially at a range. The only character that can punish consistently is Superman with his Kryptonian Crush. After Doomsday beats his opponent to a pulp through the Earth's core and back, he tosses his opponent to the ground, which ends with 35% sapped from the opponent's life bar.

USING JUMP IN ATTACKS AND CROSS UPS

The best jumping attack available to Doomsday is his mid-air hard blow. It covers the most range, has the best area of effect, and allows him to follow up with a combo on hit. For cross ups that are ambiguous, you will find that Doomsday's main cross up attack is his Falling Brimstone. This causes Doomsday to extend his body out all the way and can be ambiguous to block — especially in the corner. This just adds to Doomsday's deadly corner game.

USING AIR-TO-AIR

After landing an air-to-air heavy, Doomsday can combo into Down + Light + Juggernaut. For fighting in the air, jumping Medium is the best because of the hit box (read: area of effect). It can be used while retreating, and if Doomsday lands in time, he may be able to combo a Venom attack from a backward jumping Medium. For this to happen, Doomsday must land a late jumping Medium while he is descending. Jumping Light is also good for jumping back and hitting the opponent out of the air. The attack is quick, but Doomsday isn't able to follow up with anything for additional damage.

USING CORNER STRATEGY

When Doomsday has his opponent in the corner, he can walk back and forth out of throw range and pressure the opponent with attacks. When he scores a knockdown, he can further confuse the opponent's left or right guard with a cross up using Doomsday's Falling Brimstone jump in attack. To score a knockdown, Doomsday will want to use his throws as well as his overhead, low game utilizing his Sweeping Hook knockdown attack, and his other normal attacks canceled into Earth Shake or Venom to score a knockdown. With Doom To All activated, all of his offensive attempts while the opponent wakes up off the ground become a lot harder to defend against.

COMBOS

OPEN SPACE METERLESS:

Down + Light ~ Earth Shake — 13%
Down + Medium > Forward + Medium, Hard ~ Venom — 16%
Back + Light ~ Earth Shake — 16%
Back + Hard > Jumping Hard > Forward + Medium, Hard ~ Venom — 31%
Forward + Hard > Jumping Hard > Down + Medium > Forward + Medium ~ Earth Shake — 28%
Light, Medium, Hard > Venom — 19%
Hard ~ Earth Shake — 16%

SUPER MOVE: MASS DESTRUCTION

OPEN SPACE METER BURN:

Down + Light ~ Meter Burn Venom — 19%
Back + Light ~ Meter Burn Venom — 22%
Hard ~ Meter Burn Air Snatch — 23%
Meter Burn Earth Shake > Back + Medium, Hard, Light — 21%

CORNER METERLESS:

Light, Medium, Hard > Down + Hard — 19%
Light, Medium, Hard > Down + Medium > Hard ~ Earth Shake — 25%
Forward + Hard > Neutral Jumping Hard > Down + Medium > Hard ~ Earth Shake — 30%

THE FLASH

The Flash is a character with great basic attacks as well as special moves. His high and low mix-ups are very dangerous and can lead to plenty of damage. Flash's gameplan is to stay aggressive and always keep his opponent guessing between low and high attacks. When Flash is a full screen away, he can't really do much because he doesn't have a projectile, which can make it difficult to get close to some of the more powerful projectile characters. Flash has a Special Move called Speed Dodge that helps avoid projectiles. This helps The Flash to get in versus powerful projectile characters.

INTERACTIVE OBJECT TYPE: ACROBATIC

SUPER MOVE

SPEED ZONE
Range: Full Screen
Hit Level: Mid
Description: The Flash races around the world to build a tremendous amount of force, then delivers it with a series of punches to his dazed opponent.

CHARACTER POWER

TIME LOOP
Command: Left Trigger
Range: N/A
Description: Flash taps into the Speed Force, slowing time to make opponents move in slow motion, creating more opportunities for combos because opponents stay in the air longer. However, Flash can't block while in Time Loop and the effect ends if he's hit.

For character information updates please visit www.primagames.com/InjusticeUpdates

BEST BASIC ATTACKS

SPINNING BACKHAND

Command: Forward + Medium
Hit Level: Overhead
Range: Outside of sweep range
Description: A fast-advancing overhead move that's very good to close in on your opponent, this attack is safe when blocked.

BOOTS UP

Command: Down + Medium
Hit Level: Mid
Range: Close
Description: Boots Up is a launcher/anti-air good for stopping jump in attacks and allows for a juggle if it hits. This move is safe when blocked.

POWER KICK

Command: Back + Hard
Hit Level: Mid
Range: 1/4 Screen
Description: Flash performs a kick that causes a wall bounce and opens up the opportunity to juggle your opponent. If the Meter Burn button is used, you'll get one hit of armor and you can use it to bait an opponent's attack and counter with a Power Kick. This move is safe when blocked.

FLASHY KICK

Command: Forward + Hard
Hit Level: Overhead
Range: Close
Description: Flash performs a ground bounce move into a possible juggle. This move can also be Meter Burned to have armor and it is safe when blocked.

BEST COMBO ATTACKS

FORCED ACCELERATION

Command: Forward + Medium, Light
Hit Level: Overhead, Mid
Range: 1/4 Screen
Description: Flash performs a fast-advancing overhead that ends with three punches. This move is very fast and can be canceled into any of Flash's Special Moves for high damage.

QUICK STEP

Command: Down + Light, Down + Medium
Hit Level: Low, Low
Range: Close
Description: Quick Step hits with two fast low attacks good for pressure, and can be canceled into any of Flash's Special Moves for high damage. This move should be used in combination with Forced Acceleration to keep your opponents guessing whether they have to block high or low.

ROLLER COASTER

Command: Back + Medium, Medium, Forward + Hard
Hit Level: Mid, Mid, Mid
Range: Sweep
Description: Roller Coaster is a fast-advancing three-hit move good for getting close to your opponent.

SPECIAL MOVES

SPEED DODGE

Command:	Down, Back + Light
Hit Level:	N/A
Range:	N/A

Description: Flash vibrates his body faster than the speed of light allowing most projectiles to pass through him once the move is active.

METER BURN SPEED DODGE

Description: Flash releases a sonic blast that knocks his opponent across the screen. Speed Dodge is good for getting characters that use heavy pressure off you.

LIGHTNING CHARGE

Command:	Back, Forward + Medium
Hit Level:	Mid
Range:	3/4 Screen

Description: Lightning Charge is a fast attack great for whiff punishing moves, but it is very unsafe on block and must be used with caution.

METER BURN LIGHTNING CHARGE

Description: Flash performs a second hit after the Lightning Charge that does a bit more damage. The second hit only happens if the first part of the move connects.

LIGHTNING KICK

Command:	Down, Forward + Light
Hit Level:	Mid
Range:	Sweep

Description: A fast kick to the abdomen, Lightning Kick has decent range and can be charged and canceled by dashing backward or forward. This move is great for ending strings that would be otherwise unsafe when blocked. Lightning Kick is not completely safe though; it is punishable by the fastest moves in the game.

METER BURN LIGHTNING KICK

Description: Flash performs a series of kicks that launches the opponent into the air, giving him more juggle opportunities.

SONIC POUND

Command:	Down, Forward + Hard
Hit Level:	Overhead
Range:	Sweep

Description: Flash leaps into the air and comes back down with a devastating punch. You can control where you want to land by pressing back or forward.

METER BURN SONIC POUND

Description: Similar to the regular version, the Meter Burn variant causes a ground bounce so you can continue with a combo of your choice.

FLYING UPPERCUT

Command:	Down, Back + Hard
Hit Level:	Mid
Range:	Outside Sweep Range

Description: A fast launcher good for hitting opponents out of the air, this move is unsafe when blocked and should only be done if you know it will connect.

RUNNING MAN STANCE

Command:	Down, Down + Medium
Hit Level:	Varies
Range:	Full Screen

Description: Flash drops into a special stance. In this stance, he can run full screen and perform three different attacks while running: a mid, a low, and an overhead, depending on a Light, Medium, or Hard button press.

STRATEGY

USING FORCED ACCELERATION

This combo attack might be one of the best in the game because it is a fast overhead. It moves the character forward, and you can combo into any Special Move after it hits. This move should be used when you have conditioned your opponent to block low attacks—for example Flash's Quick Step (Down + Light, Down + Medium)—then you can start mixing them up with Forced Acceleration. When you hit the opponent with Forced Acceleration, you should cancel the move into a Meter Burn Lightning Kick and follow up with your combo of choice. Even though the move can be effective, do not spam this combo attack because if you whiff the string, it leaves you open for your opponent to counterattack.

USING QUICK STEP

This move is a two-hitter that strikes low, and is very fast and completely safe when blocked. Just like Forced Acceleration, this move should be used when you have conditioned your opponent to block standing instead of crouching. You can also cancel this move into any Special and follow up with your combo of choice.

When Quick Step is blocked, you have enough time to walk backward if your opponent tries to poke back, at which point you can then punish with Forced Acceleration for an overhead. This is one of the best ways to make your opponent guess between high and low mix-ups.

USING LIGHTNING KICK

This move is one of Flash's best Special Moves; you can cancel into this move from almost every string Flash has, and it is fairly safe on block—only punishable by the fastest moves in the game, which are mostly Super Moves (like Superman's Kryptonian Crush).

TIP The Meter Burn Lightning Kick is Flash's best combo starting special move, and pours on even more damage when activating Time Loop before a Meter Burn Lightning Kick. Since the move is only punishable by some Supers, it is safe to use for damaging blocking opponents and to end combo attacks. Because the move requires recovery time when blocked, you can't attack right away and are forced to block if your opponent counterattacks with a fast poke.

USING TIME LOOP CHARACTER POWER

Time Loop is a solid Character Power but has a few flaws. It is effective because your enemy slows down when you activate it, and you can execute combos that would not be normally possible during normal speed. Time Loop should only be used in a combo or when an opponent jumps. If you activate the move while your opponent is on the ground, you can get punished hard for it because even though the opponent is moving slowly, any hit will get you out of Time Loop. Time Loop will also stop if an opponent uses Block Escape on any of The Flash's strikes or if The Flash throws the opponent.

USING SONIC POUND

The Sonic Pound is a special overhead move that is best used in the corner. If you have your opponent in the corner and he or she blocks one of Flash's strings like Back + Medium, Medium and you cancel it into an overhead, it crosses your opponent up if you get the hit. If your opponent thinks you will use Sonic Pound after the string, you can do the Meter Burn version of it, which doesn't cross up and bounces your opponent off the ground for a combo opportunity. This 50/50 mix-up is very good because it keeps your opponent guessing if the move will or will not cross up.

The Sonic Pound can also be controlled by pressing forward or back after executing the move. This opens up more mix-up opportunities in open space and not just in the corner. You can control if you want to land in front or in back of your opponent after canceling the move from a string.

USING RUNNING MAN STANCE

This stance is very good because, when activated, Flash can duck some projectiles in the game, and then start running in to close on his opponents. Flash can perform three different types of attacks from the Running Man stance: the Charging Slide (Forward + Hard), which is a low; Lightning Charge (Forward + Light), which is a mid; and Sonic Pound (Forward + Medium), which is a two-hitter mid and overhead. The low and the mid are very unsafe on block, while the mid-overhead is only punishable by the fastest moves in the game. The Running Man is used best when you knock an opponent down and you want to make him or her guess if you will attack with the low or overhead.

If your opponent decides not to guess when you knock them down, he or she might want to use an invincible wakeup move. If you know your opponent might wake up with something, you can cancel Running Man with a backward dash right before you get really close to your opponent to bait the wakeup, and then punish accordingly.

STRATEGY AGAINST PROJECTILES

You will find that most of your opponents' key strategies versus The Flash will be to keep him as far away as possible, especially characters with powerful projectile attacks. This is where using Speed Dodge becomes an invaluable tool. The Flash's Speed Dodge Special Move becomes active once it appears on the screen, allowing him to phase through oncoming projectiles and further advance towards his opponent. Speed Dodge can phase through any single projectile and some milti-hitting projectile attacks such as Deathstroke's Guns. Certain multi-hitting projectiles such as Batman's Meter Burn Batarang cannot be avoided by Speed Dodge because the second hit occurs after Speed Dodge is active.

Once the Flash gets to half screen or closer, he can activate his Time Loop Character Power after using Speed Dodge to phase through a projectile. Doing this will cause the opponent to recover in slow motion, causing some projectile attacks to have a long enough recovery for The Flash to connect with his Lightning Charge Special Move.

TIP *You can also use Speed Dodge to phase through strikes.*

KEEPING PRESSURE

A good way to stay in your opponent's face is by mixing high and low mix-ups to keep your opponent guessing all the time without letting him or her think about what to do next. If the opponent starts doing wakeup attacks when you knock him or her down because your opponent does not want to guess on the mix up, just block the wakeup attack and punish with your combo of choice. Flash's Fastest Man Alive string is also good for pressure because it leaves him at advantage when the move is blocked. Never let your opponent get away, because you are going to have a hard time getting in again if the opponent has a good keep-away game.

INJUSTICE
GODS AMONG US

COMBOS

OPEN SPACE:

Forward + Medium, Light ~ Lightning Charge — 20%
Forward + Medium, Light ~ Meter Burn Lightning Kick > Hard, Medium ~ Lightning Charge — 35%
Forward + Medium, Light ~ Meter Burn Lightning Kick > Medium, Light > Hard, Medium ~ Lightning Charge — 39%
Jumping Medium, Forward + Medium, Light ~ Meter Burn Lightning Kick > Medium, Light > Hard, Medium ~ Lightning Charge — 36%
Down + Medium > Medium, Light > Hard, Medium ~ Lightning Charge — 23% (anti-air)

Jumping + Medium > (Walk Forward) Light, Light > Hard, Medium ~ Lightning Charge — 24% (air-to-air)
Forward + 3 > (Walk Forward) Medium, Light > Back + Medium, Medium, Forward + Hard ~ Lightning Charge — 35%

SUPER MOVE: SPEED ZONE

Back + 3 > Jumping + Hard > Back + Medium, Medium, Forward + Hard ~ Flying Uppercut — 35%
Down + Light, Medium ~ Meter Burn Lightning Kick > Medium, Light > Back + Medium, Medium, Forward + Hard ~ Lightning Charge — 39%

CORNER COMBOS:

Jumping Hard > Down + Medium > Light, Medium > Light, Medium > Light, Medium ~ Lightning Charge - 34%
(Activate Time Loop) Lightning Charge > Lightning Charge > Lightning Charge > Lightning Charge > Lightning Charge > Lightning Charge > Lightning Charge - 29%

GREEN ARROW

Green Arrow is a well-rounded character because he can be good from anywhere on the screen and can adapt his play style depending on which character he is up against. He has a lot of tools to play a good keep-away game, but there are certain characters that have better tools than him when it comes to playing from a distance, which forces you take the fight up to them. Against characters that he can't keep away, Green Arrow can use his high and low mix-ups and his frozen arrow to trade against projectiles. Green Arrow doesn't really excel at anything, but he still does have an answer for almost any situation—he can use his different types of arrows to handle any situation he is put in. Green Arrow is a character that takes time to learn because he has to play differently against every character. But when mastered, he can be very dangerous and scary to play against.

INTERACTIVE OBJECT TYPE: ACROBATIC

SUPER MOVE

ARSENAL ASSAULT
Range: 1/4 Screen
Hit Level: Unblockable
Description: Green Arrow shoots an explosive, unblockable arrow to the ground that covers 1/4 of the screen. After the Super ends, Green Arrow is still free to follow up with a combo of choice.

CHARACTER POWER

TAKE AIM
Command: Press the Power button
Description: The Take Aim Character Power is very good for zoning and mind games. When you press the Power button, Green Arrow shoots a really fast arrow that is advantage on block and then can instantly shoot another one. This Character Power has three different variations depending on the input and the Character Power button.

For character information updates please visit www.primagames.com/InjusticeUpdates

x0

BEST BASIC ATTACKS

MONEY SHOT

Command: Forward + Medium
Hit Level: Mid
Range: Outside Sweep
Description: This move is good for poking and counter-poking as it's fast and Green Arrow moves slightly forward. This move is also used to stop opponents from just randomly performing moves to try to hit you.

SPINNING RELEASE

Command: Jumping Hard
Hit Level: Overhead
Range: Close
Description: This jumping move is useful because it has a wide reach and is difficult to anti-air, since Green Arrow uses his bow to perform this move—a bow that isn't affected by counter-attacks.

SATISFACTION

Command: Back + Hard
Hit Level: Mid
Range: Outside Sweep
Description: Green Arrow grabs his bow as if were a bat and takes a mean swing at his opponent, which causes a wall bounce on hit. It's best to use the Meter Burn version of Satisfaction because it gains armor to bait one of your opponent's attacks and punish. This move is safe when blocked.

CANARY'S KISS

Command: Forward + Hard
Hit Level: Overhead
Range: Sweep
Description: Green Arrow grabs his bow with both hands and smacks his opponent on the head with it. Like Satisfaction, it's better to use the Meter Burn version of this move because of its slow speed, which your opponent can block on reaction. This move is safe when blocked.

BEST COMBO ATTACKS

QUEEN'S GAMBIT

Command: Forward + Medium, Down + Light, Hard
Hit Level: Mid, Low, Overhead
Range: Outside Sweep
Description: This is by far Green Arrow's best string because it can be used for high/low mix-ups or to combo into. This combo attack is safe on block and can be canceled into any Special Move.

LIGHT IT UP

Command: Back + Medium, Hard
Hit Level: Overhead, Mid
Range: Close
Description: This is Green Arrow's best combo attack when up close, as the first hit is a fast overhead that is difficult to block on reaction. What's even better is that Light It Up leaves Green Arrow in advantage when the opponent blocks the full string.

BEAST SLAYER

Command: Hard, Hard
Hit Level: Mid, Mid, Mid
Range: Close
Description: This string is good to use in between juggles and to end combos because it is Green Arrow's second most damaging basic combo. This move is safe when blocked and pushes the opponent far away from you.

SPECIAL MOVES

SKY ALERT

Command: Down, Back + Light
Hit Level: High
Range: Above Head
Description: This anti-Special move is great because when Green Arrow performs this move, he leans back towards the ground, which causes a lot of jumping attacks to whiff.

METER BURN SKY ALERT

Description: The Meter Burn version of this move deals more damage and covers a wider area because Green Arrow shoots four arrows instead of two, making it an even better anti-air move against opponents.

STINGER

Command: Back, Forward + Hard
Hit Level: Low
Range: 1/2 Screen
Description: The Stinger is a slide that is best used in combos or in high/low mix-ups because it is very unsafe on block and can't get punished with a full combo.

METER BURN STINGER

Description: Pressing the Meter Burn button after Stinger connects shoots an arrow and causes the move to do more damage overall.

(AIR) DEAD ON

Command: Down, Back + Light
Hit Level: Overhead
Range: Under Green Arrow
Description: Green Arrow jumps into the air and fires two arrows above his opponent's head. Green Arrow already has a move to stop jump-ins and a move to avoid getting anti-aired. With this, he can jump towards his opponent without fear of getting anti-aired, however this move is not safe when blocked.

METER BURN (AIR) DEAD ON

Description: Just like Sky Alert, the Meter Burn version of this move adds two more arrows and covers a wider area, making it harder for opponents to anti-air Green Arrow.

UP HAVEN BLAST

Command: Down, Forward + Medium
Hit Level: High
Range: Sweep Range Upward
Description: Green Arrow shoots an explosive arrow upward at an angle good for anti-airing opponents. This move is hard to punish because the recovery is so fast.

HURRICANE BOW

Command: Down, Forward + Light
Hit Level: Mid
Range: Close
Description: This move good is to use in combos only because it is very unsafe on block and can be punished with a full combo.

SAVAGE BLAST

Command: Down, Back + Medium
Hit Level: Mid
Range: Sweep
Description: Green Arrow leaps backward and shoots an explosive arrow into the ground. This is Green Arrow's get-away move; it's good for quickly escaping your opponent and creating space. This move is safe on block and is Green Arrow's best move to use on wakeup.

METER BURN SAVAGE BLAST

Description: The Meter Burn version of this move shoots an additional arrow that reaches farther than the first shot.

METER BURN UP HAVEN BLAST

Description: The Meter Burn version of Up Haven Blast fires an additional arrow that travels farther and lower than the first one, making this move a good combo ender.

STRATEGY

USING QUEEN'S GAMBIT

This string is perfect for creating high/low mix-ups, dealing chip damage, and pressuring your opponent. The good thing about this move is that the second hit is a quick low, but the third hit is an overhead. At first, your opponent will get hit by this move a couple of times, but in time he or she will learn to always block it, and this is when you start Green Arrow's high/low mix-up. If you think your opponent will stand up after he or she blocks the low to block the overhead, you can cancel the low into either the slide or the crouching Take Aim arrow. If you have a frozen arrow ready, this mix-up becomes even more dangerous because you can get a full combo if your opponent guesses wrong, and if your opponent guesses right, it won't matter because the frozen arrow is safe when blocked. If you think your opponent will stay blocking low because he or she doesn't want to get hit by the slide or the arrow, you can continue the string and hit your opponent overhead, and then follow up with whichever arrow you had readied, or you can hold the arrow, jump, and shoot the arrow down or shoot it low. Your opponent will be left constantly guessing.

USING LIGHT IT UP

This string is one of the best overhead startups in the game, mainly because you can use it along with the Queen's Gambit combo string and create even more scary high/low mix-ups. If you've conditioned your opponent to block low, this is the perfect place to start abusing this string because it is almost impossible to react to the incredibly speedy overhead. When the whole string gets blocked, you are still in advantage because your opponent will still be stuck in block stun. When you are fighting against an opponent that is hard to keep away and has an answer for all of your zoning tools, take the fight to him or her and use this string because it has no risk. You are safe if the string connects or is blocked.

USING SAVAGE BLAST

This move should be used when your opponent is rushing you down and you want to quickly get away from him or her. If your opponent knocks you down and tries to mix you up, wake-up attack with Savage Blast because it's very hard to punish and safe on block. You can play mind games with this move as well. You can use Green Arrow's Take Aim Character Power and then hold the arrow 1/2 screen away from your opponent. Then, if your opponent tries to react to it by attempting to punish, you can just release the arrow. If he or she continues to block, dash towards your opponent to scare him or her and make your opponent think you are going to grab him or her or go for pressure. If your opponent panics and throws out an attack, release Savage Blast right after dashing forward to catch your opponent's attack.

USING TAKE AIM CHARACTER POWER

Green Arrow's Character Power can be used for a variety of different situations depending on which character you are fighting against. The fire arrow does the most damage on hit and chip, and travels at the same speed as the regular arrow. The fire arrow is used best at full screen when you want to keep your opponent away. The electric arrow, on the other hand, is the fastest out of all the arrows and deals decent damage. When it is used in a juggle, it stuns your opponent in the air and makes him or her fall slower, which gives an opportunity to do combos that you wouldn't be able to do without it. The electric arrow is best used full and 1/2 screen away because of its speed, making it hard for an opponent to react to it. The electric arrow is decent for use in combos, but the frozen arrow is even better. Green Arrow's most high-damaging combos should be executed using the frozen arrow, which allows for combos that wouldn't be normally possible. This makes the frozen arrow the best of the bunch, but the other versions still have their usefulness. While the frozen arrow is the slowest out of all the arrows, it still has plenty of speed and can trade against other projectiles to get a full combo. Know all your matchups, and always be prepared to use the right arrow for each situation.

COMBOS

Forward + Medium, Down + Light, Hard ~ Frozen Arrow > Stinger — 15%
Hard, Hard ~ Stinger — 17%
Forward + Medium, Down + Light, Hard ~ Frozen Arrow > (Dash Forward) Hard, Hard ~ Stinger - 22%
Forward + Medium, Down + Light, Hard ~ Frozen Arrow > (Dash Forward) Hard, Hard ~ Meter Burn Stinger - 25%

Forward + Medium, Down + Light, Hard ~ Frozen Arrow > (Dash Forward) Back + Hard > Jumping + Hard > Hard, Hard — 28%
Forward + Medium, Down + Light, Hard ~ Frozen Arrow > (Dash Forward) Back + Hard > Jumping + Hard > Hard, Hard ~ Stinger — 31%

SUPER MOVE: ARSENAL ASSAULT

Forward + Medium, Down + Light, Hard ~ Arsenal Assault > Back + Hard > Jumping + Medium > Hard, Hard — 52%

INJUSTICE
GODS AMONG US

GREEN LANTERN

Green Lantern is one of the most complete characters in the game. He is solid on both the defensive and offensive end and does this with a good degree of safety. He does great damage, his projectile attacks make it very hard for opponents to approach or jump at him, and his quick attack strings make him a handful to deal with in close. He also has a good 50/50 mix-up when up close to keep opponents guessing. His only downside is that his damage is only great when he can use Meter Burn attacks or his Character Power. This means that you have to be extra careful about how and when you use your meter and Character Power. Spending meter for an extra 5%-9% can get you killed in the long run, as you can find yourself needing more meter or your Character Power later in the fight.

INTERACTIVE OBJECT TYPE: POWER

SUPER MOVE

BEWARE MY POWER
Hit Level: Mid
Range: Close
Description: Green Lantern teleports his opponent to Oa, then pummels him or her with a series of different constructs. This attack is full combo punished when blocked.

CHARACTER POWER

GREEN LANTERN'S LIGHT
Command: Press the Power button
Description: Green Lantern calls upon the power of the Lantern to slightly increase his damage on normal attacks and special attacks. Besides a slight damage boost on all attacks, the range of his Mini-Gun special attack is now increased, and his Lantern's Might Special Move now causes a small ground bounce.

For character information updates please visit www.primagames.com/InjusticeUpdates

BEST BASIC ATTACKS

LOWERING DROPKICK

Command: Jumping Light
Hit Level: Overhead
Range: Close
Description: Green Lantern jumps into the air with a downward-angled kick that allows him to chain into other combo attack strings versus a grounded opponent. This attack hits overhead, so it must be blocked from the standing block position.

RISING CUT

Command: Down + Medium
Hit Level: Mid
Range: Sweep
Description: Green Lantern performs an uppercut that launches the opponent. This attack is full combo punished when blocked.

DOWNWARD OVERHAND

Command: Jumping Medium
Hit Level: Overhead
Range: Sweep
Description: Green Lantern swipes downward with his fist from above, which allows him to chain into other combo attack strings versus a grounded opponent. This attack hits overhead so it must be blocked from the standing block position.

HIGH TENSION

Command: Back + Hard
Hit Level: Mid
Range: Sweep
Description: Green Lantern unleashes a big uppercut attack that will bounce his opponent off of the corner of the screen and back, giving him juggle combo opportunity. This attack can be charged by holding the Hard attack button and canceled out of with a forward or backward dash while you are charging the attack. Pressing the Meter Burn button during this attack (burns one bar of meter) will add one hit of armor. High Tension is also Green Lantern's Back, Back + Meter Burn Bounce Cancel (Bounce Cancel burns two bars of meter). This attack leaves Green Lantern at advantage when blocked, allowing him to follow up with additional attacks.

STANDING FLIP KICK

Command: Forward + Hard
Hit Level: Overhead
Range: Close
Description: Green Lantern does a flip kick that launches his opponent and creates a juggle combo opportunity. This attack hits overhead, so it must be blocked from the standing block position. This attack can be charged by holding the Hard attack button, and canceled out of with a forward or backward dash while you are charging the attack. Like High Tension, pressing the Meter Burn button during a Standing Flip Kick adds one hit of armor. Standing Flip Kick is also Green Lantern's Forward, Forward + Meter Burn Bounce Cancel. This attack leaves Green Lantern at advantage when blocked, allowing him to follow up with additional attacks.

CYCLONE KICK

Command: Jumping Hard
Hit Level: Overhead
Range: Sweep
Description: Green Lantern lands on his opponent with a flip kick that will launch when it hits. This attack leaves Green Lantern at advantage when blocked, allowing him to follow up with additional attacks. This attack hits overhead, so it must be blocked from the standing block position.

BEST COMBO ATTACKS

PARALLEL NATURE

Command:	Back + Light, Hard
Hit Level:	Low, Mid
Range:	Sweep

Description: Green Lantern leads off with a sliding low attack followed a double fist uppercut launcher. This attack is only punished by the faster Super Moves in the game when blocked. Green Lantern can be interrupted in between the first and second attack of this string by generic Down + Light attacks and Down + Medium uppercut launching attacks as well as Super Moves.

HYPERBOLIC

Command:	Medium, Medium, Hard
Hit Level:	Mid, Mid, Mid
Range:	Close

Description: Green Lantern starts off with a kick to his opponent's stomach, followed by a lunging jab, ending with a spin kick that results in a knockdown that cannot be Tech Rolled. This attack is safe when blocked.

LANTERN CORPS

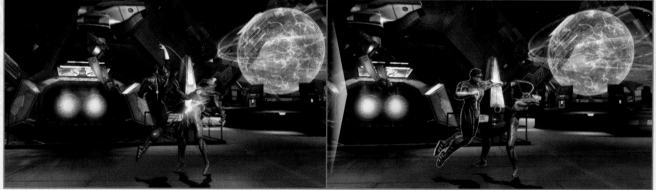

Command:	Back + Medium, Hard
Hit Level:	Mid, High
Range:	Close

Description: Green Lantern performs a fast uppercut followed by a spinning blow with a mace construct. This attack is safe when blocked. The second attack can be crouched and the opponent can full combo punish. Green Lantern can be interrupted by a Super Move in between the first and second hit of this attack string.

SPECIAL MOVES

AIR OA'S ROCKET

Command: Back, Forward + Light while in the air
Hit Level: Overhead
Range: Full Screen
Description: While airborne, Green Lantern fires a rocket construct that travels toward his opponent at a downward angle. This attack can be punished by certain attacks if the rocket either misses or is blocked while Green Lantern is too high in the air. This attack hits overhead, so it must be blocked from the standing block position.

OA'S ROCKET

Command: Back, Forward + Light
Hit Level: High
Range: Full Screen
Description: Green Lantern shoots a rocket construct that expands into a clamp grenade when it makes contact with his opponent. This attack is safe when blocked and full combo punished when crouched.

METER BURN OA'S ROCKET

Description: Pressing the Meter Burn button during Oa's Rocket will cause the rocket and/or clamp grenade to detonate, doing additional damage and launching the opponent. The detonation by itself hits the opponent mid; if the rocket is blocked first and then detonated, the detonation will still hit mid. You can detonate the rocket any time it is on the screen, even after it has been blocked or hits the opponent. This attack is safe when blocked.

ROCKET POWER

Command: (Close Range) Down, Back + Medium then hold Back; (Medium Range) Down, Back + Medium; (Far Range) Down, Back + Medium then hold Forward
Hit Level: High when in close, mid from outside sweep range
Range: Close reaches just in front of you; Medium reaches to 1/2 screen; Far reaches to 3/4 screen
Description: Green Lantern forms two rocket constructs and throws them towards his opponent at a downward angle, where they meet and explode. When done from mid to far range, this attack cannot be crouched—it must be blocked. This attack is safe when blocked.

METER BURN ROCKET POWER

Description: Pressing the Meter Burn button during Rocket Power will throw a third, more damaging, larger rocket construct that goes full screen. This attack is safe when blocked.

LANTERN'S MIGHT

Command: Down, Back + Light
Hit Level: Mid
Range: 1/3 Screen
Description: Green Lantern suspends his opponent in a field of energy, lifting him or her up and slamming the opponent over his head to the ground. This attack can reach characters as far away as 1/3 of the screen and from that range can be punished by very few characters, making this attack safe from its maximum range versus a lot of the cast. This attack is full combo punished at close range.

METER BURN LANTERN'S MIGHT

Description: Pressing the Meter Burn button during Lantern's Might will now bounce the opponent in the air, allowing you to follow up with a juggle combo. This attack is punished by a full combo up close, but from its maximum range can be only punished by a fast advancing attack.

INJUSTICE
GODS AMONG US

MINI-GUN

Command: Back, Forward + Medium
Hit Level: Mid
Range: 1/2 Screen
Description: Green Lantern forms a Gatling gun construct and shoots a wave of bullets in a sweeping motion. This attack is only punished by the faster Super Moves of the game.

TURBINE SMASH

Command: Back, Forward + Hard
Hit Level: Mid
Range: Nearly Full Screen
Description: Green Lantern materializes a jet engine turbine construct and uses it to propel himself across the stage, smashing it into his opponent. This attack travels very close to (but not quite) the entire length of the screen. This attack is punished by fast advancing attacks when blocked.

AIR TURBINE SMASH

Command: Back, Forward + Hard while in the air
Hit Level: High
Range: Nearly Full Screen
Description: Green Lantern materializes a jet engine turbine construct and uses it to propel himself across the stage while airborne. Green Lantern is vulnerable when he lands.

METER BURN MINI-GUN

Description: Pressing the Meter Burn button during Mini-Gun will now shoot multiple waves of bullets, doing additional damage. When this attack is blocked, Green Lantern is punished only by the faster Super Moves of the game.

METER BURN TURBINE SMASH

Description: Pressing the Meter Burn button during Turbine Smash now throws the turbine engine as a projectile full screen towards his opponent. This attack is safe when blocked.

METER BURN AIR TURBINE SMASH

Description: Pressing the Meter Burn button during Air Turbine Smash now throws the turbine engine full screen as a projectile while in mid-air. Green Lantern is vulnerable when he lands.

STRATEGY

USING HIGH TENSION (BACK + HARD) AND STANDING FLIP KICK (FORWARD + HARD)

High Tension should be used from sweep range, as it has a longer reach than Standing Flip Kick, allowing it to hit from ranges that Standing Flip Kick cannot. High Tension is also the better choice inside of juggle combos because it gives a better launcher, allowing for more damaging combo follow ups.

Standing Flip Kick is nearly twice as fast as High Tension, making it a much better option at close range. Standing Flip Kick is not only fast, but is also an overhead attack, allowing it to be used as a 50/50 mix-up with the low starting Parallel Nature attack string.

USING PARALLEL NATURE (BACK + LIGHT, HARD)

Parallel Nature is your best normal attack string. This string starts with an advancing, sliding low and ends in a pop up that can be canceled into your Character Power, as well as both the normal and Meter Burn versions of the Lantern's Might Special Move on reaction to the combo string hitting. When this attack string is blocked, you can cancel into your Mini-Gun or Meter Burn Mini-Gun to avoid being right next to your opponent.

Green Lantern can be universally interrupted by the entire cast in between the first and second attack of his Parallel Nature string with Down + Light, Down + Medium, or a Super Move. You can space out the first hit of this string so that it makes contact from the attack's maximum range, and this will make it harder to interrupt, but the string can still be interrupted by the same universal attacks.

You can cancel out of the first attack of the Parallel Nature string with a Back, Back + Meter Burn or Forward, Forward + Meter Burn Bounce Cancel. Using the one hit of armor of the Bounce Cancel attack, you will absorb your opponent's interrupt attempt and launch him or her for a juggle combo. The Bounce Cancel will still be interrupted if the opponent uses a Super Move.

USING OA'S ROCKET (BACK, FORWARD + LIGHT)

The start-up on this attack is pretty fast, the projectile itself travels fast, and Green Lantern recovers fast. From half to full screen, this attack is pretty abusable and one of the better keep out projectiles in the game.

The Air Oa's Rocket is used as both a keep out and anti-projectile tool. You can jump projectile attacks from a distance and counter with the air Oa's Rocket. This is a good way to avoid your opponent's oncoming projectile while shooting one of your own; you can do this attack at any point in the air, allowing you to vary the height to throw off opponents who are trying to advance towards you.

TIP Meter Burn Oa's Rocket is one of the best projectiles in the game. When this attack is blocked, you can delay when you press the Meter Burn button so your opponent has no clue when you will detonate the rocket — or if you will detonate it at all. If your opponent tries to respond in any way while the rocket is still visible, you can detonate it and launch him or her. When Oa's Rocket hits, you have plenty of time to visibly see that it has hit, confirm it, and then detonate the rocket for a juggle combo.

When an opponent attempts to crouch under your Oa's Rocket to avoid the block damage or use an attack that goes under the rocket, Meter Burn this attack as it reaches the opponent. This forces your opponent to block the attack, and in the event that your opponent has tried to use an attack to go under your Oa's Rocket, the Meter Burn version will hit and launch your opponent as it passes over him or her. You can also detonate the rocket underneath your opponent should he or she try to jump over it.

USING ROCKET POWER (DOWN, BACK + MEDIUM)

This comes in handy versus characters that have air projectiles. These characters can use air projectiles to constantly stay off of the ground in an attempt to stay away from Oa's Rocket, but you can use Rocket Power to get around this. As your opponent tries to approach, he or she may attempt to jump in towards you at the slightest sign that you may be throwing a ground projectile. This is where you can use Rocket Power to mix things up. Your opponent may take to the air, in an attempt to jump over your Oa's Rocket attack. By mixing in Rocket Power from the appropriate range, you can knock an opponent right out of the air, allowing you to connect with your Lantern's Might special attack.

TIP The Meter Burn version can be done at any time during Rocket Power. The best way to use this is to delay the Meter Burn so that your opponent does not know when it is safe to advance after seeing the first attack.

USING LANTERN'S MIGHT (DOWN, BACK + LIGHT)

As an anti-air, this attack has almost no equal. You can snatch an opponent right out of the air on reaction with little to no difficulty. This attack is one of the best space-controlling tools in the game; opponents must approach very carefully to avoid it. Lantern's Might has a maximum range of 1/3 screen, and from that range very few characters can punish you — and of those characters that can punish you from the move's maximum range, almost none of them can do so with any substantial damage.

When the normal version of this attack hits, it will not juggle, but will splat the opponent down with a knockdown that cannot be Tech Rolled. From this knockdown, you can immediately follow up with the Parallel Nature string or another Lantern's Might, and the opponent must block or use a wakeup attack. If your opponent tries to get up and jump or use a standard attack, he or she will be hit. You can back away after the knockdown, baiting a wakeup attack, and then whiff punish it with another Lantern's Might. This idea works off of basically any knockdown situation where the opponent is within the range of your Lantern's Might special attack.

TIP The Meter Burn version of Lantern's Might is Green Lantern's best move. It bounces the opponent off of the ground, allowing Green Lantern to follow up with a damaging combo. It is one of the best moves in the game, and the main reason why opponents must approach Green Lantern with caution.

USING HYPERBOLIC (MEDIUM, MEDIUM, HARD)

Green Lantern's Hyperbolic attack string is a safe, mid-hitting combo that can be hit confirmed and canceled into his Lantern's Might Special Move. Hyperbolic is the only attack string that allows you to safely hunt a combo starter as every attack hits mid, has no areas where the opponent can interrupt, and is totally safe when blocked. You can confirm when this attack string hits, or when your opponent has blocked it. When the string hits, cancel into your Lantern's Might Special Move for a launcher. When the string is blocked, you can either cancel into your Mini-Gun Special to create some space between you and your opponent, or you can follow up the blocked string with your Meter Burn Standing Flip Kick. The Hyperbolic attack string recovers at low negative frames, which means that there is very little recovery after the attack is blocked. When opponents attempt to poke back after blocking the string, using the armor on your Meter Burn Standing Flip Kick will absorb your opponent's attack and hit them.

USING RISING CUT (DOWN + MEDIUM)

This attack is the universal mid uppercut launcher that all characters have. Where Green Lantern's separates itself, though, is how it's used in close situations. The Lantern's Might Special Move will not catch opponents that jump inside sweep range or over Green Lantern's head — this is where the Rising Cut comes in. Green Lantern's fist goes straight up and over the top of his head, protecting him from any close jump in or cross up attempts.

USING MINI-GUN (BACK, FORWARD + MEDIUM)

The Mini-Gun hits four times and Meter Burn Mini-Gun hits 14 times. This means that, when timed right, it will beat most of the armor attacks in the game as most of the armor only absorbs between one and three attacks — including Super Moves. Meter Burn Mini-Gun also inflicts 20% damage when it hits, making it one of the most damaging projectile attacks in the game. After activating your Character Power, the range of your Mini-Gun is extended to nearly full screen, and the range on your Meter Burn Mini-Gun is extended to full screen.

USING AIR TURBINE SMASH (BACK, FORWARD + HARD WHILE IN AIR)

The landing recovery of the Air Turbine Smash is fairly quick. This works well in situations where you want to avoid the opponent's projectile attack while advancing towards him or her quickly. By using the Air Turbine Smash for mobility, Green Lantern flies across the screen and lands with pretty fast recovery. This attack can also be used to escape situations where you find yourself trapped in a corner, as it gives you the ability to quickly advance across the screen. Should you use the Air Turbine Smash while avoiding some of the slower-recovering projectiles, you can actually land and recover in time to punish your opponent.

USING JUMP IN ATTACKS AND CROSS UPS

Jumping Light attack is the most effective attack for a straight on jump in into a combo attack chain. Its downward angle helps it work better than the jumping Medium attack.

Jumping Medium is best used in air-to-air situations. Its long reach works great in beating and out-ranging other airborne attacks. When this attack hits in air-to-air situations, it allows you to land quickly while keeping your opponent airborne, granting you a Meter Burn Lantern's Might Special Move.

For cross ups that are ambiguous, you will find that jumping Light and Medium will not work very well or not at all. The most effective way to cross up your opponent is to use your jumping Hard attack right as you are directly over the top of his or her head. Based on when you tap Hard, your attack will hit in front or behind your opponent and it is not clearly visible as to which side, which forces your opponent to guess.

When jumping Hard is blocked, Green Lantern is at a pretty big advantage and can mix up between his Parallel Nature attack string (which hits low), his Standing Flip Kick (which hits overhead), or a throw.

Overall, jumping Hard is your absolute best jumping tool when it comes to jumping in on a grounded opponent. It has more range than any other of your jumping attacks, juggles when it hits, has advantage when it's blocked, and can cause ambiguous cross ups. One of the best ways to set up your jumping Hard is after ending juggles with your Lantern's Might Special. The normal version of Lantern's Might is a knockdown that can't be Tech Rolled. If you make the read that your opponent is going to get up blocking (respecting your other options), you can jump in with Hard and go into a juggle combo if it hits, or follow up with other attacks when it's blocked.

USING GREEN LANTERN'S LIGHT CHARACTER POWER

The main use of your Character Power is that it allows the Lantern's Might special attack to give you a juggle without having to Meter Burn. You can cancel out of normal attacks and combo attack strings into your Character Power, then cancel out of your Character Power activation into a Special attack such as Lantern's Might. Doing this does take a specific timing in order to actually connect the Special attack after you cancel into your Character Power.

USING UN-CLASHABLE DAMAGE

When your opponent is on the second life bar and he or she is caught in a combo, your opponent can use the option to Clash to escape the combo and even regain some health. This is where Green Lantern really pulls ahead of most of the cast. He has damaging combos that the opponent cannot escape because the attacks used cannot be escaped with a Clash.

COMBOS

NO METER BURN:

Down + Medium > Medium, Medium, Hard ~ Lantern's Might — 14%
Down + Medium > Back + Light, Hard ~ Power ~ Lantern's Might > Medium, Medium, Hard ~ Lantern's Might — 19%

Back + Light, Hard ~ Power ~ Lantern's Might > Medium, Medium, Hard ~ Lantern's Might — 22%
Forward + Hard > Jumping Medium > Medium, Medium, Hard ~ Lantern's Might — 26%
Forward + Hard > Back + Light, Hard ~ Power ~ Lantern's Might > Medium, Medium, Hard ~ Lantern's Might — 27%
Back + Hard > Jumping Hard > Medium, Medium, Hard ~ Lantern's Might — 29%
Jumping Hard > Back + Light, Hard ~ Power ~ Lantern's Might > Medium, Medium, Hard ~ Lantern's Might — 31%

ONE METER BURN:

Down + Medium > Meter Burn Lantern's Might > Back + Hard > Jumping Hard > Medium, Medium, Hard ~ Lantern's Might — 26%
Back + Light, Hard ~ Meter Burn Lantern's Might > Back + Hard > Jumping Hard > Medium, Medium, Hard ~ Lantern's Might — 31%
(close/mid range) Meter Burn Oa's Rocket > Forward + Medium > Back + Light, Hard ~ Power ~ Lantern's Might > Medium, Medium, Hard ~ Lantern's Might - 39%
Medium, Medium, Hard ~ Meter Burn Lantern's Might > Back + Hard > Jumping Hard > Medium, Medium, Hard ~ Lantern's Might — 33%
Down + Light ~ Meter Burn Lantern's Might > Back + Hard > Jumping Hard > Medium, Medium, Hard ~ Lantern's Might — 32%

Meter Burn Lantern's Might > Back + Hard > Jumping Hard > Medium, Medium, Hard ~ Lantern's Might — 32%
Forward + Hard > Back + Medium, Hard ~ Meter Burn Oa's Rocket > Medium, Medium, Hard ~ Lantern's Might — 36%
Anti-Air Rocket Power > Meter Burn Lantern's Might > Back + Hard > Jumping Hard > Medium, Medium, Hard ~ Lantern's Might — 37%
Air-to-Air Jumping Medium > Meter Burn Lantern's Might > Back + Hard > Jumping Hard > Medium, Medium, Hard ~ Lantern's Might — 36%
Jumping Hard > Meter Burn Lantern's Might > Back + Hard > Jumping Hard > Medium, Medium, Hard ~ Lantern's Might — 40%
Back + Hard > Jumping Hard > Back + Medium, Hard ~ Meter Burn Oa's Rocket > Medium, Medium, Hard ~ Lantern's Might — 41%

SUPER MOVE: BEWARE MY POWER

DOUBLE METER BURN:

Meter Burn Lantern's Might > Back + Hard > Jumping Medium > Back + Medium, Hard ~ Meter Burn Oa's Rocket > Medium, Medium, Hard ~ Lantern's Might — 40%
Forward + Hard > Back + Medium, Hard ~ Meter Burn Oa's Rocket > Back + Medium, Hard ~ Meter Burn Lantern's Might > Medium, Medium, Hard ~ Lantern's Might — 43%
Meter Burn Oa's Rocket > Meter Burn Lantern's Might > Back + Hard > Jumping Hard > Medium, Medium, Hard ~ Lantern's Might — 42%

CORNER METER BURN:

Meter Burn Lantern's Might > Back + Hard (let the opponent pass over your head) > Jumping Medium > Medium, Medium, Hard ~ Lantern's Might — 30%
Back + Light, Hard ~ Power ~ Lantern's Might > Medium, Medium, Hard ~ Meter Burn Oa's Rocket > Medium, Medium, Hard ~ Lantern's Hard — 33%
Forward + Hard > Back + Medium, Hard ~ Oa's Rocket (let the opponent pass over your head) > Back + Medium, Hard ~ Lantern's Might — 35%

Jumping Hard ~ Meter Burn Lantern's Might > Back + Hard (let the opponent pass over your head) > Jumping Medium > Medium, Medium, Hard ~ Lantern's Might — 38%

UN-CLASHABLE COMBOS:

Forward + Hard > Meter Burn Oa's Rocket > Forward + Hard — 25%

Meter Burn Lantern's Might > Back + Hard > Meter Burn Oa's Rocket > Forward + Hard — 29%
Meter Burn Oa's Rocket > Forward + Hard > Forward + Hard — 32%

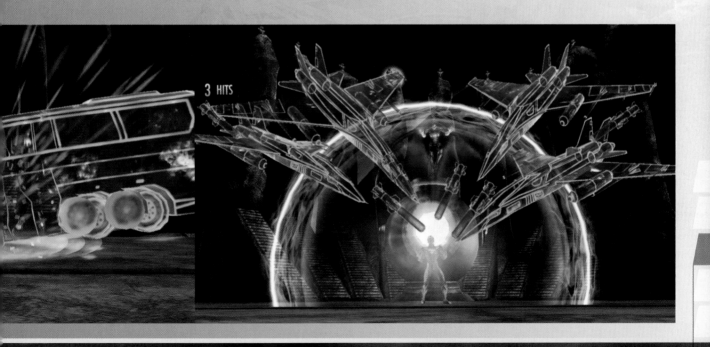

3 HITS

INJUSTICE
GODS AMONG US

HARLEY QUINN

Harley Quinn is the perfect definition of well-rounded character; she has plenty of tools and can be good from anywhere on screen, but doesn't overly excel at anything in particular. Harley has a command grab, air projectiles, and a command dash, and she can do a lot of damage without using meter, which is huge in a game where using your meter is so central to gameplay. The reason Harley doesn't excel at doing a lot of the things she does is simple: even though she has a good rush down and keep-away game, there are still some characters that can do one or both even better. That doesn't mean she loses to those characters. It just means that she can struggle with abusing certain parts of her repertoire because those characters can do it better.

INTERACTIVE OBJECT TYPE: ACROBATIC

SUPER MOVE

MALLET BOMB
Range: Full Screen
Hit Level: Mid
Description: Harley Quinn tosses a hammer that travels full screen. After the move connects, she dashes forward and leaves a cake bomb near her opponent that can be comboed out of after it explodes.

CHARACTER POWER

BAG-O-TRICKS
Command: Press the Power button
Description: Harley Quinn's Character Power has three different variations that are completely random. Sometimes she kisses a picture of The Joker, which increases her attack power for a limited time. Other times she releases an unblockable bomb (she needs to be close to an opponent for this to connect). In others still, she produces a rose, which restores heath for a short time.

For character information updates please visit www.primagames.com/InjusticeUpdates

BEST BASIC ATTACKS

OVERHEAD BASH

Command: Forward + Medium
Range: Sweep
Hit Level: Overhead
Description: Harley Quinn smacks her opponent with both of her pistols. This overhead is great because it's safe when blocked and can be canceled into any of Harley's Special Moves.

TAKE AIM

Command: Back + Medium
Hit Level: Low
Range: Outside Sweep
Description: Harley takes aim and shoots her opponent's feet. This move is a super-fast low, safe when blocked, and can be canceled into any of Harley's Special Moves for more damage.

HARLEY SWING

Command: Back + Hard
Hit Level: Mid
Range: 1/4 Screen
Description: Harley produces her silly hammer out of nowhere and hits her opponent with it, making him or her bounce off the wall and giving her a juggle opportunity. This move is safe when blocked and can be Meter Burned to have one hit of armor.

HAMMER SLAM

Command: Forward + Hard
Hit Level: Overhead
Range: 1/4 Screen
Description: Harley Quinn jumps forward with her silly hammer and hits her opponent on the head with it. This move is a ground bounce, is safe when blocked, and gives her a juggle opportunity.

BEST COMBO ATTACKS

PLEASED TO MEETCHA

Command: Medium, Up + Hard

Hit Level: Mid, Mid

Range: Close

Description: A slap to the face with her pistol that ends with a launcher kick, this is Harley's best combo attack because it does a lot of damage, is a launcher, and can be canceled into any of her Special Moves. This is the combo attack of choice to use in regular combos.

HE LOVES ME

Command: Back + Medium, Medium

Hit Level: Low, Mid

Range: Outside Sweep

Description: Harley shoots her opponent's foot, then his or her chest. If the first hit of this combo attack is blocked, the second hit won't activate. This move is good to punish low attacks.

THAT'S CUTE

Command: Forward + Medium, Hard

Hit Level: Overhead, Mid

Range: Sweep

Description: Harley smacks her opponent with both of her pistols and then launches him or her into the air. This move can be canceled into any of her Special Moves and is safe when blocked.

SPECIAL MOVES

POP POP

Command: Down, Back + Medium
Hit Level: Mid
Range: Full Screen
Description: This projectile can be charged and has three different properties. With no charge, it is a projectile that hits mid and quickly travels full screen. When charged for about two seconds, the projectile is slower but becomes an overhead. When fully charged, it becomes a slow unblockable projectile that travels full screen. Sometimes, when fully charged, the gun jams and fires a dud instead. You can also dash cancel out of this move.

METER BURN POP POP

Description: The Meter Burn version just cancels the recovery time of the projectile, allowing Harley to move immediately after performing the Special Move.

LINE OF FIRE

Command: Down, Forward + Light
Hit Level: High
Range: Full Screen
Description: A fast projectile that travels full screen and is safe when blocked.

METER BURN LINE OF FIRE

Description: The Meter Burn version of Line Of Fire adds an extra hit and does a bit more damage.

(AIR) OOPSY DAISY

Command: Down, Back + Light
Hit Level: Mid
Range: 1/2 Screen
Description: Harley fires her gun from the air to the ground. This move is a mid and safe when blocked.

METER BURN (AIR) OOPSY DAISY

Description: The Meter Burn version adds an extra shot, does more damage, and keeps Harley in the air a little longer.

HEADS UP

Command: Down, Back + Light
Hit Level: High
Range: Full Screen
Description: An anti-air projectile that hits an opponent out of the air.

METER BURN HEADS UP

Description: The Meter Burn version adds, you guessed it, an extra gunshot and does more damage.

CUPCAKE BOMB

Command: Back, Forward + Medium
Hit Level: Overhead
Range: 1/2 Screen
Description: This Special Move is an overhead projectile that reaches 1/2 screen and travels in an arc. This means that the move won't hit if thrown close to an opponent, as the projectile will fly over his or her head.

METER BURN CUPCAKE BOMB

Description: Harley throws three cupcake bombs instead of one when using the Meter Burn version of Cupcake Bomb, covering a larger area and dealing more damage.

INJUSTICE
GODS AMONG US

PLAY DOCTOR

Command: Down, Back, Forward + Light
Hit Level: High
Range: Outside Sweep
Description: Harley stabs her opponent in the back with a poison syringe. This move is an unblockable command grab that also hits your opponent when he or she is in a juggle state.

METER BURN PLAY DOCTOR

Description: Pressing the Meter Burn button during Play Doctor poisons the enemy. The opponent keeps taking damage for a short period of time.

SILLY SLIDE

Command: Back, Forward + Hard
Hit Level: Low
Range: 1/2 Screen
Description: The Silly Slide is a fast command dash good for closing in on your opponent. The Silly Slide can only be canceled into Tantrum stance.

TANTRUM STANCE

Command: Down, Back + Hard
Hit Level: Low
Range: 1/4 Screen
Description: Harley performs a drop kick that hits low, and then stays on the floor and can perform three different attacks while being in Tantrum stance. She can do a cartwheel that hits mid and causes a ground bounce by pressing the Light button, a handstand drop kick that hits low by pressing the Medium button, and a series of gunshots that also hit mid by pressing the Hard button.

STRATEGY

USING PLEASED TO MEETCHA

This string is the easiest way of starting most of Harley's most damaging combos. After landing a jumping attack on your opponent, you should always follow up with this string, and then continue with your combo of choice. The problem with Harley is that most of her combo attacks knock the opponent too far away to do anything but continue the combo with a gunshot or her Tantrum stance. This combo attack gives Harley more than enough time to follow up with a Back + Hard attack, which does plenty of damage and causes a wall bounce, leaving your opponent in a juggle state. Since you are using Back + Hard right after Pleased To Meetcha, your opponent stays in an extended juggle state because the combo is still early. Thanks to *Injustice*'s gravity system, if you had hit the opponent with a Back + Hard as part of a ten-hit combo your opponent would fall to the ground much, much faster.

USING HE LOVES ME

This string is best used against opponents that like to rush down and dash forward frequently. If the first hit of this move whiffs or is blocked, the second hit won't activate, though that isn't much of a concern given that the move is safe when blocked anyway. This move is also really good for baiting low pokes. If your opponent blocks your Down + Light move and then tries to poke back with his or her own Down + Light, you can walk backwards and then whiff punish your opponent with the He Loves Me string. The best Special Move to follow hitting your opponent is Tantrum stance because of its reach and damage potential. Make your opponent throw out random low pokes and always punish with this string.

USING THAT'S CUTE

You can use this string and Tantrum stance to create a high/low mix-up that leads into big damage. This over-head might not be especially fast, but it isn't very slow either. If you condition your opponent to block low, you can sneak in this overhead starter to begin your combos from there. This string can be canceled into Harley's Tantrum stance, which is a low, so if your opponent blocks the overhead, you can go right into the low and keep your opponent guessing constantly. You don't *have* to go for the high/low mix-up; this string is a launcher too, but it sends the opponent too far to follow up with anything but her Tantrum stance, which only does a little bit of damage. That's precisely why using Harley's Pleased To Meetcha string is better for starting combos that do more damage.

USING POP POP

This projectile move might look like it is worthless at first, but it really isn't. This move is best used when you are a full screen away from your opponent where he or she can't really react to the gun as you charge it. The projectile hits mid, so you can't duck it, which means that your opponent is forced to jump or block the incoming attack. This is when you start the mind games from full screen. You can charge the gun and, if you predict he or she is going to jump forward, just dash cancel out and punish your opponent's jump ins with an attack of your choice. If your opponent decides to stay put when you are charging the gun, just let it charge to the max because it becomes unblockable and you can follow the projectile and attack your opponent. Always keep in mind that the gun can randomly jam, negating your potential attack.

USING TANTRUM STANCE

The Tantrum stance is a really good move that can used to create a lot of mind games. The Bullet Frenzy (Hard after Tantrum stance) can only be punished by fast low attacks — everything else will whiff. Bullet Frenzy is the most safe option from Tantrum stance — the other follow-ups can be interrupted and even punished with a full combo, so you should only use those attacks in combos. Bullet Frenzy, however, is really hard to punish even though some characters can punish it with a full combo. A lot of the characters can't, so it is safe to just do the move here and there to catch your opponent off guard.

KEEPING PRESSURE

Harley can be really good up close, as her high and low mix-up is great and hard to block because of her many variations. Harley's Down + Light is especially quick; you can hit your opponent with Down + Light, then transition into Forward + Medium since your opponent will most likely be blocking low after getting hit. Light, Light, Medium leaves Harley at advantage on block, making this a good pressure string. You can follow up this string with Back + Medium, Medium if your opponent tries to poke back with a Down + Light move.

INJUSTICE
GODS AMONG US

COMBOS

Back + Light, Medium, Light ~ Line Of Fire — 18%
Back + Medium, Medium ~ Tantrum Stance > Hard — 20%
Light, Light, Medium ~ Tantrum Stance > Hard — 23%
Back + Medium, Medium ~ Tantrum Stance > Light > Tantrum Stance > Hard — 25%
Forward + Medium, Hard ~ Silly Slide > Light, Light, Medium ~ Line Of Fire — 27%
Back + Hard > Jumping + Medium > Medium, Up + Hard ~ Playing Doctor — 26%
Medium, Up + Hard > Back + Hard > Jumping + Medium > Medium, Up + Hard ~ Playing Doctor — 26%

Back + Medium, Medium ~ Tantrum Stance > Light > Back + Hard > Jumping + Medium > Medium, Up + Hard ~ Playing Doctor — 36%
Jumping Medium, Medium, Up + Hard > Back + Hard > Jumping + Medium > Medium, Up + Hard ~ Playing Doctor — 31%
Medium, Up + Hard > Back + Hard > Jumping + Medium > Medium, Up + Hard ~ Mallet Bomb — 36%
Back + Medium, Medium ~ Tantrum Stance > Light > Back + Hard > Jumping + Medium > Medium, Up + Hard ~ Mallet Bomb > Playing Doctor — 48%

SUPER MOVE: MALLET BOMB

Medium, Up + Hard > Back + Hard > Jumping + Medium > Medium, Up + Hard ~ Mallet Bomb > Playing Doctor — 39%
Medium, Up + Hard, Medium, Up + Hard, Medium, Up + Hard ~ Playing Doctor — 20% (Corner Only)

INJUSTICE
GODS AMONG US

HAWKGIRL

Hawkgirl can be very annoying to deal with because of her air control and keep-away game. She is the only character that can stay in the air for a long period of time, making it difficult for her opponents to catch her. While Hawkgirl is in the air, she can throw her powerful mace downward to stop opponents from getting too close, and the recovery of the projectile is quite speedy, so she can just keep doing it over and over again until her fly mode wears off. Even then, as soon as she drops back to the ground, she can activate her Character Power again to resume her keep-away game. Hawkgirl isn't solely good from far away; she has very good basic attacks and varied combo strings that move into lows and overheads, making her just as good close to her opponent as she is from afar. Hawkgirl's game plan is to frustrate her opponents by making them chase her until they make mistakes. If an opponent has tools to get around her zoning, she can always take the fight up to them.

INTERACTIVE OBJECT TYPE: POWER

SUPER MOVE

THE POWER OF NTH
Range: 1/2 Screen
Hit Level: Overhead
Description: Hawkgirl dashes toward her opponent and takes him or her into the skies where she beats the opponent up, then sends him or her back to the ground with a powerful blow to the face.

CHARACTER POWER

SOARING HAWK
Command: Press the Power button
Description: Soaring Hawk is one the most annoying Character Powers in the game. While in Soaring Hawk mode, Hawkgirl can fly around the screen for decent amount of time, making it really hard for a lot of the characters to catch her. Hawkgirl can perform additional attacks while she in this mode as well as perform her regular mid-air Special Moves.

For character information updates please visit www.primagames.com/InjusticeUpdates

BEST BASIC ATTACKS

LOW MACE JAB

Command: Down + Light
Hit Level: Mid
Range: Close
Description: This is a very fast attack good for punishing moves up close and for keeping your opponent in check. This move is safe when blocked.

CLOUD NINE

Command: Down + Medium
Hit Level: Mid
Range: Sweep
Description: Cloud Nine is one of the best uppercuts in the game because Hawkgirl uses her mace to perform the move, giving it good range. It rarely trades hits with other attacks, making it an almost perfect anti-air move.

ASCENSION

Command: Forward + Hard
Hit Level: Overhead
Range: Sweep
Description: This is move is a ground bounce attack that leaves the opponent in a juggle state. This move can be Meter Burn canceled to have one hit of armor, and is safe when blocked. As an added bonus, Hawkgirl hops slightly before performing this move, making her avoid some low attacks.

GREAT DIVINE

Command: Back + Hard
Hit level: Mid
Range: Sweep
Description: This move causes a wall bounce, leaving your opponent in a juggle state, is safe when blocked, and can be Meter Burned for one hit of armor.

INJUSTICE
GODS AMONG US

BEST COMBO ATTACKS

MACE MAXIMUM

Command: Light, Medium, Hard
Hit Level: High, Mid, Mid
Range: Close
Description: Hawkgirl hits her opponent in the face and stomach, and then launches him or her into the air with her mace, leaving the opponent in a juggle state. This is one of Hawkgirl's best strings to start combos and is safe when blocked.

DAWN STAR

Command: Back + Medium, Medium
Hit Level: Mid, Low
Range: Close
Description: Hawkgirl hits her opponent in the face with her mace, then goes for a low kick. This combo attack is good for mix-ups because Hawkgirl can go into an overhead instead of low after Back + Medium by pressing Back + Medium, Hard. This makes your opponent guess if the next hit will be a low or an overhead.

BLOODY WAR

Command: Hard, Medium, Back + Light
Hit Level: Mid, Mid, Mid
Range: Close
Description: A series of attacks that ends with a power kick sending your opponent across the screen, this move is good if you want to knock your opponent away to start Hawkgirl's keep-away game. This move is also safe when blocked.

SPECIAL MOVES

MACE CHARGE

Command: Back, Forward + Medium
Hit Level: Mid
Range: 1/2 Screen
Description: Hawkgirl performs a back flip, then launches herself towards her opponent with her mace. This move is a fast-advancing attack that hits mid and is safe when blocked. This move can avoid a lot of attacks up close and punish them because of the speed at which she flips backward. Mace Charge can also be used in mid-air.

METER BURN MACE CHARGE

Description: Pressing the Meter Burn button after executing the move adds an extra hit that knocks the opponent to the ground.

WING EVADE

Command: Down, Back + Medium
Hit Level: Varies
Range: 1/4 Screen
Description: Hawkgirl flaps her wings and jumps backward, avoiding her opponent's attack. Hawkgirl can perform three different attacks after performing this move: she can do a quick overhead attack by pressing the Medium button, an anti-air Mace Toss by pressing the Light button, or a quick dive kick that hits mid by pressing the Hard button.

STOMP

Command: Down + Hard
Hit Level: Overhead
Range: Close
Description: This Stomp is a quick overhead, and only punishable by the fastest attacks in the game. The Stomp is also good for crossing up opponents.

MACE TOSS

Command: Down, Back + Light
Hit Level: Mid
Range: Full Screen
Description: The Mace Toss is a really good projectile move that travels full screen. The projectile itself is high so it can be ducked, but it has other properties that make it useful. Hawkgirl delays her Mace Toss by holding down the Light button and can dash cancel out of it. She can also throw the mace upward by pressing Up after executing the move.

METER BURN MACE TOSS

Description: The Meter Burn version of Mace Toss adds an extra shoulder charge that knocks the opponent away.

(AIR) MACE TOSS

Command: Down, Forward + Light
Hit Level: High
Range: Full Screen
Description: This variant of the Mace Toss projectile has the same properties as the ground Mace Toss, but can be launched (you guessed it) from the air.

METER BURN (AIR) MACE TOSS

Description: The Meter Burn version of this attack adds an extra hit that travels downward quickly and is safe on block, depending on how high you hit your opponent.

(AIR) DOWNWARD MACE

Command: Down, Back + Light
Hit Level: Overhead
Range: 3/4 Screen
Description: The Downward Mace is similar to the Mace Toss, with the only difference being how Hawkgirl throws the mace: towards the ground at an angle.

METER BURN (AIR) DOWNWARD MACE

Description: The Meter Burn version of this move is the same as the Meter Burn (Air) Mace Toss.

INJUSTICE
GODS AMONG US

STRATEGY

USING MACE MAXIMUM (LIGHT, MEDIUM, HARD)

This is Hawkgirl's best string to start combos. It can be canceled into Hawkgirl's Character Power, letting you create some really good mind games when your opponent blocks one of her strings. When you cancel one of her strings into fly mode, you can go for an instant overhead with her Heavenward Stomp. Even though this is Hawkgirl's best string to start combos, her damage output overall is rather low because her keep-away game is too good. If she had both damage and a good zoning game, she would be a little overpowered. You can also use this string for pressure because it moves Hawkgirl while attacking and is safe on block. If your opponent gets hit, you can combo afterward, but even if the string is blocked, you can always cancel into fly mode.

USING MACE CHARGE

The Mace Charge can be used to whiff punish and evade a lot of attacks in the game. Since this move is completely safe on block, you can use it to stop opponents from rushing you down. The only downside of this move is that you can't combo after it connects, but the move itself does a lot of damage for a single-hit Special that avoids attacks *and* is speedy. Trying to whiff punish this move can also be really hard because Hawkgirl can block right after she lands, making the move completely safe on block and very hard to punish on whiff. Hawkgirl can also do this move while being in fly mode, which makes the move even more dangerous—she's already hard to catch, and if an opponent can reach her, she can just knock him or her back down with the Mace Charge.

USING DOWN STAR (BACK + MEDIUM+ MEDIUM)

This string is good for creating a high/low mix-up. When your opponent starts blocking the sweep, you can use Back + Medium, Hard, an overhead that leaves the opponent in a juggle state. Always mix it up between the two strings to keep your opponent guessing. The best follow up that Hawkgirl can do after the overhead is Down + Medium into her Mace Charge Special Move. This combo doesn't deal a lot of damage, but as stated before, Hawkgirl is a character that doesn't do much damage overall. The last hit of Down Star also avoids high attacks and the overhead (Back + Medium, Hard) avoids low attacks.

USING WING EVADE

Wing Evade is Hawkgirl's best wakeup along with Mace Charge. The good thing about Wing Evade is that you can activate her fly mode right after inputting this move. This is great, because you can avoid your opponent's mix-up on your wakeup and fly away from him or her to start Hawkgirl's keep-away game. If your opponent starts guessing correctly and jumps at you to try and punish your escape after Wing Evade, you can press the Medium button and hit your opponent before he or she can do anything. If your opponent dashes, walk backward after using Wing Evade as a wakeup. Pressing the Hard button during the evade can catch the opponent as he or she walks backward. Since Wing Evade is safe when blocked, there's no risk of retaliation. Another post-Wing Evade option is pressing the Light button to make Hawkgirl throw her mace upward for anti-airing an opponent. This move can keep an opponent guessing, but remember that her Down + Medium is technically a better anti-air option.

USING SOARING HAWK

Hawkgirl's play style revolves around her Soaring Hawk or fly mode Character Power. As explained earlier, Hawkgirl is not bad up close, but is the type of character that makes her opponent chase her and forces him or her to make mistakes so she can punish the opponent with damage. Hawkgirl has a lot of good options for keeping her opponent away from her while she is in fly mode. For characters that can't reach her when she is all the way at the top of the screen but have fast dashes or projectiles that reach up there, she can use her Mace Toss to keep the opponent from advancing forward and to stop him or her from shooting projectiles. The mace recovers instantly as soon as the opponent blocks it or gets hit by it, which means that she can be ready to throw again quickly. If you are fighting against a character that can reach Hawkgirl, you can use the Mace Charge to knock him or her back to the ground. If an opponent gets too close and jumps right at you from an angle where the Mace Toss and Mace Charge won't hit, you can always use the Heavenward Stomp to send him or her back to the ground.

MIXING IT UP

Sometimes it's good to take the fight to your opponent—even if you can beat him or her from far away—to keep your opponent on his or her toes. A smart player will always find a way around a bad match up, and that's the perfect time to start using Hawkgirl's other tools. Hawkgirl players can sometimes get repetitive and develop patterns because keep away from a lot of the characters might seem easy at first. If you fight against an opponent that can get around your zoning, that's when you start mixing up your play style. Always try to use all of Hawkgirl's tools—never limit yourself, because by just playing keep away all the time it will take you longer to get better in other areas, like defense and offense. Make your opponent fear you from anywhere on screen, not just when you are far away from them, because when your opponent finally catches up to you and starts rushing you down, you will not know what to do if you've spent most of your time learning how to stay away from your opponent instead of learning how to fight on the ground.

Back + Medium, Hard, Down + Medium ~ Mace Charge — 23%
Light, Medium, Hard > Hard, Medium, Back + Light — 23%
Light, Medium, Hard ~ Soaring Hawk > Medium ~ Mace Charge — 25%

Light, Medium, Hard > Hard, Medium ~ Mace Charge — 26%
Light, Medium, Hard ~ Soaring Hawk > Light, Medium, Hard — 26%

Light, Medium, Hard ~ Soaring Hawk > Medium ~ Meter Burn Mace Charge — 31%

SUPER MOVE: THE POWER OF NTH

Light, Light, Medium ~ The Power Of Nth — 38%

THE JOKER

The Joker plays as crazy, wild, and unpredictable in this game as he does on TV, in comics, and the movies. He can keep attacking opponents farther out with his comical long barrel revolver or by throwing laughing gas canisters. When in close, he keeps opponents guessing with wild jumping, exploding teeth, acid flower, and more. His Character Power can be deadly as it increases The Joker's movement speed, causing him to become even more unpredictable. The Joker is not a beginner character; he requires setups that necessitate time and practice to master. However, the time you spend will be well rewarded.

INTERACTIVE OBJECT TYPE: GADGET

SUPER MOVE

LET'S BE SERIOUS
Hit Level: Mid
Range: Full Screen
Description: The Joker throws a pie projectile into his opponent's face, followed by a series of strikes from his crowbar. He then delivers a shot from his revolver before clubbing the opponent with a canister of laughing gas. He finally stands over his opponent and points a bazooka right in his or her face before delivering a powerful blast. This attack is full combo punished when blocked up close. This attack can be crouched at certain ranges by some characters.

CHARACTER POWER

JOKER'S WILD
Command: Press the Power button or Down + Power button
Range: Close
Description: Pressing the Power button will cause The Joker to parry all high and mid attack strikes, while pressing Down + Power button will cause The Joker to parry all low attack strikes. After a successful parry, The Joker will retaliate with a quick knife strike and increase his HA! meter by one, with a maximum of up to three. For each HA!, The Joker will receive a slight increase in his movement speed.

For character information updates please visit www.primagames.com/InjusticeUpdates

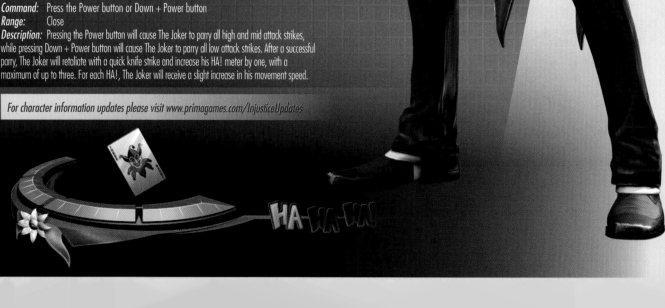

BEST BASIC ATTACKS

UPWARD CROWBAR

Command: Down + Medium
Hit Level: Mid
Range: Sweep
Description: The Joker pulls out a crowbar and uppercuts his opponent, launching him or her. This attack is full combo punished when blocked.

AIR HINGE KICK

Command: Jumping Medium
Hit Level: Overhead
Range: Close
Description: The Joker jumps into the air with a very fast kick attack that allows him to chain into other combo attack strings versus a grounded opponent. This attack hits overhead, so it must be blocked from the standing block position.

SWEEP KICK

Command: Down + Hard
Hit Level: Low
Range: Sweep
Description: The Joker performs a spinning low kick that knocks his opponent down. When this attack hits, it results in a knockdown that cannot be Tech Rolled. This attack is full combo punished when blocked up close. From this attack's maximum range, it is only punished by faster advancing normal attacks and faster advancing Special attacks.

CROWBAR SLAM

Command: Back + Hard
Hit Level: Mid
Range: Sweep
Description: The Joker bats his opponent with a crowbar, bouncing him or her off the corner of the screen and back, giving him a juggle combo opportunity. This attack can be charged by holding the Hard attack button and cancelled out of with a forward or backward dash while you are charging the attack. Pressing the Meter Burn button during this attack (burns one bar of meter) will add one hit of armor. Crowbar Slam is also The Joker's Back, Back + Meter Burn Bounce Cancel (bounce cancel burns two bars of meter). This attack leaves The Joker at advantage when blocked.

DOWNWARD CROWBAR

Command: Forward + Hard
Hit Level: Overhead
Range: Sweep
Description: The Joker smashes his opponent over the head with a crowbar, which launches his opponent and gives him a juggle combo opportunity. This attack hits overhead, so it must be blocked from the standing block position. This attack can be charged by holding the Hard attack button and cancelled out of with a forward or backwards dash while you are charging the attack. Pressing the Meter Burn button during this attack (burns one bar of meter) will add one hit of armor. Downward Crowbar is also The Joker's Forward, Forward + Meter Burn Bounce Cancel (bounce cancel burns two bars of meter). This attack leaves The Joker at advantage when blocked.

FLYING CROWBAR

Command: Jumping Hard
Hit Level: Overhead
Range: Sweep
Description: The Joker wildly jumps in the air with a crowbar attack. This attack hits overhead, so it must be blocked from the standing block position. This attack leaves The Joker at advantage when blocked, allowing him to follow up with additional attacks.

BEST COMBO ATTACKS

FULL DECK

Command: Forward + Medium, Hard, Medium
Hit Level: Mid, Mid, Mid
Range: Close
Description: The Joker swipes downward with his knife, followed by a quick jab, ending with a lunging knife attack. This attack is only punished by Superman's Super Move. This string can be interrupted by a Super Move in between the first and second attack.

CLOWN PRINCE

Command: Forward + Medium, Light
Hit Level: Mid, Overhead
Range: Close
Description: The Joker swipes downward with his knife followed by an overhead kick from his knife-tipped shoe. This attack is safe when blocked. The second attack of this string hits overhead, so it must be blocked from the standing block position.

MAD LOVE

Command: Hard, Medium
Hit Level: Mid, Mid, Mid
Range: Sweep
Description: The Joker kicks his opponent and then attacks him or her with two knife strikes. This attack is only punished by the faster Super Moves of the game. This string can be interrupted by a Super Move in between the second and third attack. This string is what The Joker uses to end his juggles.

SPECIAL MOVES

CROWBAR

Command: Back, Forward + Hard
Hit Level: Overhead
Range: 1/4 Screen
Description: The Joker beats his opponent down with his crowbar. When this attack is blocked, The Joker is punished by all normal attacks and Special attacks that reach him. This attack hits overhead, so it must be blocked in the standing block position.

LAUGHING GAS

Command: Down, Back + Light
Hit Level: High
Range: Full Screen
Description: The Joker tosses a canister of laughing gas towards his opponent. The Joker throws the Laughing Gas canister in a rainbow-like arc, causing it to hit mid as it reaches its maximum range. This attack is full combo punished when blocked at close range.

ROLLING LAUGHING GAS

Command: Down, Back + Medium
Hit Level: Low
Range: Full Screen
Description: The Joker drops a canister of laughing gas and then kicks it, sending the canister rolling towards his opponent. This attack is full combo punished when blocked at close range.

METER BURN CROWBAR

Description: Pressing the Meter Burn button during a successful Crowbar will unleash a repeated barrage of crowbar strikes.

METER BURN LAUGHING GAS

Description: Pressing the Meter Burn button during Laughing Gas while the canister is traveling in the air or after it connects with the opponent will shoot a blast from The Joker's revolver, causing the canister to explode and launching the opponent for additional damage.

METER BURN ROLLING LAUGHING GAS

Description: Pressing the Meter Burn button during Rolling Laughing Gas while the canister is rolling or after it connects with the opponent will shoot a blast from The Joker's revolver, causing the canister to explode and launching the opponent for additional damage.

BANG!

Command: Down, Forward + Light
Hit Level: High
Range: Full Screen
Description: The Joker draws his revolver and fires a shot at his opponent. This attack can be delayed by holding the Light attack button, and The Joker can cancel the delay by dashing forward or backward. This attack leaves The Joker at advantage when blocked.

CHATTERING TEETH

Command: (Close Range) Down, Back + Hard
(Medium Range) Down, Back + Hard, Up
(Far Range) Down, Back + Hard, Forward
Hit Level: Low
Range: Close reaches right in front of you;
Medium reaches to sweep range;
Far reaches 1/4 screen
Description: The Joker throws out several teeth on the ground that chatter for a very short period of time before exploding, launching the opponent.

ACID BLOSSOM

Command: Back, Forward + Medium
Hit Level: Mid
Range: Sweep
Description: The Joker shoots a quick stream of acid from the flower on his jacket. This attack is safe when blocked.

USING CROWBAR SLAM (BACK + HARD) AND DOWNWARD CROWBAR (FORWARD + HARD)

Both of these attacks are the exact same speed and cover just about the exact same range. What makes your Crowbar Slam the better option is that it is better inside of juggles and as a stand-alone attack due to the launcher it gives, which allows for easier and more damaging combos as well as setting off stage transitions.

USING UPWARD CROWBAR (DOWN + MEDIUM)

This attack is The Joker's uppercut launcher and his staple anti-air. The Joker has one of the slower uppercut attacks, so this requires you to have good timing when anti-airing your opponent's jump in attempts. This attack should only be used as an anti-air and never against a grounded opponent as this attack is full combo punished by the entire cast of characters.

USING CROWBAR (BACK, FORWARD + HARD)

Your Crowbar Special Move hits overhead and has a range of 1/4 screen. You can use that as a mix-up with your Sweep Kick which hits low. Use the Crowbar/Sweep Kick mix-up from your Sweep Kick's maximum range so that the Sweep Kick has a higher degree of safety.

USING SWEEP KICK (DOWN + HARD) AND CHATTERING TEETH

The Joker's Sweep Kick connects from a range that far exceeds the normal sweep range, and from its maximum range the attack has a higher degree of safety as it becomes harder to punish. From this attack's maximum range it is only punished by faster advancing normal attacks and faster advancing Special attacks, which not every character has. After your Sweep Kick hits, it causes a knockdown that cannot be Tech Rolled. This allows The Joker to follow up with his jumping Medium and force the opponent to guess on a normal or cross up jump in. You can also follow up the Sweep Kick knockdown with Chattering Teeth. After knocking the opponent down with your Sweeping Kick, throw out the Chattering Teeth that corresponds with the range you knocked the opponent down from. If the opponent gets up and blocks, follow up with a jumping Medium attack. This forces the opponent to block the jumping attack overhead while also having to block the Chattering Teeth low. You can vary the timing on your jumping Medium so that it connects before or after the Chattering Teeth explode.

This will keep the opponent guessing on which attack should be guarded first—should he or she block overhead then low or low then overhead? If you perform this setup with your Character Power HA! meter at full, you can jump in so fast that you can time your jumping Medium attack to connect at the exact same time the Chattering Teeth explode, causing this set up to be unblockable. If the opponent gets up with a wakeup attack, you can throw out the Chattering Teeth and still block almost every wakeup in the game as long as you throw the Chattering Teeth out fast enough. This will cause most wakeup attacks to be hit by the Chattering Teeth in their recovery. Even when many of the wakeup attacks hit The Joker in this situation, the Chattering Teeth explode beneath them and in many cases The Joker can still juggle the opponent, even if the wakeup has knocked him down.

Some wakeups recover so fast when blocked that the opponent can recover in time to block the Chattering Teeth. In several of these situations, you should intentionally get hit by the wakeup—provided you can recover in time after being hit by that particular attack to juggle your opponent. A good example of this is Green Lantern and his Lantern's Might Special Move. Green Lantern can use Lantern's Might as a wakeup and still recover in time to block

the Chattering Teeth after Lantern's Might is blocked. However, The Joker can get hit by the Lantern's Might Special, which will cause Green Lantern to now follow through with the attack. This adds more recovery to the move, which in turn causes the Chattering Teeth to explode beneath Green Lantern as he follows through with the attack. As The Joker gets up from being hit by Lantern's Might, he can connect with a jumping Medium attack while Green Lantern is still airborne, and go into a juggle combo.

After being hit by the Sweep Kick, your opponent can always jump back on reaction to you throwing out Chattering Teeth. When this happens, do not throw out Chattering Teeth, and instead continue your offense or throw.

USING CHATTERING TEETH AS A STAND-ALONE ATTACK

Chattering Teeth is effective as a shield, protecting you when your opponent attempts to go on the offensive. Throwing it in front of you can protect you from your opponent's jump in attacks, grounded attacks, and so on. Even if your opponent throws you, the Chattering Teeth will explode beneath him or her while your opponent is in the middle of his or her throw. You can cancel out of basic attacks and combo strings with Chattering Teeth, and in many cases the Chattering Teeth will explode as your opponent is hitting you out of the Chattering Teeth recovery.

USING BANG! (DOWN, FORWARD + LIGHT) AND LAUGHING GAS (DOWN, BACK + LIGHT)

The speed of this attack allows The Joker to stay back at a distance and beat out most powerful projectile-based characters in a projectile battle. Opponents will find it difficult to match this attack projectile for projectile. This is a fast projectile attack that leaves The Joker at advantage when blocked and is irritating for opponents to deal with from a distance. The Joker's advantage on this attack increases the farther away he is from his opponent when he or she blocks the attack. This means that after blocking this attack from a distance, The Joker will be able to fire off another gunshot before his opponent can get the next attack out. Your opponent will soon realize that the only way to advance is to slowly walk towards The Joker as he or she continuously crouches after every step to avoid blocking the gunshot, or to jump forward in random anticipation of the attack because it is too fast to jump over on reaction. Your BANG! gunshot has to be jumped as a guess and not on reaction, which allows the attack to set up your Laughing Gas. When at a distance, if your opponent chooses jumping as the way to advance over your BANG! gunshot, you can anticipate this and throw out your Laughing Gas canister. When the canister hits your opponent out of the air, you can Meter Burn the attack and launch the opponent, allowing you to follow up with your BANG! gunshot attack for a 21% juggle combo.

USING ACID BLOSSOM (BACK, FORWARD + MEDIUM)

This Special Move is used as The Joker's main grounded combo and juggle combo ender. When this attack hits, it keeps your opponent grounded even if he or she is already in a juggled state. This eliminates your opponent's option to use a wakeup because the Acid Blossom doesn't knock him or her down, but instead leaves your opponent standing with The Joker left at advantage.

USING AIR HINGE KICK (JUMPING MEDIUM)

This attack grants major advantage when it hits—so much advantage that The Joker has time to confirm the jumping Medium has hit and then go into his combo string. Right next to his opponent, The Joker can abuse this attack by jumping over his opponent with a fast and instant jumping Medium. This attack will hit the opponent as The Joker is on his way up and over, and when the attack connects, The Joker can land and chain right into a guaranteed combo string. Even when this attack hits at point-black range, as The Joker is on his way up, the advantage on the attack is so great that he can land behind his opponent and he or she still will not be able to block his combo string. Air Hinge Kick is one of the best jumping attacks in the game when it comes to cross up jumps. The Joker can use this attack to cross up jump his opponent at point-blank range. Also, because of just how much collision The Joker has on his back foot as he executes this attack, as well has how long the attack stays active once it's on screen, he can jump over his opponent and mix-up landing with this attack, or landing with an empty jump in and throw the opponent.

USING FLYING CROWBAR (JUMPING HARD)

This attack is very hard to anti-air when used from the right range. The Joker extends his crowbar out to a point where the opponent cannot hit him before his crowbar makes contact. This allows The Joker to abuse this attack from certain ranges.

USING FULL DECK (FORWARD + MEDIUM, HARD, MEDIUM) AND CLOWN PRINCE (FORWARD + MEDIUM, LIGHT)

When opponents get in close, you can use your Full Deck attack string to push them back. When this string hits, you can hit confirm it and end with your Acid Blossom Special Move. Some characters can crouch under the second attack of Full Deck if he or she blocks the first hit from a crouch block. When this happens, you can use your Clown Prince attack string. Both strings start exactly the same, so there is no way for the opponent to know which attack string you are using, and unlike the Full Deck attack string, Clown Prince cannot be interrupted. The Clown Prince attack string causes a knockdown that cannot be Tech Rolled, allowing you to attempt Chattering Teeth setups or dash in for more offense.

USING JOKER'S WILD CHARACTER POWER

Your Character Power is a parry that can turn all high, mid, and low strikes against your enemies. Each time you parry an attack, you gain an extra HA! in your Character Power meter. Each HA! you gain (up to a maximum of three) will increase your movement speed. You can use your Character Power to parry out of pressure situations and even interrupt certain attack strings.

INJUSTICE
GODS AMONG US

COMBOS

OPEN SPACE NO METER BURN:

Down + Medium > Forward + Medium, Hard, Medium ~ Acid Blossom — 16%
Forward + Medium, Hard, Medium ~ Acid Blossom — 17%
Chattering Teeth > Jumping Medium > Hard, Medium ~ Acid Blossom — 30%
Back + Hard > Jumping Medium > Hard, Medium ~ Acid Blossom — 30%

Chattering Teeth > Back + Hard > Jumping Medium > Hard, Medium ~ Acid Blossom — 34%

OPEN SPACE METER BURN:

Down + Medium ~ Meter Burn Rolling Laughing Gas > Back + Hard > Hard, Medium ~ Acid Blossom — 26%
Light, Light ~ Meter Burn Rolling Laughing Gas > Back + Hard > Jumping Medium > Hard, Medium ~ Acid Blossom — 34% (Will not work on Bane, Doomsday, Grundy or Lex Luthor.)
Jumping Medium, Forward + Medium, Hard ~ Meter Burn Rolling Laughing Gas > Back + Hard > Jumping Medium > Hard, Medium ~ Acid Blossom — 38% (Will not work on Bane, Doomsday, Grundy or Lex Luthor.)

Jumping Medium, Hard ~ Meter Burn Rolling Laughing Gas > Back + Hard > Jumping Medium > Hard, Medium ~ Acid Blossom — 43%

SUPER MOVE: LET'S BE SERIOUS

4 HITS

CORNER NO METER BURN:

Down + Medium > Hard, Medium ~ Acid Blossom — 18%
Back + Hard (let the opponent pass over your head) > Jumping Medium > Hard, Medium ~ Acid Blossom — 30%

Chattering Teeth > Jumping Hard > Hard, Medium ~ Acid Blossom - 33%

CORNER METER BURN:

Light, Light ~ Meter Burn Rolling Laughing Gas > Jumping Medium > Hard, Medium ~ Acid Blossom - 32%

Jumping Medium, Forward + Medium, Hard ~ Meter Burn Rolling Laughing Gas > Jumping Medium > Hard, Medium ~ Acid Blossom - 36%
Jumping Medium, Hard ~ Meter Burn Rolling Laughing Gas > Jumping Medium > Hard, Medium ~ Acid Blossom - 40%

KILLER FROST

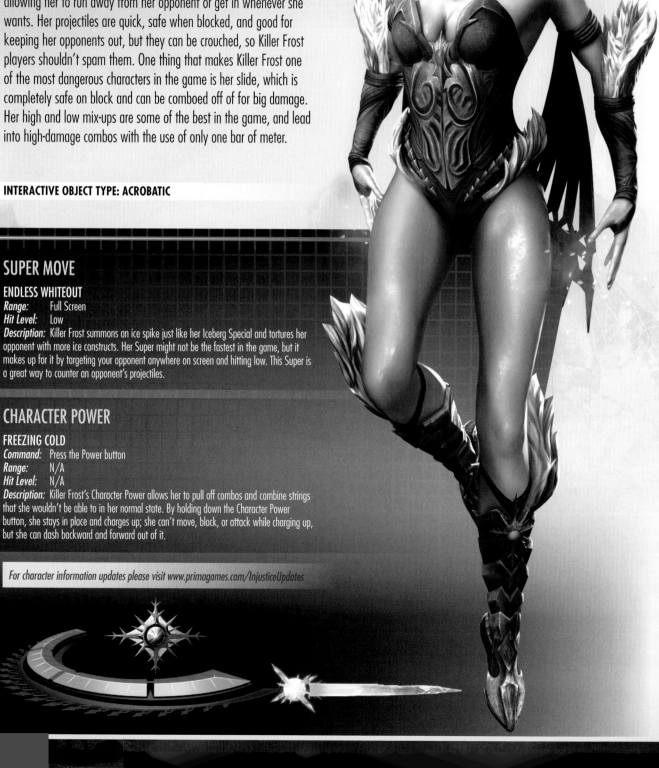

Killer Frost is a very good character with a lot of tools. She can be deadly from anywhere on screen, and her movement is also very good. Killer Frost is one of the few characters that has an air dash, allowing her to run away from her opponent or get in whenever she wants. Her projectiles are quick, safe when blocked, and good for keeping her opponents out, but they can be crouched, so Killer Frost players shouldn't spam them. One thing that makes Killer Frost one of the most dangerous characters in the game is her slide, which is completely safe on block and can be comboed off of for big damage. Her high and low mix-ups are some of the best in the game, and lead into high-damage combos with the use of only one bar of meter.

INTERACTIVE OBJECT TYPE: ACROBATIC

SUPER MOVE

ENDLESS WHITEOUT
Range: Full Screen
Hit Level: Low
Description: Killer Frost summons an ice spike just like her Iceberg Special and tortures her opponent with more ice constructs. Her Super might not be the fastest in the game, but it makes up for it by targeting your opponent anywhere on screen and hitting low. This Super is a great way to counter an opponent's projectiles.

CHARACTER POWER

FREEZING COLD
Command: Press the Power button
Range: N/A
Hit Level: N/A
Description: Killer Frost's Character Power allows her to pull off combos and combine strings that she wouldn't be able to in her normal state. By holding down the Character Power button, she stays in place and charges up; she can't move, block, or attack while charging up, but she can dash backward and forward out of it.

For character information updates please visit www.primagames.com/InjusticeUpdates

BEST BASIC ATTACKS

FREEZER BURN
Command: Back + Light
Hit Level: Low
Range: Sweep
Description: Killer Frost creates a sword made of ice and slices her opponent's legs. This move is a fast low that moves Killer Frost forward slightly, which is good for poking. This move is safe when blocked.

GLACIER KICK
Command: Up + Hard
Hit Level: Mid
Range: Sweep
Description: Two hop kicks that launch your opponent behind you and leaves him or her in a juggled state. This move is safe when blocked and can be done up to three times in a row.

GLAZE
Command: Forward + Hard
Hit Level: Overhead
Range: Sweep
Description: This is Frost's fastest overhead and possibly one of the fastest in the game. This move is safe on block and leads into combos.

FROST KICK
Command: Back + Hard
Hit level: Mid
Range: Sweep
Description: Killer Frost performs a wall bounce move that leaves the opponent in a juggle state.

BEST COMBO ATTACKS

TEMPEST

Command: Forward + Light, Light, Medium
Hit Level: Mid
Range: Close
Description: This is Killer Frost's most damaging combo attack. It's a four-hit string that can be canceled into one of her Special Moves. This move is safe when blocked.

DIAMOND DUST

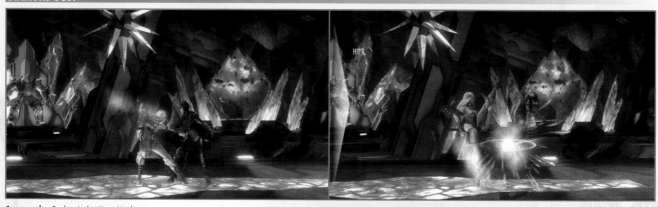

Command: Back + Light, Up + Hard
Hit Level: Low, Mid
Range: Sweep
Description: Killer Frost uses her ice sword to start a combo. This is a fast low starter that transitions into a launcher and is safe when blocked.

ARCTIC FROST

Command: Forward + Light, Light, Hard
Hit Level: Mid, Mid, Mid
Range: Close
Description: Killer Frost slaps her opponent in a dancing fashion and ends with a spinning kick. This combo attack can be canceled into any of her Specials.

SPECIAL MOVES

FROSTBITE

Command:	Down, Back + Light
Hit Level:	N/A
Range:	N/A

Description: Killer Frost's hands turn into ice and she is able to parry most high and mid attacks.

METER BURN FROSTBITE

Description: The Meter Burn version of Frostbite leaves the opponent frozen after a successful parry for a combo of choice.

ICEBERG

Command:	Down, Back + Medium
Hit Level:	Mid
Range:	Full Screen

Description: Killer Frost summons an ice spike that tracks and impales the opponent anywhere on the screen. This move is safe on block in certain areas on the screen where some opponents can't reach or don't have moves fast enough to punish it.

METER BURN ICEBERG

Description: Pressing the Meter Burn button after Iceberg connects leaves the opponent frozen in the air a little longer, making it easier to land a combo.

FLASH FREEZE

Command:	Down, Back, Forward + Medium
Hit Level:	High
Range:	1/4 Screen

Description: Killer Frost dashes towards her opponent, grabs and freezes him or her, and then slaps the opponent with her icy hands. This move is unblockable; the only way to avoid it is by crouching.

METER BURN FLASH FREEZE

Description: Pressing the Meter Burn button after Flash Freeze connects leaves the opponent frozen for a follow up combo instead of slapping him or her away.

BLACK ICE

Command:	Back, Down + Hard
Hit Level:	Low
Range:	3/4 Screen

Description: Killer Frost slides towards her opponent and, if the move connects, pops the opponent up into the air for a follow up with a combo of your choice. This move is safe when blocked.

FROZEN DAGGERS

Command:	Back, Forward + Light
Hit Level:	High
Range:	Full Screen

Description: Killer Frost launches two ice daggers at her opponent that deal a good amount of damage, especially for a projectile.

STRATEGY

USING DIAMOND DUST (BACK + LIGHT, UP + HARD)

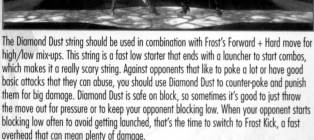

The Diamond Dust string should be used in combination with Frost's Forward + Hard move for high/low mix-ups. This string is a fast low starter that ends with a launcher to start combos, which makes it a really scary string. Against opponents that like to poke a lot or have good basic attacks that they can abuse, you should use Diamond Dust to counter-poke and punish them for big damage. Diamond Dust is safe on block, so sometimes it's good to just throw the move out for pressure or to keep your opponent blocking low. When your opponent starts blocking low often to avoid getting launched, that's the time to switch to Frost Kick, a fast overhead that can mean plenty of damage.

USING TEMPEST (FORWARD + LIGHT, LIGHT, MEDIUM)

This is Killer Frost's most damaging combo attack, which can lead into many other combos. The third of the combo's four hits can be canceled into a Special Move if you want to keep your opponent close to you, or you can let the whole attack finish and then cancel into any Special. The problem with this strategy is that you will only be able to land Iceberg after the string because your opponent will have been launched far away. Though you can still get a decent amount of damage from a Meter Burn Iceberg into the slide (Black Ice), it is best to cancel Tempest's third hit, because you can do better and more damaging combos. You also have the option to cancel out of Tempest's third hit into an Arctic Frost (Forward + Light, Light, Hard) combo that is only three hits, but deals a bit more damage.

USING FROSTBITE (DOWN, BACK + LIGHT)

Frostbite is one of the best parries in the game because it's fast and can parry most high and mid attacks. If you are blocking one of your opponent's strings and know that there is a gap in between the string that you can interrupt, you can pretty much mash Frostbite and then Meter Burn it to get a full punish. Having an instant parry in this game is pretty scary, since a lot of moves have gaps in between. If a Frost player knows all the other characters' strings that have gaps, the opponent likely can't attack her because Frost can squeeze into those gaps to punish the opponent any time she has one bar of meter. Learn and study all other characters' attacks, memorize all the gaps every string has, and you will be become one scary player to attack up close.

USING ICEBERG (DOWN, BACK + MEDIUM)

Iceberg is a Special Move that is best used offensively, but can also be utilized as a defensive tool. You can combo most of Killer Frost's strings into the Iceberg and then combo *again* out of it, which opens up a lot of possibilities. The timing on connecting another move after performing the Iceberg is a little strict, but with practice it can be perfected. Remember, you can always Meter Burn the Iceberg, which pops the opponent higher into the air, allowing for easier follow-ups. Even though this move is not safe on block, it can be used to stop characters with good projectiles. Even though you might trade hits with an opponent, Iceberg deals solid damage, so you might win the trade half the time, depending on how strong your opponent's projectile is. From full screen it is safe to spam this move, as a lot of characters don't have super fast moves that can travel full screen, save for Superman's Super or a character with a fast teleport like Ares.

USING BLACK ICE (BACK, DOWN + HARD)

Black Ice is arguably the best low attack in the game for a lot of reasons. This low travels 3/4 of the screen at a high speed, slips under high-hitting projectiles, and is completely safe when blocked. What really makes this move dangerous is Frost's ability to combo after the move hits, and her combos deal a pretty good amount of damage even without meter use. With one meter segment, she deals even more damage. You can pretty much spam this move until it hits when your opponent has no meter or doesn't have a move with armor that is meterless. When your opponent has meter, you have to be more careful when using the slide because your opponent can be waiting for it and punish you with an armored Forward or Back + Hard.

USING FROZEN DAGGERS (BACK, FORWARD + LIGHT)

Frozen Daggers are a good tool to use in a projectile war because they do more damage than most projectiles, are quick, and are only punishable by the fastest attacks in the game—plus the opponent has to be close. If the daggers are blocked from full screen, the opponent can't move right away because you can keep him or her in check with the Iceberg Special Move. That means your opponent has to block before he or she can do anything. When Killer Frost has the health lead, she can pretty much run away from her opponent and start her keep-away game. It can be hard for certain characters to hit Frost when she wants to run away, because her air dash and ground back dash are great, plus the opponent has to always worry about her Frozen Daggers, Iceberg, and slide. Opponents fighting Killer Frost can't just dash forward; they have to think carefully how they want to get in.

COMBOS

Black Ice > Forward + Light, Light, Medium ~ Iceberg — 24%
Black Ice > Up + Hard > Light, Light ~ Frozen Daggers — 26%
Forward + Light, Light, Hard ~ Iceberg > Light, Light ~Frozen Daggers — 29%
Forward + Light, Light, Medium (First Hit) ~ Black Ice > Up + Hard > Up + Hard > Forward + Light, Light ~ Frozen Daggers — 35%
Forward + Light, Light, Hard ~ Black Ice > Up + Hard > Up + Hard > Forward + Light, Light ~ Frozen Daggers — 39%
Back + Light, Up + Hard > Up + Hard > Up + Hard > Forward + Light, Light, Medium (First Hit) ~ Meter Burn Iceberg > Back + Hard > Frozen Daggers — 41%
Forward + Light, Light, Hard ~ Black Ice > Up + Hard > Up + Hard > Forward + Light, Light, Medium (First Hit) ~ Iceberg — 40%
Back + Hard > Jumping + Hard > Forward + Light, Light, Hard ~ Meter Burn Iceberg > Forward + Light, Light ~ Frozen Daggers — 38%
Black Ice > Up + Hard > Up + Hard > Forward + Light, Light, Medium (First Hit) ~ Meter Burn Iceberg > Back + Hard > Frozen Dagger — 42%

Forward + Light, Light, Hard ~ Black Ice > Up + Hard > Up + Hard > Forward + Light, Light, Medium (First Hit) ~ Meter Burn Iceberg > Back + Hard > Frozen Daggers — 47%
Down + Medium > Black Ice > Up + Hard > Forward + Light, Light, Medium (First Hit) ~ Meter Burn Iceberg > Back + Hard > Frozen Daggers — 29%

Back + Hard > Jumping + Hard > Forward + Light, Light, Hard ~ Flash Freeze — 47%

TIP *While in Freezing Cold mode: Forward + Light, Light, Hard ~ Black Ice > Up + Hard (do as many reps as possible) > Forward + Light, Light, Medium (First Hit) ~ Meter Burn Iceberg > Back + Hard > Frozen Daggers — damage varies depending on how many times you loop Up + Hard*

While in Freezing Cold mode: Forward + Light, Light, Hard (do as many reps as possible) ~ Meter Burn Iceberg > Back + Hard > Black Ice > Up + Hard > Forward + Light, Light, Medium (First Hit) ~ Iceberg — damage varies (corner only)

SUPER MOVE: ENDLESS WHITEOUT

3 HITS

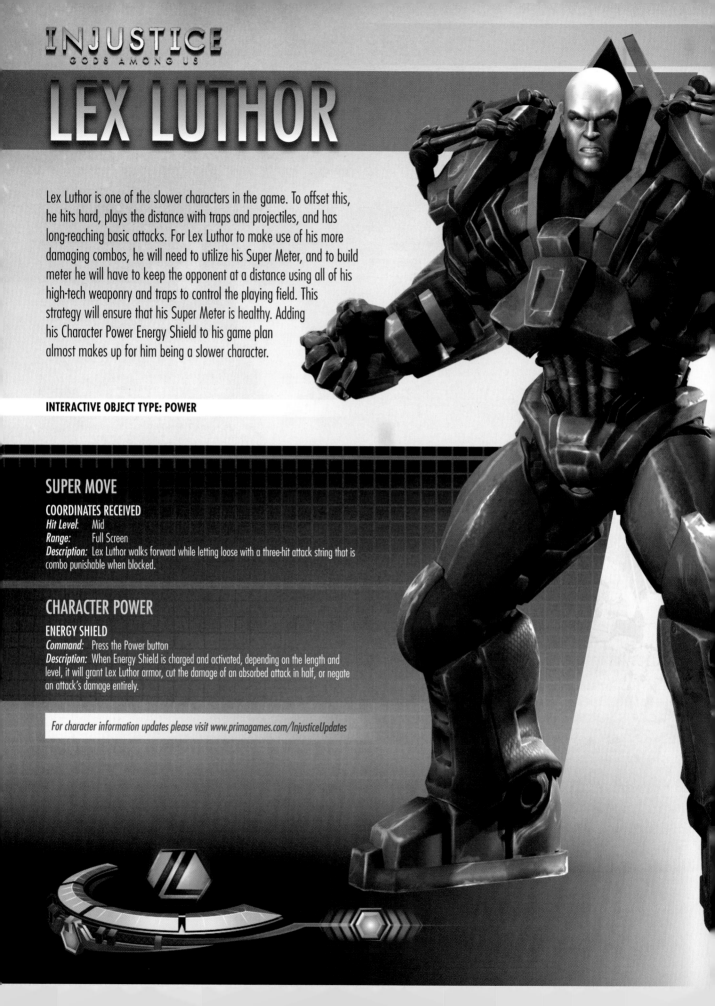

INJUSTICE
GODS AMONG US

LEX LUTHOR

Lex Luthor is one of the slower characters in the game. To offset this, he hits hard, plays the distance with traps and projectiles, and has long-reaching basic attacks. For Lex Luthor to make use of his more damaging combos, he will need to utilize his Super Meter, and to build meter he will have to keep the opponent at a distance using all of his high-tech weaponry and traps to control the playing field. This strategy will ensure that his Super Meter is healthy. Adding his Character Power Energy Shield to his game plan almost makes up for him being a slower character.

INTERACTIVE OBJECT TYPE: POWER

SUPER MOVE

COORDINATES RECEIVED
Hit Level: Mid
Range: Full Screen
Description: Lex Luthor walks forward while letting loose with a three-hit attack string that is combo punishable when blocked.

CHARACTER POWER

ENERGY SHIELD
Command: Press the Power button
Description: When Energy Shield is charged and activated, depending on the length and level, it will grant Lex Luthor armor, cut the damage of an absorbed attack in half, or negate an attack's damage entirely.

For character information updates please visit www.primagames.com/InjusticeUpdates

BEST BASIC ATTACKS

HYPER AXE

Command: Jumping Hard
Hit Level: Overhead
Range: Sweep
Description: Lex Luthor swings an axe that covers full sweep range and arcs in a wide vertical swath front of him.

LOW SHOT

Command: Down + Light
Hit Level: Mid
Range: Sweep
Description: Lex Luthor performs a shot out of his hand that hits the length of sweep range and is safe when blocked.

LOW PUSH KICK

Command: Down + Hard
Hit Level: Low
Range: Sweep
Description: A low-crouching attack where Lex Luthor extends his foot and knocks the opponent down. The Low Push Kick is unsafe when blocked, but can be spaced out to make it harder to punish.

ION PUSH

Command: Back + Hard
Hit Level: Mid
Range: Sweep
Description: A wall bounce attack that has good range covering sweep distance that is also safe when blocked.

DOUBLE SHOT

Command: Forward + Hard
Hit Level: Overhead
Range: Sweep
Description: An overhead bounce attack that covers all of sweep distance and is safe when blocked.

SKY FALL

Command: Up + Hard
Hit Level: High
Range: Close
Description: A quick attack that reaches into the air and hits an airborne opponent that is close to Lex Luthor's head.

DOWNWARD DESTRUCTION

Command: Forward + Medium
Hit Level: Overhead
Range: Close
Description: A fast overhead attack that hits inside of sweep distance, it is unsafe when blocked but can be spaced out to where it is too far away to reach.

PHOTON KICK

Command: Hard
Hit Level: Mid
Range: Sweep
Description: A kick that extends into sweep ranges and knocks the opponent backwards. The Photon Kick is safe when blocked.

BEST COMBO ATTACKS

HIGHEST CURRENCY

Command: Back + Light, Hard

Hit Level: Low

Range: Close

Description: A low combo starter that staggers long enough to cancel into a Special for longer attack strings, Highest Currency can only be punished by Superman's Super Move when blocked.

CRIMINAL MIND

Command: Light, Light, Medium

Hit Level: High, High, Overhead

Range: Close

Description: Three-hit combo starter attack that is 100% safe when blocked and cannot be interrupted.

SPECIAL MOVES

GRAVITY PULL

Command: Down, Back + Medium
Hit Level: Mid
Range: 1/2 Screen
Description: Lex Luthor pulls the opponent toward him to deliver a blast that sends him or her flying across the screen. Gravity Pull is very unsafe when blocked, but at a distance can be hard to punish.

METER BURN GRAVITY PULL

Description: Pressing the Meter Burn button during Gravity Pull will stagger an opponent instead of blasting him or her away, leaving the opponent open to a follow up with an attack of Lex Luthor's choice.

LEX PROBE

Command: Down, Back + Hard
Hit Level: Mid
Range: Full Screen
Description: Lex Luthor summons a probe that will shoot the opponent anywhere on the screen.

METER BURN LEX PROBE

Description: Pressing the Meter Burn button with Lex Probe will summon two probes that will shoot the opponent and knock him or her down.

GRAVITY MINE

Command: Down, Down + Hard for Mid
　　　　　　 Down, Down + Hard, Back for Close
　　　　　　 Down, Down + Hard, Forward for Far
Hit Level: Low
Range: Close, Mid, Far
Description: Lex Luthor tosses a Gravity Mine on the ground that will hit stagger the opponent long enough for a follow up. This move is safe when blocked.

METER BURN GRAVITY MINE

Description: Pressing the Meter Burn button during Gravity Mine will detonate the mine, launching the opponent into the air.

LANCE BLAST

Command: Down, Forward + Light
Hit Level: Mid
Range: Full Screen
Description: Lex Luthor pulls out his lance and shoots a blast horizontally that travels full screen and is safe when blocked.

UP LANCE BLAST

Command: Down, Back + Light
Hit Level: Mid
Range: Vertical 1/3
Description: Instead of shooting his blast horizontally, Lex Luthor fires it vertically, which will hit any airborne opponent. Like the horizontal version, this attack is safe when blocked.

CORP CHARGE (CAN BE PERFORMED WHILE AIRBORNE)

Command: Back, Forward + Medium
Hit Level: Mid
Range: Any
Description: Lex Luthor uses the jets equipped to his suit to fly forward, quickly knocking the opponent down. Combo punishable when blocked.

ORBITAL STRIKE

Command: Down, Forward + Hard
Hit Level: Unblockable
Range: Any
Description: Lex Luthor calls a satellite to home in on the opponent and hit him or her with a laser.

METER BURN ORBITAL STRIKE

Description: Pressing the Meter Burn button during Orbital Strike will summon rockets instead of a laser, hitting the opponent and launching him or her into the air.

STRATEGY

USING LOW SHOT (DOWN + LIGHT)

Low Shot is a fast poke that is best used as a quick attack to frustrate an opponent up close. Use it whenever an opponent is getting overzealous with pressure. On hit, this grants enough advantage for a 50/50 mix-up attempt using Downward Destruction or High Currency.

USING LOW PUSH KICK (DOWN + HARD)

Low Push Kick does indeed hit low and knocks the opponent down and backward, giving lex Luthor enough space to start laying traps and zoning his opponent. It can be used as a whiff punish or a counter-poke up close after blocking an attack, and is good to just toss out in sweep range as well. Having more range than most characters' normals, it should be a go-to attack.

USING SKY FALL (UP + HARD)

Sky Fall is great when an opponent is in the air and near Lex Luthor. When this hits, it will knock the opponent far away from Lex Luthor, allowing him enough time to set his mines and probes so they can force the opponent into a situation where Lex Luthor can score damage with his projectiles.

USING DOWNWARD DESTRUCTION (FORWARD + MEDIUM)

Lex Luthor's best overhead attack, Downward Destruction is fast and safe when blocked. It's best to use the move whenever the opponent is crouching up close, but is also great in situations where Lex Luthor will have advantage, such as after blocking an attack that leaves an opponent recovering, when Low Shot hits, after landing a blocked jumping attack, and for when opponents are expecting Highest Currency. It knocks the opponent back on hit, which is where Lex Luthor wants his opponent to be, and it also can be Special canceled. The ideal Special to cancel into would be Meter Burn Gravity Pull, since it sets up big damage. With Highest Currency, Downward Destruction becomes a very strong 50/50 game up close and should be an opponent's biggest worry up close. The attack is extremely useful whenever Lex Luthor has advantage, such as when Lex Probes are on the screen to force the opponent to block, allowing Lex Luthor to do his Downward Destruction or Highest Currency mix-up.

USING PHOTON KICK (HARD)

Photon Kick is one of Lex Luthor's best normal attacks up close. It executes quickly and covers full sweep distance while knocking the opponent backward onto the ground. It can be used as a poke, whiff punish, and to keep the opponent out whenever he or she gets into range. It is completely safe when blocked, so there is never a reason not to use this attack in sweep distance.

USING ION PUSH (BACK + HARD)

Ion Push is a safe wall bounce attack that can be used specifically for combos after landing a Meter Burn Gravity Pull, and as a poke in sweep distance. Ion Push also can gain a hit of armor with Meter Burn. This is useful for getting aggressive opponents off of Lex Luthor when they are in range.

USING DOUBLE SHOT (FORWARD + HARD)

Double Shot can be used in sweep distance as a safe overhead to start a combo. It also can be used with Meter Burn to armor through any of the opponent's attacks or projectiles as a single hit.

USING HIGHEST CURRENCY (BACK + LIGHT, HARD)

A two-hit low attack string that can be special canceled, Highest Currency works best when used with Meter Burn Gravity Pull, since it sets up big damage. The last hit in Highest Currency is totally safe when blocked unless the attack trying to punish you is Superman's Kryptonian Crush. The main goal is to build a lot of meter so Lex Luthor can use Meter Burn Gravity Pull after landing Highest Currency, however Highest Currency into Meter Burn Gravity Pull cannot be hit confirmed, so you have to know it is going to hit. Using this as a poke can be risky, since Gravity Pull is extremely unsafe when blocked and combo punishable. To make the reward count for the risk, make sure you have meter for a Meter Burn Gravity Pull, so when it hits you get maximum damage. Another strategy is using the first hit of Highest Currency as a poke; it is 100% safe and is a true block string with Lance Blast. When people become used to blocking Back + Light canceled to Lance Blast, they won't be thinking about Downward Destruction, and you can sneak that in as an overhead or finish the Highest Currency string, depending on how they are blocking the poke. If they are crouching, hit them with Downward Destruction; if they are standing, finish the string. You can also grab them if you aren't confident about going for the 50/50 .

USING CRIMINAL MIND (LIGHT, LIGHT, MEDIUM)

Criminal Mind is a safe combo starter when blocked, and cannot be interrupted by anything in the game, plus the last hit launches for a Gravity Pull follow up. Criminal Mind doesn't have to be canceled into Gravity Pull for it to work, since the last hit gives you enough time to confirm that the opponent was successfully hit before you decide to perform Gravity Pull. Criminal Mind can be used up close when blocking unsafe attacks that are punishable when guarded, and after landing a jumping attack.

USING GRAVITY PULL (DOWN, BACK + MEDIUM)

Gravity Pull is how Lex Luthor nets his damage. Using Meter Burn with this attack gives Lex Luthor combo opportunities that aren't normally possible with his normal Gravity Pull. This is important, because Lex Luthor isn't a combo-centric character, and this is the best and most consistent way for him to score big damage. While the opponent is trying to get around Gravity Mines, Lex Probes, Orbital Strikes, and Lance Blasts, he or she is susceptible to getting caught by a Gravity Pull and losing a lot of his or her life bar. Gravity Pull can also be used to pull the opponent into the range of Gravity Mines and Lex Probes, which will combo the opponent if he or she isn't blocking. Gravity Pull will grab opponents out of any attack they are executing with the right timing. This is a great counter-zoning tool at half screen, and is worth the risk of just tossing it out from that range. Unfortunately, this comes with a draw back, as it leaves Lex Luthor very open when blocked up close and is combo punishable. From farther away, it is much harder to punish Lex Lurthor when blocking Gravity Pull.

USING GRAVITY MINE (DOWN, DOWN + HARD)

Gravity Mine is best used as a zoning tool for keeping the opponent at specific ranges. However, the Meter Burn isn't worth it, which is best used for Gravity Pull. Gravity Mine is there to either catch an opponent trying to run away from Orbital Strike, or to control a certain space on the playing field, allowing Lex Luthor to set up all of his Special Moves on the opponent. Whenever a Gravity Mine is on the screen, use Orbital Strike, Lance Blast, Lex Probe, or Gravity Pull, depending on what the opponent is doing. If the opponent is staying on the defensive, use Orbital Strike and Lex Probe. If the opponent is trying to advance forward, you can use Corps Charge or Lance Blast.

USING ORBITAL STRIKE (DOWN, FORWARD + HARD)

Orbital Strike is an attack that homes in on the opponent for an unblockable attack. It executes quickly and will keep the opponent from wanting to stand still for too long. The Meter Burn version of the attack hits three times and allows Lex Luthor to use Gravity Pull to follow up a combo at 3/4 of the screen. Orbital Strike forces an opponent to move around, and this can cause him or her to jump and land on a Gravity Mine, get hit by Lance Blast, or move in the range of a Lex Probe—all of which allows Lex Luthor to continue his zoning. Orbital Strike should be Lex Luthor's most used Special Move from a distance.

USING LEX PROBE (DOWN, BACK + HARD)

Lex Probe is another proximity Special Move, good for controlling a great deal of space in front of Lex Luthor . With Meter Burn, he throws out two probes that cover the same amount of space, but instead of shooting once it will fire twice. This makes dealing with Lex Luthor's projectiles even more difficult; use this attack to slow the opponent, allowing Lex Luthor to move around freely. Lex Probes also work great offensively too, allowing Lex Luthor to pressure his opponent and force him or her to want to block. If the probe hits the opponent, Lex Luthor can get a free combo if in range, making blocking in this situation an opponent's best option. Unfortunately for that opponent, Lex Luthor has an up-close 50/50 mix-up, or he can charge Lance Blast up and hit the opponent with an unblockable blast. The Meter Burn version will launch the opponent into the air, allowing Lex Luthor to Gravity Pull him or her in for damage, Meter Burn the Gravity Pull for a full combo, or just pull off a Back + Hard attack to combo without spending meter.

USING LANCE BLAST/UP LANCE BLAST
(DOWN, FORWARD/BACK + LIGHT)

Lance Blast is Lex Luthor's standard projectile attack that travels full screen, and he can charge the attack or dash cancel out of it. When charging, it has three levels. The first level is when you'd normally perform the attack, and when blocked it pushes back. The second level will cause the projectile to launch the opponent on hit. The third is an unblockable attack that only travels a short distance. This works well with all of his Special Moves, especially when the opponent gets close. This strategy, however, works best when the opponent hesitates due to a Lex Probe or a Gravity Mine on the screen. When the opponent begins to jump or back dash to avoid a charged Lance Blast, Lex Luthor can dash cancel forward or backward, which will allow Lex Luthor to perform another attack to punish the opponent in his or her recovery. Lance Blast is totally safe when blocked.

USING CORP CHARGE (BACK, FORWARD + MEDIUM)

Corps Charge is mainly used as a whiff punisher or to catch opponents off guard when trying to advance or retreat, or as a whiff punisher outside the range of Lex Luthor's normals. Another way you can use Corps Charge is when the opponent tries to run away from Lex Probes, Gravity Mines, Orbital Strikes, or a charged Lance Blast. Corps Charge can also be used as a combo ender.

USING ENERGY SHIELD CHARACTER POWER

If Lex Luthor needed anything else to make his zoning complete it's this, his Character Power. If an opponent finally gets through Lex Luthor's projectile obstacle course nonsense, he or she still has to deal with Lex Luthor being able to absorb attacks. If the opponent tries to hit him, he can just hit an opponent out of whatever attack the opponent tries—more than likely an attack that pushes the opponent full screen or starts a combo. Lex Luthor can charge his shield up to three levels: At level 1, he has armor and absorbs one attack; at level 2 it cuts the attack's damage in half and preserves armor; and at level 3, he still has armor and the attack causes no damage. Using this along with everything else Lex Luthor has is a pain even when you are finally next to him. The only downside is he has to charge the Power up, but the rewards are worth it.

USING COORDINATES RECEIVED

Coordinates Received is a safe Super Move that has armor, so it can blow through Special Moves. Its only downside is the lack of range, so it must be used up close. However, seeing that Lex Luthor has one of the best ranged tactics in the game, this makes his Super Move useful. Most characters are going to try to get next to Lex Luthor to stop him from attacking, but by that time he should have a full bar of meter. One false move and Lex Luthor unleashes his Super.

USING JUMP IN ATTACKS AND CROSS UPS

Lex Luthor's jumping Medium is his cross up attack, and jumping Hard is his best jump attack, as it covers a wide range in front of him. This is also another tactic to use to make it even harder for opponents to approach him. Jumping Hard will be one of Lex Luthor's most used attacks.

USING AIR-TO-AIR

Lex Luthor's best air-to-air is definitely his jumping Hard. It out ranges every air-to-air attack in the game and makes it so Lex Luthor can attack while retreating or advancing. If an opponent gets too close, jump backward and use Lex Luthor's jumping Hard to give yourself space. If you want to advance toward the opponent and attack at the same time to cover a big range in front of you, then use jumping Hard like an attacking shield to help you control the distance between yourself and your opponent.

COMBOS

NO METER BURN:

Back + Light, Hard ~ Gravity Pull — 14%
Forward + Medium ~ Gravity Pull — 19%
Jumping Hard > Corp Charge — 19%
Light, Light, Medium ~ Gravity Pull — 17%

SUPER MOVE: COORDINATES RECEIVED

ONE METER BURN:

Meter Burn Gravity Pull > Back + Hard > Jumping Hard > Forward + Medium ~ Gravity Pull — 34%
Meter Burn Orbital Strike > Gravity Pull — 22%

NIGHTWING

Nightwing is one of the few characters in the game with different stances, dubbed Escrima and Staff. Both stances have pros and cons that help offset each other. Using Escrima, Nightwing is a very nimble acrobat, allowing him to jump very high and move with a fast advancing forward dash, making it easier for him to get around projectiles. For attacking, however, he has to get in close to deal any damage, and can be easily out-ranged. His Staff stance lets him control the ground more, having a shorter jump, but allowing him to attack from the air while staying very close to the ground, and making it difficult to anti-air him with normal attacks. In Staff he can attack safely from a distance with longer-ranged attacks, but has trouble getting around projectiles.

INTERACTIVE OBJECT TYPE: GADGET

SUPER MOVE

DARK AS NIGHT
Hit Level: Mid
Range: Sweep
Description: Nightwing performs a sweeping ranged mid attack that is safe when blocked. It is combo punishable when blocked at point-blank range, but at a distance the only character that can punish Dark As Night is Superman's own Super Move.

CHARACTER POWER

STYLE CHANGE
Command: Press the Power button
Description: Nightwing's Style Change swaps between his short-ranged Escrima stance and his longer-ranged Staff stance.

For character information updates please visit www.primagames.com/InjusticeUpdates

BEST ESCRIMA STANCE BASIC ATTACKS

OVERHEAD STRIKE

Command: Back + Medium
Hit Level: Overhead
Range: Sweep
Description: Nightwing extends forward in sweep distance with an overhead attack that bounces the opponent. This move can be canceled into Specials and Super Moves on hit or block. Overhead Strike is safe against every character in the game but Superman and his Kryptonian Crush.

CIRCULAR POWER

Command: Forward + Hard
Hit Level: Overhead
Range: Sweep
Description: Nightwing flips forward and lands with an overhead attack that bounces opponents high enough for a combo. Circular Power can be Meter Burned to gain a hit of armor, and is totally safe when blocked.

SPINNING BLAST

Command: Back + Hard
Hit Level: Mid
Range: Sweep
Description: Nightwing sways backward, then charges forward to deliver a Transition attack that also wall bounces for a combo attempt. Meter Burning this move adds a hit of armor, and is totally safe when blocked.

ESCRIMA STRIKE

Command: Down + Light
Hit Level: Mid
Range: Sweep
Description: Nightwing extends forward into sweep distance with an overhead attack that bounces the opponent. Escrima Strike can be canceled into Special and Super Moves and is totally safe when blocked.

EXTENDED KICK

Command: Jumping Hard
Hit Level: Overhead
Range: Close
Description: An airborne jumping attack where Nightwing extends both of his legs downward for a double kick that juggles on hit.

SPINNING HEEL KICK

Command: Up + Hard
Hit Level: Overhead
Range: Sweep
Description: An overhead kick that jumps over low attacks and delivers a knockdown that can't be Tech Rolled out of, the Spinning Heel Kick is totally safe when blocked.

BIRD'S NEST

Command: Up + Hard, Down + Hard
Hit Level: Low
Range: Sweep
Description: A low knockdown attack that can't be Tech Rolled, the first part of Bird's Nest's animation jumps over low attacks and is totally safe when blocked.

INJUSTICE
GODS AMONG US

BEST STAFF STANCE BASIC ATTACKS

FACE POKE

Command: Light
Hit Level: Mid
Range: 1/4 Screen
Description: A staff poke that extends for 1/4 of the screen, Face Poke can be followed up into a combo attack ender or canceled into a Special or Super. This move is totally safe when blocked.

OVERHEAD STRIKE

Command: Medium
Hit Level: Overhead
Range: 1/4 Screen
Description: A long-range overhead strike that bounces the opponent on hit and is safe when blocked. This move is safe against every character in the game but Superman with his Kryptonian Crush. From a distance it is 100% safe when blocked, even against Superman.

CROUCHING TALON

Command: Down + Light
Hit Level: Mid
Range: Close
Description: Crouching Talon is a safe-when-blocked crouching mid poke.

HAWKEYE

Command: Down + Hard
Hit Level: Low
Range: 1/4 Screen
Description: This long-range sweep hits low and will knock the opponent down without a chance for a Tech Roll. Hawkeye is combo punishable when blocked, but can be made safe against most characters from a distance.

AIR POKE

Command: Jumping Light
Hit Level: Overhead
Range: Sweep
Description: Nightwing jabs with his staff while jumping to cover a majority of sweep range.

STAFF SMACK

Command: Jumping Hard
Hit Level: Overhead
Range: Sweep
Description: Nightwing performs an airborne rising attack while jumping.

BEST ESCRIMA COMBO ATTACKS

WIDE WING

Command: Forward + Medium, Light, Hard
Hit Level: Mid, Mid, Mid, Mid
Range: Close
Description: A three-hit combo string that can be Special and Super canceled, Wide Wing's last hit produces a knockdown. This string cannot be interrupted, and the first and last hits are totally safe when blocked. The second hit is safe when blocked against every attack but Superman's Kryptonian Smash.

SURRENDER NOW

Command: Back + Light, Hard
Hit Level: Mid, Low
Range: Inside Sweep
Description: This is a two-hit string that leads into a sweeping knockdown. It is 100% safe when blocked, and the string cannot be interrupted.

BEST STAFF COMBO ATTACKS

OUTSIDER

Command: Light, Forward + Light
Hit Level: Mid, Low
Range: Sweep
Description: A fast, long-range mid to low poke that can be Special canceled for a combo, Outsider is totally safe when blocked.

LAST CHANCE

Command: Light, Down + Hard
Hit Level: Mid, Low
Range: Sweep
Description: A long-range quick poke that ends in a low knockdown that can't be Tech Rolled, this string is interruptable by Super Moves and fast normal attacks. It is also unsafe when blocked.

WING SPAN

Command: Light, Forward + Medium
Hit Level: Mid, Overhead
Range: Sweep
Description: Wing Span is a mid that transitions quickly to an overhead and knocks the opponent down. This string can be interrupted by fast normals and Supers, but is safe when blocked.

ESCRIMA SPECIAL MOVES

(AIR) WINGDING

Command: Down, Back + Light
Hit Level: Overhead
Range: 1/2 Screen
Description: Nightwing throws three WingDings in a downward arc that stun the opponent on hit. This attack can be punished when blocked.

METER BURN (AIR) WINGDING

Description: Pressing the Meter Burn button during (Air) WingDing will toss an additional WingDing that knocks the opponent down on hit.

GROUND SPARK

Command: Down, Back + Medium
Hit Level: Low
Range: Full Screen
Description: Ground Spark is a fast-traveling, low-hitting projectile that will stagger an opponent. It can be held to delay when it executes, and can be dash canceled out of. This move is safe when blocked.

METER BURN GROUND SPARK

Description: Pressing the Meter Burn button during Ground Spark will increase the size and damage of the projectile, and knocks the opponent down on hit. This move is safe when blocked.

ESCRIMA FURY

Command: Down, Forward + Medium
Hit Level: Mid
Range: Close
Description: Nightwing performs a five-hit combo that launches the opponent into the air for a juggle. This move is combo punishable when blocked.

METER BURN ESCRIMA FURY

Description: Pressing the Meter Burn button after landing Escrima Fury will increase the number of hits from five to nine, launching the opponent into the air for a juggle.

FLIP KICK

Command:	Down, Back + Hard
Hit Level:	Overhead
Range:	Sweep

Description: Nightwing performs a flip kick that advances forward and hits overhead, knocking the opponent down for a knockdown that can't be Tech Rolled, but is combo punishable when blocked.

METER BURN FLIP KICK

Description: Pressing the Meter Burn button during Flip Kick will cause Flip Kick to extend into a second overhead attack that launches for a juggle follow up and is safe when blocked.

SCATTER BOMB

Command:	Down, Back + Light
Hit Level:	Mid
Range:	Close

Description: Nightwing throws a Scatter Bomb vertically that will knock airborne opponents out of the air. This move is safe when blocked.

METER BURN SCATTER BOMB

Description: Pressing the Meter Burn button during Scatter Bomb will cause the bomb to explode for two extra hits, causing additional damage.

STAFF SPECIAL MOVES

STAFF SPIN

Command:	Down, Back + Hard
Hit Level:	Mid
Range:	1/2 Screen

Description: Nightwing twirls his Staff around five times, ending in Tech Roll-proof knockdown. This move is totally safe when blocked.

METER BURN STAFF SPIN

Description: Pressing the Meter Burn button after landing Staff Spin will cause the last hit of the attack to become a wall bounce that allows Nightwing to follow up with a combo, and is totally safe when blocked.

GROUND BLAST

Command:	Down, Back + Medium
Hit Level:	Low
Range:	Anywhere

Description: Nightwing slams his Staff into the ground, creating a staggering effect if the opponent isn't blocking while his or her feet are touching the ground. This move is totally safe when blocked.

METER BURN GROUND BLAST

Description: Pressing the Meter Burn button during Ground Blast will deliver a second blast that knocks the opponent down, preventing a Tech Roll. Like the normal version, this move is totally safe when blocked.

FLYING GRAYSON

Command:	Back + Forward + Hard
Hit Level:	High
Range:	1/2 Screen

Description: Nightwing uses his Staff to propel himself through the air, delivering a flying kick that knocks the opponent back. Flying Grayson is safe when blocked against the whole cast, save for Superman's Kryptonian Crush.

STRATEGY (ESCRIMA)

USING ESCRIMA SPINNING BLAST (BACK + HARD) AND ESCRIMA CIRCULAR POWER (FORWARD + HARD)

Both attacks, when used with Meter Burn, gain a hit of armor, and with their speed it makes them very viable in melee range as they travel through the opponent's attacks and projectiles. This strategy gives Nightwing the opportunity to land big damage combos. Circular Power is an overhead bounce attack that avoids low in its starting animation, while Spinning Blast takes a step back, which can cause some attacks by your opponent up close to whiff. For use without meter, use Circular Power when the opponent is trying to attack you with crouching attacks. Spinning Blast can be used to force attacks to miss right before it hits.

USING OVERHEAD STRIKE (BACK + MEDIUM)

Overhead Strike ground bounces on hit, travels the full sweep distance, and best of all is safe when blocked by most of the roster except Superman's all-powerful Kryptonian Crush. It can be Special and Super canceled, and is a great poke to use in sweep range or to use as a whiff punisher at the same distance.

USING WIDE WING (FORWARD + MEDIUM, LIGHT, HARD)

Wide Wing is a three-hit string that can be Special and Super canceled. Unfortunately, it's disadvantageous when blocked because the last hit will miss the opponent, but it can be made safe when blocked by Special canceling. It's a good counter-poke string for up-close distance if you think the opponent won't be guarding, but it's best to use Wide Wing in situations after Nightwing has frame advantage (i.e., can recover faster than his opponent).

USING ESCRIMA STRIKE (DOWN + LIGHT)

Escrima Strike is a low thrust that is best as a retaliation poke up close, and can be canceled into Special Moves. It also has a follow up that knocks down on normal hit. Use Escrima Strike with Flip Kick to cross the opponent up and knock him or her down.

USING SURRENDER NOW (BACK + LIGHT, HARD)

Surrender Now is a two-hit mid to low string that extends forward. The first hit can be canceled into Flip Kick for a 50/50 knockdown mix-up. Use this as an opening poke and as a whiff punisher.

USING SPINNING HEEL KICK (UP + HARD)

Spinning Heel Kick is safe when blocked overhead and will hit the opponent for a knockdown that can't be Tech Rolled away from. Use this to set up pressure on an opponent's wakeup and go for cross ups. Spinning Heel Kick is slow to start up, but it does have the ability to jump over low attacks.

USING BIRD'S NEST (UP + HARD, DOWN + HARD)

Bird's Nest is a very deceptive low to block because the start-up animation is the exact same as Spinning Heel Kick, and the opponent will be looking for the overhead attack and attempt to block while standing. When hit, the opponent is put into a knockdown situation that can't be Tech Rolled, just like Spinning Heel Kick, so the same strategy applies.

USING EXTENDED KICK (JUMPING HARD)

Extended Kick is the best jumping attack in Nightwing's arsenal. It can be used as an instant overhead and is very difficult to anti-air by using basic attacks. For this reason alone, Nightwing can jump in much easier than most characters, so use this to your advantage and bully your opponent from the air.

USING (AIR) WINGDING (DOWN, BACK + LIGHT)

(Air) WingDing is a projectile attack that can only be executed in mid-air, and is great for counter-zoning and to zone in general. The Meter Burn version throws an additional WingDing that knocks back on hit, making it great to use when the opponent thinks all the WingDings have been thrown, stopping the opponent in his or her tracks.

USING GROUND SPARK (DOWN, BACK + MEDIUM)

Ground Spark is Nightwing's ground projectile that travels full screen. He can hold and delay when he releases it, activate it immediately, or even avoid releasing it altogether with a dash cancel. Nightwing can use Ground Spark to continue pressure by dash canceling out during block strings. Where he can cancel into Specials, he can cancel into Ground Spark and then dash cancel out of it to apply more pressure, giving him mix-up opportunities for a throw, lows, and overheads. The Meter Burn version of this attack deals more damage and knocks down.

USING ESCRIMA FURY (DOWN, FORWARD + MEDIUM)

Escrima Fury is Nightwing's Special that sets up a lot of his damage in Escrima stance, jugglewise. It's unsafe when blocked, so it's best to use during a string that he is able to hit confirm into, or in a situation where it is guaranteed. Tossing Escrima Fury out at the wrong time will give the opponent an opportunity to punish Nightwing, so it must be used precisely. The Meter Burn version is nine hits for more damage, and still launches into the air.

USING FLIP KICK (DOWN, BACK + HEAVY)

Flip Kick is one of Nightwing's top Specials in Escrima stance. Up close, it can cross up, hits overhead, and is safe when blocked. This is a very abusable Special Move, and can keep every opponent on his or her toes. It knocks down on hit and gives Nightwing a throw attempt, forcing the opponent to use a wakeup attack that can be baited and punished. The Meter Burn version hits twice and launches the target into the air for a combo.

USING SCATTER BOMB (DOWN, BACK + LIGHT)

Scatter Bomb is a short-ranged projectile attack that hits vertically in front of Nightwing, thus making it a useful anti-air attack. The Meter Burn version creates a second hit and keeps an opponent in the air a little longer for a combo attempt.

STRATEGY (STAFF)

USING FACE POKE (LIGHT)

Face Poke is a long-range attack that can transition into Wing Span, an overhead that creates a knockdown or Outsider. A low attack that can be canceled into a Special Move, Face Poke is also great for keeping opponents at bay who try to rush in. This is one of Nightwing's main normal attacks in his Staff stance.

USING OVERHEAD STRIKE (MEDIUM)

Overhead Strike is a fast (wait for it...) overhead that launches an opponent into the air for a combo. It's safe when blocked, and can be used along with his Staff stance/Hawkeye as a regular standing mix-up, since Hawkeye hits low and is a long-range sweep.

USING HAWKEYE (DOWN + HEAVY)

Hawkeye is a long-range, low poke that is a knockdown on hit, and functions well as a whiff punisher or as a good spacing tool in general. Mix with Overhead Strike to get the best out of Hawkeye's potential. Opponents may get annoyed and start blocking low, at which point Nightwing should sneak in with an Overhead Strike.

USING CROUCHING TALON (DOWN + LIGHT)

Crouching Talon is Nightwing's fastest normal in Staff stance, and can be canceled into Special attacks and his Super Move. This is best used as a counter-poke up close and to get Nightwing out of tight situations.

USING AIR POKE (JUMPING LIGHT)

Air Poke is used as a jumping attack that allows Nightwing to control the ground in front of him and attack at the same time. Acting as an offensive shield, this will allow Nightwing to move forward while attacking.

USING STAFF SMACK (JUMPING HARD)

Staff Smack is a jumping attack that works much like Air Poke, but instead it controls the air if the opponent tries to match Nightwing there. It can also be used as a jumping attack to lead into a combo on the ground.

USING STAFF SPIN (DOWN, BACK + HARD)

Staff Spin is a safe-when-blocked Special Move that knocks down on hit, and is great to use after Nightwing's staff normals like Crouching Talon and Face Poke. The Meter Burn version of this attack causes a wall bounce and allows Nightwing to follow up with a combo.

USING GROUND BLAST (DOWN, BACK + MEDIUM)

Ground Blast is a Staff stance Special that hits the opponent anywhere on the screen. The Meter Burn version of this attack hits twice and knocks down on hit. Better still, when blocked, it pushes back and is a great way to build meter.

USING FLYING GRAYSON (BACK, FORWARD + HEAVY)

Flying Grayson is a long-range attack that travels 3/4 of the screen and hits overhead. It's safe when blocked and is really great for moving Nightwing close to his opponent as well as knocking him or her down, but is best used outside of sweep distance or farther.

USING STYLE CHANGE CHARACTER POWER

Style Change is specifically used for transitioning between Nightwing's Escrima and Staff stances. Some situations and characters are best fought with different stances. Escrima is great for pressuring up close, but a riskier way to score big damage, however it creates more opportunities for dealing damage to the opponent. Staff stance is great for playing a slower-paced but safer game with longer-ranged pokes and whittling down the opponent in a more systematic way. Using both stances at the right times can throw off the opponent.

USING DARK AS NIGHT

Dark As Night has armor for the duration of its active frames, but it doesn't have a lot of range, so it's best used up close or being comboed into.

USING JUMP IN ATTACKS AND CROSS UPS:

Nightwing shines in the air, being an acrobatic Gadget-based character. His Escrima stance jumping Hard is among the best jumping attacks in the game, having an area of effect that is very difficult to anti-air, and if used next to the opponent will become an instant overhead that is very tough to guard. Nightwing's jumping Hard can abuse jumping in for free, since more than likely he will beat out all opponents' anti-air attempts. Jumping Medium from Escrima can be used as a cross up, but that is the only reason for using it over jumping Hard.

In Staff stance, jumping Light is his best normal in the air, since it can also hit overhead and he can attack while advancing forward in the air safely. In Staff stance, Nightwing has a very low jump arc, so it is very difficult to anti-air him.

USING AIR-TO-AIR

Nightwing's best air-to-air attack by far is Escrima jumping Hard; most normal attacks have a hard time competing with Nightwing in the air because of the hit box that it possesses. Nightwing also has (Air) WingDing that he can use to hit an opponent out of the air and keep him or her at a distance. Nightwing can cancel jumping Hard into (Air) WingDing for a quick combo to add more damage when jumping Hard hits. Nightwing's Staff attack jumping Hard is good as an air-to-air similar to Face Poke, but it hits airborne targets instead of grounded ones.

ESCRIMA COMBOS

NO METER BURN:

Escrima Fury > Forward + Hard > Jumping Hard ~ (Air) WingDing — 26%
Back + Medium > Escrima Fury > Jumping Hard ~ (Air) WingDing — 27%
Forward + Hard > Back + Medium~Escrima Fury > Jumping Hard ~ (Air) WingDing — 31%
Back + Light, Light ~ Escrima Fury > Forward + Hard > Jumping Hard ~ (Air) WingDing — 31%
Forward + Medium, Light, Hard ~ Escrima Fury > Forward + Hard > Jumping Hard ~ (Air) WingDing — 32%
Back + Heavy > Back + Medium ~ Escrima Fury > Jumping Hard ~ (Air) WingDing — 31%

ONE METER BURN:

Meter Burn Escrima Fury > Forward + Hard > Jumping Hard ~ (Air) WingDing — 31%
Meter Burn Flip Kick > Back + Hard > Jumping Hard ~ (Air) WingDing — 30%

CORNER:

Escrima Fury > Back + Hard > Jumping Hard ~ (Air) WingDing — 26%
Back + Medium > Escrima Fury > Jumping Hard ~ (Air) WingDing — 27%
Forward + Hard > Back + Medium ~ Escrima Fury > Jumping Hard ~ (Air) WingDing — 31%
Back + Hard > Jumping Hard ~ (Air) WingDing — 27%

CORNER ONE METER BURN:

Meter Burn Flip Kick > Back + Hard > Jumping Hard ~ (Air) WingDing — 30%
Meter Burn Escrima Fury > Back + Hard > Jumping Hard ~ (Air) WingDing — 31%

STAFF COMBOS

NO METER BURN:

Light, Forward + Light ~ Staff Spin — 17%
Down + Light ~ Staff Spin — 12%
Medium > Hard > Light ~ Flying Grayson — 28%
Jumping Hard > Light ~ Flying Grayson — 27%

CORNER NO METER:

Medium > Hard > Light, Forward + Light ~ Flying Grayson — 29%

CORNER METER BURN:

Light, Forward + Light ~ Meter Burn Ground Blast > Light, Forward + Light ~ Flying Grayson — 31%
Light, Forward + Light ~Meter Burn Staff Spin > Down + Light ~ Staff Spin - 31%
Jumping Hard > Light ~ Meter Burn Staff Spin > Down + Light ~ Staff Spin - 37%

INJUSTICE
GODS AMONG US

RAVEN

Raven is a character with powerful zoning tools and a good keep-away game, but also has tools to get around zoning for those characters that have a better keep away game than her. Raven's Empty Void move can absorb projectiles and build a little bit of meter in the process. Opponents have to think before spamming projectiles against Raven because when she absorbs any projectile, she can Meter Burn the move and return an unblockable projectile that deals good damage. Raven's keep-away game gets even better when she activates her Demon Stance, which grants her new moves like a teleport that positions her in front of or behind her enemies and a full screen telekinetic move that is safe when blocked. Raven also has a lot of good basic attacks and combos that deal a lot of damage, so she is not only good from a distance, but can fight her opponents up close.

INTERACTIVE OBJECT TYPE: ACROBATIC

SUPER MOVE

DEADLY SIN
Hit Level: Mid
Range: Sweep
Description: Raven transports her opponent to another dimension where demons attack the victim. After that damage, Raven's father, Trigon, shoots a beam that sends the opponent back to reality.

CHARACTER POWER

DEMON STANCE
Command: Press the Power button
Description: Raven unleashes the evil within and turns into a demonic version of herself that replaces some of her Special Moves and unlocks new ones for a short period of time. She gets a teleport, a full-screen telekinetic attack, and a beam that erupts from the ground. This makes it almost impossible for characters with a good keep-away game to keep her out while she is in Demon Stance.

For character information updates please visit www.primagames.com/InjusticeUpdates

BEST BASIC ATTACKS

FOREST RAVEN

Command: Hard
Range: Close
Hit Level: Mid, Mid
Description: Raven performs a two-hit launcher that is safe when blocked and can be canceled into any of her Special Moves.

RAVEN'S FURY

Command: Jumping Hard
Hit Level: Overhead
Range: Close
Description: This jumping attack is deceptive because it is hard to tell where she is going to land when she jumps at her opponent, making the opponent guess if the move will pass overhead for a cross up or not.

TOURNIQUET

Command: Back + Hard
Hit Level: Mid
Range: Sweep
Description: Raven takes a step back and charges with a powerful strike that causes a wall bounce on hit and can be followed up with a combo of choice. This move is safe when blocked and can be Meter Burned for one hit of armor. You can also charge the attack by holding the Hard button or dash cancel out of it.

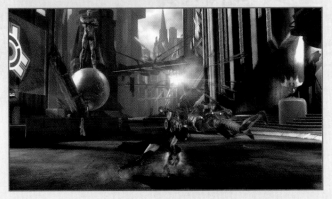

LINKING TALON

Command: Forward + Hard
Hit Level: Overhead
Range: Sweep
Description: A powerful overhead attack that causes a ground bounce, Linking Talon can be charged by holding the Hard button and canceled out of by dashing backward or forward. The Meter Burn version adds one hit of armor.

BEST COMBO ATTACKS

TITAN TRASH

Command: Forward + Medium, Medium, Medium
Hit Level: Mid, Mid
Range: Close
Description: Raven performs three spinning back hands that hit mid. This is Raven's most damaging combo attack, is safe when blocked, and can be canceled into any of her Special Moves. This string is a good way to start and end most of her combos.

TEARS OF SORROW

Command: Back + Light, Medium
Hit Level: Low, Low
Range: Sweep
Description: Tears Of Sorrow issues two quick low attacks that can be canceled into any Special Moves. This move is safe when blocked, and the second hit of this string is quite fast and will often beat out other basic attacks.

TWILIGHT'S END

Command: Back + Medium, Hard
Hit Level: Mid, Mid
Range: Sweep
Description: This is a two-hit string that sends the opponent across the screen and is safe when blocked. This string is good because Raven can play a really good keep-away game, and by sending her opponents across the screen she can give them a hard time trying to get in.

SPECIAL MOVES

EMPTY VOID

Command: Down, Back + Light
Hit Level: Mid
Range: Full Screen
Description: This Special Move absorbs high projectiles and builds a little bit of meter. This attack is best used against opponents that like to spam projectiles.

METER BURN EMPTY VOID

Description: After absorbing the projectile, you can press the Meter Burn button and return a more powerful projectile that is unblockable to your opponent. Holding down and the Meter Burn button will send the projectile down from above the opponent's head—this is also unblockable.

SOUL CRUSH

Command: Down, Forward + Medium
Hit Level: Mid
Range: 3/4 Screen
Description: The Soul Crush is a telekinetic attack that covers 3/4 of the screen, making it a good zoning tool. The move is safe on block if done at max range. Around mid range, it can only be punished by fast attacks that move the opponent closer. This means that Raven can use Soul Crush freely against a large portion of the roster without fear of their advancing attacks slipping in.

METER BURN SOUL CRUSH

Description: The Meter Burn version of Soul Crush launches the opponent into the air and allows Raven to follow up with more attacks.

SINGULARITY

Command: Down, Back + Medium
Hit Level: Mid
Range: 1/4 Screen
Description: Singularity is very similar to Soul Crush in terms of what the move does. The only differences are that Singularity only covers 1/4 of the screen and is a little slower. On the plus side, the move is safer on block and does a little more damage.

METER BURN SINGULARITY

Description: By pressing the Meter Burn button after Singularity connects, Raven bounces her opponent off the ground and is able to follow up with additional attacks. This is one of Raven's best ways to start high-damaging combos because the opponent is launched very high in the air, which makes many of Raven's attacks available for follow up.

SHADOW RAVEN

Command: Down, Forward + Light
Hit Level: High
Range: Full Screen
Description: Shadow Raven is her standard projectile that travels full screen and inflicts a decent amount of damage on impact.

EVENT HORIZON (DEMON STANCE)

Command:	Down, Back + Medium
Hit Level:	Mid
Range:	Full Screen

Description: Event Horizon functions almost like an upgraded version of Raven's Soul Crush. Unlike Soul Crush, which covers only 3/4 of the screen, Event Horizon covers the full screen, is safer on block, and does more damage.

METER BURN EVENT HORIZON

Description: By pressing the Meter Burn button after landing Event Horizon, Raven summons a claw that will hold the opponent close, allowing for a follow-up combo of your choice.

NEGATIVE MASS (DEMON STANCE)

Command:	Down, Forward + Light
Hit Level:	Mid
Range:	Varies

Description: Negative Mass is a stream of dark energy that is birthed from the ground and knocks down the opponent. This move is safe on block and is good for keeping opponents away. The move can be used closer or farther from Raven by pressing Back or Forward after performing the move.

METER BURN NEGATIVE MASS

Description: The Meter Burn version of Negative Mass summons a demon that uppercuts the opponent after the move connects.

FRONT/BEHIND DARK TRANSMISSION (DEMON STANCE)

Command:	Down, Back + Hard or Down, Forward + Hard
Hit Level:	N/A
Range:	N/A

Description: Dark Transmission is a fast teleport that allows Raven to quickly move in front or behind her opponent. Dark Transmission can also be performed in mid-air.

STRATEGY

USING TITAN TRASH (FORWARD + MEDIUM, MEDIUM, MEDIUM)

The Titan Trash string is Raven's go-to attack to start most of her combos because it deals the most damage. This string is very hard to punish because all hits are mid and the string is safe on block, so it can be used for pressure as well. This string is also easy to hit confirm into Singularity (Down, Back + Medium). When Raven wants to take the fight to her opponent, this string is very good for closing in because Raven advances forward while doing this string. The only downside about this move is that it leaves Raven pretty open when it whiffs, giving her opponent a chance to punish with a full combo. This means that even though the move is both effective and safe when blocked, it shouldn't be spammed because your opponent will capitalize on it.

USING TEARS OF SORROW (BACK + LIGHT, MEDIUM)

This string is useful for pressure and for whiff punishing an opponent that abuses low attacks. You can always buffer this string into Singularity when you are playing a poking game against your opponent because, if it whiffs, Singularity won't activate. If it hits, however, Singularity can then be Meter Burned into a full combo afterwards. This string does not reach far, but if spaced well, you can punish almost any low attack in the game as the second hits quickly and beats many lows.

USING EMPTY VOID (DOWN, BACK + LIGHT)

Empty Void is Raven's perfect counter to opponents that are abusing projectiles. This Special Move can be used in plenty of ways that are crucial to how Raven handles projectile-heavy characters. Raven is a meter monster, which means that she will have at least one bar most of the time unless she just finished performing a Super Move. She builds meter quickly because of her long-range Soul Crush, which must be blocked and forces the opponent to stay grounded because it can connect even in the air. Every time Soul Crush is blocked, Raven gains meter, and she gets even more if it successfully connects. Meter is central to using Empty Void. Raven can shoot back any projectile that she absorbs when you press the Meter Burn button after absorption. The tricky part is that the projectile you shoot back is unblockable and travels quickly, making it hard to react to. Even if an opponent anticipates the projectile and jumps early, Raven can send the projectile down from above the opponent's head, which is also unblockable.

USING SOUL CRUSH (DOWN, FORWARD + MEDIUM)

The Soul Crush is one of—if not *the*—best Special Move in Raven's arsenal. It isn't safe on block, but only a few characters (like Superman or The Flash) can punish it from max distance. Other characters can't even punish her when she is close, which means that she can spam this move against a lot of the characters in the game. Basically, if the opponent has no fast advancing move that reaches at least 1/4 of the screen right after Soul Crush is blocked, Raven can keep using Soul Crush from that distance without ever having to worry about getting punished when the move is blocked. The Meter Burn version of Soul Crush can only be used when the move hits, so it is good to use in between a combo because the move causes a ground bounce.

USING SINGULARITY (DOWN, BACK + MEDIUM)

This Special Move is on par with Soul Crush in terms of usefulness. Here we have another move that can be spammed against a lot of characters. The only differences are that this move only reaches 1/4 of the screen, but is much safer on block than Soul Crush, which makes Raven great up close, not just from far away. In this way, Raven has two Special Moves that can be very annoying and lead into big damage if Meter Burned when the move connects. Singularity is also good for punishing strings that are not safe on whiff, and can be used as wakeup attack against opponents that try to mix you up when they knock you down. It is safe to do a wakeup with Singularity because even if the opponent baits you into performing the move, there is a good chance he or she won't have a move fast enough to punish it.

USING SHADOW RAVEN (DOWN, FORWARD + LIGHT)

Raven's projectile also plays a big role in her keep-away game, because even though the move can be ducked, it is speedy and she can keep her opponents in check with Soul Crush should they try do anything after crouching under the projectile. If the opponent stays crouched after the projectile whiffs (expecting Raven to do Soul Crush), you can just throw another projectile and keep the opponent guessing whether you are going to throw another projectile or switch to Soul Crush. Always try to mix it up. Raven's projectile might seem easy to get around at first, but when you learn how to use it in combination with Soul Crush, it becomes a very hard projectile to deal with.

USING DEMON STANCE CHARACTER POWER

Raven lets the evil within consume her, transforming her into a demonic version of herself. Raven is already hard to keep out when she is not in Demon Stance, but when activated, keeping her at bay becomes almost impossible. When Raven is in Demon Stance, Event Horizon hits full screen and stops opponents from throwing projectiles—not because of the move itself, but because of what can happen if the projectiles pass through each other and both characters take a hit. Event Horizon pulls the opponent to Raven and does a decent amount of damage in the process. You can only combo after the move if you Meter Burn it, however. If Raven trades with a projectile after the move is already activated and pulls the opponent to her, the opponent stays stunned and Raven has a chance for a full combo. So even though she takes damage from her enemies' projectiles, it is better to bait it and trade on purpose to get a full combo rather than waste a bar on a Meter Burn. Raven can also use her teleports to get around projectiles when she is in Demon Stance. If the opponent's projectile has a large window of recovery, she can teleport *and* get a full combo.

COMBOS

Light, Light, Forward + Medium ~ Singularity — 17%
Forward + Medium, Medium, Medium ~ Singularity — 21%
Down + Medium > Meter Burn Singularity > Back + Hard > Jumping + Medium > Forward + Medium, Medium, Medium ~ Soul Crush — 31%

Back + Light, Medium ~ Meter Burn Singularity > Forward + Medium, Medium, Medium — Singularity — 32%
Back + Light ~ Meter Burn Singularity > Jumping + Hard > Forward + Medium, Medium, Medium ~ Singularity — 38%
Forward + Medium, Medium, Medium ~ Meter Burn Singularity > Jumping + Hard > Forward + Medium, Medium, Medium ~ Singularity — 41%
Forward + Medium, Medium, Medium ~ Meter Burn Singularity > Back + Hard > Jumping + Medium > Forward + Medium, Medium, Medium ~ Soul Crush — 41%
Forward + Medium, Medium, Medium ~ Meter Burn Singularity > Forward + Medium, Medium, Medium ~ Meter Burn Soul Crush > Forward Medium, Medium, Medium ~ Soul Crush — 41%
Jumping + Medium, Forward + Medium, Medium, Medium ~ Meter Burn Singularity > Back + Hard > Jumping + Medium > Forward + Medium, Medium, Medium ~ Soul Crush — 44%

SUPER MOVE: DEADLY SIN

Jumping + Medium > Forward + Medium, Medium, Medium ~ Meter Burn Singularity > Back + Hard > Jumping + Medium > Forward + Medium, Medium, Medium ~ Meter Burn Soul Crush > Forward + Medium, Medium, Medium ~ Soul Crush – 47%

SHAZAM!

Shazam's whole goal is to spend as much of the fight as possible close to his opponent. He is absolutely devastating once he gets into his mix-up game where he actually has unblockable setups allowing him to reset his opponent. Shazam's biggest weakness is that he can struggle to get in close, and when he finally does get in, he plays a high risk/medium reward style. Making one or two wrong decisions can easily cost you the match.

INTERACTIVE OBJECT TYPE: POWER

SUPER MOVE

THE POWER OF SHAZAM!
Hit Level: Mid
Range: Sweep
Description: Shazam blasts his opponent into the sky with a powerful punch, sending him or her into the clouds where he lands more attacks before throwing the opponent back to the ground. This attack is only punished by fast advancing normal attacks and special attacks that can reach Shazam.

CHARACTER POWER

SOLOMON'S JUDGMENT
Command: Press the Power button
Description: Shazam summons the power of lightning around his fists, causing all of his punching attacks to inflict additional damage.

For character information updates please visit www.primagames.com/InjusticeUpdates

BASIC ATTACKS

LOW JAB

Command: Down + Light
Hit Level: Mid
Range: Close
Description: Shazam performs a crouching jab. This attack is safe when blocked and leaves Shazam at advantage when it hits.

JUMPING STRIKE

Command: Jumping Light
Hit Level: Overhead
Range: Close
Description: Shazam jumps into the air with flying knee attack that allows him to chain into other combo attack strings versus a grounded opponent. This attack hits overhead, so it must be blocked in the standing position.

THUNDERING ELBOW

Command: Back + Medium
Hit Level: Overhead
Range: 1/4 Screen
Description: Shazam performs a jumping elbow smash that launches his opponent. This attack hits overhead, so it must be blocked from the standing block position. This attack is punished by fast normal attacks and fast Special Moves when blocked.

LIFTING CUT

Command: Down + Medium
Hit Level: Mid
Range: Close
Description: Shazam smashes his opponent into the air with a double fisted uppercut. This attack is only punished by Superman's Super Move.

MERCURY'S SIDEKICK

Command: Jumping Medium
Hit Level: Overhead
Range: Close
Description: Shazam jumps into the air with a side kick attack that allows him to chain into other combo attack strings versus a grounded opponent. This attack hits overhead, so it must be blocked in the standing block position.

SWEEPING KICK

Command: Down + Hard
Hit Level: Low
Range: Sweep
Description: Shazam crouches down and sweeps his opponent's feet out from under them. When this attack hits, the knockdown cannot be Tech Rolled. This attack is full combo punished when blocked.

POWER CROSS

Command: Back + Hard
Hit Level: Mid
Range: Close
Description: Shazam unloads a straight power punch, bouncing his opponent off of the corner of the screen and back, giving him juggle combo opportunity. This attack can be charged by holding the Hard attack button and cancelled out of with a forward or backward dash while you are charging the attack. Pressing the Meter Burn button during this attack (burns one bar of meter) will add one hit of armor. Power Cross is also Shazam's Back, Back + Meter Burn Bounce Cancel (bounce cancel burns two bars or meter). This attack leaves Shazam at advantage when blocked, allowing him to follow up with additional attacks.

MIGHTY SLAM

Command: Forward + Hard
Hit Level: Overhead
Range: 1/4 Screen
Description: Shazam hammers his opponent with a fierce overhead punch that launches and gives him a juggle combo opportunity. This attack hits overhead, so it must be blocked from the standing block position. This attack can be charged by holding the Hard attack button and cancelled out of with a forward or backward dash while you are charging the attack. Pressing the Meter Burn button during this attack (burns one bar of meter) will add one hit of armor. Mighty Slam is also Shazam's Forward, Forward + Meter Burn Bounce Cancel (bounce cancel burns two bars or meter). This attack leaves Shazam at advantage when blocked, allowing him to follow up with additional attacks.

ACHILLES' FIST

Command: Jumping Hard
Hit Level: Overhead
Range: Close
Description: Shazam punches at a downward angle while airborne. This attack hits overhead, so it must be blocked from the standing block position. This attack leaves Shazam at advantage when blocked, allowing him to follow up with additional attacks.

BEST COMBO ATTACKS

HERCULES' STRENGTH

Command: Light, Light, Medium
Hit Level: High, Mid, Mid
Range: Close
Description: Shazam delivers two quick hook punches followed by an uppercut launcher that knocks the opponent up high and back across the screen. This attack is safe when blocked. If the first attack of this string is crouched, Shazam can be full combo punished.

ONE-TWO KICK

Command: Medium, Medium
Hit Level: Mid, Mid
Range: Close
Description: Shazam opens up with a knee attack, followed by a spinning kick that knocks the opponent back. This attack is full combo punishable by fast normal attacks and fast special attacks when blocked.

MIGHTY CHARGE

Command: Back + Medium, Hard
Hit Level: Overhead, Mid
Range: 1/4 Screen
Description: Shazam performs a jumping elbow attack that launches his opponent and then finishes him or her off with a rising shoulder attack. The first hit of this string hits overhead, and must be blocked from the standing block position. This attack is punished by fast normal attacks and fast special attacks when blocked.

SPECIAL MOVES

ATLAS TORPEDO

Command: Back, Forward + Medium
Hit Level: Overhead
Range: 3/4 Screen
Description: Shazam torpedoes towards his opponent encased in a field of energy. This attack is punished by fast advancing normal attacks and fast advancing Special Moves when executed and blocked at close range. This attack is full combo punished when executed and blocked from a distance.

METER BURN ATLAS TORPEDO

Description: Pressing the Meter Burn button during a successful Atlas Torpedo will cause Shazam to grab his opponent and throw him or her to the ground for additional damage.

BOLT OF ZEUS

Command: Down, Back + Medium
Hit Level: High
Range: Full Screen
Description: Shazam throws a lightning bolt towards his opponent. This attack is punished by fast normal attacks and fast Special Moves when blocked at close range. This attack is full combo punished if crouched at close range.

METER BURN BOLT OF ZEUS

Description: Pressing the Meter Burn button during Bolt Of Zeus will summon a more powerful bolt of lightning that hits mid and causes increased damage.

HERCULEAN MIGHT

Command: Down, Back, Forward + Light
Hit Level: High Throw
Range: 1/4 Screen
Description: Shazam leaps towards his opponent, binding him or her with a grab, and slamming him or her to the ground while blasting the opponent with a bolt of lightning. This attack is a command throw and is unblockable and unbreakable. This attack can be crouched, allowing the opponent to full combo punish Shazam.

METER BURN HERCULEAN MIGHT

Description: Pressing the Meter Burn button during a successful Herculean Might will cause Shazam to bounce his opponent into the air, giving him a juggle combo opportunity. You can cancel the recovery on a successful Meter Burn Herculean Might with a jump, granting added combo opportunities.

ACHILLES' CLUTCH

Command: Down, Back + Light
Hit Level: Mid Throw
Range: Close
Description: Shazam grabs his opponent then jumps up and slams the opponent to the ground. This is a command throw that hits mid, meaning it will grab an opponent who is crouching. This attack will miss if the opponent is stand blocking, allowing him or her to full combo punish Shazam.

METER BURN ACHILLES' CLUTCH

Description: Pressing the Meter Burn button during a successful Achilles' Clutch will cause Shazam to follow up with a dive kick that launches his opponent.

ADVANCING MERCURY STORM

Command: Down, Forward + Hard
Hit Level: N/A
Range: N/A
Description: Shazam turns into pure energy and teleports towards his opponent. Shazam is vulnerable during this attack's startup and again as he reappears.

ELUDING MERCURY STORM

Command: Down, Back + Hard
Hit Level: N/A
Range: N/A
Description: Shazam turns into pure energy and teleports away from his opponent. Shazam is vulnerable during this attack's startup and again as he reappears.

USING POWER CROSS (BACK + HARD) AND MIGHTY SLAM (FORWARD + HARD)

Power Cross is used inside of combos and Mighty Slam is used in the neutral game. Inside of juggles, Power Cross bounces the opponent off of the screen, which allows for more damaging follow ups. In the neutral game, Power Cross suffers because it has very little range and hits high. Mighty Slam is better in the neutral game because of its range and it hits mid.

USING LOW JAB (DOWN + LIGHT)

When in close, this is a great attack for poking. When it hits, it leaves Shazam at major advantage. You can follow up a successful Low Jab with Shazam's Lifting Cut uppercut launcher or his Sweeping Kick (Down + Hard), and the opponent cannot interrupt either of those follow-ups unless he or she uses a Super Move. After getting hit by the Low Jab, once your opponent realizes that he or she cannot interrupt your sweep and/or uppercut follow-up, you can now go into a mix-up between Shazam's Herculean Might (Down, Back, Forward + Light) unblockable high command throw and your Thundering Elbow (Back + Medium) overhead attack/Achilles' Clutch (Down, Back + Light) mid command throw. After getting hit by your Low Jab, the opponent can back dash away from your Sweeping Kick and/or Lifting Cut follow-up. You can punish your opponent's back dash attempt by following up with Thundering Elbow, and you will hit your opponent as he or she is back dashing away.

USING LIFTING CUT (DOWN + MEDIUM)

Shazam's uppercut is his staple anti-air. This attack doesn't have the best range, so an opponent has to be close or right on top of you in order for this attack to connect. Learn the attack's range and it should prove to be a reliable anti-air. You can also use Lifting Cut when in close as a way to follow up when Shazam has hit his opponent with an attack that leaves him at advantage.

USING SWEEPING KICK (DOWN + HARD)

Sweeping Kick is a crouching sweep with a knockdown that cannot be Tech Rolled. Upon knocking your opponent down with this attack, your Herculean Might command throw is guaranteed unless the opponent uses a wakeup attack. After Sweeping Kick connects, if your Herculean Might command throw is timed right, your opponent will not be able to crouch, strike, or jump out of it. The opponent's only option is to wakeup attack, which can be baited and punished.

Shazam can end basically every juggle with his Sweeping Kick, setting up a reset situation with his Meter Burn Herculean Might. You may be sacrificing some damage by ending your juggles with your Sweeping Kick attack, but if the opponent doesn't use a wakeup attack, your Meter Burn Herculean Might command throw is guaranteed and you will re-launch the opponent for another juggle combo. Always remember that the opponent is forced to use a wakeup attack to avoid a reset combo situation; this will allow you to read that the wakeup is coming. Bait it and punish it.

USING THUNDERING ELBOW (BACK + MEDIUM)

Thundering Elbow reaches 1/4 screen and hits overhead. It is one of your staple tools when approaching your opponent. This is an overhead attack, so it will hit opponents who are crouched. The range of this attack along with the easy-to-execute command makes Thundering Elbow a great tool for whiff punishing your opponent.

USING HERCULEAN MIGHT (DOWN, BACK, FORWARD + LIGHT)

Herculean Might has a range of 1/4 screen and has a similar jumping, lunging forward startup to Thundering Elbow. Herculean Might is an unblockable command throw that hits high. Herculean Might is too fast to react to, and this means that opponents have to commit to crouching in order to avoid it. This attack is also a great whiff punisher against attacks that do not allow your opponent to recover in crouch.

> **TIP** What makes this attack so deadly is the Meter Burn Herculean Might. By Meter Burning the attack, it will now launch the opponent, granting Shazam a juggle combo opportunity. Meter Burn Herculean Might is basically a 1/4 screen range unblockable high launcher that is too fast for your opponent to react against. Meter Burn Herculean Might is one of Shazam's main combo starters as it will launch the opponent, granting Shazam a juggle combo opportunity. This attack is also used inside of juggles as one of Shazam's main attacks used to extend combos.

USING THUNDERING ELBOW WITH HERCULEAN MIGHT

Thundering Elbow and Herculean Might can be hard to react to when the opponent is guarding against one or the other. While approaching the opponent, he or she must pre-commit to defending against Herculean Might, as it is too fast for an opponent to react to. Pre-committing to crouching under Herculean Might will cause the opponent to get hit by Thundering Elbow. Thundering Elbow happens fast enough and has a similar enough startup to Herculean Might, allowing you to hit an opponent who is in crouch, attempting to avoid the Herculean Might command throw. This now forces the opponent to have to stand block to guard the overhead Thundering Elbow, which will cause the opponent to get hit by the Herculean Might command throw. Mixing up when you use these two attacks as you approach your opponent is one of the biggest keys to Shazam's success.

USING MIGHTY CHARGE (BACK + MEDIUM, HARD)

This combo starts off with your Thundering Elbow attack as the first hit of the string. When an opponent consistently baits and punishes your Thundering Elbow attack, you can use the follow-up attack to the string, turning your Thundering Elbow attack into a Mighty Charge attack string. After blocking the first attack of the string, if your opponent attempts to punish your Thundering Elbow, he or she will be hit by the follow-up in this attack string.

USING ACHILLES' CLUTCH (DOWN, BACK + LIGHT)

This attack should be used in close range as a punisher when an opponent is crouching in an attempt to avoid your Herculean Might command throw. Your Achilles' Clutch command throw hits mid, so it will grab all crouching opponents.

> **TIP** Meter Burn Achilles' Clutch is one of Shazam's main combo starters as it will launch the opponent, granting Shazam a juggle combo opportunity. This attack is also used inside of juggles as one of Shazam's main attacks to extend combos.

USING HERCULES' STRENGTH (LIGHT, LIGHT, MEDIUM)

The Hercules' Strength attack string pays off to the fullest when used against a cornered opponent. In open space, this string will knock the opponent back for minimal damage. In corners it will launch the opponent right in front of Shazam and allow him to follow up with a damaging juggle combo.

USING ATLAS TORPEDO (BACK, FORWARD + MEDIUM)

Atlas Torpedo is used as a cancel from attack strings where your opponent would normally attempt to back dash out of a command throw cancel. This will force the opponent to either stop back dashing out of the command throw cancels, or constantly get hit by the cancel into Atlas Torpedo.

USING ONE-TWO KICK (MEDIUM, MEDIUM)

After the opponent blocks your One-Two Kick, you can cancel into your Herculean Might command throw and it will hit the opponent unless the opponent either crouches under the command throw or back dashes after blocking the second attack of the string. If the opponent chooses to crouch under Herculean Might command throw cancel, you can cancel the One-Two Kick into your Achilles' Clutch mid command throw, which will grab the crouching opponent. The opponent can avoid all mix-ups involving a Herculean Might and Achilles' Clutch cancel out of the One-Two Kick by back dashing after blocking the second attack of the string. By canceling the One-Two Kick string into your Atlas Torpedo, you will hit the opponent as he or she is back dashing. Your opponent is basically put in a position where he or she has to get hit by the Atlas Torpedo unless the opponent stops back dashing out of the command throw mix-up.

USING ADVANCING MERCURY STORM (DOWN, FORWARD + HARD) AND ELUDING MERCURY STORM (DOWN, BACK + HARD)

Advancing Mercury Storm can be used in anticipation of a projectile attack as a way to pass through the projectile and get closer to the opponent. Depending on how close you are to the opponent and the recovery on the projectile that you pass through, you can recover from your Advancing Mercury Storm in time to full combo punish your opponent. You can also use your Advancing Mercury Storm as a way to pass through your opponent and his or her attacks to escape a cornered situation. Eluding Mercury Storm can be used as an escape tool when you are attempting to create space between you and your opponent. Eluding Mercury Storm can be done in anticipation of your opponent attacking or using a projectile, and pass through them.

Both the Advancing and Eluding Mercury Storm can be cancelled into from most attacks and attack strings. By canceling into either Mercury Storm you can give a higher degree of safety to an attack that is normally full combo punished by the entire cast. When cancelling into either Mercury Storm from an attack string, Shazam can be punished by any Super Move that will reach him or by certain specials that will track his movement, but opponents have to know which Mercury Storm he is cancelling into and execute a counter-attack in front or behind them. In order to pass through strikes and projectiles, you must execute your Advancing or Eluding Mercury Storm in anticipation of the attack and not on reaction to it. Both Advancing and Eluding Mercury Storm can only pass through attacks after their startup, which does take time to become active. This requires you to anticipate the attack and go into either Mercury Storm before the attack makes contact.

USING BOLT OF ZEUS (DOWN, BACK + MEDIUM)

This projectile attack is average at best. It's not fast enough to help Shazam win out in a projectile war against the more powerful projectile characters, but it will help against those types of characters by giving him some sort of damage option from a distance so that he can close out matches without always having to rush in on his opponent.

> **TIP** The Meter Burn Bolt Of Zeus hits mid, making it a good tool for those "end of the life bar" situations where you don't want your opponent to be able to crouch under your projectiles to avoid taking the block damage.

USING JUMPING ATTACKS

Jumping Light is your best jumping attack when looking to chain into an attack combo against a grounded opponent. This attack doesn't have much range, so it has to be done close in order to hit your opponent. Jumping Medium has the most range of any of your jumping attacks but it also has a higher collision than the other jumping attacks, making it easy for opponents to crouch under unless its executed very close to your opponent and very low to the ground. This attack is best used for air-to-air situations where you can put the range of this attack to good use. Shazam can land a juggle combo if he connects with his jumping Medium in a jumping towards his opponent air-to-air or neutral air-to-air situation, but he cannot juggle after a jumping backwards air-to-air situation. Jumping Hard has moderate range and will connect easily against a crouching opponent. The only downside to your jumping Hard attack is that it is very hard to land a juggle when it hits a crouching opponent.

USING SOLOMON'S JUDGMENT CHARACTER POWER

Shazam's Character Power can be activated anytime it is available. It adds increased damage anytime your opponent blocks or is hit by any of Shazam's punch attacks.

COMBOS

NO METER BURN:

Down + Medium > Herculean Might — 13%
Back + Medium ~ Herculean Might — 14%
Down + Medium (Short Step Forward) > Medium, Medium ~ Herculean Might — 15%

Medium, Medium ~ Herculean Might — 17%
Air-to-Air Neutral Jump Medium > Herculean Might — 18%
(Jumping Towards the Opponent) Air-to-Air Jumping Medium > Medium, Medium ~ Herculean Might — 20%
Forward + Hard > Jumping Hard > Down + Hard — 24%
Forward + Hard > Jumping Hard > Medium, Medium ~ Herculean Might — 29%
Forward + Medium, Medium, Hard > Medium, Medium ~ Herculean Might - 24%

(With Opponent in the Corner) Light, Light, Medium > Light, Light, Medium > Light, Light, Medium > Light, Light, Medium ~ Achilles' Clutch — 32%
(With Opponent in the Corner) Forward + Medium, Medium, Hard > Light, Light, Medium > Light, Light, Medium > Light, Light, Medium ~ Achilles' Clutch — 34%

SUPER MOVE: THE POWER OF SHAZAM!

METER BURN:

Down + Medium > Meter Burn Herculean Might > Back + Hard > Jumping Hard > Down + Hard — 24%
Down + Medium > Meter Burn Herculean Might > Back + Hard > Forward + Medium, Medium, Hard ~ Herculean Might - 25%
Meter Burn Achilles' Clutch > Down + Hard — 20%

Meter Burn Achilles' Clutch > Medium, Medium ~ Herculean Might — 27%
Medium, Medium ~ Meter Burn Herculean Might > Back + Hard > Jumping Hard > Down + Hard — 27%
Meter Burn Herculean Might > Back + Hard > Jumping Hard > Down + Hard — 28%
Back + Medium ~ Meter Burn Herculean Might > Back + Hard > Jumping Hard > Down + Hard — 28%
Medium, Medium ~ Meter Burn Herculean Might > Back + Hard > Forward + Medium, Medium, Hard ~ Herculean Might - 29%
Meter Burn Herculean Might > Back + Hard > Jumping Medium > Forward + Medium, Medium, Hard ~ Herculean Might - 34%

Back + Medium ~ Meter Burn Herculean Might > Back + Hard > Jumping Medium > Forward + Medium, Medium, Hard ~ Herculean Might - 34%
Forward + Medium, Medium, Hard > Medium, Medium ~ Meter Burn Herculean Might > Back + Hard > Forward + Medium, Medium, Hard ~ Herculean Might - 35%
Forward + Hard > Jumping Medium > Forward + Medium, Medium, Hard ~ Meter Burn Herculean Might > Forward + Medium, Medium, Hard ~ Herculean Might - 38%
Meter Burn Achilles' Clutch > Medium, Medium ~ Meter Burn Herculean Might > Forward + Medium, Medium, Hard ~ Herculean Might - 37%

INJUSTICE
GODS AMONG US

SINESTRO

Sinestro is one of the best characters in the game when it comes to a mid-ranged and full-screen game. His ability to not only keep you away, but put you in mix-ups from across the screen, can make him frustrating for opponents to fight against. His Character Power is also one of the best; it allows him to defend better, attack with a higher degree of safety, and form combos in situations where he normally couldn't. Sinestro also puts his opponents into situations where the damage is guaranteed by doing a series of attacks that cannot be escaped with a Clash. Sinestro can struggle if he is forced to fight up close for too long. If opponents can find their way up close often or for an extended period of time, this will neutralize a lot of Sinestro's strengths.

INTERACTIVE OBJECT TYPE: POWER

SUPER MOVE

SINESTRO'S MIGHT
Hit Level: Mid
Range: 1/3 Screen
Description: Sinestro drags his opponents through a portal, teleporting them into deep space where he slams them with two meteors, then blasts them down to earth. This attack is punished by fast normal attacks, fast Special Moves, and faster Super Moves when blocked at point-blank range. From sweep range, this attack is only punished by Superman's Super Move when blocked. This attack is safe when blocked from its maximum range.

CHARACTER POWER

BEWARE YOUR FEARS
Command: Press and hold the Power button
Description: Sinestro charges up his Fear meter, which creates a construct that hovers over him. Pressing the Power button fires off one blast of energy towards the opponent's location. After firing off three blasts of energy, the construct disappears and must be charged up again.

For character information updates please visit www.primagames.com/InjusticeUpdates

BEST BASIC ATTACKS

ASCENDING CONSTRUCT

Command: Down + Medium
Hit Level: Mid
Range: Sweep
Description: Sinestro summons a construct upwards, delivering a launching uppercut. This attack is punished by fast normal attacks and fast Specials when blocked.

RING HAMMERFIST

Command: Back + Medium
Hit Level: Overhead
Range: Close
Description: Sinestro hammers down on his opponent with a punch attack that bounces him or her off of the ground and launches the opponent. This attack hits overhead, so it must be blocked from the standing block position. This attack is punished by fast normal attacks and fast Specials when blocked.

DESCENDING STAB

Command: Jumping Medium
Hit Level: Overhead
Range: Sweep
Description: Sinestro jumps into the air while extending an axe construct, which allows him to chain into other combo attack strings versus a grounded opponent. This attack hits overhead, so it must be blocked from the standing block position.

COMET KICK

Command: Hard
Hit Level: Mid
Range: Close
Description: Sinestro strikes his opponent with a backwards flip kick. This attack is safe when blocked.

LOW AXE SWING

Command: Down + Hard
Hit Level: Low
Range: Sweep
Description: Sinestro uses an axe construct to knock his opponent off his or her feet with a knockdown that cannot be Tech Rolled. This attack is full combo punished when blocked.

SMASHING FIST

Command: Back + Hard
Hit Level: Mid
Range: 1/4 Screen
Description: Sinestro uses a construct to smash his opponent with an uppercut, bouncing him or her off of the corner of the screen and back, giving him a juggle combo opportunity. This attack can be charged by holding the Hard attack button and cancelled out of with forward or backward dash while you are charging the attack. Pressing the Meter Burn button during this attack (burns one bar of meter) will add one hit of armor. Smashing Fist is also Sinestro's Back, Back + Meter Burn Bounce Cancel (bounce cancel burns two bars or meter). This attack leaves Sinestro at advantage when blocked, allowing him to follow up with additional attacks.

THRASHING HAMMER FIST

Command: Forward + Hard
Hit Level: Overhead
Range: Close
Description: Sinestro uses a construct to hammer down on his opponent with an attack that launches and gives him a juggle combo opportunity. This attack hits overhead so it must be blocked from the standing block position. This attack can be charged by holding the Hard attack button and cancelled out of with a forward or backwards dash while you are charging the attack. Pressing the Meter Burn button during this attack (burns one bar of meter) will add one hit of armor. Thrashing Hammer Fist is also Sinestro's Forward, Forward + Meter Burn Bounce Cancel (bounce cancel burns two bars of meter). This attack leaves Sinestro at advantage when blocked, allowing him to follow up with additional attacks.

DOWNWARD SLICE

Command: Jumping Hard
Hit Level: Overhead
Range: Close
Description: Sinestro jumps into the air, swiping downward with an axe construct. This attack hits overhead, so it must be blocked from the standing block position. This attack leaves Sinestro at advantage when blocked, allowing him to follow up with additional attacks.

INJUSTICE
GODS AMONG US

BEST COMBO ATTACKS

ZERO COMPASSION

Command: Back + Light, Hard
Hit Level: Mid, Mid
Range: 1/4 Screen
Description: Sinestro materializes an axe construct and thrusts it into his opponent, and then again uses the construct to uppercut the opponent into the air for a pop up. This attack is punished by fast normal attacks and fast special attacks. This string can be interrupted in between the first and second attack by using a Super Move.

IN BLACKEST DAY

Command: Back + Medium, Light, Hard
Hit Level: Overhead, Low, Mid
Range: Close
Description: Sinestro bounces his opponents off of the ground and then hits them with two spike constructs. After the first attack is blocked at close range, the two follow-up attacks will miss. The second hit of this attack will not miss when blocked from the string's maximum range, but the opponent can interrupt the string in between the first two attacks with a Super Move. This attack string starts with an overhead, so it must be blocked from the standing block position. This is Sinestro's staple combo ender. You should end almost every juggle with this attack string as it knocks the opponent back to almost full screen, the range where Sinestro is at his best.

POWER BURN

Command: Forward + Medium, Down + Light, Hard
Hit Level: Mid, Low, Mid
Range: Close
Description: Sinestro kicks his opponent in the stomach, followed by a fireball to his or her feet, and ends with a smashing shield construct to his or her face. This attack is safe when blocked, but an opponent can interrupt this string in between the first and second attack by using a Super Move.

SPECIAL MOVES

FEAR BLAST

Command: Down, Forward + Light
Hit Level: Starts high but descends as it goes forward, eventually hitting mid at 3/4 through full screen range.
Range: Full Screen
Description: Sinestro constructs fear into a projectile and blasts it at his opponent. This attack is full combo punished when blocked at closer ranges, and can be punished from sweep range to almost full screen by fast attacks that can reach Sinestro.

METER BURN FEAR BLAST

Description: Pressing the Meter Burn button during Fear Blast will fire off two additional projectiles, doing more damage. This attack is only punished by the faster Super Moves of the game when blocked at close range, and full combo punished when crouched at close range. From close range to 3/4 screen, an opponent can interrupt this attack in between the first and second Fear Blast with a Super Move.

IMPACT EVENT

Command: Down, Back + Medium
Hit Level: Overhead
Range: Full Screen
Description: Sinestro summons a meteor construct, crashing down on top of his opponent. This attack is full combo punished when blocked up close. This attack is full combo punished when blocked at closer ranges, and can be punished from sweep range to full screen by attacks that can reach Sinestro.

METER BURN IMPACT EVENT

Description: Pressing the Meter Burn button during a successful Impact Event will summon a second meteor construct that bounces his opponent off the ground, doing additional damage.

ARACHNID STING

Command: Down, Forward + Medium
Hit Level: High
Range: Close
Description: Sinestro constructs four arachnid legs from his back, using it to uppercut his opponent. This attack is full combo punished when blocked or crouched.

METER BURN ARACHNID STING

Description: Pressing the Meter Burn button during Arachnid Sting will launch the ends of the construct towards the opponent. The ends of the construct hit high, so they can be crouched but cannot be blocked because they are unblockable.

AIR AXE OF TERROR

Command: Down, Back + Light while in air
Hit Level: Mid
Range: Sweep
Description: Sinestro constructs an axe on the ground below him and pulls it up towards him. This attack is safe when blocked.

FINAL SHACKLES

Command: Down, Back + Light
Hit Level: Mid
Range: Full Screen
Description: Sinestro binds his opponent in shackles of fear, allowing him to follow up with more attacks. This attack is full combo punished when blocked at closer ranges, and can be punished from sweep range to full screen by attacks that can reach Sinestro.

INJUSTICE
GODS AMONG US
STRATEGY

USING SMASHING FIST (BACK + HARD) AND THRASHING HAMMER FIST (FORWARD + HARD)

Smashing Fist should be used over Thrashing Hammer Fist at all times. Smashing Fist is faster, has more range, and leads to a better launcher resulting in easier and more damaging combos.

USING COMET KICK (HARD)

This attack can be used as a getaway move while in close. When Comet Kick is blocked, you have the option for a trap. You can cancel into the Event Impact special attack, inflicting block damage. Opponents can reversal or even just forward or backward dash past the Event Impact special and punish Sinestro; this is where you have the option to now cancel into Final Shackles instead. There is no way to interrupt or dash past a cancel into Final Shackles off of this attack — the opponent must block it. If the opponent tries to jump, dash, Super Move, or so on, he or she will be hit by the Final Shackles, leaving you close enough to get a full combo. However, remember that Final Shackles is not safe when blocked, so your opponent can punish you if he or she guesses correctly and blocks the attack.

USING ZERO COMPASSION (BACK + LIGHT, HARD)

This attack string is your primary whiff punisher. The range on the first attack of Zero Compassion reaches 1/4 screen distance and the attack string as a whole moves Sinestro forward, making the string a natural for converting whiffs to damage. Any time your opponent misses attacks while trying to approach or retreat from you, use Zero Compassion to punish the missed attacks and launch your opponent for a juggle combo.

USING ASCENDING CONSTRUCT (DOWN + MEDIUM)

This is the best uppercut in the game. The construct appears in front of Sinestro, giving it great range, and travels up over his head, which will cause it to anti-air even cross up jumps. When you connect with this attack, it launches, giving you a juggle combo.

USING POWER BURN (FORWARD + MEDIUM, DOWN + LIGHT, HARD)

This is Sinestro's main attack string. You will notice that most of Sinestro's attack strings that lead to damaging juggles are unsafe, but this combo allows you to attack at close range with a string that leads to a damaging juggle with complete safety when blocked. In open space, you will need to use the first two attacks of this string (which can be hit confirmed), and then cancel into Final Shackles. When the opponent is cornered, you can use all three attacks of this string to combo them by using a Down + Light to juggle your opponent after the entire Power Burn string has hit.

USING RING HAMMER FIST (BACK + MEDIUM)

This is a fast overhead attack that bounces your opponent off of the ground for a juggle combo. When this attack hits, you can cancel into Final Shackles and combo your opponent. Ring Hammer Fist can be punished by faster attacks and is universally punished by Down + Light into a Special Move Cancel. However, canceling into Final Shackles after Ring Hammer Fist will catch your opponent's punishment attempt. Your opponent can remain blocking after Ring Hammer Fist and block the Final Shackles Special Move cancel, then punish you with their combo of choice. This however has now made your opponent hesitant to punish your Ring Hammer Fist by itself. This grants you a little freedom to use Ring Hammer Fist as a hit confirmed launcher, then follow up with Down + Light into a Final Shackles Special Move cancel. The opponent respecting your option to cancel into Final Shackles has now given you the illusion of safety.

By spacing Ring Hammer Fist properly you can use Back + Medium, Light which is your Ring Hemmer Fist as the initial attack followed by the second hit of the Blackest Day attack string. When spaced correctly, the second attack of Blackest Day will not miss the opponent, making your Ring hammer Fist safe on block.

USING LOW AXE SWING (DOWN + HARD)

This low attack can be used as a 50/50 mix-up with your Ring Hammer Fist overhead attack. Low Axe Swing causes a knockdown that cannot be Tech Rolled, forcing your opponent to get up right in front of you; this will give you a guaranteed well-timed throw attempt unless the opponent uses a wakeup attack. You also have the option to follow up with a cross up with your jumping Hard, or fake the cross up, and instead empty jump and then land and perform a throw, Ring Hammer Fist, or Low Axe Swing.

USING AIR AXE OF TERROR (DOWN, BACK + LIGHT WHILE IN AIR)

You can use this attack as you are jumping towards your opponent at close range. If timed right and done at the right height, this attack can counter your opponent's anti-air attempt. If you land this attack close enough to your opponent, you will land and recover in time to juggle him or her.

USING FEAR BLAST (DOWN, FORWARD + LIGHT)

Fear Blast and Meter Burn Fear Blast are best used from about 3/4 screen to full screen range; this is the attack's optimal range. From Fear Blast's optimal range, the attack will hit mid on all characters except The Flash (as he crouches lower than any other character). While The Flash can crouch under the Fear Blast even from its optimal range, he will not be able to crouch under the two additional projectiles of the Meter Burn Fear Blast when done from its optimal range. Big characters can't really crouch under the Fear Blast at all; Lex Luthor can't duck the Fear Blast from any range and Bane and Doomsday can only crouch under the Fear Blast when they are right next to Sinestro. When Fear Blast is blocked from its optimal range, Sinestro can fire off Fear Blast after Fear Blast as fast as possible. If the opponent tries to dash after blocking the Fear Blast, he or she will be hit by the next one. While the opponent cannot dash through repeated Fear Blasts when done at the optimal range, he or she can jump over the follow-up Fear Blast and advance to a range where he or she can crouch under it. Any time you knock the opponent back to 3/4 screen to full screen range, you can follow up with a Fear Blast or Meter Burn Fear Blast and most characters are forced to block it.

USING IMPACT EVENT (DOWN, BACK + MEDIUM)

After blocking a Meter Burn Fear Blast, the opponent can jump over a follow-up Fear Blast and advance. When this happens, follow up your blocked Meter Burn Fear Blast with your Impact Event Special. If the opponent tries to jump, Impact Event will hit him or her out of the air. You can Meter Burn Impact Event, which will launch your opponent and allow you to follow up with a guaranteed Final Shackles. After blocking a Meter Burn Fear Blast, the opponent can dash out of your Impact Event follow-up and advance. Any time you notice your opponent using jumping as a way to close the gap from 3/4 screen to full screen, a well-timed Impact Event can hit the opponent out of mid air.

USING FINAL SHACKLES (DOWN, BACK + LIGHT)

After blocking a Fear Blast from the attack's optimal range or Meter Burn Fear Blast, the opponent can dash under the Impact Event follow-up and advance. When this happens, follow up your optimal range blocked Fear Blast or Meter Burn Fear Blast with your Final Shackles Special attack. If the opponent tries to dash under the Impact Event, he or she will get caught by Final Shackles, giving Sinestro an opportunity to combo his opponent even from across the screen. After blocking a Fear Blast from the attack's optimal range or a Meter Burn Fear Blast, the opponent can jump out of your Final Shackles follow-up and advance. Opponents will get caught by Final Shackles any time they dash, not just in a projectile trap situation. Final Shackles can also be used as a cancel after pokes as a way to catch opponents attempting to counter-poke Sinestro after blocking his attacks.

USING JUMPING ATTACKS

Jumping Medium has more range then jumping Hard, which will allow Sinestro to jump in towards his opponent from a farther distance. Jumping Hard works great at close range as straight forward or neutral jump in attack and is also his best cross up attack option.

USING BEWARE YOUR FEARS CHARACTER POWER

Your Character Power must have all three bars charged before the construct appears. After using all three shots, the construct disappears and you must charge all three bars again. Your Character Power will also disappear upon getting hit by or hitting your opponent with a Super Move, as well as upon hitting your opponent through or getting hit through a Level Transition yourself. Beware Your Fears allows you to shoot a blast of energy totally independent from what Sinestro is doing. You can shoot an energy blast when blocking an opponent's attacks and interrupt them mid attack. You can also shoot an energy blast while attacking your opponent, allowing you to maintain pressure or make moves that are punishable safe. When the blast of energy hits your opponent, it results in a small knockdown, giving Sinestro a combo opportunity. Your Character Power also allows you to shoot an energy blast after any move hits, giving you the ability to extend combos or create combos in situations where you normally wouldn't be able to.

Using this Character Power to extend bigger juggles is usually a waste; if you already have your opponent caught in a damaging combo, there is no need to use your Character Power to barely extend the damage. Instead, use your Character Power to help create combos where there normally is no combo opportunity, to punish opponents out of their attacks while you are blocking/retreating, or to keep pressure/make unsafe attacks now safe if you are on the offensive.

Your Character Power can also be chained immediately into any attack or Special Move. When opponents are trying to advance in on your projectile game, shoot a Character Power blast, followed immediately by your Impact Event/Meter Burn Impact Event Special Move. If the blast hits, your Impact Event will also hit. This prevents the opponent from dashing or jumping towards. When in close, chain your Character Power into your Smashing Fist (Back + Hard) attack. If the Character Power hits, the Smashing Fist will connect and launch the opponent for a damaging combo. If the Character Power and Smashing Fist are blocked, Sinestro is left at advantage, allowing you press your attack or use the advantage to retreat.

TIP *Having your Character Power out at all times is your main focus. Anytime you end a full screen juggle with Final Shackles you should begin to charge your Character Power.*

COMBOS

OPEN SPACE:

Down + Medium > Back + Light ~ Final Shackles > Back + Hard > Jumping Hard > Back + Medium, Light, Hard — 21%
Back + Medium ~ Final Shackles > Back + Hard > Jumping Hard > Back + Medium, Light, Hard — 24%
Back + Light, Hard > Back + Light ~ Final Shackles > Back + Hard > Jumping Hard > Back + Medium, Light, Hard — 26%
Air Axe Of Terror > Down + Light ~ Final Shackles > Back + Hard > Jumping Hard > Back + Medium, Light, Hard — 27%

Forward + Medium, Down + Light ~ Final Shackles > Back + Hard > Jumping Hard > Back + Medium, Light, Hard — 26%
Back + Hard > Jumping Hard > Back + Medium, Back + Hard ~ Final Shackles > Jumping Medium, Back + Medium, Light, Hard — 34%
Back + Light, Hard > Jumping Hard > Down + Light ~ Final Shackles > Back + Hard > Jumping Medium > Back + Medium, Light, Hard - 31%
Jumping Hard > Down + Light ~ Final Shackles > Back + Hard > Jumping Hard > Back + Medium, Light, Hard - 32%

CORNER:

Down + Medium > Hard ~ Final Shackles > Back + Hard (let the opponent pass over your head) > Jumping Medium > Back + Medium, Light, Hard — 24%
Forward + Medium, Down + Light, Hard > Down + Light ~ Final Shackles > Neutral Jump Medium, Forward + Medium, Down + Light, Hard — 25%
Forward + Medium, Down + Light, Hard > Down + Light ~ Final Shackles > Back + Hard (let the opponent pass over your head) > Jumping Medium > Back + Medium, Light, Hard — 29%

Back + Light, Hard > Hard ~ Final Shackles > Back + Hard (let the opponent pass over your head) > Jumping Medium > Back + Medium, Light, Hard — 29%

SUPER MOVE: SINESTRO'S MIGHT

METER BURN:

(mid to far range) Final Shackles > Meter Burn Impact Event > Fear Blast — 15%

(mid to far range) Meter Burn Impact Event > Fear Blast — 20%

(close) Meter Burn Impact Event > (Walk Forward) Back + Light ~ Final Shackles > Back + Hard > Jumping Hard > Back + Medium, Light, Hard - 34%

(corner only, from just outside of sweep range to close range) Meter Burn Impact Event > Hard ~ Final Shackles > Back + Hard (let the opponent pass over your head) > Jumping Medium > Back + Medium, Light, Hard — 37%

CHARACTER POWER COMBOS:

(mid to far range) Power ~ Impact Event — 13%

(mid to far range) Final Shackles > Meter Burn Impact Event > Fear Blast > Power — 18%

(mid to far range) Meter Burn Impact Event > Power ~ Impact Event — 25%

(close) Power ~ Back + Hard > Jumping Hard > Back + Medium, Light, Hard — 34%

(corner only) Air Axe Of Terror > Power > Hard ~ Final Shackles > Back + Hard (let the opponent pass over your head) > Jumping Medium > Back + Medium, Light, Hard — 34%

Power ~ Meter Burn Impact Event > Power ~ Impact Event - 29%

Air Axe Of Terror > Power > Back + Hard > Jumping Hard > Back + Medium ~ Final Shackles > Jump In Medium, Back + Medium, Light, Hard - 37%

INJUSTICE
GODS AMONG US

SOLOMON GRUNDY

Up close, Solomon Grundy will give his opponents nightmares with a barrage of hit level mix-ups and unblockable attacks. From up to half of the screen, Grundy also has a plethora of armored attacks to help him close space and inflict damage on his opponent. Grundy can, however, struggle at times if he finds himself stuck at a far distance for too long. He does have tools to help him fight from a distance for a short period of time, but the longer his opponent stays away from him, the harder the match becomes for Grundy.

INTERACTIVE OBJECT TYPE: POWER

SUPER MOVE

GRAVE DIGGER
Hit Level: Unblockable Mid Throw
Range: Close
Description: When Grundy activates his Super, he is now in a mode where all of his attacks become a super throw for a limited amount of time. This deadly grab can be used to catch opponents standing, crouching, or jumping in the air. While active, Grundy now moves faster, jumps farther, and can't be knocked down.

CHARACTER POWER

PAIN CHAIN
Command: Press the Power button
Hit Level: Unblockable Mid Throw
Range: Close
Description: Grundy is able to perform a series of throws that link into each other and grant specific abilities based on how many are landed and which chain is used. Pressing the Meter Burn button when performing this attack will add one hit of armor.

For character information updates please visit www.primagames.com/InjusticeUpdates

BEST BASIC ATTACKS

GUT PUNCH

Command: Down + Light
Hit Level: Mid
Range: Close
Description: Grundy unleashes a quick crouching jab. This attack leaves Grundy at advantage when blocked, allowing him to follow up with additional attacks.

RISING BACKHAND

Command: Down + Medium
Hit Level: Mid
Range: Close
Description: Grundy uppercuts his opponent with a backhand slap, launching him or her into the air. This attack is full combo punishable.

SWAMPY STOMP

Command: Back + Medium
Hit Level: Low
Range: Close
Description: Grundy stomps the ground, knocking his opponent down. This attack is safe when blocked.

GRUNDY BLAST

Command: Back + Hard
Hit Level: Mid
Range: Close
Description: Grundy uppercuts his opponent, causing him or her to bounce off of the corner of the screen and back to him, giving him a combo opportunity. This attack can be charged by holding the Hard attack button and cancelled out of with a forward or backward dash while you are charging the attack. Pressing the Meter Burn button during this attack (burns one bar of meter) will add one hit of armor. Grundy Blast is also Grundy's Back, Back + Meter Burn Bounce Cancel (bounce cancel burns two bars or meter). This attack leaves Grundy at advantage when blocked.

GRUNDY CRUSH

Command: Forward + Hard
Range: Sweep
Description: Grundy delivers a crushing overhead that launches the opponent and gives him a combo opportunity. This attack hits overhead, so it must be blocked from the standing block position. This attack can be charged by holding the Hard attack button and cancelled out of with a forward or backward dash while you are charging the attack. Pressing the Meter Burn button during this attack (burns one bar of meter) will add one hit of armor. Grundy Crush is also Grundy's Forward, Forward + Meter Burn Bounce Cancel (bounce cancel burns two bars of meter). This attack leaves Grundy at advantage when blocked.

BEST COMBO ATTACKS

DEATH TO ALL

Command: Forward + Light, Medium
Hit Level: Low, Mid
Range: Sweep
Description: Grundy lets fly with a low kick and then a quick jab to the opponent's stomach. This attack is only punished by Superman's Super Move.

INJUSTICE
GODS AMONG US

SPECIAL MOVES

CLEAVER SPIN

Command: Down, Back + Light
Hit Level: Overhead
Range: 1/3 Screen
Description: Grundy pulls a cleaver from his back and attacks his opponent with a spinning cleaver strike that knocks the opponent down when it hits. This attack is full combo punished when blocked. This attack hits overhead, so it must be blocked from the standing block position.

METER BURN CLEAVER SPIN

Description: Pressing the Meter Burn button during Cleaver Spin adds one hit of armor to the attack and causes the opponent to bounce higher, giving Grundy a juggle combo opportunity. This attack is full combo punished when blocked, and like all overhead attacks must be blocked from the standing block position.

WALKING CORPSE

Command: Back, Forward + Hard
Hit Level: Unblockable Mid Throw
Range: Nearly 1/2 Screen
Description: Grundy runs towards his opponent, then grabs him or her before delivering a headbutt that knocks his opponent to the ground. This attack can be cancelled by tapping Down, Back before the throw connects, and has three hits of armor.

METER BURN WALKING CORPSE

Description: Pressing the Meter Burn button during a successful Walking Corpse adds an additional throw that bounces the opponent off the opposite corner of the screen, resulting in a knockdown that can't be Tech Rolled.

GRAVE ROT

Command: Down, Back + Hard
Range: Close
Description: Grundy emits unblockable rotten fumes that can poison the opponent ad inflict damage when he or she comes into contact with him.

METER BURN GRAVE ROT

Description: Pressing the Meter Burn button on the startup of Grave Rot increases the damage of the poison fumes.

DEAD AIR

Command: Back, Forward + Medium
Hit Level: Mid
Range: Close
Description: Grundy grabs his opponent and throws him or her over his shoulder, resulting in a knockdown that cannot be Tech Rolled. This attack is full combo punished when blocked.

METER BURN DEAD AIR

Description: Pressing the Meter Burn button during a successful Dead Air tosses the opponent in the air, allowing Grundy to follow up with a combo. This attack is full combo punished when blocked.

SWAMP HANDS

Command: Down, Back + Medium
Hit Level: Low
Range: Full Screen
Description: Grundy stomps the ground, making a swamp puddle appear under his opponent's feet. Hands then rise from the ground and trip up his opponent, knocking him or her down. This attack leaves Grundy at very small advantage when blocked.

TO THE GRAVE

Command: Down, Forward + Light
Hit Level: Air
Range: Close
Description: Grundy grabs his opponent out of the air and slams him or her to the ground.

METER BURN SWAMP HANDS

Description: Pressing the Meter Burn button during Swamp Hands adds one hit of armor and will cause the hands to hold the opponent in place for an extended period of time, allowing Grundy to follow up with a combo. This attack leaves Grundy at very small advantage when blocked.

STRATEGY

USING GRUNDY BLAST (BACK + HARD) AND GRUNDY CRUSH (FORWARD + HARD)

Neither Grundy Blast nor Grundy Crush has good range, as you have to be close for either attack to connect. Grundy Blast is slightly faster and results in better, easier, and more damaging combos. If you find yourself in a situation where you have to use one of these attacks, Grundy Blast is the better choice.

USING GUT PUNCH (DOWN + LIGHT)

This attack is a quick crouching poke that Grundy can use as he approaches his opponent at close range or as a counter-poke. If you time it properly, Grundy can activate his Super Move after this attack hits and your opponent will not be able to escape the throw follow-up.

USING WALKING CORPSE (BACK, FORWARD + HARD)

Walking Corpse is a quick advancing command throw. From about 1/2 screen or closer, this attack allows you to advance in on characters trying to keep you out with projectile attacks or ranged strikes. Walking Corpse has three hits of armor, so it will go through almost anything the opponent can throw at you and forces an opponent to play around it, rather than Grundy having to play around his opponent's keep-out attempts. You can cancel out of the command throw by tapping Down, Back before the command throw connects. This will cause Grundy to quickly dash towards his opponent and stop right in front of them. Even though you cancelled out of the command throw, the dash will retain the three hits of armor.

TIP Your Meter Burn Walking Corpse causes Grundy to throw the opponent over his shoulder and slam him or her off of the opposite corner of the screen. The opponent gets slammed down and is within a single dash distance of Grundy. This throw results in a knockdown with no danger of being Tech Rolled, as the opponent takes a long time to recover from the slam. This gives Grundy enough time to activate his Grave Rot Special Move and Walking Corpse again. The follow up Walking Corpse is guaranteed unless the opponent uses a wakeup attack. It is possible to continuously follow up one Meter Burn Walking Corpse after another until the opponent escapes with a wakeup attack, or Grundy uses all of his Super Meter. You can slightly delay your follow up Walking Corpse, allowing you to use the armor to absorb the opponent's wakeup attack and grab them after their wakeup attack invincibility has worn off. Doing this, however, will now grant the opponent enough time to recover and back dash out of the Walking Corpse.

USING SWAMP HANDS (DOWN, BACK + MEDIUM)

Swamp Hands is a great tool to counter projectile attacks when you find yourself at a far distance from the opponent. Swamp Hands does equal or more damage than most normal projectile attacks, which helps Grundy to not fall behind in the likelihood of a trade. Swamp Hands can be timed to beat out or trade with some of the quicker projectile attacks in the game. In a situation where your Swamp Hands attack trades with a projectile, most projectiles do not knock down, whereas this attack does. This allows Grundy to attack with another Swamp Hands as his opponent is getting up.

Your Meter Burn Swamp Hands will hold the opponent in place and allow Grundy to combo them. The Meter Burn version has armor, so in the event of a projectile trade, Grundy can take the projectile and dash forward (even as far as full screen), and full combo or at minimum land a Walking Corpse or Pain Chain throw.

TIP Your Meter Burn Swamp Hands will grab your opponent and hold him or her in place for a short period of time. If you are far from the opponent, you can follow up with your normal Swamp Hands attack for a combo that will work from anywhere on screen. At closer ranges, Grundy can follow up his Meter Burn Swamp Hands with a full combo. Both your normal and Meter Burn versions of Swamp Hands are safe when blocked, making them a safe low option when used as a mix-up with the normal or Meter Burn versions of the Cleaver Spin overhead attack, with the Meter Burn versions of both attacks being the preferred option. You can cancel out of normal attacks with your Meter Burn Swamp Hands or Meter Burn Cleaver Spin and the opponent must guess which option to block.

USING CLEAVER SPIN (DOWN, BACK + LIGHT)

Your Cleaver Spin hits overhead and is best used as a cancel off of normal attacks, as a mix up with your Swamp Hands (Down, Back + Medium) low hitting Special Move. Cleaver Spin doesn't have any form of armor on it, so it doesn't have any real practical use as a stand-alone attack.

TIP Your Meter Burn Cleaver Spin also hits overhead, but will launch the opponent. You can use it like the normal version of Cleaver Spin, as a mix-up with Swamp Hands, by canceling into the attack off of normal attacks. This attack has one hit of armor, so it allows you to absorb and go through your opponent's keep-out attempt as you approach him or her from as far away as 1/3 screen distance. If you intend to use the Cleaver Spin as a mix-up with Swamp Hands, use the Meter Burn version, as both versions of Cleaver Spin are full combo punished, but the Meter Burn version will grant you a juggle combo.

USING GRAVE ROT (DOWN, BACK + HARD)

Grave Rot and Meter Burn Grave Rot will cause the opponent to take unblockable damage any time he or she is right next to Grundy. Even if the opponent is hitting you, he or she still takes damage from the Grave Rot fumes. If you catch your opponent in a combo while Grave Rot is active, the poison fumes will continue to damage the opponent during the combo. You should activate your normal version of Grave Rot any time you get an opening to do so.

USING DEAD AIR (BACK, FORWARD + MEDIUM)

There really isn't a use for the normal version of the attack because it does not launch the opponent, and the Meter Burn version should only be used inside of combos as a way to launch the opponent after landing a ground combo. This attack should never be used as a stand-alone move because unlike some of Grundy's other command throws, this attack is blockable and punished by a full combo afterwards.

USING TO THE GRAVE (DOWN, FORWARD + LIGHT) AND RISING BACKHAND (DOWN + MEDIUM)

To The Grave and Rising Backhand are Grundy's two main and most reliable attacks to anti-air his opponent with. To The Grave is the less damaging option, but it is also the most reliable one as well. Rising Backhand may not be as reliable, but it does launch the opponent, allowing Grundy to follow up with a juggle combo.

Where your To The Grave air throw has the edge as an anti-air is that it causes a knockdown that cannot be Tech Rolled, and allows Grundy to come in for a Walking Corpse attempt or other set ups.

USING DEATH TO ALL (FORWARD + LIGHT, MEDIUM)

You can use this attack chain as you approach the opponent, taking advantage of the string's range and forward movement. This attack string can be hit confirmed, allowing you to cancel into normal/Meter Burn Swamp Hands or Meter Burn Dead Air Specials. When this string is blocked, you can cancel into your Meter Burn Cleaver Spin or normal/Meter Burn Swamp Hands, and the cancel into Swamp Hands can be interrupted by a fast poke or escaped by a back dash. The cancel into Meter Burn Cleaver Spin cannot be interrupted due to the attack having one hit of armor, and it can't be escaped with a back dash.

USING SWAMPY STOMP (BACK + MEDIUM)

After this attack is blocked, Grundy should cancel into his Cleaver Spin, Swamp Hands, or Pain Chain Character Power command throw. After your opponent blocks your Swampy Stomp, using your normal/Meter Burn Cleaver Spin Overhead attack or normal/Meter Burn Swamp Hands Low attack creates a 50/50 mix-up with both of the Meter Burn options resulting in a combo. After Swampy Stomp is blocked, you can cancel into your Pain Chain Character Power command throw, which is unblockable and cannot be crouched. If your opponent is attempting to block the Cleaver Spin/Swamp Hands mix-up, he or she will be hit by your Pain Chain throw. The opponent can back dash out of the Pain Chain throw option by immediately back dashing after blocking your Swampy Stomp. However, your opponent cannot back dash out of the Cleaver Spin or Walking Corpse, causing him or her to get hit by either attack. The most reliable mix-up after your opponent blocks your Swampy Stomp is to mainly follow up with your normal/Meter Burn Cleaver Spin or normal/Meter Burn Swamp Hands, then mix in the Pain Chain command throw to catch your opponent trying to block the overhead/low mix up. Cleaver Spin, Swamp Hands, Pain Chain, and Walking Corpse will all connect after your Swampy Stomp attack hits.

USING PAIN CHAIN CHARACTER POWER

Your Pain Chain Character Power is an unblockable, fast, mid command throw. You can Meter Burn this attack to gain one hit of armor, which you can use to escape pressure situations, as you approach your opponent, or to beat out certain wakeups as your opponent is getting up. After connecting with your Pain Chain command throw, you have three chain throw options to choose from, all resulting in different buffs: Power, Health, and Defense. These buffs stay with Grundy for the remainder of the match or until he lands another Pain Chain. The Power Chain will cause Grundy's damage output to increase, the Health Chain will cause Grundy to take less damage when he is hit, and the Defense Chain will cause Grundy to take less block damage.

The chain throw option you use will depend on the character you are up against. For example, if you find yourself up against a powerful projectile character, then you will want to use your Health or Defense Chain so you take less attack damage or less block damage. Each chain inflicts different damage to the opponent. The Health Chain is the most damaging, followed by the Power Chain, and the Defense Chain is the least damaging chain throw. To connect each part of the chain throw, input the following command to the next throw near the end of the previous throw.

PAIN CHAIN FOLLOW-UPS:

Power Chain: Forward, Back + Power – Grundy receives a damage increase on all of his attacks

Power Final Hit: Down, Forward + Power – Grundy deals even more damage on all of his attacks

Health Chain: Down, Down + Power – Grundy now takes less damage

Health Final Hit: Up, Up + Power – Grundy takes even less damage

Defense Chain: Down, Up + Power – Grundy takes reduced block damage

Defense Final Hit: Up, Down + Power – Grundy now takes even less block damage

COMBOS

NO METER BURN:

Back + Medium ~ Swamp Hands — 12%
Back + Medium ~ Cleaver Spin — 13%
Forward + Light, Medium ~ Swamp Hands — 13%

Down + Medium > Light, Light ~ Pain Chain — 24% for Power Chain/27% for Health Chain/21% for Defense Chain
Back + Medium ~ Pain Chain — 27% for Power Chain/32% for Health Chain/23% for Defense Chain
Back + Hard > Jumping Hard > Light, Light ~ Pain Chain — 39% for Power Chain/42% for Health Chain/36% for Defense Chain

SUPER MOVE: GRAVE DIGGER

SOLOMON GRUNDY

METER BURN:

Meter Burn Cleaver Spin > Light, Light ~ Pain Chain — 32% for Power Chain/36% for Health Chain/29% for Defense Chain
Back + Medium ~ Meter Burn Cleaver Spin > Light, Light ~ Pain Chain — 33% for Power Chain/37% for Health Chain/30% for Defense Chain
Forward + Light, Medium ~ Meter Burn Dead Air > Light, Light ~ Pain Chain — 37% for Power Chain/41% for Health Chain/34% for Defense Chain
Forward + Light, Medium ~ Meter Burn Swamp Hands (Dash Forward) > Back + Hard > Jumping Hard > Light, Light ~ Pain Chain — 43% for Power Chain/46% for Health Chain/41% for Defense Chain

Back + Medium ~ Meter Burn Swamp Hands (dash forward) > Back + Hard > Jumping Hard > Light, Light ~ Pain Chain — 44% for Power Chain/47% for Health Chain/41% for Defense Chain
Light, Light ~ Meter Burn Dead Air > Light, Light ~ Pain Chain — 38% for Power Chain/42% for Health Chain/35% for Defense Chain
Light, Light ~ Meter Burn Swamp Hands (Dash Forward) > Back + Hard > Jumping Hard > Light, Light ~ Pain Chain — 44% for Power Chain/47% for Health Chain/42% for Defense Chain

CORNER:

Back + Medium ~ Meter Burn Swamp Hands > Neutral Jump Medium, Back + Light, Hard ~ Pain Chain — 44% for Power Chain/48% for Health Chain/41% for Defense Chain
Forward + Light, Medium ~ Meter Burn Swamp Hands > Neutral Jump Medium, Back + Light, Hard ~ Pain Chain — 44% for Power Chain/48% for Health Chain/41% for Defense Chain

(with Grundy's back to the corner) Meter Burn Walking Corpse > Down + Light ~ Pain Chain — 48% for Power Chain/53% for Health Chain/44% for Defense Chain

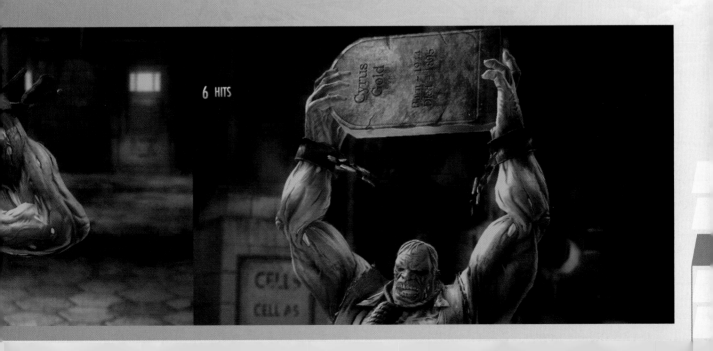

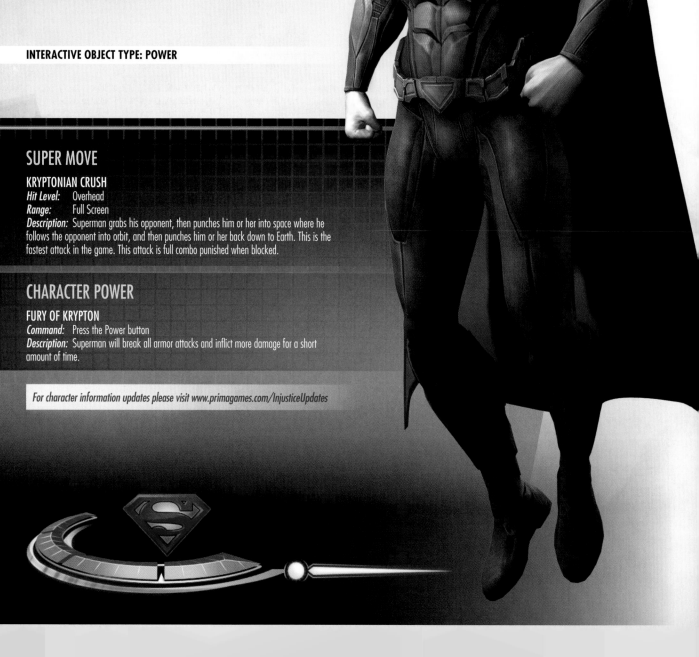

INJUSTICE
GODS AMONG US

SUPERMAN

Superman is a well-rounded character. Offensively, his 50/50 mix-up can be devastating. Trying to keep Superman out is no easy task, as he has an Air Dash that allows him to advance over and around almost all of his opponent's options. Even if you manage to keep Superman at bay, he has a good air and ground projectile that allows him to fight even at far ranges. The only flaw Superman has is that his low option in his 50/50 mix-up is very unsafe, and this is his main go-to mix-up. Opponents can devastate Superman with one good read and change the match in their favor.

INTERACTIVE OBJECT TYPE: POWER

SUPER MOVE

KRYPTONIAN CRUSH
Hit Level: Overhead
Range: Full Screen
Description: Superman grabs his opponent, then punches him or her into space where he follows the opponent into orbit, and then punches him or her back down to Earth. This is the fastest attack in the game. This attack is full combo punished when blocked.

CHARACTER POWER

FURY OF KRYPTON
Command: Press the Power button
Description: Superman will break all armor attacks and inflict more damage for a short amount of time.

For character information updates please visit www.primagames.com/InjusticeUpdates

BEST BASIC ATTACKS

UPPERCUT
Command: Down + Medium
Hit Level: Mid
Range: Close
Description: Superman delivers an Uppercut that will launch his opponent. This attack is safe when blocked.

DOUBLE FIST
Command: Jumping Medium
Hit Level: Overhead
Range: Sweep
Description: Superman jumps into the air with both fists extended, which allows him to chain into other combo attack strings versus a grounded opponent. This attack hits overhead, so it must be blocked from the standing block position.

CHARGE PUNCH
Command: Back + Hard
Hit Level: Mid
Range: Sweep
Description: Superman unleashes a big uppercut attack that will bounce his opponent off of the corner of the screen and back, giving him a juggle combo opportunity. This attack can be charged by holding the Hard attack button and cancelled out of with a forward or backward dash while you are charging the attack. Pressing the Meter Burn button during this attack (burns one bar of meter) will add one hit of armor. Charge Punch is also Superman's Back, Back + Meter Burn Bounce Cancel (bounce cancel burns two bars or meter). This attack leaves Superman at advantage when blocked, allowing him to follow up with additional attacks.

CHARGE OVERHEAD
Command: Forward + Hard
Hit Level: Overhead
Range: Close
Description: Superman does an overhead punch that launches the opponent and gives him a juggle combo opportunity. This attack hits overhead, so it must be blocked from the standing block position. This attack can be charged by holding the Hard attack button and cancelled out of with a forward or backward dash while you are charging the attack. Pressing the Meter Burn button during this attack (burns one bar of meter) will add one hit of armor. Charge Overhead is also Superman's Forward, Forward + Meter Burn Bounce Cancel (bounce cancel burns two bars of meter). This attack leaves Superman at advantage when blocked, allowing him to follow up with additional attacks.

LOW POKE
Command: Down + Hard
Hit Level: Low
Range: Close
Description: Superman punches his opponent in the legs, resulting in a knockdown that cannot be Tech Rolled. This attack is only punished by Super Moves when blocked.

FLYING LOW
Command: Down + Forward + Hard
Hit Level: Low
Range: 1/3 Screen
Description: Superman flies low towards his opponent's legs and knocks the opponent down. This attack is full combo punished when blocked.

BEST COMBO ATTACKS

THE LAST SON

Command: Medium, Medium, Hard
Hit Level: Mid, Mid, Overhead
Range: Close
Description: Superman performs a three-hit punch string that ends in an overhead launcher that must be blocked from the standing block position. This string is safe when blocked.

SOLITUDE STRIKES

Command: Forward + Medium, Hard
Hit Level: Mid, Mid
Range: Sweep
Description: Superman swoops towards his opponent with a two-hit punch combination that ends with an Uppercut launcher. This attack is only punished by Superman's Super Move.

UNSTOPPABLE

Command: Back + Medium, Hard
Hit Level: Mid, Mid
Range: Close
Description: Superman delivers a spinning punch, and then finishes off with a punch to the opponent's stomach that results in a knockdown that cannot be Tech Rolled. This attack is safe when blocked.

SPECIAL MOVES

SUPER BREATH

Command:	Down, Back + Medium
Hit Level:	Mid
Range:	Sweep

Description: Superman uses his Super Breath to blow his opponent across the screen. When blocked, Superman is left at advantage, allowing him to follow up with additional attacks.

METER BURN SUPER BREATH

Description: Pressing the Meter Burn button at the startup of Super Breath will freeze opponents in place. When blocked, this attack is only punished by Superman's Super Move.

HEAT VISION

Command:	Down, Back + Light
Hit Level:	Mid
Range:	Full Screen

Description: Superman shoots his Heat Vision with a sweeping blast that starts in front of him and continues across the length of the screen. When blocked at closer ranges this attack is extremely unsafe.

METER BURN HEAT VISION

Description: Pressing the Meter Burn button during Heat Vision shoots an additional powerful blast that strikes overhead and knocks the opponent across the screen to deliver more damage. This attack ends with an overhead, so it must be blocked from the standing block position. When blocked at closer ranges this attack is extremely unsafe.

AIR HEAT VISION

Command:	Down, Back + Light while in the air
Hit Level:	Mid
Range:	Full Screen

Description: At any point while in mid-air Superman can shoot his Heat Vision. When blocked at closer ranges this attack is extremely unsafe.

METER BURN AIR HEAT VISION

Description: Pressing the Meter Burn button during Air Heat Vision shoots an additional powerful blast that hits overhead and knocks the opponent across the screen and does more damage. This attack ends with an overhead, so it must be blocked from the standing block position. When blocked at closer ranges this attack is extremely unsafe.

RISING GRAB

Command:	Down, Forward + Medium
Hit Level:	High
Range:	Close

Description: Superman jumps into the air, grabbing his opponent and slamming him or her down to the ground. This attack is full combo punished when it is blocked or misses. When this attack hits, Superman can cancel into his Air Heat Vision as he slams the opponent to the ground.

METER BURN RISING GRAB

Description: Pressing the Meter Burn button during a successful Rising Grab will cause Superman to slam his opponent down even harder, doing additional damage. This attack is full combo punished when it is blocked or misses. When this attack hits, Superman can cancel into his Air Heat Vision as he slams the opponent to the ground.

FLYING PUNCH

Command:	Back, Forward + Hard
Hit Level:	Mid
Range:	Sweep

Description: Superman lunges at his opponent with a flying punch that knocks the opponent back when it hits. This attack is full combo punished when blocked.

METER BURN FLYING PUNCH

Description: Pressing the Meter Burn button during Flying Punch adds two additional attacks that hit overhead for more damage and a more powerful knockdown. This attack is only punished by the fastest Super Moves in the game when blocked. Opponents can interrupt this attack in between the first and second hit with a Super Move. This attack ends with an overhead, so it must be blocked from the standing block position.

INJUSTICE
GODS AMONG US

FLYING GROUND SMASH

Command:	Down + Hard while in air
Hit Level:	Overhead
Range:	1/4 Screen

Description: Superman plunges down on his opponent from above. Superman can be combo punished when this attack is blocked or whiffs, but he will be considered airborne when punished. This is an overhead attack so it must be blocked from the standing position.

HEAT ZAP

Command:	Down, Back + Hard
Hit Level:	High
Range:	Full Screen

Description: Superman shoots a straight eye laser. This attack is punished by fast attacks if crouched at close range. This attack leaves Superman at advantage when blocked.

LOW SCOOP

Command:	Down, Forward + Light
Hit Level:	Low
Range:	Close

Description: Superman scoops his opponent up by the feet and launches him or her into the air. This attack is full combo punished when blocked.

METER BURN FLYING GROUND SMASH

Description: Pressing the Meter Burn button during a successful Flying Ground Smash lifts the opponent up and slams him or her to the ground, doing additional damage. Superman can be combo punished when this attack is blocked or whiffs, but he will be considered airborne when punished. This is an overhead attack, so it must be blocked from the standing block position.

STRATEGY

USING CHARGE PUNCH (BACK + HARD) AND CHARGE OVERHEAD (FORWARD + HARD)

Charge Punch has more uses than the Charge Overhead. In open space, Charge Punch nets more damage than Charge Overhead both by itself and inside of juggles due to the wall bounce allowing for more damaging combo options. When you have the opponent cornered, use Charge Overhead over Charge Punch, unless you are hunting a Level Transition. Superman's Charge Punch will send the opponent flying over his head, making any juggle you do knock your opponent out of the corner. Charge Overhead will launch the opponent right in front of you and give you a damaging combo while still keeping your opponent cornered. After your opponent blocks your Charge Punch or Charge Overhead, you are left at advantage. You can follow up on your advantage with your Solitude Strikes (Forward + Medium, Hard) attack string, and the opponent cannot interrupt the attack unless he or she back dashes or uses a Super Move. If the opponent attempts to back dash, you can follow up with your Flying Punch or Flying Ground Smash to hit your opponent as they are back dashing away.

USING THE LAST SON (MEDIUM, MEDIUM, HARD) AND LOW SCOOP (DOWN, FORWARD + LIGHT)

This string is where Superman's primary 50/50 mix-up comes from and the attack string that you will want to use when you are right next to your opponent. The entire string is mid and the last hit finishes with an overhead launcher, so the opponent must block the final attack standing. The mix-up comes from being able to cancel out of the string with Superman's Down, Forward + Light Low Scoop. By using the first two attacks of The Last Son, then canceling to Low Scoop, you create a low/overhead mix-up where the opponent must guess. Low Scoop and the overhead of the string both launch, so Superman gets a juggle no matter which option connects. The only thing to remember here is that the final attack of The Last Son is completely safe, whereas Low Scoop is punished by a full combo from the entire cast. The biggest drawback to the The Last Son attack string is that it can be interrupted by a Super Move in between each strike. Your opponent can back dash out of the last attack of The Last Son string, even if he or she is in a corner. This is again where Low Scoop comes into play. The opponent cannot back dash out of Low Scoop when you cancel into it after the second hit of The Last Son string. The opponent again finds himself or herself in a situation where he or she must block Low Scoop, which again opens up the option of finishing The Last Son string with the overhead launcher.

USING SOLITUDE STRIKES (FORWARD + MEDIUM, HARD)

This attack string is used to help Superman bully his way up close. Once you get into sweep range, you can use this attack string to close distance on your opponent while safely hunting for a juggle combo starter. This attack is also your main whiff punisher as it's your best advancing attack string.

USING UNSTOPPABLE (BACK + MEDIUM, HARD)

When this attack string hits, your opponent is knocked down and cannot Tech Roll. This allows you to advance toward your opponent and follow up with more offense. The opponent does have the option to use a wakeup attack as you come in to continue your pressure, but the wakeup can be baited and punished accordingly.

USING BASIC KNOCKDOWN ATTACKS

Down + Hard Low Poke is a heavy punch to your opponent's feet and results in a knockdown where the opponent cannot Tech Roll away to safety. When approaching your opponent, you can use this attack to gain a knockdown and then continue pressure. The opponent will then have to deal with any pressure or mix-ups you decide to use unless he or she chooses to use a wakeup attack, but you can scout this and punish accordingly. Down Forward + Hard Flying Low covers a surprising amount of ground. You can catch opponents off guard as you approach with this attack.

USING SUPER BREATH (DOWN, BACK + MEDIUM)

Superman's Super Breath leaves him at major advantage when blocked. This allows him to follow up with his Solitude Strikes (Forward + Medium, Hard) attack string and the opponent cannot interrupt the attack unless he or she back dashes or uses a Super Move. If the opponent attempts to back dash, you can follow up with your Flying Punch or Flying Ground Smash to hit your opponent as they are back dashing away. You can cancel into Super Breath from basic and combo string attacks, allowing you to continue pressure after your strikes are blocked.

> **TIP** The Meter Burn Super Breath is used inside combos to freeze opponents and give Superman a bigger, more damaging combo. Even on an already-juggled opponent, Meter Burn Super Breath will freeze the opponent in a grounded state, allowing Superman to continue his combo.

USING HEAT VISION (DOWN, BACK + LIGHT) AND HEAT ZAP (DOWN, BACK + HARD)

The absolute closest range you want to use Heat Vision is half screen, and even that is very risky against some characters. The ground version of this attack has a decent startup speed and travels across the screen at a decent pace. Where this attack truly excels is its air version. The Air Heat Vision can be done while Superman is at any point of his jump, be it on the way up or down. Superman can use the Air Heat Vision to make it tough for characters to advance towards him, or to jump over his opponent's projectile and punish him or her with one of his own from up to full screen. One of the main ways this attack helps is that it makes Superman an aggressive character with the option to still deal out damage from a distance, and the fact that he has an air projectile allows him to do this while avoiding his opponent's projectile attacks. Superman is not bound to always having to commit to approaching his opponent; in situations where he may be forced to fight at a range for a period of time, this attack allows him to do so without too much difficulty. Heat Zap inflicts 6 1/2% just in block damage, and 12% when it hits. This out-damages just about every projectile in the game for block damage and is one of the more damaging projectile attacks on hit as well. Superman can sit at 3/4 to full screen and fire off Heat Zap after Heat Zap, and then use his Air Heat Vision to jump over the opponent's counter projectile attack and punish him or her with one of his own.

USING RISING GRAB (DOWN, FORWARD + MEDIUM)

This is one Superman's primary anti-air tools. This attack will beat out all incoming airborne attacks. This attack is also used as a combo ender where you want to reverse positions. When you land the Rising Grab, you can cancel at the end of the attack with Superman's Heat Vision for added damage. If you do not cancel at the end of this attack, it causes a knockdown that cannot be Tech Rolled.

USING UPPERCUT (DOWN + MEDIUM)

Superman's Uppercut is his most damaging anti-air. It is his only real reliable way to anti-air with an attack that will allow him to go into a combo. With proper timing, this attack can prove to be a consistent anti-air.

USING DOUBLE FIST JUMPING ATTACK (JUMPING MEDIUM)

This is your best jumping attack option. This attack allows Superman to chain into a combo attack against a grounded opponent on block or hit. This is your staple jumping attack; use this attack anytime you are hunting a jump in combo starter, be it off of a straight on jump in or when you are dropping down onto the opponent from your Air Dash. Your Double Fist jumping attack is also great for air-to-air situations. Superman can go right into a juggle combo after landing a jumping towards or neutral jump Double Fist jumping attack.

USING FLYING GROUND SMASH (DOWN + HARD WHILE IN AIR)

After jumping over projectile attacks from a range where you cannot reach the opponent for a jump in combo starter, you can use the Flying Ground Smash to close that distance and punish your opponent. Flying Ground Smash will also auto-face and track the opponent should you jump or Air Dash over him or her.

USING KRYPTONIAN CRUSH

This is by far the fastest attack in the game. Superman's Super Move is the ultimate punishing tool, punishing some moves that are safe to every other move in the game.

USING AIR DASH

One of few characters that has an Air Dash, Superman can use his Air Dash while jumping over projectiles, and then land with a drop down attack and go right into a full combo. His Air Dash makes it difficult for opponents to use projectile attacks on him from half screen or closer.

Superman can use his Air Dash to punish an opponent's anti-air attempts, or he can jump towards his opponent and Air Dash as he is on the way down. This can cause your opponent's anti-air attempt to miss as Superman Air Dashes over them, allowing him to drop down with an attack and go into a full combo. From just inside of full screen range, Superman can punish projectiles by jumping forward, and then Air Dashing into his Flying Ground Smash. Superman can use his Air Dash as an escape tool. He can Air Dash backward or Air Dash himself out of any corner situation. You can Air Dash low to the ground by doing an instant Air Dash. By tapping Up + Forward and then immediately tapping Forward, you can buffer both the jump and dash commands, allowing you to execute a fast and low to the ground Air Dash.

USING FURY OF KRYPTON CHARACTER POWER

When Superman activates Fury Of Krypton, his attacks will beat out any form of armor including other Super Moves and he also gains a slight damage increase. Superman can cancel out of attack strings and basic attacks mid-juggle with Fury Of Krypton, and then cancel out of the activation with his Super Move, landing a powered-up Super Move on a juggled opponent.

INJUSTICE
GODS AMONG US

COMBOS

OPEN SPACE NO METER BURN:

Down + Medium > Forward + Medium, Hard > Forward + Medium, Hard ~ Flying Punch — 17%
Forward + Medium, Hard > Forward + Medium, Hard > Forward + Medium, Hard ~ Flying Punch — 22%
Medium, Medium ~ Low Scoop > Forward + Medium, Hard > Forward+ Medium, Hard ~ Flying Punch — 23%
Air-to-Air Jumping Medium > Forward + Medium, Hard > Forward + Medium, Hard ~ Flying Punch — 23%

Medium, Medium, Hard > Forward + Medium, Hard > Forward + Medium, Hard ~ Flying Punch — 24%
Back + Hard > Jumping Hard > Back + Medium, Hard ~ Flying Punch — 30%

OPEN SPACE METER BURN:

Down + Medium > Forward + Medium, Hard ~ Meter Burn Super Breath > (Dash Forward) Back + Hard > Jumping Hard > Hard ~ Flying Punch – 27%
Forward + Medium, Hard ~ Meter Burn Super Breath (short step forward) > Back + Hard > Jumping Hard > Back + Medium, Hard ~ Flying Punch — 34%
Medium, Medium, Hard > Forward + Medium, Hard ~ Meter Burn Super Breath > Jump In Medium, Medium, Medium ~ Low Scoop > Hard ~ Flying Punch — 35%
Air-to-Air Jumping Medium > Forward + Medium, Hard ~ Meter Burn Super Breath > Jump In Medium, Medium, Medium ~ Low Scoop > Hard ~ Flying Punch — 35%

Medium, Medium ~ Low Scoop > Light ~ Meter Burn Super Breath > Back + Hard > Jumping Hard > Back + Medium, Hard ~ Flying Punch — 35%
Back + Hard > Jumping Hard > Forward + Medium, Hard ~ Meter Burn Super Breath > Jump In Medium, Medium, Medium ~ Low Scoop > Hard ~ Flying Punch — 40%

SUPER MOVE: KRYPTONIAN CRUSH

212

CORNER NO METER BURN:

Medium, Medium ~ Low Scoop > Back + Medium, Hard ~ Flying Punch — 21%

Forward + Medium, Hard > Medium, Medium, Hard > Light, Light, Light ~ Low Scoop > Hard ~ Flying Punch — 29%
Medium, Medium, Hard > Medium, Medium, Hard > Light, Light, Light ~ Low Scoop > Hard ~ Flying Punch — 32%
Forward + Hard > Medium, Medium, Hard > Light, Light, Light ~ Low Scoop > Hard ~ Flying Punch — 32%

CORNER METER BURN:

Medium, Medium ~ Low Scoop > Back + Medium, Hard ~ Meter Burn Super Breath > Neutral Jump Medium, Hard ~ Flying Punch — 30%
Forward + Medium, Hard > Medium, Medium, Hard > Light, Light, Light ~ Low Scoop > Hard ~ Meter Burn Super Breath > Neutral Jump Medium, Hard ~ Flying Punch — 37%

Medium, Medium, Hard > Medium, Medium, Hard > Light, Light, Light ~ Low Scoop > Hard ~ Meter Burn Super Breath > Neutral Jump Medium, Hard ~ Flying Punch — 41%
Forward + Hard > Medium, Medium, Hard > Light, Light, Light ~ Low Scoop > Hard ~ Meter Burn Super Breath > Neutral Jump Medium, Hard ~ Flying Punch — 40%

WONDER WOMAN

Wonder Woman has one of the most effective 50/50 mix-ups in the entire game. She also has great mobility and great air attacks. Her parry is the absolute best parry in the game, as it parries both strikes and projectiles. Her Sword stance is not too effective though. The main benefit to Sword stance is the ability to receive less block damage, which would help her greatly versus characters with powerful projectiles if her parry in Lasso stance wasn't a much better asset. Her Lasso stance parry not only parries projectiles, but Wonder Woman takes no damage from the attack and she also builds meter for just performing parry. Lasso stance is the stance that you should be in, as it has better damage, better mobility, better 50/50 mix-ups, better range, and a parry. The only downside to Wonder Woman is that she has trouble when she finds herself down in the life lead versus a powerful projectile character. Her ability to parry projectiles becomes less useful when she is now forced to approach her opponent in an attempt to regain the life lead and win the fight.

INTERACTIVE OBJECT TYPE: POWER

SUPER MOVE

JUSTICE JAVELIN
Hit Level: Mid
Range: 1/2 Screen
Description: Wonder Woman unleashes a devastating assault with the help of her Amazonian sisters, ending with one final deadly blow from her sword. This attack is full combo punished when blocked.

CHARACTER POWER

STYLE CHANGE
Command: Press the Power button
Description: Wonder Woman can switch between her Lasso and Sword stance. From Lasso stance, Wonder Woman is faster, more mobile, and deals more damage. From Sword stance, Wonder Woman takes reduced block damage, but also deals less damage and moves slower with less mobility. Wonder Woman also loses access to a few Special Move options while in Sword stance as well as her Air Dash.

For character information updates please visit www.primagames.com/InjusticeUpdates

BEST LASSO STANCE ATTACKS

QUICK KICK

Command: Jumping Light
Hit Level: Overhead
Range: Close
Description: Wonder Woman performs a fast-jumping kick attack that allows her to chain into other combo attack strings versus a grounded opponent. This attack hits overhead, so it must be blocked in the standing position.

RISING LASSO

Command: Down + Medium
Hit Level: Mid
Range: Close
Description: Wonder Woman crouches down and whips her lasso over her head. This attack launches when it hits and is safe when blocked.

AMAZON'S BLAST

Command: Back + Hard
Hit Level: Mid
Range: Sweep
Description: Wonder Woman winds up and unloads with a thunderous spinning uppercut launcher that bounces her opponent off the corner of the screen and back, giving her a juggle combo opportunity. This attack can be charged by holding the Hard attack button and cancelled out of with a forward or backward dash while you are charging the attack. Pressing the Meter Burn button during this attack (burns one bar of meter) will add one hit of armor. Amazon's Blast is also Wonder Woman's Back, Back + Meter Burn Bounce Cancel (bounce cancel burns two bars of meter). This attack leaves Wonder Woman at advantage when blocked, allowing her to follow up with additional attacks.

AMAZON'S HEEL

Command: Forward + Hard
Hit Level: Overhead
Range: Close
Description: Wonder Woman performs a jumping overhead heel strike that launches the opponent and gives her a juggle combo opportunity. This attack hits overhead, so it must be blocked from the standing block position. This attack can be charged by holding the Hard attack button and cancelled out of with a forward or backward dash while you are charging the attack. Pressing the Meter Burn button during this attack (burns one bar of meter) will add one hit of armor. Amazon's Heel is also Wonder Woman's Forward, Forward + Meter Burn Bounce Cancel (bounce cancel burns two bars of meter). This attack leaves Wonder Woman at advantage when blocked, allowing her to follow up with additional attacks.

AIR LASSO SLAM

Command: Jumping Hard
Hit Level: Overhead
Range: Sweep
Description: Wonder Woman whips her lasso down onto her opponent from above. This attack hits overhead, so it must be blocked from the standing block position. This attack causes a small launch when it hits. When this attack is blocked, Wonder Woman is at advantage and can follow up with additional attacks.

BEST LASSO STANCE COMBO ATTACKS

GODS AND MORTALS

Command: Back + Light, Light, Hard
Hit Level: Mid, Mid, Mid
Range: Close
Description: Wonder Woman attacks with two punches to her opponent's body, followed by a kick that launches. This attack is safe when blocked.

DESTINY CALLING

Command: Medium, Hard
Hit Level: Mid, Mid
Range: Close
Description: Wonder Woman punches her opponent and then follows up with a spin kick that launches. This attack is punished by fast normal attacks and fast Special attacks when blocked.

HEPHAESTUS RUSH

Command: Back + Medium, Hard
Hit Level: Overhead, Mid
Range: 1/4 Screen
Description: Wonder Woman whips her lasso on top of her opponent's head, bouncing him or her off of the ground and then finishing the opponent off with a horizontal lasso strike. This attack is safe when blocked.

ATHENA'S WISDOM

Command: Hard, Hard
Hit Level: Low, Mid
Range: Close
Description: Wonder Woman kicks her opponent once in the feet and then again in the legs, resulting in a launch. This attack is safe when blocked. The opponent can interrupt Wonder Woman in between the first and second hit of this attack string with a Super Move.

BEST SWORD STANCE BASIC ATTACKS

LOW POKE

Command: Down + Light
Hit Level: Mid
Range: Close
Description: Wonder Woman jabs her sword into the legs of her opponent. This attack is safe when blocked.

UPWARD STAB

Command: Down + Medium
Hit Level: Mid
Range: Close
Description: Wonder Woman launches her opponent with a sword uppercut. This attack is safe when blocked.

WARRIOR'S BASH

Command: Forward + Hard
Hit Level: Overhead
Range: Close
Description: Wonder Woman launches her opponent by bashing him or her over the head with her shield. This attack hits overhead, so it must be blocked from the standing block position. This attack can be charged by holding the Hard attack button and cancelled out of with a forward or backward dash while you are charging the attack. Pressing the Meter Burn button during this attack (burns one bar of meter) will add one hit of armor. Warrior's Bash is also a Forward, Forward + Meter Burn Bounce Cancel (bounce cancel burns two bars of meter). This attack leaves Wonder Woman at advantage when blocked, allowing her to follow up with additional attacks.

SWORD SLAM

Command:	Jumping Hard
Hit Level:	Overhead
Range:	Sweep

Description: Wonder Woman swings her sword downward while airborne. This attack leaves you at advantage when blocked, allowing you to follow up with additional attacks. This attack hits overhead so it must be blocked from the standing block position.

BEST SWORD STANCE COMBO ATTACKS

AEGIS WRATH

Command:	Back + Medium, Light
Hit Level:	Low, Overhead
Range:	Sweep

Description: Wonder Woman stabs her opponent in the legs and then follows up with a jumping sword thrust. The second attack in this string hits overhead, so it must be blocked from the standing position. This attack is punished by fast normal attacks and fast Specials when blocked.

JUSTICE

Command:	Back + Medium, Hard
Hit Level:	Low, Low
Range:	Sweep

Description: Wonder Woman stabs her opponent in the legs and then follows through with a spinning sword sweep. This attack is only punished by Superman's Super Move.

BEST LASSO SPECIAL MOVES

STRAIGHT TIARA

Command:	Back, Forward + Medium
Hit Level:	High
Range:	1/2 Screen

Description: Wonder Woman throws her tiara straight towards her opponent. This attack is safe from a distance, but full combo punished if blocked up close.

AMAZONIAN UPPERCUT

Command:	Down, Forward + Hard
Hit Level:	Mid
Range:	Sweep

Description: Wonder Woman unloads on her opponent with a jumping uppercut. This attack is full combo punished when blocked.

AIR AMAZONIAN SMASH

Command:	Down, Back + Hard while in air
Hit Level:	Overhead
Range:	1/4 Screen

Description: Wonder Woman plunges down onto her opponent with a diving punch. This attack is an overhead so it must be blocked from the standing block position. This attack is punished only by the faster Super Moves of the game when blocked.

METER BURN STRAIGHT TIARA

Description: Pressing the Meter Burn button during Straight Tiara will cause the tiara to hit the opponent on its return to Wonder Woman, doing additional damage. This attack is safe when blocked.

METER BURN AMAZONIAN UPPERCUT

Description: Pressing the Meter Burn button during a successful Amazonian Uppercut will cause Wonder Woman follow through with her Demi-Goddess' Might flying punch attack, doing additional damage.

METER BURN AIR AMAZONIAN SMASH

Description: Pressing the Meter Burn button during Air Amazonian Smash will cause Wonder Woman follow through with her Amazonian Uppercut for additional damage. This attack is an overhead so it must be blocked from the standing block position. This attack is only punished by Superman's Super Move when blocked.

INJUSTICE
GODS AMONG US

LASSO GRAB

Command: Down, Forward + Light
Hit Level: High
Range: 1/4 Screen
Description: Wonder Woman grabs her opponent with her lasso and then pulls him or her toward her before punching the opponent away. This attack leaves Wonder Woman at advantage when blocked, allowing her to follow up with additional attacks. Opponents can crouch this attack and full combo punish Wonder Woman.

METER BURN LASSO GRAB

Description: Pressing the Meter Burn button during Lasso Grab does additional damage and, for a short period of time, will increase Wonder Woman's damage output while decreasing her opponent's damage output.

LASSO SPIN

Command: Down, Back + Hard
Hit Level: Mid
Range: Close
Description: Wonder Woman performs a spin attack, using her lasso to launch her opponent. This attack is punished by fast normal attacks and fast Specials.

UP TIARA

Command: Down, Back + Medium
Hit Level: High
Range: 1/4 Screen
Description: Wonder Woman throws her tiara upwards at an angle. This attack can be combo punished by most characters when blocked.

AIR STRAIGHT TIARA

Command: Back, Forward + Medium while in air
Range: 1/2 Screen
Description: While in mid-air Wonder Woman throws her tiara straight in front of her.

AIR DEMI-GODDESS' MIGHT

Command: Down, Forward + Hard while in air
Range: 3/4 Screen
Description: Wonder Woman performs a fast air flying punch.

BRACELETS OF SUBMISSION

Command: Down, Back + Light
Description: Wonder Woman will parry any high or mid normal attack as well as any projectile. After a successful parry, Wonder Woman's damage output is increased for a short period of time.

AIR DOWN TIARA

Command: Down, Back + Medium while in air
Hit Level: High or Overhead based on the height you execute the attack
Range: 1/2 Screen
Description: While in mid-air, Wonder Woman throws her tiara downward at her opponent. This attack will hit overhead when done at lower heights where it must be blocked from the standing block position. This attack is only safe if done from a distance.

SWORD STANCE SPECIAL MOVES

SHIELD TOSS

Command: Back, Forward + Medium
Hit Level: High
Range: 1/2 Screen
Description: Wonder Woman throws her shield straight towards her opponent. This attack is safe when blocked.

METER BURN SHIELD TOSS

Description: Pressing the Meter Burn button during Shield Toss will cause the shield to hit the opponent on its return to Wonder Woman, doing additional damage. This attack is safe when blocked.

AMALTHEA BASH

Command: Back, Forward + Hard
Hit Level: Mid
Range: 1/3 Screen
Description: Wonder Woman charges at her opponent, bashing him or her with her shield. This attack is full combo punished when blocked.

METER BURN AMALTHEA BASH

Description: Pressing the Meter Burn button during Amalthea Bash will follow up with another bashing shield charge that knocks the opponent down, doing additional damage. This attack leaves Wonder Woman at advantage when blocked, allowing her to follow up with additional attacks.

AIR DOWN SHIELD
Command: Down, Back + Medium
Hit Level: Overhead
Range: 1/2 Screen
Description: While in mid-air, Wonder Woman throws her shield downward at her opponent. This attack hits overhead, so it must be blocked from the standing block position. The safety of this attack varies based on the height it is thrown from; the lower it is thrown, the safer it is.

SHIELD STRIKE

Command: Down, Back + Light
Range: Close
Description: Shield Strike is a fast attack that will also parry high and mid strikes. When Shield Strike parries an attack, Wonder Woman will automatically follow up with a sword strike attack. Pressing Medium, Hard after the sword strike will have Wonder Woman follow up with two additional sword strikes. This attack is only punished by Superman's Super Move.

UP SHIELD

Command: Down, Back + Medium
Hit Level: High
Range: 1/4 Screen
Description: Wonder Woman throws her shield upwards at an angle. This attack is only punished by Superman's Super Move when blocked. This attack is full combo punished if crouched at close range.

USING AMAZON'S BLAST (BACK + HARD) AND AMAZON'S HEEL (FORWARD + HARD)

Amazon's Blast is better in almost every way. It has more range, allows for easier juggles, and has a higher combo damage output potential. The only time that you would use Amazon's Heel over Amazon's Blast would be to avoid setting off a Level Transition.

USING RISING LASSO (DOWN + HARD)

Rising Lasso is one of the best uppercuts in the game. This is Wonder Woman's primary anti-air tool, allowing her to consistently punish jumping opponents with a launcher, giving her a juggle combo.

USING HEPHAESTUS RUSH (BACK + MEDIUM, HARD) AND ATHENA'S WISDOM (HARD, HARD)

The first attack of the Hephaestus Rush string is one of Wonder Woman's best attacks; it has amazing reach and is key in setting up Wonder Woman's 50/50 game. This attack hits overhead, so Wonder Woman can use this to create a 50/50 mix-up between this attack string and the low-starting Athena's Wisdom attack string. The first attack of the Hephaestus Rush attack string can be cancelled into Wonder Woman's Super Move or, if up close, can be cancelled into her Lasso Spin launcher. If you are not close enough for a cancel into your Lasso Spin attack, you should use both hits of the Hephaestus Rush attack string.

Athena's Wisdom is the attack string that is used as the low option in Wonder Woman's 50/50 mix-up game. You cancel the Athena's Wisdom attack string into the Lasso Spin launcher for a damaging combo. This attack is most effective when used as a mix-up with the overhead Hephaestus Rush attack string.

USING GODS AND MORTALS (BACK + LIGHT, LIGHT, HARD)

This attack string has two main uses: 1) It's used as a punishing tool when blocking unsafe attacks or as a whiff punisher and 2) It's used inside of combos, be it in the middle or as an ender.

USING LASSO STANCE JUMPING ATTACKS

Jumping Light is your best tool versus a grounded opponent; it's your best attack when looking to land a jump in attack that will allow you to go into an attack string combo starter. Jumping Hard is great for air-to-air situations as it's fast and also out-ranges a lot of the other jumping attacks in the game. In air-to-air situations you can buffer in Wonder Woman's Air Demi-Goddess' Might (Down, Forward + Hard) attack as a follow-up. This way, if your air-to-air jumping Hard connects, Wonder Woman will cancel into Air Demi-Goddess' Might for a 21% two-hit combo. If jumping Hard does not make contact, Air Demi-Goddess' Might will not activate, and Wonder Woman will land normally. Jumping Hard also leads to big damage if it hits a grounded opponent in the standing position. When jumping Hard is blocked, Wonder Woman is at advantage and can follow up with additional attacks.

USING AIR AMAZONIAN SMASH (DOWN, BACK + HARD WHILE IN AIR)

As a Wonder Woman player, you will find that opponents will throw just about everything at you in an attempt to stay away. This is because of how effective her 50/50 game is. You can use her Air Amazonian Smash as a way to bully your way in. This attack also makes it hard to anti-air Wonder Woman due to the speed of the attack, and it can also be done from any height. You can fool your opponent into thinking that a normal jump in is coming, then Air Amazonian Smash him or her right out of the anti-air attempt. Using this attack at the right times can make your opponent think twice about anti-air attempts, which now frees up your ability to jump in towards your opponent.

USING AIR DASH

Wonder Woman's Air Dash is a mobility tool that also opens up her ability to go on the offensive. She can jump and Air Dash over projectile attacks, then drop down onto her opponent. You can also use her Air Dash to fool opponents trying to anti-air you by Air Dashing past their anti-air attempt, then dropping down for a full combo punish. Wonder Woman can use her Air Dash as an escape tool as well. She can Air Dash backward or Air Dash herself out of any corner situation. She can also Air Dash low to the ground by doing an instant Air Dash: by tapping Up + Forward, then immediately tapping Forward, you can buffer both the jump and dash commands, allowing you to execute a fast and low-to-the-ground Air Dash.

USING TIARA PROJECTILE SPECIAL ATTACKS

Wonder Woman's Straight Tiara is your standard mid-ranged ground projectile. The range on this attack is about 1/2 screen, so be sure to be within that range or closer when you use it. When this attack gets blocked, Wonder Woman can Meter Burn the tiara to hit the opponent on its return, and this can catch opponents who are too eager to respond after blocking the normal version of the attack. You can also Meter Burn this attack when it hits for additional damage. Up Tiara is best used from just outside of 1/4 screen distance; from this range you can anti-air opponents who are attempting to jump over a Straight Tiara. Air Straight Tiara can be used both to punish opponents who attempt to jump in over a ground Straight Tiara, in air-to-air situations to prevent opponents from following you mid-air, or as a way to stop opponents from using jumping as a way to close distance. Air Down Tiara allows Wonder Woman to jump over oncoming projectiles while delivering one of her own. Opponents can crouch under this attack if it is performed while Wonder Women is higher in the air. However, if the attack is performed lower to the ground, the opponent will not be able to crouch under this attack as it will hit overhead.

USING BRACELETS OF SUBMISSION (DOWN, BACK + LIGHT)

This is one of the best parries in the game. Not only does it parry all high and mid strikes, but it also parries projectiles. Wonder Woman can actually get the life lead and force her opponent to come to her because of her ability to not just parry his or her projectiles without taking any damage, but build a good amount of meter for it as well. After landing a successful parry on a high or mid strike, Wonder Woman gets a guaranteed attack based on the recovery of the move she parries. For fast recovering attacks, the only attack guaranteed is her Justice Javelin Super Move or Down + Light ~ Lasso Spin. When parrying attacks that have more recovery, she can follow up the successful parry with her Gods And Mortals attack string. Wonder Woman can also parry multiple hits in succession, allowing her to parry entire attack strings in some cases.

USING SWORD STANCE

The Aegis Wrath (Back+ Medium, Light) and Justice (Back + Medium, Hard) attack strings are an overhead/low mix-up on the last hit of the string. Jumping Hard is Wonder Woman's best jumping attack in this stance. It has a good range and is great for cross up jumps. When it's blocked, Wonder Woman is at advantage and can follow up with additional attacks.

Amalthea Bash (Back, Forward + Hard) is one of your best attacks in this stance. It travels far and staggers your opponent if it hits, giving you enough advantage to follow up with more attacks. This attack is unsafe, but when blocked, you can confirm your opponent's block and Meter Burn the attack, now leaving Wonder Woman at advantage. However, opponents can use a Super Move and interrupt your Meter Burn follow-up unless you commit to the Meter Burn ender rather than delaying it while trying to confirm the hit or block.

COMBOS

OPEN SPACE LASSO STANCE:

Down + Medium > Back + Light, Light, Hard > Back + Light, Light, Hard ~ Lasso Grab — 25%
(right next to your opponent) Back + Medium ~ Lasso Spin > Back + Light, Light, Hard ~ Lasso Grab — 27%

Hard, Hard ~ Lasso Spin > Jumping Medium > Medium, Hard ~ Lasso Grab — 31%
Lasso Spin > Lasso Spin > Back + Light, Light, Hard > Medium, Hard ~ Lasso Grab — 30%
Down + Light ~ Lasso Spin > Back + Hard > Jumping Hard > Back + Light, Light, Hard ~ Lasso Grab — 33%
(against a standing opponent only) Jumping Hard > Back + Light, Light, Hard > Back + Light, Light, Hard ~ Lasso Grab — 38%

Hard, Hard ~ Lasso Spin > Back + Hard > Jumping Hard > Back + Light, Light, Hard ~ Lasso Grab — 38%
Back + Hard > Jumping Hard > Back + Light, Light, Hard > Back + Light, Light, Hard ~ Lasso Grab — 40%
Back + Light, Light, Hard ~ Lasso Spin > Back + Hard > Jumping Hard > Back + Light, Light, Hard ~ Lasso Grab — 40%

CORNER LASSO STANCE:

Down + Medium > Lasso Spin > Back + Light, Light, Hard > Medium, Hard ~ Lasso Grab — 24%

Back + Medium ~ Lasso Spin > Back + Light, Light, Hard > Medium, Hard ~ Lasso Grab — 31%
Hard, Hard ~ Lasso Spin > Lasso Spin > Back + Light, Light, Hard > Medium, Hard ~ Lasso Grab — 34%
Back + Light, Light, Hard ~ Lasso Spin > Back + Hard > Neutral Jump Medium > Back + Light, Light, Hard > Medium, Hard ~ Amazonian Uppercut — 39%
Back + Hard > Neutral Jump Hard > Back + Light, Light, Hard > Medium, Hard ~ Lasso Grab — 38%
Lasso Spin > Back + Hard > Neutral Jump Hard > Back + Light, Light, Hard > Medium, Hard ~ Lasso Grab — 37%

INJUSTICE
GODS AMONG US

SINGLE PLAYER

THE MANY FACES OF BATTLE

One of the most intriguing parts of *Injustice: Gods Among Us* is the variety of different ways in which to square off against your opponents. A lengthy Story Mode picks up right where the *Injustice* comic mini-series left off, with all hell breaking loose across Metropolis. Through it, you'll get to experience a constantly changing cast of heroes and villains that serve as a narrative-driven way of exploring the more than two dozen different characters available for play in other modes. If you're looking to find a favorite, Story Mode is a perfect way to see — and do battle against — the whole *Injustice* roster. Story Mode isn't the *only* way to get a little fiction to go along with your fights, however. S.T.A.R. Labs offers a mind-boggling 260 challenges, each with three unique goals to attempt above and beyond just beating the snot out of your opponent, and Battles provide the ultimate ladder-based challenge with a multitude of alternate takes on the normal *Injustice* rules. Battles aren't to be undertaken blithely, as they're all-or-nothing challenges — you get one shot to take down the entire ladder of randomly chosen characters, and if you fall in battle, it's back to the beginning.

STORY MODE

PROLOGUE

Metropolis has been decimated. In an instant, an atomic-level fission reaction hummed to life, turning to fusion and detonating. One moment, millions of lives existed. The next, they were gone, evaporated in the heat and radiation of the same forces that power the stars. The person responsible could never have been guessed: Superman, his mind reeling from The Scarecrow's fear toxin, had carried what he thought was Doomsday up into space. In reality, it was the love of his life, Lois, and their unborn child who perished in the cold vacuum of space. As she did, the transmitter hidden inside her triggered a nuclear bomb in the heart of Metropolis, claiming five million lives. It was a plan concocted by The Joker and carried out with the kind of heartless precision that only the Clown Prince of Crime could manage. As the events of *Injustice*'s Story Mode play out, Superman pays a visit to The Joker's holding cell with one thing on his mind.

Worlds away, another set of super heroes are doing battle with evil, engaging in a massive brawl over the gleaming, quite intact spires of Metropolis. As Green Lantern, Shazam, Superman, Wonder Woman, and Aquaman battle arch-enemies on the ground, an assault happening far above the planet's surface is playing out, led by Lex Luthor as he invades the Watchtower with Catwoman, Bane, and Solomon Grundy. Nightwing requests the help of his old mentor, Batman, who headed to Arkham Asylum for an investigation of his own...

CHAPTER 1: BATMAN

The Joker never seems to stay in Arkham Asylum for long, but when The Dark Knight is summoned to investigate his disappearance, a trap is foiled, revealing the true threat.

Opponent: Deathstroke

Stage: Arkham Asylum

TIP Deathstroke excels at long-range games of keep-away. His ranged ability is mostly horizontal, though, so jump in early or use Batman's Grapple Lunge and/or slide kick to close distance and keep applying pressure to avoid eating stray rounds from his many shots. The TVs and cooling pipe are good ways to apply extra damage. Just remember that the explosion hits diagonally, not directly below the TVs.

Back in Metropolis, the whole group of heroes are holding their own, but Doomsday takes the combined efforts of everyone on hand — at least until Superman decides to do the whole swoop-in-and-carry-the-bad-guy-off routine. With Deathstroke out of the way, Batman is free to head up to the Watchtower to put a stop to Lex Luthor's plans, but not before meeting an old rival.

Opponent: Bane

Stage: Watchtower

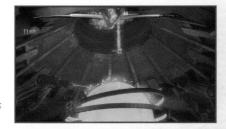

TIP Bane is almost the complete opposite of Deathstroke in that he wants to get in close. Keep him at bay as best you can, and watch for the armor that many of his special moves have as they wind up. Concentrate less on trying to interrupt his attacks and instead stay agile. The sooner you can bait him over to the left, the better your chances of using the shuttlecraft to roast the big lug or using a Level Transition attack to continue the battle below.

BATARANG BEATDOWN

After polishing off Bane, it's time to confront Lex Luthor directly, but *Injustice*'s Story Mode introduces some interesting mini-games before certain big fights. This first challenge is relatively light; simply match the on-screen button prompts to chuck batarangs at the armored villain as he stomps toward Batman. With each new round of prompts, Lex Luthor will walk faster and require more hits, but by successfully repelling him, Batman can start the subsequent fight with all his health, while Lex Luthor will have to make do with a fair chunk of his first life bar already whittled down. Of course, if he actually reaches Batman during this mini-game, the injuries sustained here carry over into the next round. Worse, if the fight itself is a loss, you'll have to repeat this whole mini-game before the rematch can begin, so be quick with those button presses.

Opponent: Lex Luthor

Stage: Watchtower

TIP Lex Luthor just loves his Gravity Pull — and why not? It's an effective way of drawing enemies in and then spitting them back out, effectively controlling space in a single move. Thankfully, Bats has more than a few long-range options of his own, but be mindful of all those hovering bots flying around. Lex is almost as fond of chucking them your way too, and his hits are potent.

After rounding up the bad guys, peace aboard the Watchtower seems to have been restored. But no sooner do the heroes take a breather than a warning klaxon begins to blare. The Joker and Harley have their hands on a nuke, courtesy of Lex Luthor, and as the Prologue made clear, The Joker and atom bombs are a very, very bad combination. As the heroic group races to stop The Joker from detonating the nuke, something strange begins to happen. The Joker, Batman, Green Lantern, Wonder Woman, Green Arrow, and Aquaman are surrounded by a strange blue glow, and Batman and his nemesis are pulled into a place that's eerily familiar. The Joker's fondness for his rival apparently runs out, though, and in this strange new world, a new battle begins.

Opponent: The Joker

Stage: Metropolis

TIP Metropolis' first appearance can be a little overwhelming if this is the first time you've actually seen it. It doesn't help that there's quite a bit going on in the level, but if you want a full tour, just use Level Transition moves near the right side of the first two areas, then the left side of the Museum to head back to Street level. In addition to getting a clear picture of the sole three-level stage in the game, you'll destroy big chunks of The Joker's life in the process.

The rivals' give and take is cut short as the local armored constabulary, who seem to hold Batman of all people in rather low regard, arrive with rifles at the ready. Possessing one of the keenest minds on the planet has its advantages, though, and after using a little sonic crowd control, Batman is consumed by a puff of smoke faster than you can say "ninja vanish." Meanwhile, the other heroes transported to this place try to suss out where they've ended up.

INJUSTICE
GODS AMONG US

A rooftop pow-wow sees Wonder Woman, Green Lantern, Green Arrow, and Aquaman deciding they're definitely not where they should be. With plenty of investigating to do, Green Lantern heads to the first place he can think of: Ferris Aircraft. There, he discovers a very different looking Raven and Cyborg torturing a mask-less Deathstroke for information. With no choice but to stop such barbarism, Green Lantern steps in.

Opponent: Raven

Stage: Ferris Aircraft

TIP *It can take a bit to adjust to Green Lantern's new moves and his Power abilities. What better way to do so than to grab every possible Interactive Object in this level and use them to bludgeon the snot out of Raven? Staying on the offensive is good, as her reach with some of her soul-powered Special Moves is disorienting to say the least. Remember that both the turbine to the left and rockets on the right edge of the level are reusable.*

Cyborg, not surprisingly, doesn't take well to the beating his friend got, and he quickly attempts to settle the score.

Opponent: Cyborg

Stage: Ferris Aircraft

TIP *The one-time Justice League metal man is much, much more of a long-range character than his partner. Expect plenty of incoming blasts from Cyborg's cannon. As a Power character, all the things Green Lantern can do (Interactive Objects-wise), so can Cyborg, so watch out for that big missile in the middle of the level. Counter with projectiles of your own and slip in where possible to unload a series of quick combos — might we recommend some of the ones found in Green Lantern's Character chapter?*

After freeing the one-eyed mercenary and getting some troubling news, Hal gets a distress call from Wonder Woman, who has come under attack by Sinestro in the alleys of Gotham City. He quickly heads back to help out the Amazon, and confront his one-time ally.

WILL VS. FEAR

Another mini-game ensues as soon as Green Lantern manages to catch up to Sinestro. Like the Lex Luthor battle before it, correctly following the button prompts will start Hal with a full life bar, while Sinestro will have some of his trimmed away. The button prompts this time around are a little more complicated, requiring multiple presses and a bit of button mashing at the end. Take a moment to memorize your system's buttons if you don't know them off the top of your head, then be ready to respond quickly to counter Sinestro's constructs with some of your own.

Opponent: Sinestro

Stage: Gotham City

TIP *Sinestro is dangerous mostly because of how quick many of his attacks are. Being able to conjure boulders to drop from the sky is a nifty trick, so be ready to block as you advance in to pound away. This part of Gotham City isn't terribly rich with Interactive Objects, so make use of the dumpster, chemical truck, and fire hydrant if you wish, but don't neglect Green Lantern's ability to easily loop into combos.*

There's scarcely time to check on Diana before another threat appears: this world's Hal Jordan, apparently quite content to join Sinestro in wearing a yellow ring and embracing the power of fear. Bad idea, Yellow Lantern.

Opponent: Yellow Lantern

Stage: Gotham City

TIP *Again, there's not a lot of opportunity to unload with nearby objects, and this Hal has the same moves you do. Try to avoid trading projectiles and just close in to make the most of your Hard strikes for bounces into longer combo strings. This is still early into Story Mode, so these opponents don't tend to hit with heavy combos. Press the attack and you'll kick your ass in no time.*

An approaching police presence forces a hasty retreat, and Green Lantern, Green Arrow, and Wonder Woman opt to walk and talk — until they encounter a familiar cape and cowl. Elsewhere, another iconic cape wearer monitors feedback from his vast security network, learning of a group of newcomers that could mean trouble.

CHAPTER 3: AQUAMAN

Miles deeper, Aquaman returns to his kingdom, only to be mistaken for this world's ruler. Playing it off, he plans to research the history of this dimension and nearly pulls off the ruse before reading the treaty conditions that his doppelganger had agreed to: unconditional subservience to Superman's jackbooted rule. As his pride swells, he rejects the terms—a move The Flash and Shazam don't seem to agree with.

Opponent:	The Flash
Stage:	Atlantis

TIP Forget using any Level Transitions here; Atlantis is just one section, but there's plenty here with which to beat on The Scarlet Speedster. If he tries to close in near the edges of the level (which is all The Flash can really do, so go hog wild with Aquaman's heavily ranged attacks), break the tanks to unleash a wall of water—something The Flash can't do with nearly as much height as an Acrobatic-type character.

The Flash's defeat leaves little time for gloating, as Shazam quickly tries to put an end to the Atlantean uprising. After a missed blast, he steels himself for the fight to come, as does Aquaman.

Opponent:	Shazam
Stage:	Atlantis

TIP Shazam doesn't suffer from the same long-range deficit as his partner, but he's vulnerable to cross-ups and a barrage of quick attacks. Get in close to keep up the pressure and the AI won't be able to handle your onslaught.

Further proof that alternate versions of ourselves sport facial hair is presented as this world's *real* Aquaman attempts to subdue his double. This is, of course, a rather stupid move given that this world's Aquaman could likely best his own men easily, but at least it makes for a fun fight before the twin lords of the sea square off properly.

Opponent:	Aquaman
Stage:	Atlantis

TIP All that range advantage that you had on the previous two characters is negated by this mirror match, but even the bearded Aquaman can't handle a steady stream of thrown tridents. Be ready for the AI to start using Meter Burn versions of the special moves around this fight, too.

After dealing with Superman's emissaries and his alternate self, Aquaman's streak of beatdowns ends rather dramatically. Ares has frozen the Atlantis guard and provokes the Fish Whisperer into yet another duel.

Opponent:	Ares
Stage:	Atlantis

TIP The biggest thing to watch out for with Ares is the strength of his attacks. They have plenty of damage potential, so use ranged attacks where possible to keep him at bay. If he gets in close, Aquaman's throw naturally pushes enemies away, and is a good way to keep distance. Don't neglect the objects strewn around this throne room either. If you don't use them Ares just might.

A friendly chat later and Ares sends Aquaman back to meet up with his fellow travelers. Much has happened while under water. This world's Batman has explained that normal humans can be "upgraded" with Kryptonian nanotech in the form of a simple pill, making them stronger and more resilient. Upon learning of the struggle between this world's Batman and Superman, the group has no choice: they must help to regain control from a Kryptonian gone mad, and fortunately they have an ace in the hole. Back in his Fortress of Solitude, Superman seems to have found some rebound comfort in the form of a very differently attired Wonder Woman, but news that the trail of this dimension's newcomers is starting to grow warmer spells danger for the transplanted heroes.

INJUSTICE
GODS AMONG US

Batman wasn't the only one to escape in the billowing smoke. The Joker has "borrowed" one of the soldiers' transports and headed back to his native Gotham City, where he's reunited with Gotham City's protector. It would appear the Clown has become a bit more battle-ready, though, and with a laugh and a sneer, another brawl ensues.

Opponent: Batman

Stage: Gotham City

TIP The Joker is a bit of a handful at first, but his Hard strikes can do plenty of damage to The Dark Knight. The nearby dumpster, unlike in the previous Green Lantern fights in this area, can be reused by The Joker (and Batman, so be careful).
Don't forget about it in the middle of this fight. If Interactive Objects are your bag, don't forget that Gotham City's rooftops are only a Level Transition attack away.

Even in this same-but-different parallel universe, Batman's luck holds true. Just as The Joker is about to gas the Bat for good, Superman's cronies show up to capture the Caped Crusader. Thinking himself lucky to escape, The Joker is confronted by a vengeful Harley.

Opponent: Harley Quinn

Stage: Gotham City

TIP Harley's not much of a handful, even this alternate reality version of her. Her AI doesn't really have much in the way of anti-air attacks, so jump in and keep on the attack, making sure to save up some meter for when she
Clashes—something that starts happening a bit more often going forward.

Defeated by someone who can't possibly be anyone but her Puddin', Harley realizes that if this isn't her former love, it's someone close enough and brings him to his doppelganger's lair. Meanwhile, the captive Batman is scanned by Superman and his true nature is revealed. At the same time, a seemingly revived Joker is busy sharing his discovery of the Kryptonian nanomachines with his henchmen, creating an army of nigh-invulnerable lackeys. Even as Hawkgirl and Nightwing crash the party, The Joker seems confident that his newfound strength is more than enough for the winged warrior.

Opponent: Hawkgirl

Stage: Joker's Asylum

TIP Play defensively when squaring off against Hawkgirl, as she has options at almost any range. At longer ranges, she can throw her mace, so try not to leave a full screen between the two of you. Jumping attacks are dangerous, as she has
plenty of anti-air moves, and the AI is starting to ramp up to use them. The starting Mess Hall area is a bit dangerous, so try to initiate a Level Transition to get back up into the Cell Block, then remove the TVs with explosives quickly to create an open space.

Just as The Joker attempts to clip Hawkgirl's wings, Nightwing takes notice and charges, initiating yet another mini-game.

IN THE CARDS

The Joker's mini-game is refreshingly different from the rest. Sure, you'll still use the same buttons, but you must tap them in sets of two and three in rapid succession to ward off Nightwing's approach. As the rounds continue, the number of flicked cards needed to stop Batman's protege increases, so keep calm and work in groups, tapping quickly and cleanly before moving to the next group. A mis-pressed button halts the whole process and gives Nightwing a few precious seconds to close the distance, at which point The Joker will start the subsequent fight lower on health.

Opponent: Nightwing

Stage: Joker's Asylum

TIP Nightwing is nothing if not quick, and can easily string together his attacks into lengthy pummeling sessions. Keep him from initiating those strings in the first place by piling on damage with aggressive strings of your own. Don't
be afraid to Meter Burn some of your more powerful strikes to shave off health early on, and remember that Level Transitions can provide more Interactive Objects (as well as more damage).

Party crashing turns into a team sport as the original universe's Green Arrow, Wonder Woman, Aquaman, and Green Lantern join this universe's Batman in tracking down The Joker. Hawkgirl, freshly revived from her beating, grabs Nightwing and swoops off to safety shortly before it's revealed that this world's Harley is actually one of the good guys. Aboard the Watchtower, Superman works with Cyborg to figure out how to follow the others into the alternate dimension. Earthward back in that alternate universe, this world's decidedly non-villainous Lex Luthor and a rested Deathstroke plan a covert break-in while the rest of the Insurgency begins executing their own intrusion elsewhere.

CHAPTER 5: GREEN ARROW

Wayne Manor has been put on lockdown as this world's Superman tirelessly searches for his Batman. Thankfully, Batman in any universe is still a brilliant tactician, and sneaking into his own family's estate home is a non-issue. As the group skulks around the dilapidated Wayne Manor, they come across Killer Frost and Solomon Grundy doing some searching of their own. It's fightin' time.

BULL'S-EYE

Another mini-game so soon? Yep, and this one truly *is* different from anything else in the game. Green Arrow has to nock and fire arrows to repel the lumbering Solomon Grundy before he can get in striking distance. It's a fairly simple process at first—just aim with the left stick and fire using the on-screen prompts—Grundy begins chucking more knives and lobbing chairs Green Arrow's way with each round. Thankfully, the arrows don't have to be surgically precise, just hit some part of the incoming attacks. Don't forget to quickly switch back to attacking Grundy, though, since he's the true threat. Pepper him with enough arrows and the battle will begin with a nice health advantage. Let him get too close, though, and it's you who will need to overcome a damage deficit.

Opponent:	Solomon Grundy		Opponent:	Wonder Woman
Stage:	Wayne Manor		Stage:	Batcave

TIP *Grundy is surprisingly quick for his size, and unlike someone like Bane, he has a long-range option that includes a stomp to produce incapacitating hands underneath Green Arrow. Your agility while controlling Green Arrow is your best asset, along with being able to fire plenty of long-range projectiles. If Grundy gets in close, remember that the Interactive Objects at the edges and center of this Great Room can offer a quick escape.*

TIP *Wonder Woman is a formidable opponent because of her two-stance nature. When she's airborne, watch for longer-range attacks, including her lasso, which can daze. Stay close and try to keep the combos coming, then back off when she changes to her ground-based, sword-wielding stance. Her shield throw in this stance is quite quick, but Green Arrow's slide kick can help you sneak in for a few quick attacks before returning to ranged strikes.*

Once the hulking zombie is put out of commission by a well-timed Green Lantern swoop, a decidedly different threat presents herself. Killer Frost sends Wonder Woman to the deep chill and turns her attention on Green Arrow.

With this world's Wonder Woman out of the picture, it almost seems like the combined skills of the Insurgency have the situation under control, pulling Black Adam back down to ground level. A surprise blast incapacitates nearly everyone, though, leaving Green Arrow to subdue the Egyptian magician.

Opponent:	Killer Frost		Opponent:	Black Adam
Stage:	Wayne Manor		Stage:	Batcave

TIP *Like Grundy, Killer Frost has the ability to summon a ground-based attack that can strike with little warning. It's quick enough to interrupt attempts to use Interactive Objects (unless you Meter Burn them to absorb the attack) and along with her ranged attacks, she will keep you on your toes. Stay mobile, zipping in to pepper her with attacks that remove her knack for throwing projectiles. If attempting Green Arrow's Super Move, remember that it must hit at medium range, and Killer's Frost's ability to slide kick in to close distance can cause it to whiff.*

TIP *Black Adam's ability to summon objects that can then attack on a whim makes him difficult to anticipate. Though he has plenty of ranged options, he likes to play a closer game, using the orbs that surround his body to inflict extra damage. Use Green Arrow's ranged attacks to pester, and when Black Adam closes in, try to make the most of juggles (the Batcomputer in the background is a great way to heap on a bit of damage to a normal combo) to prevent him from summoning more magical assistants.*

As the crew at Wayne Manor clean up, Superman confides in his best friend, not knowing Lex Luthor is bankrolling the Insurgency, and reveals where the original universe's Batman is being held. This universe's Batman, as always, has a plan: a weapon he devised to take down Superman has been hidden in the long-abandoned Batcave. Using the DNA signatures of these doppelgangers, Batman is finally able to unearth the ultimate weapon to stop the Man of Steel. No sooner is it freed than Black Adam and Wonder Woman infiltrate the Batcave and a new set of duels begins.

Though the invading duo has been taken care of, the kryptonite-based weapon was damaged in the melee, and repairs will be necessary. The Superman incapacitation plan has hit a stumbling block.

Elsewhere, though, here's better news: back in the original universe, Superman is using the combined speed and intellect of The Flash and Cyborg to open his own portal to the alternate universe in the hopes of saving their friends. Unfortunately, an overload teleports Cyborg into the alternate universe where a case of mistaken identity has Cy facing down Deathstroke.

Opponent: Deathstroke

Stage: Insurgency

TIP Use Cyborg's ability to rip off and throw Interactive Object chunks of the level to your advantage. He's a Power character, but has a few projectile attacks of his own to help mix things up. Unfortunately, Deathstroke's repertoire

is based around his own ability to attack from afar, so get in close and really put Cyborg's heavy hitting attacks to good use. It can be difficult to close the distance once Deathstroke starts firing, so get in early and stay right on the mercenary.

Given Lex Luthor's reputation in the universe Cyborg just came from, it's understandable that he'd think this Lex Luthor was a villain too, so get ready for a tussle against ol' baldy.

Opponent: Lex Luthor

Stage: Insurgency

TIP It's a battle of the mechanical men here, but Lex Luthor is definitely the slower of the two. Use this to your advantage to zip in and land a few strikes, then back off to pepper the burly brawler with a few longer-range shots.

Lex Luthor's AI makes better use of his move sets this time around, so be wary of incoming orbital strikes and his ability to add armor. If he's glowing, switch to more powerful attacks to break through the added defenses.

Mercifully, Lex Luthor's allies show up to explain the situation to a very confused Cyborg. Meanwhile, Superman has followed their trail to the Batcave, and thanks to a few tiny shards of kryptonite, realizes what they're up to. Meanwhile, the assembled Insurgency goes over their plan of attack: the original universe's Batman is being held on Stryker's Island, and getting him out is going to take some high-powered distraction to offset the infiltration. Luckily, Cyborg's ability to disguise himself is perfect for a trip to the Hall of Justice—even if it means Deathstroke has to tag along. When this universe's Catwoman shows up, though, Cyborg's cover is blown.

Opponent: Catwoman

Stage: Hall of Justice

TIP Catwoman is fast, and she uses that speed to get in close to attack, given that she has no real long-range attacks. This, fortunately, is where Cyborg does his best work, so just keep on the attack to prevent Catwoman from throwing you off your rhythm.

Catwoman isn't the only enemy in this Great Hall. This universe's Cyborg knows himself quite well, and hacks into his double's systems. What follows is a good old-fashioned hack-off as the two try to breach each other's defenses before settling things the hard way.

Opponent: Cyborg

Stage: Hall of Justice

TIP Try to stay relatively close to your doppelganger, since as you well know by now, his ranged blast is great at preventing a quick rush in. There are plenty of Interactive Objects to grab and toss, and doing so early can

keep your menacing twin from doing the same to you.

Nothing stands in Cyborg's way now, and he and Deathstroke regroup to use the Hall of Justice's teleporter to head up to the Watchtower.

CHAPTER 7: DEATHSTROKE

Once again, the infiltration team splits up, with Deathstroke doing a little exploration. In a perfect show of his ability to pre-plan, a set of carefully placed explosives soften up The Flash and Shazam before he goes to work on them in earnest.

Opponent:	Shazam
Stage:	Watchtower

TIP *Welcome to the joy that is Deathstroke's ability to harass with the best of 'em. This wide open fight is a perfect chance to test out his various methods of laying down firepower, but even when Shazam gets in close, Deathstroke is well prepared to push enemies back. If you need breathing room, the shuttlecraft at the far left end of this upper level lets Deathstroke activate it and jump out of the corner.*

The Flash comes to just in time to realize his partner has already been taken out. With no choice but to engage Deathstroke, a new battle begins.

Opponent:	The Flash
Stage:	Watchtower

TIP *What happens when a character that has to get in close to cause any damage is up against a character that excels at keeping enemies away? You're about to find out. Play with the Interactive Objects in the Watchtower; Deathstroke's Gadget ability to plant explosives or just flip off objects can keep him away from close encounters. It also perfectly complements his long-range move possibilities. Those long-range attacks are great for when The Flash slows time to make his move toward you.*

With the barrier surrounding Batman's location dropped (plus the Watchtower's self-destruct activated for good measure), Deathstroke and Cyborg have a little chat with Lex Luthor, who elects to deal with his lifelong friend personally—so long as the Insurgency can find a weapon at Ferris Aircraft. Meanwhile, Harley can't deny her heart and lets The Joker go free even as Superman and The Flash back in the original universe prepare to make another attempt at opening a portal. Elsewhere, Wonder Woman and Killer Frost are using Ferris Aircraft computers to investigate the tears that pulled the characters across universes when Deathstroke returns to the very spot where he was tortured earlier. Payback time.

Opponent:	Killer Frost
Stage:	Ferris Aircraft

TIP *This second duel with Killer Frost plays out largely the same as with Green Arrow—keep moving to avoid any ice spike traps and unload with plenty of ranged attacks. The jet engine on the left end of the stage as well as the rockets at the far right both have plenty of uses, so don't forget about them in the heat of battle.*

Wonder Woman, not surprisingly, finds a way to slip her bonds after Killer Frost has been taken out, leaving Deathstroke no choice but to take aim at the Amazon.

Opponent:	Wonder Woman
Stage:	Ferris Aircraft

TIP *Deathstroke's ability to attack from afar will come in handy here, as Wonder Woman more or less has a run of the place with her Power abilities. Try to avoid the center of the level unless using the missile to create distance, and close the gap when Wonder Woman switches to her sword and shield stance. If attempting to use the tool chest or pressurized tanks, fire off a few rifle rounds to distract so your Interactive Object throws aren't interrupted.*

Lex Luthor's intel was right; Ferris Aircraft did indeed have a weapon that could be used against this world's Superman. Deathstroke grabs it while Batman and Green Arrow prepare to infiltrate Stryker's Island.

The breakout has begun, and Aquaman is ready with his distraction. Fear the lord of the seas as he rises from the water on the back of a giant... crustacean?! When it's joined by dozens of others, though, this little distraction doesn't seem quite as foolhardy. As Batman and Green Arrow cross Stryker's Island's Yard, however, Nightwing and Catwoman decide to complicate things. Time for a little reunion.

Opponent:	Catwoman
Stage:	Stryker's Island

TIP *Catwoman's speed, coupled with AI that is slowly becoming more and more capable of linking moves into combos and blocking simple attacks, can be a handful. Throws, thankfully, are still useful, and Batman's ability to place explosives on the weights and generator at the left and right ends of the Yard, respectively, can really help to punish Catwoman's need to strike from close range. Bait her in and plant an explosive as you leap away, but jump short to maximize follow-up attack potential.*

Nightwing certainly seems to be getting the upper hand on Green Arrow until Batman steps in and makes a surprising revelation: this red-suited version of Nightwing isn't Dick Grayson. It's Bruce's own son, Damian Wayne. After a gravely cutting remark, father and son begin their brawl.

Opponent:	Nightwing
Stage:	Stryker's Island

TIP *Never underestimate the power of daddy issues. Nightwing is fast, agile, and sports two different move sets. In his Staff stance, avoid jumping in where possible, as the staff has decent range and the AI will anticipate the move. When the staff breaks back into two clubs for his Escrima style, Nightwing has a ground-travelling electric spark to avoid. Try to hang back, controlling spacing with batarangs, and use the Grapple Lunge to close the distance to attack with high-damage combos. Parrying can also have fantastic results if you have the timing down.*

Aquaman's distraction is working like a charm. The onslaught is keeping Superman's forces busy while this universe's Batman and Green Lantern are able to slip in and release the original universe's Dark Knight. Just as they're about to escape, though, Raven introduces a wrinkle into things.

TARGET PRACTICE

With Raven controlling Green Arrow's actions, Batman has no choice but to try to close the distance before the arrows can hurt him. It's been a while since one of these mini-games, but this one basically plays out like the rest, only in reverse. Pay attention to the on-screen button prompts, and be ready to hit a button *sequence* (read: one at a time, not simultaneously) in the second round on. Should Batman make it to Green Arrow cleanly, he'll start the next fight with full health. Poor Green Arrow's probably going to have his pride bruised, though.

Opponent:	Green Arrow
Stage:	Stryker's Island

TIP *Green Arrow's ability to fire diagonally and horizontally can make getting in close a little difficult, but use sliding kicks and the Grapple Pull to slip in between shots and unload with everything you've got. Poor Oliver might be under Raven's control, but he still hits like he's giving it his all and the AI will make decent use of the Freeze Arrow to add more damage if you stay far enough away. Stay on top of him to overwhelm his ranged game.*

Her control broken, Raven finally opts to handle Batman more directly, but she's no match for *two* Batmen. The still-injured (and cowl-less) Batman clocks her in the head, and he and Green Arrow are able to slip out while the Batman from this alternate universe confronts Yellow Hal Jordan.

Opponent:	Yellow Lantern
Stage:	Stryker's Island

TIP *This yellow ring-wearing version of the Green Lantern is absolutely smitten with his ability to toss projectiles. He'll unload with his chain gun, blast away with fireballs, and regularly lift Batman whenever you're close. Rather than trying to trade projectiles, use Interactive Objects like the mounted turret to the left of this Cell Block area or the cryo tank on the right to freeze Hal in his tracks. A Level Transition attack back down to the Yard offers more objects to use against this Lantern if needed.*

No more distractions remain. Batman is finally able to meet up with his double and Green Arrow amid an absolutely brutal series of beatdowns by Superman. Wonder Woman is nearly strangled, Aquaman goes staff-less, Green Lantern nearly has his back broken... and that's all before Supes sees the Batmen escaping. A well-timed jump and teleportation one-two seem to make it clear where they're headed, and Superman rockets up to the Watchtower — right before the self-destruct Deathstroke initiated blows the whole station to bits. The Man of Steel easily shrugs off the blast, but as he looks to Earth, he hears a familiar voice.

CHAPTER 9: LEX LUTHOR

Time for a little time travel. Jumping back three hours, just as the plan to rescue Batman is starting to gel, Lex Luthor has put the finishing touches on his anti-Superman weapon. Clearly the decision to end a lifelong friendship is weighing heavily on him, but he downs one of the Kryptonian nanomachine pills, climbs into his suit, and heads to Metropolis. Along the way, a couple of homing missiles cut his flight short, but as it would happen, his subsequent crash reunites him with the now-free Joker and Harley. Taking orders from the clown now, Harley attacks.

Opponent: Harley Quinn

Stage: Metropolis

TIP *Lex Luthor's suit of armor makes him an extremely potent fighter—potentially one of the strongest in the game—but there's a trade-off: his normal movement is painfully slow. Thankfully, his dashes are fairly quick, and his ability to trade projectiles or slip in for seriously meaty blows should make short work of Harley. Being a Power character, he's got access to the nearby hovercar. After using one, another takes its place in a few seconds, so go to town.*

Let it never be said that The Joker isn't completely demented. If not for Lex Luthor's beam, the clown likely would have killed the one person that truly loved him. That might explain why he quickly attacks Lex Luthor.

Opponent: The Joker

Stage: Metropolis

TIP *The Joker's MO for this fight is to get in close and overwhelm Lex Luthor with his moves. Thankfully, the mechanized suit-wearing hero is more than capable of holding his own. In fact, his chest slam is a great way to quickly create distance, which can then be followed up with ranged attacks. Better still, Metropolis offers three distinct areas filled with Interactive Objects to throw The Joker's way.*

It's hard to blame Harley for wanting vengeance, but she shows some restraint when given the chance to do what The Joker couldn't—which is good, because over at Stryker's Island, things are getting rather intense. Green Lantern has to battle not just his double, but this universe's Hawkgirl and Black Adam. Thankfully, Lex Luthor's missiles take the heat off Green Lantern as Lex Luthor pulls the threats back into Metropolis for another showdown, does his best Top Gun impression, and fires off missiles that set Hawkgirl down in the Plaza at the Hall of Justice.

Opponent: Hawkgirl

Stage: Hall of Justice

TIP *Hawkgirl is quick, and has plenty of aerial attacks that should make it obvious that jumping around is a bad idea, but Lex Luthor has his Character Power, which adds armor to his already bulky suit. Use it to absorb impacts and pound the crap out of Hawkgirl, then retaliate with chest slams, the suck/blast combo of Gravity Pull, and some ranged attacks. Lex Luthor's Super Move also has the advantage of starting with four punches, any of which will kick off the final blow if they connect.*

Lex Luthor still has his eye on Hawkgirl's belt, but he's going to have to deal with Shazam first if he wants it. Thankfully, he *really* wants it.

Opponent: Shazam

Stage: Hall of Justice

TIP *Be especially wary of Shazam's fondness for using some of the various Interactive Objects around the Hall of Justice. In fact, since you're both Power characters, try to eliminate the extra interactive elements before he can use them, then remember to bulk up with Lex Luthor's Character Power (which won't interrupt a move if Shazam's lightning-powered barrel roll hits), and charge in for big hits.*

With the lingering threats of Shazam and Hawkgirl out of the way, it's time to call in their boss. Lex Luthor calls out to his friend, and prepares for the ultimate showdown—whoops, a last-ditch attack from Shazam fries Lex Luthor's circuits and destroys the last chance the Insurgency had of stopping Superman's One Earth reign.

CHAPTER 10: THE FLASH

Superman's cabal discusses the repercussions of not just a group of interlopers, but two Batmen now out in the wild. Though his supremacy seems assured now, Superman's actions have become brutal and dangerous. Dissent is sowed in the ranks and when one of their own is killed without hesitation, some of Superman's inner circle start to worry. The Flash finally can take no more, but before he's allowed to leave, he has to deal with a yellow ring-wearing Lantern.

TIP *You try telling a guy who can run at the speed of light that he should stop. Even Lantern's force field isn't enough to stop The Flash from vibrating through, but that doesn't mean there isn't going to be a fight before The Flash can leave.*

Opponent:	Yellow Lantern
Stage:	Fortress of Solitude

TIP *This Yellow version of the Green Lantern isn't all that different from his doppelganger, but The Flash represents the first character that you've played until now that doesn't have any ranged attacks. The Flash has to*

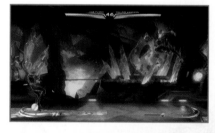

get in close, which isn't easy when there are so many projectiles flying, but thankfully his Character Power is slowing time — and projectiles.

Well look what overgrown undead simpleton is back from his suborbital trip. Time to see who wins in a fight of speed vs. strength.

Opponent:	Solomon Grundy
Stage:	Fortress of Solitude

TIP *Make the most of every opportunity to use The Flash's dash punch to tack on an extra hit or two any time an attack pops Solomon Grundy up into the air. He's a big guy who hits hard, and The Flash has to fight him up close,*

which means every hit needs to be made with the idea of producing as much damage as possible. Thankfully, the teleporter at the far right end of the stage works off a juggled character to add a chance to keep up the attacks, so use it often.

Having dealt with a Lantern and a zombie, The Flash is finally free to leave the Fortress of Solitude. As he screams toward Gotham City, he makes a slight detour to disarm a small army and confront Sinestro, who uses his ring to fling The Flash all the way over to the dusky Wayne Manor where the battle continues.

Opponent:	Sinestro
Stage:	Wayne Manor Night

TIP *The hardest part about fighting Sinestro is his ability to generate seemingly endless projectiles — and his Meter Burn version of them produces three times as many. Use The Flash's Character Power to slow time and zip in quickly*

to pepper Sinestro with hits that keep him juggled in the air. The left and right sides of this stage can be dangerous, but The Flash has the ability to slam Sinestro's head into the nearby car for big damage. Use a Level Transition attack near the right side if you want to head into the Great Room for a few objects The Flash can throw.

It took centuries to build the pyramids, but when you can run at the speed of light, you can build your own to house the leader of the Sinestro Corps in seconds. The Flash dashes away to join up with the Insurgency, but finds a suspicious Green Arrow preparing for battle.

Opponent:	Green Arrow
Stage:	Insurgency

TIP *Once again, this matchup seems a little unfair, with a ranged character being able to unload on The Flash. Slow time to get in close and pummel the archer, or take him for a tour around the Insurgency base by using Transition*

Attacks at the left edge of both levels of this stage.

With the Green Arrow's fears assuaged, The Flash works quickly to explain Superman's plans to the rest of the resistance.

CHAPTER 11: WONDER WOMAN

As the group works on a new plan, all hell breaks loose, and the secret base is compromised. Nearly every super-powered brawler at Superman's disposal has come to fight, starting with a juiced-up, Venom-powered Bane.

CHARMED BRACELETS

Bane should know better than to try to hurt Wonder Woman with mere bullets, but this mini-game gives you a chance to practice your button knowledge. Quickly tap out the sequence of numbers for the first few rounds, then mash *all* of them to keep the meter above the on-screen line to withstand the final burst of attacks and go into the following fight with full health.

Opponent:	Bane
Stage:	Insurgency

TIP *In a refreshing switch after having to constantly get in close, Wonder Woman has plenty of options for doling out punishment. Being a Power character (as is Bane), she can use the monitors in the center, or initiate a Level Transition attack to move to Luthor's Lab at the other end of the complex for more Interactive Objects. Stay on your toes while fighting Bane. His ability to absorb impacts and keep attacking can interrupt attempts at long combo strings. Stick to dishing out quick, guerrilla-style attacks to slowly whittle down his health.*

With Bane out of the picture, it's time to help defeat some of the other enem—whoops, teleported to Themyscira by none other than Ares. This won't be a friendly chat...

Opponent:	Ares
Stage:	Themyscira

TIP *The Amazonian home is littered with all manner of objects to be grabbed and thrown, and given the ability of Ares to dish out plenty of damage with his attacks, it's best to rip anything not bolted down and chuck it at him ASAP. The*  *AI likes to keep Ares as a short-range fighter, which suits Wonder Woman's sword and shield stance nicely.*

A defeated Ares shows Diana something troubling: a vast army of Amazons preparing for battle down at the Port. It would appear this universe's Wonder Woman is rallying her sisters for an all-out assault, but before the inevitable confrontation can take place, Raven must be dealt with first.

Opponent:	Raven
Stage:	Themyscira

TIP *This fight against Raven won't go nearly as easily as the last few. She's not just quick, she has ranged attacks that can hit from extremely far away and are difficult to anticipate fast enough to properly block. Try to stay in close*  *to avoid some of her projectiles, but keep up a steady defense and counter when an attack string is successfully blocked. The AI is starting to get really aggressive from this point on, and it'll use everything a character has to stop you.*

The original universe's Wonder Woman tries to reason with her double, but her words fall on deaf ears. If this army is to be dispersed, it will have to happen *after* their leader has been stymied with extreme prejudice.

Opponent:	Wonder Woman
Stage:	Themyscira

TIP *Mirror matches are always difficult, but Wonder Woman in the hands of the more advanced AI can be an absolute beast. She's quick while in her floating stance and brutal when using a sword and shield. Try to counter her stance*  *switches with some of your own, and don't be afraid to trash the place or take the fight back up to the Temple area above by using the right-most Level Transition area. Wonder Woman's fondness for throwing her shield in sword and shield stance can make getting in difficult, so use any Interactive Objects you can to damage, then close the distance.*

With her double out of commission, Wonder Woman is able to calm the ire of her sisters, explaining their true purpose as Amazons. Rather than stoking men's anger, they're meant to temper it, and with a rallying speech, she repurposes the army for the final confrontation with Superman's own. It's a good thing too, as Metropolis is a war zone, with Superman cutting off routes into and out of the city and using a controlled Doomsday to wreak havoc. With the battle raging above, the two Batmen debate their final options, and decide to settle their differences with fisticuffs.

Opponent:	Batman
Stage:	Batcave

TIP *Yet another mirror match has Batman fighting, well, Batman. Again, the AI here will use the full suite of moves, but Batman is more than capable of defeating himself using a careful combination of grapples, sliding kicks, and some of the lengthier combos found in our Character section. The key is to keep this world's Batman on the defensive, popping him up for juggled attacks so he can't do the same. Cape parries can also be effective, but be ready to block low to counter sliding kicks.*

Their differences settled, the Batmen decide there's only one option left: the portal that drew the original universe's Batman must be used again to bring Superman over to fight himself. Nothing else can stop him. As the portal hums to life, you can almost hear the John Williams refrain...

The Man of Steel gets the full rundown from Batman: things are bad, and they're only going to get worse as this world's Superman flexes his One Earth muscle. Up on street level, super-powered beings duke it out with seemingly no end in sight. They need a way to tip the scales. They need Superman. And Superman needs to teach Black Adam a thing or two about collateral damage.

TRAFFIC JAM

This final mini-game against Black Adam is the most intense of them all—not just because it requires precision and quick timing, and not just because it's the lengthiest of the bunch, but because if you miss shooting any of these cars by following the on-screen prompts, you'll start the upcoming match with less than full health (though at least Black Adam will as well if you managed to shoot him in between waves of thrown cars). Stay calm, and tap the buttons as they appear, rhythmically. The last thing you want to do at this point is second-guess a button press and end up eating a car.

Opponent:	Black Adam
Stage:	Gotham City

TIP Black Adam is deadly for all the same reasons he was when you first fought him as Green Arrow; he can conjure energy orbs that cause damage even as you attack him, can dole out tons of projectiles that hit when he wants them to, and hits with plenty of force even with normal attacks. Bait him into the left corner of the Alley to use a Level Transition while using Superman's heat vision in the air to chip away at his health, then Level Transition back down to the Alley to add more damage. The more you can eat away at that first life bar while keeping your own, the better your chances of felling this sorcerer and moving on.

Superman helps Adam cool down, bests Sinestro without a single punch, reminds Green Lantern of his true colors, and stops Aquaman's portable tsunami all in quick succession. Must be nice to be so powerful, but it's that last part that triggers yet another battle against this universe's lord of the seas.

Opponent:	Aquaman
Stage:	Metropolis

TIP The key to defeating Aquaman is in never letting him get close. Superman's airborne heat vision has a huge arc, and his dash punch is a fast way to create distance after it hits. Using the two together along with some of the heavier Interactive Objects around should make short work of this fight.

With the One Earth forces decimated, Superman needs only to find his double and beat some sense into him. But before he can do that, there's the little matter of a genetically modified killing machine. Superman grabs Doomsday and carries him to the Fortress of Solitude for the showdown you knew was coming.

Opponent:	Doomsday
Stage:	Fortress of Solitude

TIP The best way to overcome Doomsday's annoying overabundance of defense is to tap into Superman's Character Power. By juicing up his blows, even smaller combos can make a lasting impact. Better, though, is to try to lure him over to the right side of the stage, where the juggle-friendly Interactive Object and Level Transition area sit neatly close together. There's no better place to take a big chunk of life out of the monster than by linking these two together. Remember, too, that Superman's Super Move is the fastest in the game; nothing beats it—certainly not one of Doomsday's normal attacks, so once his first life bar is gone, let loose with the big punch.

With the ultimate anti-Superman weapon out of commission in the Phantom Zone, there's only one objective left: Superman himself. Steel yourself, because this one's going to be brutal.

Opponent:	Superman
Stage:	Fortress of Solitude

TIP Keep a close eye on your Character Power, and use it whenever available, because your double certainly will. If the Power isn't activated or recharging, you're wasting its potential. This tortured Superman will also throw quite a bit, so try to stay on the move, zipping in and out for quick Power-assisted combos. Be wary of thrown objects. If your double gets near an Interactive Object, he'll use it, so try to beat him to the punch early, and make sure your hits are juiced up whenever possible.

Pat yourself on the back as you enjoy the conclusion to the story. You've managed to save not one, but potentially two worlds from the despotic rule of a man driven mad by loss and grief. Who's to say the Superman from the original universe would have reacted any differently? Fortunately, it doesn't look like anyone else will have to find out. For completing Story Mode, you've earned the Godfall alternate Superman outfit to wear as a badge of honor. More challenges await in the rest of the Single Player modes, however. Are you ready for them?

BATTLES

Your ticket to some of the best XP gains available in Single Player, Battles present a set of themed challenges that can be undertaken in a variety of ways. In some cases, the character you'll play as is randomly chosen, and in all of them, the order and actual enemies you'll face is also randomized. As a result, there's no clear strategy here other than to get to know the whole roster as best you can to make the most of your character's attacks and avoid the AI's different moves when they attack.

That AI is tuned to become harder toward the final matches (usually 10 per Battle), so don't think things will be a cakewalk after the first few fights go smoothly. When coupled with an XP booster from the Archives, Battles can be a great way to quickly gain levels in a relatively short amount of time, getting you that much closer to new unlocks and customizations of your Hero Card. Finishing any Battle with a character unlocks his or her ending movie, viewable in the Archives.

The first few Battles are available from the start and are mostly self-explanatory, but the rest must be purchased in the Archives. Consider these default options a kind of training ground. Once you've gotten comfortable with the basics, you can head to the Archives and start buying new ones. (Don't forget to consult the Archives chapter to see where each Battle is hidden and use the descriptions below to find something that suits you.)

REGULAR

Objective: Defeat a series of randomly chosen heroes and villains set at your desired difficulty.

HEROES ONLY

Objective: Can you stand against the might of the world's most powerful heroes?

VILLAINS ONLY

Objective: Test your skill against the most dangerous villains the universe has ever known!

POISONED

Objective: Poison courses through your veins, constantly draining your health!

SURVIVOR

Objective: Your health meter carries over from match to match! Perform feats of exceptional skill to obtain bonus health.

TIP As the first possible Battle that can be unlocked in the Archives, Survivor presents an interesting added dimension to normal fights. That is, your actions determine how much of your health you get back between matches. Winning the match, connecting with a Super, and using Interactive Objects or Level Transitions all translate to a small measure of health restoration between fights. Use this to your advantage, capitalizing on the easier AI for the first few fights to make sure you're completely topped off before starting the next; use every interactible, use Supers, and try to avoid taking unnecessary damage.

MIRROR MATCH

Objective: Fight as your opponent in a series of mirror matches!

TIP There's no better way to learn to play as and against the entire cast than playing against your own character. Consult the previous Characters chapter for go-to combos and a deeper understanding of how to use your available moves; they'll be absolutely necessary for the later fights when the AI has been really cranked up.

MYSTERY

Objective: Each match grants a mystery buff or debuff to your fighter!

TIP Though it can often throw some curveballs in how it randomly assigns benefits or penalties, Mystery fights can mean huge XP rewards when coupled with a booster. Note that like Fully Charged, when your character's Super Meter is buffed, you can't actually use Super Moves, so Meter Burn every attack and Interactive Object throw if you're a Power character. Other buffs include wildly increased damage (great for the heavy hitters like Solomon Grundy, Lex, and Doomsday, but scary when you're up against them) and a speed increase that makes everyone faster than even The Flash normally is!

INJUSTICE
GODS AMONG US

FULLY CHARGED

Objective: Both you and your opponent have unlimited Super Meter, but Super Moves are disabled!

TIP Like the similar Mystery Battle variant, there's no Supers allowed here, but every other move can (and should) be Meter Burned. This is your chance to unleash some of the most potent combo strings in the game with no penalty to your Super Meter, so go nuts!

COMBO HEAVEN

Objective: You must perform a combo of the required number of hits and win the match! Transitions and Super Moves are disabled.

TIP Our Characters section is one of the best ways to learn some go-to strings that will meet the requirements for each fight. Note that they aren't necessarily the longest strings, but to win a fight, you'll often need to complete a string multiple times, which is why learning the timing of a character's best strings is so invaluable.

HELP FROM ABOVE

Objective: Your opponent's health will be restored to full every 30 seconds!

TIP Though the description says the opponent gets all their health back, what it actually means is that life bar. Don't be hasty here; concentrate on pounding out the biggest combos at the start of a countdown to eat away at the first life bar, then repeat after the next countdown. If you're ticking close to the end of another 30 second countdown and haven't chewed through at least 50% of the opponents life, go on the defensive and wait for the buff from on high before switching back to Heavy attacks. Always, always keep an eye on the clock. It's the ultimate decider in your offensive/defensive strategy.

INJURED

Objective: Begin each match with only a quarter of your maximum health!

TIP Defense is the name of the game here. You won't get any chances to gain back health, so while early fights aren't terribly difficult, all it takes is a longer string from the higher-tuned AI toward the end and you're out of commission. Use the environment as much as possible, and consider attempting this at least at first with a ranged character that can control space better than close-up characters like The Flash.

GIVE AND TAKE

Objective: You and your opponent gain health on each landed attack! You must defeat your opponent before time runs out.

TIP Though there is some limited scaling of the damage (meaning bigger characters that hit hard can gain a little more life back), the real trade here is in the number of hits. This is a combo-rich set of battles, where a nailed string can literally reverse the health situation if pulled off well. Don't attempt this Battle until you really know your character's moves inside and out.

SIDEKICK

Objective: Two opponents per match on a single arena will push your abilities to the max!

TIP The character groupings here tend to follow logical lines (so The Joker and Harley, Solomon Grundy and Doomsday, etc.). Effectively having to do double the number of fights, though, means huge XP payouts at the end if you can pull off multiple Supers and finish with plenty of health. Though it's unquestionably difficult toward the end, this is one of the best go-to XP grinding Battles in the game.

SPEED RUN

Objective: Can you defeat all of your opponents in under 3 minutes total?

TIP Don't be fooled by the description; while you do technically only have 180 seconds to finish off the entire ladder, simple actions like using Interactive Objects and Level Transitions adds more time to the clock. Use this to your advantage in the early fights by absolutely pouring on the attacks. Bounce Interactive Objects like fountains and computer terminals can be used over and over again to net more time, but consider using them as part of a combo to avoid getting penalized for whiffs by later opponents.

RANDOM FIGHTER

Objective: Fight each opponent with a randomly chosen hero or villain!

TIP Again, knowledge of the entire cast is your best tool here. Pausing to check out the moves list might help in the early fights, but knowing a move set inside and out is vital to surviving later. Of course, if you're looking for practice, this isn't a bad way to earn XP while doing it.

COUNTDOWN

Objective: You must defeat each of your opponents in under 30 seconds!

TIP It might go without saying, but we'll say it anyway: use heavy hitting characters at first to get a feel for just how quickly 30 seconds goes by. Don't think you can cheese this either by having more health than your opponent when the clock runs out; this is an all or nothing attempt, so go hard and fast.

UNSTOPPABLE!

Objective: Defeat all of your opponents without losing a single match!

TIP Some other Battles will let you continue if you fail the objective, but there's no such advantage here. You either rise to the top of the heap on your first attempt, or you start all the way at the bottom. Some of this can be a luck-of-the-draw setup, but plenty goes into character selection too. Who do you know best, and who can withstand the high-level AI best? Characters like Lex Luthor with his obscenely wide jumping Hard attack can add a little insurance, but this is still one of the last Battles for a reason.

THE MAX

Objective: You have one chance to defeat all of your opponents at maximum difficulty!

TIP The AI in Injustice, when cranked up to max difficulty, is about as cheap as you would imagine for a fighting game; button inputs are read instantly, leading to plenty of blocks of even long attack strings, to say nothing for its aggression and speed. Characters with knockback attacks and using the Hard unblockables are a great way to create precious seconds of breathing room, but the only way to win here is to use your longest, most effective combos to juggle and damage as much as possible. Anything else will simply be read and avoided.

FULL HOUSE

Objective: Try to defeat the entire cast of *Injustice*!

TIP This isn't quite as insane as it might sound. Pick the character you know the best and just get through one fight at a time. This is a marathon, but it's basically like going through the Story Mode without any of the cutscenes or context for the fight. You're going to make absolutely huge amounts of XP (especially with a booster) if you can make it through the whole gauntlet, so go here if you're looking to grind out some new levels to get new Archives unlockables.

IMPOSSIBLE!

Objective: Attempt to defeat the entire cast of *Injustice* with a single health meter!

TIP Okay, now we're starting to get a little insane. The biggest issue with Impossible! is that whole single health meter thing, but like Survivor, your actions during battle—from Super Moves (a big one) to Interactive Objects— will net you more health between fights. This is a marathon, not a sprint, so don't go taking heavy risks lest you get punished for them and have to carry that penalty forward into future fights. The longer you can go while maintaining your full health, the better off you'll be.

S.T.A.R. LABS MISSIONS

In order to train heroes from across the globe,
S.T.A.R. Labs has created a wealth of character-specific missions that
replicate a series of challenging circumstances to overcome. Try to achieve
three stars in every mission for the ultimate prize!

Think of the S.T.A.R. Labs offerings as bite-sized stories that do more with the basics of gameplay than any other mode could. This is the chance to get to know every character's move sets, but also have a little fun with their personalities and abilities. There's a frankly daunting number of challenges to play through — 240 of them in total — but they represent a way to get to know the ins and outs of the whole cast one character at a time, while allowing for more varied styles of gameplay.

We obviously can't cover tips for every one of these missions or we'd end up with a book you'd need super-strength to lift, but we've tried to pick out one interesting or especially challenging fight and outline how best to nab all three of those stars needed to unlock future challenges. Take the S.T.A.R. Labs a bit at a time. Take it from us; you really don't want to try to marathon the whole set, as there are more than a few shared themes between the characters, but there's absolutely no better way to break up the more straightforward gameplay of *Injustice* than to dip into the Labs for a few play sessions. Though they're a means to score some XP, don't consider S.T.A.R. Labs to be a major place to mine big XP gains for levels. That's exactly what the Battles are for.

SUPERMAN

GETTING STARTED

The Flash tries to reason with Superman about letting his emotions get in the way. Complete the moves listed on the top of the screen before saving Lois.

Mission 1
- » Strengthen your skills
- » Land a 5-hit combo
- » Execute a combo greater than 30%

THE YELLOW SUN

Determined to get past Bane, Superman uses the sun's power to build his strength. Stand in the rays of the sun to charge Superman's health.

Mission 2
- » Defeat Bane
- » Land a Level Transition
- » Win with 50 or more seconds remaining

KRYPTONITE BATARANGS

Lex has attached a mind-control device to Batman. Defeat Batman while avoiding his Kryptonite batarangs.

Mission 3
- » Defeat Batman
- » Use an Interactive object
- » Avoid getting hit by a Batarang

HEATING UP

Overcome the Alternate Superman that Lex brought to Earth. Hit the matching on-screen button to power up your heat vision.

Mission 4
- » Win the battle
- » Win without missing any button inputs
- » Cross the line 5 times

RAIN OF FIRE

Cyborg has been reprogrammed by Lex to take down Superman. Watch out for the falling debris from nearby buildings.

Mission 5
- » Defeat Cyborg
- » Win without getting hit by more than 5 pieces of debris
- » Connect 10 Special Moves

METEOR FROM KRYPTON

Superman has been weakened by Kryptonite dropped by Lex. Survive for 20 seconds without being hit by Catwoman's attacks.

Mission 6
- » Stay alive for 20 seconds
- » Land a 4-hit juggle combo
- » Throw twice

SAVE THE HUMAN

Lex's henchmen are attacking civilians. Protect the civilians by using your Heat Zap and Ground Smash to stop the incoming threats.

Mission 7
- » Save the citizen
- » Don't miss an incoming threat
- » Crush the bugs

NOXIOUS FUMES

Superman attempts to question Poison Ivy about Lois's location, but discovers Lex has freed The Joker and armed him with Kryptonite poison.

Mission 8
- » Defeat Joker
- » Win with a throw
- » Win without using any Special Ability

MAN OF STEEL

Three of the strongest villains in the universe have been sent to destroy Superman. Use your Super Move as the final blow.

Mission 9
- » Defeat all villains
- » Win using only punches
- » Connect 10 Special Moves on one opponent

KRYPTONITE PLATED

LexCorp has developed a Kryptonite energy source for Luthor's power armor. Damage Lex 10 times to deplete the energy source and save Lois.

Mission 10
- » Defeat Lex
- » Win without jumping
- » Win with a Super Move

BATMAN

SPARRING PRACTICE

Batman must hone his skills before going after Arkham's deadliest villains. Execute the moves listed on top of the screen to spar.

Mission 11
- » Show Nightwing how rusty you are
- » Land a 10-hit combo
- » Hit Nightwing 15 times in the head

BAFFLED BATS

Scarecrow's fear-inducing poison fills the air. Capture Raven before Scarecrow's madness overcomes Batman's reality.

Mission 12
- » Apprehend Raven
- » Use an interactive object
- » Win a Clash

GRENADES AND GRUNDY

Solomon Grundy, a zombie, is tough to damage with hand-to-hand combat. Use the undead grenades located around the Batcave to do significant damage.

Mission 13
- » Apprehend Grundy
- » Win without missing a grenade
- » Win without using grenades

PIE IN THE FACE

Stop The Joker and Harley from trying to escape Arkham. Avoid their attacks of incoming pies and chattering teeth to reach the evil duo.

Mission 14
- » Reach The Joker and Harley
- » Don't go backwards
- » Avoid 10 pies

KILLER CROC

Killer Croc has opened the cells in Stryker's Island. Use Batman's batarang to stop the prisoners from escaping.

Mission 15
- » Apprehend Killer Croc
- » Dodge 10 charges
- » Flawless Victory

DEATHSTROKE DESTROY

The Joker is covering Deathstroke's attempt to escape via an APC. Destroy the APC while avoiding incoming missiles from The Joker.

Mission 16
- » Destroy the APC
- » Win with at least 10 seconds remaining
- » Make 5 rockets hit the APC

EVIL DUO

Batman has finally caught up with The Joker and Harley again. This time stop the Evil Duo and send them back to Arkham!

Mission 17
- » Apprehend Harley and The Joker
- » Win using only Special Moves
- » Execute a combo greater than 30%

CAT NAP

While tracking Catwoman to a heist, Batman came upon an injured guard. Protect him by deflecting rockets with Batman's Parry.

Mission 18
- » Save the guard and stop Catwoman
- » Reflect the rocket at the last second
- » Don't miss a parry

HELI-BATTLE

Lex is trying to fly convicts out of the prison. Defeat the soldiers while avoiding helicopter gunfire, and then pick up a missile to take the helicopter down.

Mission 19
- » Destroy the helicopter
- » Survive 8 seconds while fighting the guards without getting hit
- » Execute a combo greater than 20%

DARK KNIGHT VISION

Bane, the last of the Arkham escapees, has shut down the power. Batman's night vision is fragile, so be careful not to get hit.

Mission 20
- » Apprehend Bane
- » Win with a throw
- » Never reach max Super Meter

CATWOMAN

CAT BURGLAR

Mission 21

Knock out the museum guards to access the roof by completing the list of displayed moves.

» Sharpen your skills
» Land a 10-hit combo
» Land 10 Low attacks

AVOID THE LIGHTS

Mission 22

In order to gain access into the museum, Catwoman must avoid the moving spotlights and destroy the air vent.

» Break into the museum
» Don't move backwards
» Complete the path backwards

ISIS

Mission 23

Use Isis to sneak past the guards in order to obtain information on the location of the Batcave.

» Reach the end of the museum
» Don't move backwards
» Meow 25 times

RUMBLE IN THE MUSEUM

Mission 24

Using Catwoman's nimble reflexes, defeat 20 guards in under 40 seconds before the alarm goes off.

» Defeat the guards
» Win without dashing
» Flawless Victory

SAFE CRACKER

Mission 25

The museum break-in led Catwoman to a safe at Wayne Manor. Hit Wayne's safe to crack it open within 30 seconds.

» Break into the safe
» Break into the safe using only Light attacks
» Win with more than 15 seconds remaining

BLOODLETTING

Mission 26

Catwoman was injured opening the safe containing the Batcave map. Complete the list of moves in the tracker before you pass out from blood loss.

» Complete the listed moves
» Complete the list in order
» Survive 8 seconds without being hit

BATTERS UP

Mission 27

Catwoman has finally found the Batcave, but bats are attacking! Kill the bats, but be sure not to get hit five times.

» Stop the bats
» Don't get hit by any bats
» Hit the red bat

CAT'S EYE

Mission 28

Nightwing should know better than to fight a cat in the dark. Use your goggles' night vision to defeat Nightwing.

» Defeat Nightwing with the lights out
» Destroy the Batrobot
» Win with a Level Transition

GOING UP?

Mission 29

Navigate Catwoman through the security system of lasers and traps in order to reach the Batcave's elevator.

» Reach the elevator
» Complete the path backwards
» Win without jumping

THE GETAWAY

Mission 30

Catwoman has finally located the Batmobile. Defeat both Nightwing and Batman, then activate the switch to release your prize.

» Steal the Batmobile
» Win with full second life bar
» Throw 6 times

THE FLASH

SPARKS

Mission 31

You must act quickly to stop Lex, but he's sent Deathstroke to slow you down. Attack him with the moves listed above to get by him, and back to your mission!

» Work on your skills
» Complete without missing a move
» Land a 6-hit juggle combo

THE SCARLET SPEEDSTER

Mission 32

Grundy is destroying Metropolis to distract The Flash. Save humans before they get crushed by falling debris.

» Defeat Grundy
» Get 10 citizens to safety
» Land an 8-hit combo

SLOW DOWN

Mission 33

Another roadblock! With only minutes until the bomb detonates, Grundy and Doomsday stand in your way. Use your Character Power to help defeat them.

» Defeat all villains
» Win without using Character Power
» Win with a Super Move

RACE AROUND THE WORLD

Mission 34

Race Superman around the globe to be the first to find info on Lex. Tap any button to fill the boost meter.

» Get there first
» Win by 50 laps
» Use only 1 boost

PRESSURE CHAMBER

Mission 35

Watchtower has info on Luthor, but Doomsday is depressurizing the station! The Flash must activate the switch on the left to close the airlock at the right time.

» Defeat Doomsday
» Don't lose any air
» Use no Super Meter

WHEN IT RAINS

Mission 36

Lex has sent Black Adam to place detonators at Wayne Manor. Defeat your enemy while avoiding falling debris from Watchtower.

» Defeat Black Adam
» Win with 30 or more seconds remaining
» Win after getting First Hit

GRUNDY SMASH

Mission 37

Grundy is trying to stop The Flash from disarming Lex's bombs. Avoid the rocks by using your Character Power to slow down time.

» Reach Grundy
» Avoid 15 rocks
» Don't duck any rocks

NICKED

Mission 38

Only Catwoman stands between you and Luthor! The Flash will regain his Character Power when the timer hits zero — use it to even the odds.

» Defeat Catwoman
» Win without using your Character Power
» Use your Character Power 4 times

LOCKED ON

Mission 39

Stop Lex from completing his evil plan. Eliminate Lex while avoiding the targeted laser strikes.

» Defeat Lex
» Survive 8 seconds without being hit
» Win a Clash

GO BOOM!

Mission 40

Luthor is trying to slow you down by using experimental shield technology. When Luthor's shield activates damage will be reflected back at the attacker.

» Defeat Lex
» Land a 4 Hit Juggle Combo
» Win without using Character Power

SHAZAM

STRENGTH OF HERCULES

Mission 41

Show Batman each of your moves at the top of the screen before starting the search for Black Adam.

» Become proficient with the power of SHAZAM
» Land a 6-hit juggle combo
» Execute a combo greater than 40%

POWER OF ZEUS

Mission 42

Black Adam cut all power to Ferris, which will melt down unless restored. Shazam can restore power by standing near the generators until fully charged.

» Keep all 3 generators powered up
» Win without using Character Power
» Connect 3 Meter Burn Special Moves and win

CLOUDY DAY

Mission 43

Black Adam took out a contract on your life. Defeat Deathstroke while avoiding the lightning strikes, which will turn Shazam back into Billy Batson.

» Defeat Deathstroke
» Execute a combo greater than 30%
» Win without filling your Super Meter to full

BLOOD BANK

Mission 44

Shazam and Lex have been infected with vampiric poison that regens health with each hit. Shazam is also bleeding out!!

» Win the battle
» Win a Clash
» Land a Level Transition

CAN'T SEE ME

Mission 45

Lex has brainwashed Cyborg and sent him after Shazam. Defeat a cloaked Cyborg and return to your search.

» Defeat Cyborg
» Survive 8 seconds without being hit
» Never reach max Super Meter

WISDOM OF SOLOMON

Mission 46

Lex is assisting Black Adam in obtaining an ancient Egyptian artifact. Complete the list of moves on the right side of the screen before time runs out.

» Complete the listed moves
» Complete the list in order
» Win with 20 or more seconds remaining

ANTARCTIC

Mission 47

Catwoman is locked in Arkham, but is protecting Black Adam's location. Penguin will attack the closest fighter to him with his umbrella.

» Defeat Catwoman
» Don't get put to sleep
» Get put to sleep 3 times

MERCURY'S SPEED

Mission 48

Reports are coming of Black Adam attacking Gotham! No time to waste. Soar through the air while smashing through the rocks.

» Reach the max distance
» Destroy 30 normal rocks
» Destroy 75 normal rocks

SHAZAM

Mission 49

You have finally caught up to Black Adam. Perform the higher-damaging combo to receive one letter of SHAZAM. First to spell out SHAZAM wins.

» Spell SHAZAM first
» Use an Interactive Object
» Use no Super Meter

AIR BATTLE

Mission 50

Black Adam has taken to the air! Blast him with everything you've got.

» Defeat Black Adam
» Win with at least 10% health or less remaining
» Destroy all Interactables

BANE

BODY BUILDER

Mission 51

Before Bane sets out to find more Venom, he must train. Execute each move at the top of the screen.

» Preserve your remaining supply of Venom
» Land a 4-hit juggle combo
» Land a 5-hit combo

ZAP ZAP

Mission 52

It seems that other villains are interested in the Venom as well. Defeat Harley while avoiding the lightning attacks.

» Defeat Harley
» Win with a lightning strike
» During a combo, have a lightning strike hit

GIVE ME LIFE

Mission 53

While searching a cave for Venom, Bane was bit by a vampiric bat. Each hit that lands will regain a portion of health lost during the fight.

» Defeat Deathstroke
» Connect 10 Special Moves
» Use no Super Meter

STAY ALIVE

Mission 54

Bane is weakened and desperately needs more Venom, but The Flash has been sent to protect the supply. Survive for 20 seconds without being hit by any attacks.

» Don't get hit for 20 seconds
» Use an Interactive Object
» Land 3 throws

VENOM RAGE

Mission 55

Continually use Bane's Character Power to regain life. Insufficient life regeneration will result in failure.

» Stay alive
» Juice 20 times
» Survive 8 seconds without being hit

PULVERIZE AND THRASH

Mission 56

You must retrieve more Venom. Defeat 20 Joker Thugs before time expires to get one step closer.

» Defeat the Joker's Thugs
» Use an Interactive Object
» Win with a full second Health Bar

ICE BOX

Mission 57

Stop Doomsday from getting the last of the Venom. Fight Doomsday while avoiding the falling ice conjured by Killer Frost.

» Defeat Doomsday
» Become frozen 10 times
» Win a Clash

FENDER-BENDER

Mission 58

Bane wants to keep Batman from being able to escape with the Venom. Destroy the Batmobile before time expires, and watch out for its defenses.

» Stop the Batmobile
» Win with 10 seconds remaining
» Make 12 rockets hit the Batmobile

JUICED UP

Mission 59

The lack of Venom is making Bane enraged! You have 15 seconds to defeat Nightwing and advance towards the Venom supply.

» Win before time runs out
» Win without jumping
» Win with a throw

BREAK THE BAT

Mission 60

You must weaken Batman and perform Bane's Backbreaker. Defeat Batman to obtain the Venom you so badly need.

» Break the Bat
» Break the Bat on your first try
» Land a Level Transition

HARLEY QUINN

BEST SERVED COLD

Mission 61

Harley's first stop to find answers begins with Batman. Execute each move at the top of the screen to reach the next location.

» Introduce Batman to your skills
» Land an 8-hit combo
» Land 40 chest hits

HIGH NOON

Mission 62

If there was a contract on The Joker, Deathstroke probably had it. Execute the command at the top of the screen just as time hits zero to outdraw Deathstroke.

» Defeat Deathstroke
» Win all 5 shots
» Shoot at the last second

DEADSHOT

Mission 63

Harley has been ambushed! Stay alive for 60 seconds while dodging incoming rockets and grenades.

» Stay alive for 60 seconds
» Win without dashing
» Win without jumping

TWO-FACE

Mission 64

Stop Catwoman and find the answers you're looking for. Two-Face is on the scene, and will flip his coin to determine who he'll shoot next.

» Defeat Catwoman
» Survive 15 seconds without being hit
» Connect 3 Meter Burn Special Moves and win

THUG'S LIFE

Mission 65

Harley thinks a band of Joker's Thugs are behind Joker's death. Stop enough of the Joker thugs by pressing the correct button sequence.

» Stop the Joker Thugs
» Hit 16 Joker Thugs
» Perfect aim

SIDE SPLITTING

Mission 66

This Joker Thug might have info. Shoot the pies and chattering teeth.

» Stop the attacks
» Don't miss an object
» Land a hit with less than 5 seconds left

KISSES!

Mission 67

The last battle has left Harley injured and her health is depleting. Use your Character Power to regain health. Contain Catwoman long enough to get answers.

» Defeat Catwoman
» Perform 75 kisses
» Win with a Super Move

CAT GOT YOUR TONGUE

Mission 68

Now that Harley has Catwoman alone, she can finally get some answers. Press the correct buttons to keep both meters above the lines until time runs out.

» Complete the mission
» Win with 1 full meter
» Win without dropping below 25% stress

PIPSQUEAK

Mission 69

The trail has led Harley to Luthor, who has shrunk her down with an experimental weapon. Jump and slide to avoid the lasers while collecting cubes to weaken Lex's defenses.

» Reach the end
» Perform a slide 10 times
» Collect all of the Nanocubes

DECEPTION

Mission 70

Luthor has the answers Harley is looking for! Get Lex to tell you why The Joker faked his demise.

» Stop Lex
» Land a 4-hit juggle combo
» Never reach max Super Meter

DEATHSTROKE

TRAINED PROFESSIONAL

Mission 71

Deathstroke wants to test his skills before his next contract. Execute each move at the top of the screen.

» Learn your trade
» Land a 6-hit juggle combo
» Connect 10 Special Moves

NEVER ENOUGH

Mission 72

Fire a grenade at Green Arrow. Each shot is affected by wind.

» Defeat Green Arrow
» Hit with first shot
» Don't miss

ASSASSIN'S STRIKE

Mission 73

Deathstroke must progress past the rock trap. Slice incoming attacks.

» Slice the rocks
» Don't miss a rock
» Swing 75 times

BURN WITH ME

Mission 74

Another day, another target to eliminate. Time your movements carefully to avoid the erupting fire.

» Defeat Harley
» Never reach max Super Meter
» Win without jumping

BOMB, SHIELD, AND SWORD

Mission 75

Bomb beats Sword, Shield beats Bomb, Sword beats Shield.

» Win best out of 5
» Perfect score
» Tie 5 times

TARGET ACQUIRED

Mission 76

Lex is trying to stop you from completing your contract. Eliminate Green Lantern while avoiding the targeted laser strikes.

» Defeat Green Lantern
» Win after getting First Hit
» Connect 3 Meter Burn Special Moves and win

PIPE BOMB

Mission 77

You must get past the pipes to get to your contract. Press the corresponding button on screen to shoot a bomb at a selected pipe. Time your shot when steam is not present.

» Hit the pipes
» Don't miss a bomb
» Hit the fire

LASER TARGETING

Mission 78

In order to fulfill your contract on Bane, you must battle him while avoiding the laser hazards triggered by Luthor's men.

» Defeat Bane
» Get hit by 10 lasers
» Hit Bane with 10 lasers

NOW YOU SEE ME

Mission 79

Deathstroke has located his next two targets. Eliminate Cyborg and Lex while their cloaking devices are active.

» Defeat Cyborg and Lex
» Win after getting First Hit
» Win with a Super Move

EAGLE EYE

Mission 80

Lex isn't getting away this time! When he launches his missiles into the air, destroy them before causing additional damage.

» Stop Lex
» Hit all missiles
» Win without using combos

GREEN ARROW

THE EMERALD ARCHER

Mission 81

Green Arrow wants to train before fulfilling his father's dying wish. Execute each move at the top of the screen.

- » Follow through with your skills
- » Land an 8-hit combo
- » Land a 4-hit juggle combo

WHITE OUT

Mission 82

Time to cross Lex's name off the list. You have been blinded by a flash grenade. Take down Lex while your vision is impaired.

- » Defeat Lex
- » Survive 8 seconds without being hit
- » Win with a Level Transition

CROWD CONTROL

Mission 83

Green Arrow has tracked a group of corrupt police officers from the list. Shoot the correct arrows at the oncoming color-coded officers.

- » Win the battle
- » Don't use the wrong arrow type
- » Use wrong arrow type 3 times

SEA KING

Mission 84

Aquaman has been brainwashed and only Green Arrow can stop him. While underwater your movements will be slower.

- » Defeat Aquaman
- » Never reach max Super Meter
- » Win with a throw

BIG SHOT

Mission 85

Merlyn is impersonating Green Arrow. Shoot at him. Each shot is affected by wind.

- » Win the battle
- » Land the first hit
- » Don't miss

SHARPSHOOTER

Mission 86

Press the correct buttons to stop the robot soldiers. This elite force is protecting those in the black book. Stop at least 13 robots.

- » Hit 13 targets to progress
- » Hit 16 targets
- » Perfect score

GLASS HOUSE

Mission 87

Killer Frost, number six in the black book, has set off a cave-in in the Batcave. Be careful of your attacks or you might accelerate the damage.

- » Survive the collapse
- » Win with a Super Move
- » Win after getting First Hit

THE HARDER THEY FALL

Mission 88

According to the list, Green Arrow must put an end to Sinestro. Over the course of the fight he will become more powerful.

- » Defeat Sinestro
- » Land a Level Transition
- » Win before Sinestro reaches his max difficulty

AIM HIGH

Mission 89

As the falling rocks plummet, run over to their corresponding locations and shoot upwards to destroy them.

- » Destroy the rocks
- » Don't whiff with an arrow
- » Don't get hit

BROKEN ARROW

Mission 90

If Bane inflicts too much damage, Green Arrow will drop his bow. Pick it back up, and regain your abilities.

- » Defeat Bane
- » Win after getting First Hit
- » Win after getting First Hit

LEX LUTHOR

SUIT UP

Mission 91

Security is malfunctioning! Lex must navigate past security lasers and drones to reach his power suit.

- » Locate Lex's Armor
- » Don't get hit
- » Jump 20 times

ENTER LEX

Mission 92

Lex must train with his new power suit before his mission to Atlantis. Execute each move at the top of the screen.

- » See what the power suit can do
- » Land a 4-hit juggle combo
- » Throw 6 times

THERE AND BACK AGAIN

Mission 93

Cyborg has been sent to defeat Lex before he reaches Atlantis. Move your energy shield to deflect Cyborg's bouncing rockets.

- » Defeat Cyborg
- » Score the first point
- » Perfect score

ORB MALFUNCTION

Mission 94

Lex's plan to take Atlantis interferes with Killer Frost's desire to freeze the planet. Her cold presence causes one of Lex's orbs to malfunction and attack Lex every 10 seconds.

- » Defeat Killer Frost
- » Win without using a Character Power
- » Win with a Super Move

PULLING THE TRIGGER

Mission 95

Malfunctioning orbs are attacking Lex. Shoot at the orbs by pressing the correct button on screen. Stop at least 13 orbs to advance.

- » Hit 13 targets to progress
- » Hi 16 targets
- » Perfect score

BURN THE EVIDENCE

Mission 96

Defeat the enemies to recover pieces of evidence that would expose Lex's plan.

- » Destroy every piece of evidence
- » Collect all pieces of evidence before burning
- » Never reach max Super Meter

LANTERN'S DEFENSE

Mission 97

Green Lantern will do everything in his power to keep Lex from Atlantis. Over the course of the fight Green Lantern will become more powerful.

- » Defeat Green Lantern
- » Win before Green Lantern reaches his max difficulty
- » Win a Clash

AIR STRIKE

Mission 98

In order to reach Atlantis you must first weaken the outer defenses. Press the on-screen buttons to destroy each target. Destroy 25 mines to progress.

- » Stop 25 mines
- » Stop 40 mines
- » Stop 50 mines

GO DEEP

Mission 99

It is time for Lex's assault! Avoid depth charges while diving to reach Atlantis. Collect air bubbles to fill your oxygen meter.

- » Reach Atlantis
- » Avoid all depth charges
- » Collect 20 air bubbles

BIG FISH

Mission 100

Defeat Aquaman while he is powered up to take Atlantis. Your movements will be slower underwater.

- » Defeat Aquaman
- » Win without using Character Power
- » Never reach max Super Meter

NIGHTWING

WOKE UP TIED UP

Mission 101

Break free from the gurney by using the displayed button commands. Once free, defeat your captors by executing the moves at the top of the screen.

- » Break free and defeat the guards
- » Land an 8-hit combo
- » Throw twice

HIDE AND SEEK

Mission 102

Now that Nightwing has escaped his confines, use your night vision to navigate past the security lasers. You have 40 seconds to reach the end.

- » Reach the end
- » Win with 20 or more seconds remaining
- » Win with 10 or more seconds remaining

BAD GAS

Mission 103

Standing within Solomon Grundy's gas cloud causes Nightwing damage. Defeat Grundy as the gas cloud grows over time until the screen is covered.

- » Defeat Grundy
- » Connect 10 Special Moves
- » Connect 3 Meter Burn Special Moves and win

DEAD MAN'S HAND

Mission 104

Grundy is back for more, defeat him while avoiding the Swamp Hands. The Swamp hands can be destroyed with Nightwing's projectile attacks.

- » Defeat Grundy
- » Survive 8 seconds without being hit
- » Destroy 10 Swamp hands

STICKS OF FURY

Mission 105

Show Bane who's the boss by landing 50 hits on him before time expires.

- » Defeat Bane
- » Win without using Character Power
- » Land a 10-hit combo

FREEZER BURN

Mission 106

Killer Frost has conjured an ice storm. Defeat her while avoiding the falling ice.

- » Defeat Killer Frost
- » Win with full second Health Bar
- » Win a Clash

PAINT THIS

Mission 107

Sinestro and Raven team up to take down Wayne Manor. Nightwing must stop Sinestro while avoiding incoming projectiles thrown by Raven.

- » Defeat Sinestro
- » Win after getting First Hit
- » Hit 10 times to the head

LOOK OUT!

Mission 108

Use night vision to navigate past the security lasers and watch out for the guards. You have 60 seconds to reach the end.

- » Reach the end
- » Win with 20 or more seconds remaining
- » Win with 10 or more seconds remaining

JUST ADD WATER

Mission 109

While underwater Nightwing's movements will be slower. Aquaman fights at normal speed.

- » Defeat Aquaman
- » Win with a throw
- » Never reach max Super Meter

THAT'S THE BOMB

Mission 110

Defeat Raven while she is in Demon stance.

- » Defeat Raven
- » Use no Super Meter
- » Perform an 8-hit juggle combo

GREEN LANTERN

SHINE BRIGHT

Mission 111

Before Green Lantern sets out on his hunt for Sinestro, he must train. Execute the moves at the top of the screen.

- » Become acquainted with your green Power Ring
- » Land a 15-hit combo
- » Hit 20 times to the legs

ARMAGEDDON

Mission 112

Use the correct button commands to shoot down approaching meteors. Large meteors require you to mash all buttons.

- » Save the earth from doom
- » Don't miss a rock
- » Allow 5 rocks to come close

SCARECROW

Mission 113

Deathstroke has a contract to protect Sinestro from Hal, and has allied himself with Scarecrow. Stop them before the madness overcomes Hal.

- » Defeat Deathstroke
- » Win without using Character Power
- » Land a 4-hit juggle combo

HEADACHE

Mission 114

Luthor has taken control over Doomsday. Perform enough head attacks to break Doomsday free from Lex's strings.

- » Break the mind control
- » Survive 15 seconds without being hit
- » Win after getting First Hit

NONE SHALL PASS

Mission 115

Green Lantern has come across Bane for the last time. Defeat him while avoiding exploding floor fires conjured by Raven.

- » Win the battle
- » Don't get hit by the explosions
- » Use an explosion in a combo

FROZEN SKIES

Mission 116

Killer Frost has conjured an ice storm. Defeat her while avoiding the ice shards. An unknown force has sped up your movement.

- » Defeat Killer Frost
- » Win a Clash
- » 5 falling ice blocks

KILOWOG

Mission 117

Kilowog has arrived to help Green Lantern. When near, he will deliver a powerful attack.

- » Defeat Joker
- » Don't use Kilowog
- » Throw 6 times

OUTFIELD

Mission 118

Defend against Sinestro's constructs coming from the air.

- » Swing at the constructs
- » Don't miss a construct
- » Swing 85 times

GREEN LANTERN'S LIGHT

Mission 119

Use all of your might to defeat Sinestro! Once Sinestro's health is low, execute the commands to overpower him.

- » Win the ring battle
- » Execute a combo greater than 30%
- » Connect 10 Special Moves

ULTIMATE BATTLE

Mission 120

Sinestro has taken to the air. Blast him with everything you can.

- » Defeat Sinestro
- » Win with 10% health or less remaining
- » Destroy all Interactive Objects

CYBORG

REBIRTH

Mission 121

Pick up weapons to gain Special Moves to add to Cyborg's arsenal. All Specials have been disabled.

- » Defeat Raven
- » Connect 10 Special Moves
- » Win without picking up a weapon

TRAINING CAMP

Mission 122

Execute each move at the top of the screen in an attempt to gain control of your abilities.

- » Learn your new abilities
- » Land an 8-hit juggle combo
- » Execute a combo greater than 40%

SPRUNG A LEAK

Mission 123

The strain on your new abilities has caused some side effects. Defeat Grundy before Cyborg drains of fluids.

- » Defeat Grundy
- » Win with full second Health Bar
- » Win with a Super Move

WHAT IS YOUR MALFUNCTION

Mission 124

Cyborg is malfunctioning and his controls are not responding correctly. Defeat Bane with Cyborg's controls reversed.

- » Defeat Bane
- » Never reach max Super Meter
- » Win after getting first hit

BROKEN LEGS

Mission 125

The electrified floor defense mechanism has disabled Cyborg's jumping capabilities. Use Cyborg's grapple move to avoid the electricity.

- » Stop Lex
- » Win a Clash
- » Win with a throw

ROCKET! ROCKET!

Mission 126

Lex Luthor, the brains behind your attempted kidnapping, has sent waves of missiles towards you. Seven hits results in failure, so try to avoid them.

- » Avoid the rockets
- » Don't get hit by a rocket
- » Win with one chance remaining

NEED A NURSE

Mission 127

The last battle strained Cyborg's systems and damaged his life support. Use your Character Power to regain health.

- » Defeat Catwoman
- » Win with full health
- » Win without using Character Power

ERROR MACRO

Mission 128

Destroy Luthor's "Defense System 01" prototype robot before it powers up. Be careful, as Lex is attacking you with lasers from a safe location.

- » Destroy Defense System 01
- » Win with 5 seconds or less remaining
- » Win with 10 seconds or more remaining

LUTHOR BEATDOWN

Mission 129

With Cyborg back to full power, he must defeat Lex while performing the moves listed in the tracker before time runs out.

- » Complete the listed moves
- » Complete the list in order
- » Execute a combo greater than 30%

INJUSTICE FOR ALL

Mission 130

The Justice League is impressed with your skills in defeating Luthor. Show them what you are made of.

- » Impress the Justice League
- » Win with full second health bar
- » Execute a combo greater than 40%

HAWKGIRL

HAWK'S NEST

Mission 131

Hawkgirl wants to train before heading out to face Luthor. Execute each move at the top of the screen.

- » Mold your Thanagarian combat skills
- » Land a 4-hit juggle combo
- » Connect 10 Special Moves

HIGH TENSION

Mission 132

Luthor has captured Cyborg and mind controlled him to protect his secret. Lex's security system is active, so jump to avoid the electric floor.

- » Defeat Cyborg
- » Don't get electrocuted by the floor
- » Win a Clash

CAN OPENER

Mission 133

Hawkgirl has retrieved Cyborg, but she can't wait until his cybernetics are repaired. Press the correct buttons to keep the 4 meters above the lines to get answers.

- » Complete the mission
- » Win with 1 full meter
- » Keep all meters above the line

SCARED HAWK

Mission 134

Bane has teamed up with Scarecrow to stop Hawkgirl. Defeat Bane before the madness overcomes Hawkgirl.

- » Defeat Bane
- » Land a 30% combo
- » Throw 6 times

SOARING HAWK

Mission 135

There is a crisis in Gotham! Hawkgirl must get there as quickly as possible. Soar through the air while smashing through the rocks.

- » Reach the max distance
- » Destroy 30 normal rocks
- » Destroy 75 normal rocks

FALLING MACE

Mission 136

Deathstroke has been hired to stop Hawkgirl. If too much damage is inflicted, she will drop her mace.

- » Defeat Deathstroke
- » Connect 3 Meter Burn Special Moves and win
- » Win with a Super Move

DISTRESS CALL

Mission 137

A distress call has gone out from Watchtower! Reach the station by flying upward while avoiding the falling rocks.

- » Complete the mission
- » Win with one hit remaining
- » Win without getting hit

FORTITUDE

Mission 138

Hawkgirl has arrived just in time at Watchtower. Stop each of the evil invaders before it's too late.

- » Defeat everyone
- » Never reach max Super Meter
- » Win with 10% health or less remaining

THE POWER OF NTH

Mission 139

Lex has promised Ares a weapon made of Nth if he helps him defeat Hawkgirl. Complete the list of moves in the tracker before time expires to obtain Lex's whereabouts.

- » Defeat Ares
- » Win without flying
- » Survive 8 seconds without being hit

MAJOR DAMAGE

Mission 140

If too much damage is inflicted, Luthor will activate his special Satlaser. Continuously attack him to interrupt the attack.

- » Defeat Lex
- » Win without getting hit by a laser strike
- » Use no Super Meter

THE JOKER

JOKER'S WILD

The Joker has made his way out of his cell and is ready to get back to his old tricks. Execute each move at the top of the screen.

Mission 141

- » Retain your sense of humor
- » Connect 10 Special Moves
- » Execute a combo greater than 30%

RIDDLE ME THIS

Nightwing has caught wind of The Joker's escape from Arkham. Each question mark The Riddler drops will contain a random effect.

Mission 142

- » Defeat Nightwing
- » Pick up 10 Question Marks
- » Win without using combos

HEART BROKEN

Harley is trying to get in on The Joker's fun! Over the course of the fight she will become more angry.

Mission 143

- » Defeat Harley
- » Throw twice
- » Win after Harley reaches her max difficulty

CATNIP

Catwoman doesn't like the idea of competing with The Joker! While fighting Catwoman, fend off Isis by performing the on-screen commands.

Mission 144

- » Defeat Catwoman
- » Win without missing any button inputs
- » Win with full second Health Bar

JOKER VENOM

Joker's Thugs are raining poison all over Gotham to cause havoc! Defeat Green Arrow while avoiding poisonous rain.

Mission 145

- » Defeat Green Arrow
- » Win without jumping
- » Win with Heavy Attack

DOWNSIZED

The Joker forces Atom to shrink in order to collect Lex's deadly nanobot technology. Execute the correct button commands to reach the finish line.

Mission 146

- » Reach the end
- » Collect all nanocubes
- » Perform a slide 10 times

SLOW ME DOWN

Hawkgirl is helping Killer Frost take back the nanobot tech you just stole. Mash any button to break free from the ice and defeat her.

Mission 147

- » Defeat Hawkgirl
- » Break free 5 times
- » Execute a combo greater than 20%

BOMBS AWAY

The Joker needs to destroy part of Arkham Asylum and free his henchmen. Plant bombs at all 3 locations. You have 60 seconds.

Mission 148

- » Plant all bombs
- » Win without getting hit while planting
- » Survive 8 seconds without being hit

HEADS OR TAILS

Catwoman is back, but this time The Joker won't let her get away! Two-Face will also flip his coin to determine who he'll shoot next.

Mission 149

- » Defeat Catwoman
- » Win with Light Attack
- » Throw 6 times

IT TAKES TWO

To even the odds, The Joker has joined forces with his beloved Harley. Harley Quinn will aid in your fight.

Mission 150

- » Defeat Batman
- » Never reach max Super Meter
- » Win without using Harley Quinn

DOOMSDAY

IT BEGINS

Doomsday has been captive for years, and must train before seeking his revenge. Execute each move at the top of the screen.

Mission 151

- » Rejuvenate your combat skills
- » Complete without missing a move
- » Hit Nightwing 15 times in the head

RIDDLE ME THAT!

Get Lex to tell you the location of Superman by defeating him. Defeat Lex while The Riddler drops surprises.

Mission 152

- » Defeat Lex
- » Pick up 10 Question Marks
- » Never reach max Super Meter

DEMONSTRATION OF POWER

Green Lantern has arrived in Metropolis to stop Doomsday. Mash any button to push back the incoming bus construct.

Mission 153

- » Stop the bus construct
- » Win with 10 or more seconds remaining
- » Win with 1 second remaining

POISON TOUCH

The Flash has been infected with a toxic contagion, but that won't stop Doomsday! The last one hit will be infected with the virus.

Mission 154

- » Win the battle
- » Use no Super Meter
- » Land a 12-hit combo

FALLING ICE

Killer Frost has conjured an ice storm. Defeat her while avoiding the falling ice.

Mission 155

- » Defeat Killer Frost
- » Become frozen 10 times
- » Win a Clash

SUPER POWER

Break through Lex's shield to stop him from unleashing a devastating attack.

Mission 156

- » Defeat Lex
- » Win without getting hit by a laser strike
- » Never reach max Super Meter

WASPS' NEST

Looks like a Justice League trap! Destroy all the wasps before they can damage you with their venomous sting 10 times, knocking you out.

Mission 157

- » Stop the wasps
- » Don't get hit by any wasps
- » Stop the fire wasp

DOOMSDAY'S REVENGE

Defeat Green Lantern while he is powered up.

Mission 158

- » Defeat Green Lantern
- » Win without using Character Power
- » Execute a combo greater than 40%

SEARCH FOR SUPERMAN

Further weaken the Justice League by defeating Wonder Woman. Avoid being hit by the tentacles that have joined the fight to help protect Superman.

Mission 159

- » Defeat Wonder Woman
- » Don't get hit by any tentacles
- » Win with a tentacle attack

D-DAY

Time has come to exact your revenge! Stop Superman while he is enraged. With Superman's death, your vengeance on the Justice League will be complete.

Mission 160

- » Defeat Superman
- » Hit 10 times to the head
- » Win with a Level Transition

SINESTRO

SINESTRO CORPS

Mission 161

Now that he is free again, Sinestro must hone his dormant skills. Execute each move at the top of the screen.

» Familiarize yourself with the yellow Power Ring
» Land a 6-hit juggle combo
» Hit 20 times to the legs

OA NOES

Mission 162

A deadly assassin has been sent to stop Sinestro. Execute the command at the top of the screen just as time hits zero to outdraw Deathstroke.

» Defeat Deathstroke
» Win all 5 exchanges
» Shoot at the last second

SLIPPERY WHEN WET

Mission 163

While underwater Sinestro's movements will be slower. Aquaman fights at normal speed.

» Defeat Aquaman
» Win after getting First Hit
» Throw twice

SEE YOU NEXT FALL

Mission 164

Sinestro has discovered that Lex has possession of a Lantern's ring. Break through the ring's shield while avoiding the laser hazards.

» Defeat Lex
» Use no Super Meter
» Hit Lex with 10 lasers

GREEN WITH ENVY

Mission 165

Show Green Arrow how much the color green reminds Sinestro of the Lanterns. Land 60 hits before Green Arrow does.

» Win the battle
» Land a Level Transition
» Don't let your opponent reach 30 hits

IN THE WIND

Mission 166

Green Lantern jumps in to protect Earth! Hold for a more powerful shot and watch out for the wind.

» Win the battle
» Hit with first shot
» Don't miss

TO RULE THEM ALL

Mission 167

Catwoman has obtained a red Power Ring and has gained new powers. Defeat Catwoman while she uses the red Power Ring against you.

» Retrieve the ring
» Survive 8 seconds without being hit
» Connect 3 Meter Burn Special Moves and win

OUT OF OPTIONS

Mission 168

As the mines appear, press the on-screen buttons to destroy each target. Smash at least 30 mines.

» Stop 30 mines
» Stop 40 mines
» Stop 50 mines

SINESTRO'S POWER

Mission 169

Sinestro must protect the Earth from meteors so that he may rule it. Use the correct button commands to shoot down approaching meteors.

» Save the Earth from doom
» Don't miss a rock
» Allow 5 rocks to come close

BACKUP

Mission 170

Atrocitus has arrived to help Sinestro take control of Earth. When near Atrocitus he will deliver a powerful attack.

» Defeat Green Lantern
» Win without using Atrocitus
» Connect 10 Special Moves

RAVEN

REGAINING CONTROL

Mission 171

Raven's inner-self is surfacing! Train to regain control by executing each move at the top of the screen.

» Regain control of yourself
» Land a 10-hit combo
» Complete without missing a move

BLEEDING OUT

Mission 172

The struggle with your inner-self is causing you to bleed out and lose all of your health.

» Defeat Killer Frost
» Win a Clash
» Win with a Super Move

RAVEN ATTACK

Mission 173

Use the Shadow Raven to destroy the incoming bats.

» Defeat the bats
» Don't get hit
» Destroy 5 or more bats at once with an explosion

ROCK N ROLL

Mission 174

Reach Bane before he crushes you with heavy boulders.

» Complete the mission
» Avoid 15 rocks
» No ducking

FRIEND IN NEED

Mission 175

Raven's rage has put Nightwing in great danger! Free him by executing the sequence of on-screen commands.

» Save Nightwing
» Win with 10 seconds or more remaining
» Win without missing a button

TITANS GO

Mission 176

The demon Trigon has possessed Raven to hurt her friends! Defeat the Titans.

» Win the battle
» Win with a Super Move
» Never reach max Super Meter

TRIGON'S PAIN

Mission 177

Trigon's demonic force has sped up time. Be the first to perform 100 hits.

» Defeat Ares
» Don't let your opponent reach 50 hits
» Win without jumping

PASS THE POISON

Mission 178

Green Arrow has been infected with a toxic contagion, but that won't stop Raven! The last one hit will be infected with the virus.

» Defeat Green Arrow
» Throw 6 times
» Connect 10 Special Moves

LIFE STEAL

Mission 179

Trigon's evil power over Raven is overwhelming! Steal health by landing attacks against Hawkgirl.

» Win the battle
» Survive 8 seconds without being hit
» Win after getting First Hit

RETURN OF TRIGON

Mission 180

Trigon comes forth to confront Raven directly, father to daughter. Defeat Trigon to prove where your allegiances lie.

» Defeat Trigon
» Win with full second Health Bar
» Connect 10 Special Moves

AQUAMAN

ATLANTEAN WARRIOR

Mission 181

In order to protect Atlantis, Aquaman must hone his skills. Execute each move at the top of the screen.

» Prepare yourself to defend Atlantis
» Land a 10-hit combo
» Hit 15 times to the legs

ASSASSIN'S CONTRACT

Mission 182

Deathstroke is coming for Aquaman, so head him off by going to him! Stop Deathstroke and watch out for Penguin's umbrella attack on the closest fighter.

» Defeat Deathstroke
» Don't get put to sleep
» Get put to sleep 5 times

KING OF ATLANTIS

Mission 183

Deathstroke informed you that Bane is coming after you! Go to him, and complete the moves to the right of the screen before time runs out.

» Complete the listed moves
» Complete the list in order
» Win without blocking

FALLING LASERS

Mission 184

Cyborg has attempted to set a trap for Aquaman so he can take over Atlantis. Show him how slippery you are while avoiding the lasers.

» Defeat Cyborg
» Get hit by 10 lasers
» Hit Cyborg with 10 lasers

BACK ALLEY

Mission 185

Standing within Grundy's gas cloud causes Aquaman damage. Defeat Grundy as the gas cloud grows over time until the screen is covered.

» Defeat Grundy
» Use no Super Meter
» Never reach max Super Meter

BIG SMASH

Mission 186

Sinestro is attempting to build a construct that can destroy Atlantis itself. Over the course of the fight he will become more powerful.

» Defeat Sinestro
» Connect 3 Meter Burn Special Moves and win
» Win after Sinestro reaches his max difficulty

LOST TRIDENT

Mission 187

Doomsday has reached the Throne Room! When too much damage is taken, Aquaman will drop his trident.

» Defeat Doomsday
» Win with Heavy Attack
» Win with a Super Move

HOT SPOT

Mission 188

Black Adam is trying to get to Atlantis himself. Defeat him while avoiding exploding floor fires conjured by Raven.

» Win the battle
» Don't get hit by the explosions
» Use an explosion in a combo

JAWS OF LIFE

Mission 189

Press the correct corresponding buttons on screen to telepathically tell the incoming rabid shark not to eat you.

» Talk the shark out of eating you
» Win and let the shark get close
» Don't miss a button

OLYMPIAN CHAMPION

Mission 190

Ares has recruited a group of villains to aid him. Defeat them one at a time, then take out Ares.

» Defeat all villains
» Perform a 6-hit juggle combo
» Win with a Super Move

SOLOMON GRUNDY

BORN ON A MONDAY

Mission 191

Before Solomon Grundy sets out to find Hawkgirl he must first train with Batman. Execute each move at the top of the screen.

» Become aware of your skills
» Land a 10-hit combo
» Execute a combo greater than 30%

THROW DOWN

Mission 192

Perform all of Grundy's Character Power Multi-throws in order to get information on Hawkgirl.

» Defeat all villains
» Flawless Victory
» Win after getting First Hit

BRUTE STRENGTH

Mission 193

Bane has challenged you to a contest of strength. Be the first to perform 50 hits. An unknown force has sped up time.

» Defeat Bane
» Never reach max Super Meter
» Don't let your opponent reach 30 hits

HARD RAIN

Mission 194

Defeat Superman while hazardous rain falls from the sky. Green raindrops replenish health while red raindrops deplete health.

» Defeat Superman
» Use an interactive object
» Win without collecting any red raindrops

ZOMBIE HANDS

Mission 195

The Joker wants Hawkgirl to stay hidden. Collecting orbs increases your Super Meter. Only while The Joker is caught in Meter Burn Zombie Hands will Grundy cause damage.

» Defeat The Joker
» Collect 25 falling orbs
» Never reach max Super Meter

AVALANCHE

Mission 196

Bane interrupts Grundy's search for Hawkgirl by throwing obstacles in his path.

» Smash through the rocks
» Don't miss a rock
» Swing 75 times

LIGHTNING STORM

Mission 197

Black Adam has created a storm of lightning above Gotham. Defeat Black Adam while avoiding the lightning strikes.

» Defeat Black Adam
» Win with a lightning strike
» During a combo have a lightning strike hit

SWAMP GAS

Mission 198

A gas cloud will start to enlarge over time. Defeat your opponent before it covers the entire screen.

» Defeat Bane
» Never reach max Super Meter
» Land a 5-hit combo

TOXIC OVERLOAD

Mission 199

Another of Hawkgirl's captors blocks your way. Stand in the green light to regain health and receive a strength boost.

» Defeat Ares
» Use no Super Meter
» Win with 30 or more seconds remaining

FRIENDS FOREVER

Mission 200

Grundy has finally located Hawkgirl! Free her by defeating Lex.

» Defeat Lex
» Connect 3 Meter Burn Special Moves and win
» Never reach max Super Meter

KILLER FROST

ICE MIST

Mission 201

Escape the Fortress without tripping the security system. Killer Frost's Ice Mist will reveal the invisible lasers up close.

- » Get past the lasers
- » Win with 10 seconds or more remaining
- » Don't go backwards

FROSTBITE

Mission 202

In preparation to create a new Ice Age, Killer Frost needs to sharpen her skills. Execute each move at the top of the screen.

- » Hone your skills for a new Ice Age
- » Land a 4-hit juggle combo
- » Execute a combo greater than 30%

SCREW LOOSE

Mission 203

The Fortress is falling apart! Make it out before it crumbles. Be careful of your attacks or you might accelerate the damage.

- » Defeat Wonder Woman
- » Use no Super Meter
- » Win with a throw

LIFE DRAIN

Mission 204

Bats outside of Wayne Manor have infected you with vampiric poisoning! Each hit that lands will regain lost health during the fight.

- » Defeat Nightwing
- » Win after getting First Hit
- » Hit 10 times to the head

THE RIDDLER'S SURPRISE

Mission 205

Killer Frost searches Arkham for Mr. Freeze, her perfect sidekick. Defeat the guard while The Riddler drops surprises.

- » Defeat the guard
- » Pick up 10 Question Marks
- » Land an 4-hit juggle combo

A STRONG DEFENSE

Mission 206

Killer Frost needs Lex's technology to bring on the next ice age. When Luthor's shield activates damage will be reflected back at the attacker.

- » Defeat Lex
- » Connect 3 Meter Burn Special Moves and win
- » Win without ducking

HOT AND COLD

Mission 207

Killer Frost is using the Watch Tower to freeze Earth, but something is wrong! She will lose health from heat, but will heal in the cold.

- » Defeat Black Adam
- » Only use Heavy attacks
- » Execute a combo greater than 30%

MELTING POINT

Mission 208

The room is rapidly heating up and will damage Killer Frost. Activate the switch to vent the heat to prevent a meltdown.

- » Survive the heat
- » Take no heat damage
- » Win with a Super Move

FIRE AND ICE

Mission 209

Batman has upgraded his batarangs to stop Killer Frost. Defeat Batman while avoiding his heat batarangs.

- » Defeat Batman
- » Survive 8 seconds without being hit
- » Win with a throw

ICEBREAKER

Mission 210

The last fight caused so much damage that everything is crumbling down. Find the door, break it down to escape, and fulfill your icy destiny.

- » Escape Arkham
- » Win with 5 or less seconds remaining
- » Don't get hit

BLACK ADAM

MIGHTY HUMAN

Mission 211

Black Adam has returned from exile to test his skills. Execute each move at the top of the screen.

- » Hone your ancient skills
- » Land a 10-hit combo
- » Complete without missing a move

FLIP OF THE COIN

Mission 212

Send a message to Shazam by defeating Batman. Two-Face will also flip his coin to determine who he'll shoot next.

- » Defeat Batman
- » Connect 10 Special Moves
- » Win a Clash

DRY LIGHTNING

Mission 213

An unknown presence has created a storm of lightning above Gotham. Defeat Ares while avoiding the lightning strikes.

- » Defeat Ares
- » Win with a lightning strike
- » During a combo have a lightning strike hit

WHAT YOU GET

Mission 214

Lex is testing a new defense technology and sends a missile barrage at Black Adam. Five missile hits results in failure.

- » Avoid the objects
- » Don't get hit by a rocket
- » Win with one chance remaining

REFLECTION

Mission 215

Angered at Lex for a failed attempt on his life, Black Adam seeks revenge. When Luthor's shield activates damage will be reflected back at the attacker.

- » Defeat Lex
- » Throw 6 times
- » Survive 8 seconds without being hit

SPLAT

Mission 216

Use the correct button commands to zap down approaching meteors.

- » Save the earth from doom
- » Don't miss a rock
- » Allow 5 rocks to come close

DISCHARGE

Mission 217

LexCorp's hoverbots are able to harness your power when in range. Smash them to regain your power.

- » Defeat Bane
- » Connect 10 Special Moves
- » Execute a combo greater than 30%

RAZZLE DAZZLE

Mission 218

Move your energy shield to deflect Cyborg's bouncing rockets. First to miss 3 rockets loses.

- » Defeat Cyborg
- » Score the first point
- » Perfect score

SHAZAM

Mission 219

Black Adam is racing to be the first to say SHAZAM. Perform a combo with greater damage to speak each letter.

- » Defeat Shazam
- » Use an Interactive Object
- » Use no Super Meter

ICE BREAKER

Mission 220

Shazam has teamed up with Killer Frost to defeat his arch enemy. Defeat your foe in a final battle while avoiding the falling ice.

- » Win the battle
- » Win after getting hit by Super Mover
- » Win a Clash

WONDER WOMAN

AMAZONIAN TRAINING

Mission 221

Train with the Amazonian before attempting to take on Ares. Execute each move at the top of the screen.

- » Master your Amazonian might to face Ares.
- » Land an 8-hit combo
- » Execute a Combo greater than 40%

LIGHTS OUT

Mission 222

Each attack Raven lands will darken the screen. Each attack Wonder Woman lands will brighten the screen.

- » Defeat Raven
- » Stop the screen from becoming 60% dark
- » Win a Clash

METEOR SHOWER

Mission 223

Ares has conjured a meteor storm while Black Adam attacks. Defeat him while avoiding the flaming rock.

- » Defeat Black Adam
- » Win with a Super Move
- » max Super Meter

AN AMAZONIAN'S POWER

Mission 224

Wonder Woman was hurt in the last battle and is slowly losing health. Complete the list of moves in the tracker before time expires.

- » Complete the listed moves
- » Win with full second Health Bar
- » Complete the list in order

SISTERS

Mission 225

Wonder Woman aids in your fight for a short time. Wonder Woman may only be used once.

- » Defeat Doomsday
- » Win without using Wonder Woman
- » Win with a Super Move

PURIFIED RAIN

Mission 226

An energy storm has rolled in. Each raindrop collected fills your Super Meter.

- » Defeat Ares
- » Collect 25 raindrops
- » Hit 10 times to the head

CATCHING A THIEF

Mission 227

Grundy has stolen an Amazonian gemstone for Ares. Execute the correct sequence of commands in time to stop him from getting away!

- » Don't let Grundy get away
- » Win without missing any button inputs
- » Pull Grundy in after he is almost free

WHO'S THERE?

Mission 228

Ares is controlling Cyborg to put an end to the Amazonians. Defeat Cyborg while his cloaking device is active.

- » Defeat Cyborg
- » Survive 8 seconds without being hit
- » Execute a combo greater than 40%

INNER STRENGTH

Mission 229

Superman will help you train for the fight ahead.
Be the first to perform 100 hits.

- » Win the battle
- » Execute a combo greater than 20%
- » Don't let your opponent reach 50 hits

LAST STAND

Mission 230

Ares has taken a final stand against Wonder Woman. He has summoned Grundy, Bane, and Doomsday to his side! Defeat them all, including Ares.

- » Defeat Ares
- » Connect 10 Special Moves
- » Survive 8 seconds without being hit

ARES

THE GOD'S WAR

Mission 231

Time to seek out and punish the Justice League, starting with Green Arrow. Execute each move at the top of the screen.

- » Master your godly powers
- » Land a 4-hit juggle combo
- » Execute a combo greater than 30%

A ROCK AND A HARD PLACE

Mission 232

A group of Amazonians have launched a barrage of rocks at Ares. Slice incoming rocks.

- » Slice the rocks
- » Don't miss a rock
- » Swing 100 times

BATTLE OF THE TITANS

Mission 233

Superman must pay for his hand in banishing Ares to Hades. Defeat an enraged Superman.

- » Defeat Superman
- » Connect 10 Special Moves
- » Win without using Character Power

UNDERWATER WARFARE

Mission 234

Prove to Aquaman that even Earth's seas belong to you. Defeat Aquaman while underwater.

- » Defeat Aquaman
- » Win after getting First Hit
- » Land a 5 Hit Combo

RUST BUCKET

Mission 235

Ares' armor has rusted from his underwater battle with Aquaman. Tap any directional button to shake the rust off your armor.

- » Win the battle
- » Connect 3 Meter Burn Special Moves and win
- » Break free 5 times

CLOAK OF THE GODS

Mission 236

Ares desires to fool the Amazonians by sneaking into Themyscira. Stay invisible without getting hit until time runs out.

- » Fool the Amazonian and sneak into Themyscira
- » Throw 6 times
- » Land an 8 Hit Combo

SPEARS AWAY

Mission 237

Ares charges forward towards Themyscira, meeting a barrage of spears. Perform Ares' teleport technique to evade then defeat Hawkgirl.

- » Avoid the spears
- » Don't get hit by a spear
- » Win with a Super Move

RAIN AND POUR

Mission 238

Defeat The Flash while hazardous rain falls from the sky. Green raindrops replenish health while red raindrops deplete health.

- » Defeat The Flash
- » Use an interactive object
- » Land a Level Transition

LASSO TIED

Mission 239

Wonder Woman has entrapped Ares with her lasso.

- » Keep Wonder Woman from escaping
- » Win after getting First Hit
- » Never reach max Super Meter

REIGN SUPREME

Mission 240

The time has come to conquer Themyscira! Defeat its guards and their champion Wonder Woman.

- » Defeat Wonder Woman and the Amazonians
- » Win a Clash
- » Win with full second Health Bar

ARCHIVES

HIDDEN TREASURE

The Archives are your ticket to a huge amount of unlockable content, from a few new costumes to background music to new Battles and concept art. The first time you enter the Archives, though, they'll all be locked away, with nary a clue as to what lies beneath for many of them. Since most of the Archives' content can only be revealed by using Armory Keys and Access Cards, we thought we'd help you see where these goodies are so you can plan your path to unlocking everything. If you have a favorite music track, would like to view a specific bit of concept art, or want to know where some of the more difficult and rewarding Battles are, you've come to the right place.

EXTRAS

You'll find a bevy of additional Battles to unlock in the first group of 15 squares here, while the right six squares hide Hero Card Portrait Packs. The former is a great way to build XP if you're trying to level up, while the latter offer a brief, but interesting, peek at some of DC Comics' best artwork over the years. At the top of the list are items you can purchase multiple times: Match Boost tokens. These handy XP multipliers require you to have reached a specific level, but once you've crossed that threshold, the rewards are well worth the asking price.

MATCH BOOSTERS	COST	LEVEL REQUIRED	DURATION
2X	1 Access Card	5	5 Matches
3X	3 Access Cards	10	10 Matches
4X	5 Access Cards	25	25 Matches
5X	10 Access Cards	50	50 Matches

ITEM LOCATION	DESCRIPTION
A1	Battle: Injured
A2	Battle: Countdown
A3	Battle: Speed Run
A4	Battle: Help From Above
A5	Battle: Fully Charged
A6	Hero Card Pack #1
A7	Hero Card Pack #2
B1	Battle: Unstoppable!
B2	Battle: Combo Heaven
B3	Battle: Mirror Match
B4	Battle: Sidekick
B5	Battle: Impossible!
B6	Hero Card Pack #3
B7	Hero Card Pack #4
C1	Battle: Random Fighter
C2	Battle: Mystery
C3	Battle: Give and Take
C4	Battle: Full House
C5	Battle: The Max
C6	Hero Card Pack #5
C7	Hero Card Pack #6

INJUSTICE
GODS AMONG US

CHARACTERS

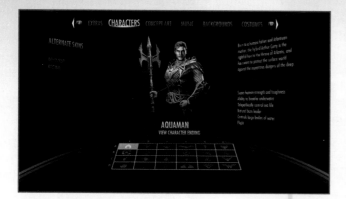

CONCEPT ART

The Characters section of the Archives is sort of a catch-all for anything related to the cast. From here, you can view any unlocked alternate costumes on 3D models, re-watch an ending movie that you earned by finishing a Battle with a particular character, and read up on the cast in their character bios. Interestingly, the alternates for each character also explain a little more about them, so if you've been curious about how some of the different takes on these DC icons have been represented, there's more than just a new texture thrown on top. While the parallel universe skins are all unlocked over in the Costumes section of the Archives, some characters have additional outfits and looks that are earned by completing certain requirements in the game. We'll explain those below.

There's often no better way to see into the creative process of a video game than to view the concept art that helped to birth the vision of the finished product. *Injustice* is particularly special because these aren't just brand-new creations, but carefully and respectfully realized versions of time-tested icons. From the character designs to the backgrounds they inhabit, the Concept Art section has a wealth of behind-the-scenes peeks into the game.

CHARACTER LOCATION	COSTUMES	HOW TO UNLOCK
A1	Aquaman, Regime	Default, Purchase in Archives
A2	Ares, Regime	Default, Purchase in Archives
A3	Bane, Regime	Default, Purchase in Archives
A4	Batman, Insurgency	Default, Purchase in Archives
A5	Black Adam, Regime	Default, Purchase in Archives
A6	Catwoman, Regime	Default, Purchase in Archives
B1	Cyborg, Regime	Default, Purchase in Archives
B2	Deathstroke, Insurgency	Default, Purchase in Archives
B3	Doomsday, Regime	Default, Purchase in Archives
B4	Flash, Regime, Elseworld, New 52	Default, Purchase in Archives, Earn 3 Stars in All S.T.A.R. Labs Challenges
B5	Green Arrow, Insurgency	Default, Purchase in Archives
B6	Green Lantern, Regime, Yellow Lantern	Default, Purchase in Archives, Win One Ranked Online Match
C1	Harley Quinn, Insurgency	Default, Purchase in Archives
C2	Hawkgirl, Regime	Default, Purchase in Archives
C3	Joker, Insurgency	Default, Purchase in Archives
C4	Killer Frost, Regime	Default, Purchase in Archives
C5	Lex Luthor, Insurgency, Kryptonite Suit	Default, Purchase in Archives, Earn 1 Star in All S.T.A.R. Labs Challenges
C6	Nightwing, Regime, New 52	Default, Purchase in Archives, Reach Level 30
D1	Raven, Regime	Default, Purchase in Archives
D2	Shazam, Regime, New 52	Default, Purchase in Archives, Complete All Shazam S.T.A.R. Labs Challenges
D3	Sinestro, Regime	Default, Purchase in Archives
D4	Solomon Grundy, Regime, Boss Grundy	Default, Purchase in Archives, Complete Classic Battle
D5	Superman, Regime, Godfall	Default, Purchase in Archives, Complete Story Mode
D6	Wonder Woman, Regime	Default, Purchase in Archives

CONCEPT LOCATION	DESCRIPTION
A1	Aquaman Concept
A2	Ares Concept
A3	Bane Concept
A4	Batman Concept
A5	Black Adam Concept
A6	Catwoman Concept
A7	Cyborg Concept
A8	Deathstroke Concept
B1	Doomsday Concept
B2	Flash Concept
B3	Green Arrow Concept
B4	Green Lantern Concept
B5	Harley Quinn Concept
B6	Hawkgirl Concept
B7	Joker Concept
B8	Killer Frost Concept
C1	Lex Luthor Concept
C2	Nightwing Concept
C3	Raven Concept
C4	Sinestro Concept
C5	Shazam Concept
C6	Solomon Grundy Concept
C7	Superman Concept
C8	Wonder Woman Concept
D1	Arkham Asylum Concept
D2	Atlantis Concept
D3	Batcave Concept
D4	Ferris Aircraft Concept
D5	Fortress of Solitude Concept
D6	Gotham City Concept
D7	Insurgency Concept
E1	Hall of Justice Concept
E2	Metropolis Concept
E3	Stryker's Island Concept
E4	Themyscira Concept
E5	Watchtower Concept
E6	Wayne Manor Concept

MUSIC

As responsible for setting the mood and tone of a battle as the visuals, a game's soundtrack can be bombastic, melancholy, upbeat, or subdued, and the *Injustice* soundtrack covers all those bases and more. If you'd like to listen to the game's tracks unfettered by the sound of faces being pummeled and dumpsters being thrown around, this is the place to come.

TRACK LOCATION	DESCRIPTION
A1	Arkham Asylum - Cell Block
A2	Arkham Asylum - Mess Hall
A3	Atlantis - Throne Room
A4	Atlantis - Throne Room Alternate
A5	Batcave - Crime Lab
A6	Batcave - Lagoon
A7	Ferris Aircraft - Hangar
B1	Fortress of Solitude - Laboratory
B2	Fortress of Solitude - Menagerie
B3	Gotham City - Rooftop
B4	Gotham City - Alley
B5	Hall of Justice - Plaza
B6	Hall of Justice - Great Hall
B7	Insurgency - Command Center
C1	Insurgency - Luthor's Lab
C2	Metropolis - Street
C3	Metropolis - Rooftop
C4	Metropolis - Museum
C5	Stryker's Island - Cell Block
C6	Stryker's Island - Yard
C7	Themyscira - Temple
D1	Themyscira - Port
D2	Watchtower - Bridge
D3	Watchtower - Reactor
D4	Wayne Manor - Entrance
D5	Wayne Manor - Great Room

BACKGROUNDS

Teeming with detail and highly dynamic, the various stages where you'll do battle are more than just a pretty backdrop for all those punches and kicks. They respond in real time to the impacts around them. Objects can be wrenched from their resting place or thrown or lobbed or slammed, and all the while in the background, in response to the destruction wrought by the ongoing fight, the stage continually falls apart. If you'd like to take a peek at some of this destruction, you need only visit this section of the Archives.

BACKGROUND LOCATION	DESCRIPTION
A1	Arkham Asylum - Cell Block
A2	Arkham Asylum - Mess Hall
A3	Joker's Asylum - Cell Block
A4	Joker's Asylum - Mess Hall
A5	Atlantis - Throne Room
A6	Batcave - Crime Lab
B1	Batcave - Lagoon
B2	Ferris Aircraft - Hangar
B3	Fortress of Solitude - Laboratory
B4	Fortress of Solitude - Menagerie
B5	Gotham City - Rooftop
B6	Gotham City - Alley
C1	Hall of Justice - Plaza
C2	Hall of Justice - Great Hall
C3	Insurgency - Command Center
C4	Insurgency - Luthor's Lab
C5	Metropolis - Street
C6	Metropolis - Rooftop
D1	Metropolis - Museum
D2	Stryker's Island - Cell Block
D3	Stryker's Island - Yard
D4	Themyscira - Temple
D5	Themyscira - Port
D6	Watchtower - Bridge
E1	Watchtower - Reactor
E2	Wayne Manor - Entrance
E3	Wayne Manor - Great Room
E4	Wayne Manor Night - Entrance
E5	Wayne Manor Night - Great Room

COSTUMES

Your favorite heroes and villains aren't just restricted to a single set of duds. If you'd rather fight as the alternate universe version of most of them, those costumes can be bought and used both online and off as much as you want. Just plunk down the Armory Keys (as opposed to the Access Cards everything else is unlocked with), and these costumes are yours.

COSTUME LOCATION	DESCRIPTION
A1	Aquaman Regime
A2	Ares Regime
A3	Bane Regime
A4	Batman Insurgency
A5	Black Adam Regime
A6	Catwoman Regime
B1	Cyborg Regime
B2	Deathstroke Insurgency
B3	Doomsday Regime
B4	Flash Regime
B5	Green Arrow Insurgency
B6	Green Lantern Regime
C1	Harley Quinn Insurgency
C2	Hawkgirl Regime
C3	Joker Insurgency
C4	Killer Frost Regime
C5	Lex Luthor Insurgency
C6	Nightwing Regime
D1	Raven Regime
D2	Shazam Regime
D3	Sinestro Regime
D4	Solomon Grundy Regime
D5	Superman Regime
D6	Wonder Woman Regime

INJUSTICE
GODS AMONG US
COLLECTOR'S EDITION

AQUAMAN
Alternate Earth V
Costume

AQUAMAN
Prime Costume

ARES
Alternate Earth V
Costume

ARES
Prime Costume

INJUSTICE
GODS AMONG US

BANE
Prime Costume

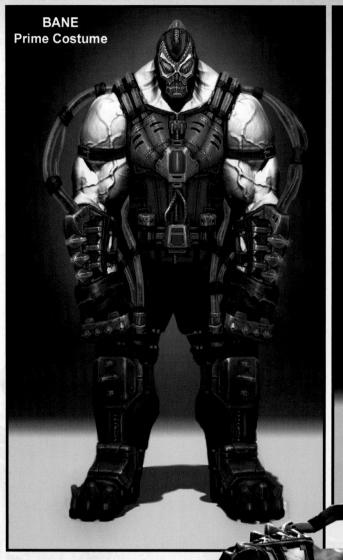

BANE
Alternate Earth V
Costume

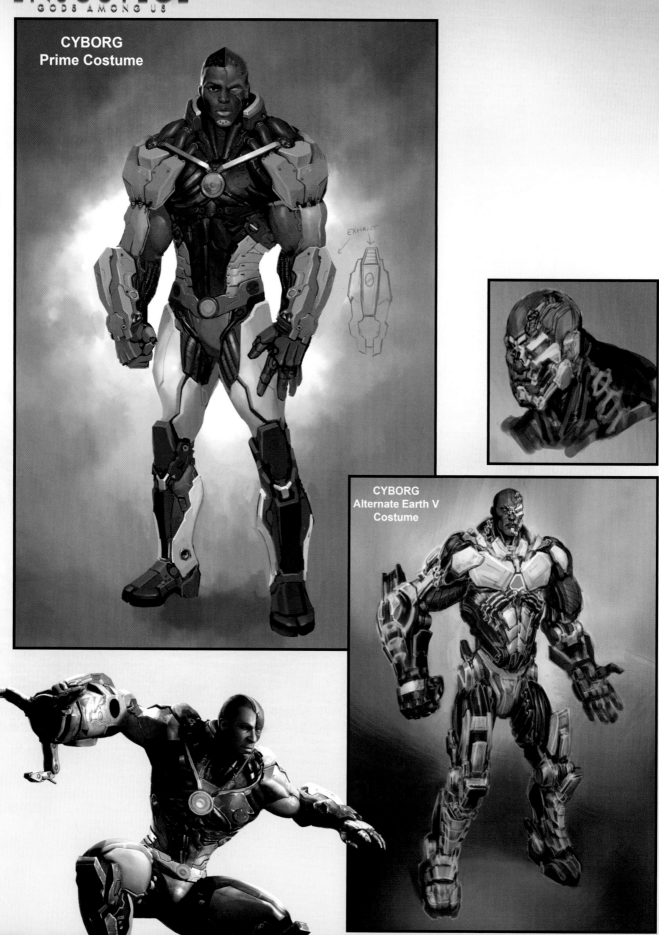

INJUSTICE
GODS AMONG US

CYBORG
Prime Costume

EXHAUST

CYBORG
Alternate Earth V
Costume

DEATHSTROKE
Prime Costume

DEATHSTROKE
Alternate Earth V
Costume

DOOMSDAY
Alternate Earth V
Costume

DOOMSDAY
Prime Costume

FLASH
Alternate Earth V
costume

FLASH
Prime Costume

GREEN ARROW
Prime Costume

GREEN ARROW
Alternate Earth V
Costume

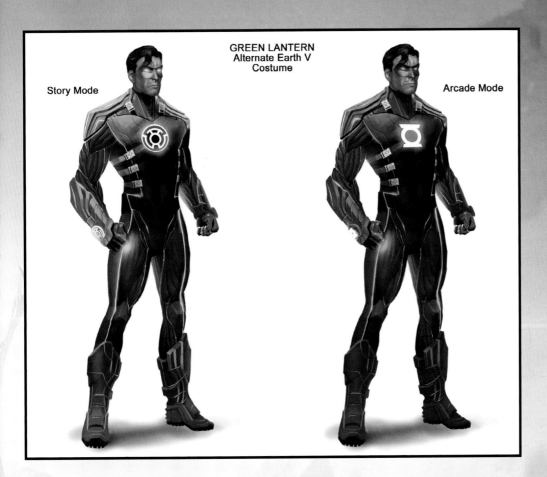

GREEN LANTERN
Alternate Earth V
Costume

Story Mode

Arcade Mode

GREEN LANTERN
Prime Costume

INJUSTICE
GODS AMONG US

HARLEY QUINN
Prime Costume
REVISED

HAWKGIRL
Alternate Earth V
Costume

HAWKGIRL
Prime Costume

INJUSTICE
GODS AMONG US

THE JOKER
Alternate Earth V
Costume

THE JOKER
Prime Costume

KILLER FROST
Prime Costume

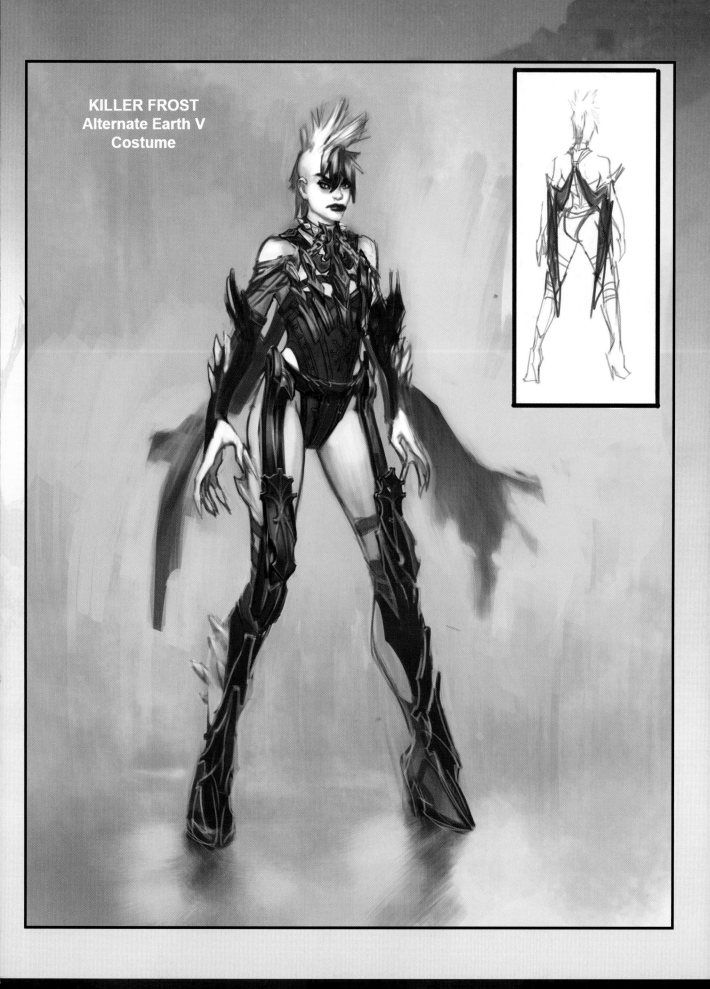

KILLER FROST
Alternate Earth V
Costume

NIGHTWING
Prime Costume
Revised

This logo (w/beak always facing left) will be used on the costume

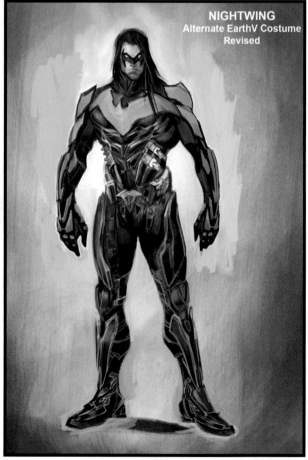

NIGHTWING
Alternate EarthV Costume
Revised

SHAZAM
Prime Costume

SHAZAM
Alternate Earth V
Costume - REVISED

SINESTRO
Alternate Earth V
Costume

SINESTRO
Prime Costume

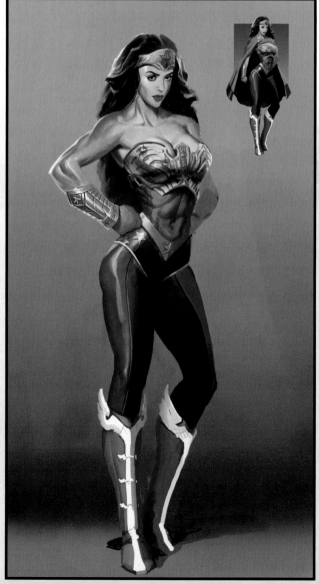

ENVIRONMENTAL STAGE CONCEPTS

ARKHAM ASYLUM

ATLANTIS

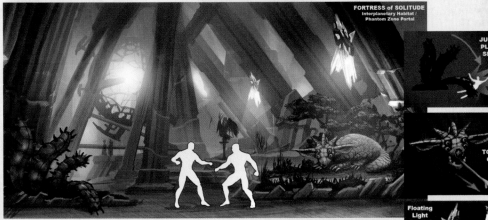

FORTRESS of SOLITUDE
Interplanetary Habitat /
Phantom Zone Portal

JUSTIN
PLANT
SLUG

TONGUE
GRAB

Floating
Light
Crystal

INJUSTICE
GODS AMONG US

WAYNE MANOR

Interactive Objects

INSURGENCY

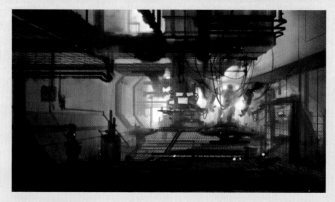

THE WATCHTOWER

INJUSTICE
GODS AMONG US

THEMYSCIRA

HALL OF JUSTICE

EXCLUSIVE COMIC BOOK CHAPTER
FROM THE CREATORS OF MORTAL KOMBAT
INJUSTICE
GODS AMONG US
DC COMICS™
DCCOMICS.COM
™ and © 2013 DC Comics. All Rights Reserved.

SHE IS A WARRIOR BORN.

SHE WAS RAISED AND TRAINED FOR THE FIELD OF BATTLE.

SHE LEFT HER ISLAND ON A MISSION OF PEACE.

MERCY

Writer: TOM TAYLOR
Art and Color by: DAVID YARDIN
Letters by: WES ABBOTT
Wonder Woman Cover Art by:
JHEREMY RAAPACK
with ANDREW ELDER
Assistant Editor: SARAH GAYDOS
Senior Editor: JIM CHADWICK

SHE DOES NOT LOOK PEACEFUL.

I ADMIRE SO MUCH IN THE PRINCESS.

HER ABILITY. HER **POWER.**

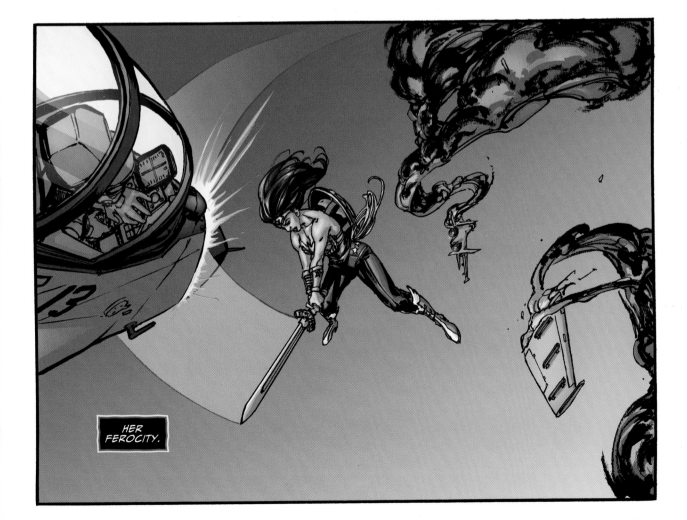

HER FEROCITY.

SUPERMAN, I HAD TO MAKE AN EXAMPLE OF A FEW, BUT THE REST OF THE FIGHTERS ARE RETREATING BACK OVER THE BORDER INTO QURAC.

UNDERSTOOD. I'LL PROTECT THE CITY UNTIL I'M SURE THE SHELLING HAS STOPPED, AND THEN I'LL JOIN YOU.

UNF!

DIANA!

IT'S ALL RIGHT. IT'S NOTHING.

JUST A FEW TANKS.

DESPITE HER DESIRE FOR PEACE, SHE REVELS IN WAR.

KRAOOOOOOOM

I KNOW--

--I KNOW WAR.

DID YOU JUST HEADBUTT A TANK?

ARES!

YOU LEFT THEMYSCIRA AS AN AMBASSADOR FOR PEACE AND NOW YOU *HEADBUTT* TANKS?

SOMETIMES PEACE NEEDS TO BE FOUGHT FOR.

OF COURSE.

THOOOM

WHAT DO YOU WANT HERE, GOD OF WAR?

FOR NOW, I JUST WANT TO WATCH YOU WORK.

I HAVE SEEN EVERY WAR THAT HAS TAKEN PLACE ON THIS PLANET BUT WATCHING SUPERHUMANS WAR WITH HUMAN ARMIES... WELL, THAT'S SOMETHING TRULY SPECIAL.

I AM NOT AT *WAR* WITH QURAC.

QURAC HAS IGNORED THE REQUEST FOR A CEASEFIRE. IT CONTINUES TO BOMBARD NEIGHBORING JUSDAL DESPITE THE COUNTRY BEING LARGELY DEFENSELESS.

WE ARE SIMPLY STOPPING THIS BOMBARDMENT.

GRRSCH

ONCE THE SHELLING HAS STOPPED, THE CONFLICT WILL END AS ALL CONFLICTS DO-- WITH A CONVERSATION.

YOU FIGHT BESIDE THE SUPERMAN.

YOU BELIEVE IN HIS CAUSE?

I DO.

DROP YOUR WEAPONS.

TURN.

AND RUN AWAY.

YOU ARE TOO MERCIFUL.

WILL YOU TAKE HER PLACE?

WILL YOU LIE IN HIS BED?

LOIS WAS AN INCREDIBLE WOMAN.

THAT DOES NOT ANSWER MY QUESTION.

I WILL LET HIM GRIEVE.

AND THEN?

HE IS THE GREATEST MAN I HAVE EVER KNOWN.

I WILL BE WHATEVER HE NEEDS ME TO BE.

YOU FEAR THIS UNION, DON'T YOU?

WHY ELSE WOULD YOU BE TAKING SUCH AN INTEREST?

YOU'RE RIGHT TO FEAR. YOU FEAR SUPERMAN BECAUSE YOU BELIEVE HE COULD SUCCEED. WHAT BECOMES OF THE GOD OF WAR IN A WORLD WITHOUT CONFLICT?

MAYBE YOU COULD BECOME THE GOD OF SOMETHING ELSE? SOMETHING LESS VIOLENT.

SAY IT WITH ME. 'I AM THE DREADED ARES, GOD OF PONIES!'

BE MINDFUL HOW YOU SPEAK TO ME.

YOU KNOW I PREFER WORDS OVER VIOLENCE, SO I WILL ASK YOU TO TAKE YOUR HAND OFF ME IF YOU WANT TO KEEP IT.

IF YOU SEEK THIS UNION, IT WOULD BE SAFER TO KILL YOU NOW.

YOU CAN'T THREATEN ME, DAUGHTER OF THEMYSCIRA. LOOK AROUND YOU. LOOK AT THIS DESTRUCTION. I AM FUELED BY THIS.

HNGH.

IT WILL BE EASY. ZEUS HIMSELF COULD NOT STAND AGAINST ME HERE. I AM AS POWERFUL IN THIS PLACE AS I HAVE EVER--

YOU DARE!

THOOM

HOW...?

NARGH!

ON THE DAY YOUR CHILDREN ARE BORN, AMAZON, I WILL BE THERE TO STOP THEM TAKING THEIR FIRST BREATH.

YOU CAN HAVE YOUR HAND BACK WHEN YOU CAN BE TRUSTED WITH IT.

YOU ACCUSED ME OF BEING TOO MERCIFUL, ARES.

ARGHH!!

DIANA!

IT'S OKAY, SUPERMAN. GODS DON'T DIE SO EASILY.

THEY DON'T DIE. BUT THEY DO FADE.

COME. LET US SPEAK TO THE QURAC GOVERNMENT ABOUT A LASTING PEACE. LET US ENSURE THIS WAR GOD FADES.

DO GODS FEEL PAIN?

NOT AS MORTALS DO. BUT YOU PIN A GOD TO THE GROUND BY DRIVING A SWORD THROUGH HIS SPINAL COLUMN AND I IMAGINE IT STINGS A BIT.

THIS. THIS IS WHY I FEAR THE AMAZON AND THE SUPERMAN TOGETHER.

HE COULD NOT DO THIS ALONE. BUT THE PRINCESS DOES NOT HAVE HIS RESTRAINT.

SHE WILL DO WHAT HE CAN'T.

AND IF SHE TAKES AWAY HIS RESTRAINT...

THE WORLD COULD NOT FIGHT AGAINST THAT.

AND IN A WORLD THAT CANNOT FIGHT, WHAT WOULD I BECOME?

PONIES...

END

INJUSTICE
GODS AMONG US

PRIMA Official Game Guide

Written by:
Sam Bishop, Carl White, Emmanuel Brito, and Bill Menoutis

Prima Games
An Imprint of Random House, Inc.
3000 Lava Ridge Court, Suite 100
Roseville, CA 95661
www.primagames.com

Product Manager:	Jesse Anderson
Design & Layout:	Marc W. Riegel
Cover Design:	Melissa Jeneé Smith
Copyedit:	Julia Mascardo

Australian warranty statement:

This product comes with guarantees that cannot be excluded under the Australian Consumer Law. You are entitled to a replacement or refund for a major failure and for compensation for any other reasonably foreseeable loss or damage. You are also entitled to have the goods repaired or replaced if the goods fail to be of acceptable quality and the failure does not amount to a major failure.

This product comes with a 1 year warranty from date of purchase. Defects in the product must have appeared within 1 year, from date of purchase in order to claim the warranty.

All warranty claims must be facilitated back through the retailer of purchase, in accordance with the retailer's returns policies and procedures. Any cost incurred, as a result of returning the product to the retailer of purchase are the full responsibility of the consumer.

AU wholesale distributor: Bluemouth Interactive Pty Ltd, Suite 1502, 9 Yarra Street, South Yarra, Victoria, 3141. (+613 9646 4011)

Email: support@bluemouth.com.au

This project would have not been possible without the support of Ed Lin, Craig Mitchell, Raymond So, Irene Chan, Sharis Gharibi, Kehau Rodenhurst, Ryan Brennan, Scott Warr, Victoria Setian, Peter Wyse, Ed Boon, Steve Beran, Shaun Himmerick, Adam Urbano, John Edwards, Paulo Garcia, Warren Wilkes, Hector Sanchez, Brian Goodman, Pat McCallum, Thomas Zellers, Kristen Chin, Melanie Swartz, Erin Piepergerdes, Ben Elliott, JJ Zingale, and Josh Anderson.

THE STRATEGISTS

EMMANUEL BRITO
Emmanuel "CDjr" Brito is a competitive fighting game player from The Bronx, New York. He started playing video games at the age of 7, developing a fondness for not just fighters, but shooters, RPGs, and action games. He has won many *Mortal Kombat 9* tournaments, both majors and locals, but his best performances were at MLG Columbus where he took First Place and EVO 2012 where he finished Second. Outside of gaming he likes to hang out with friends, go to the gym, play basketball, and learn about new things every day. Emmanuel was responsible for the **Black Adam, Cyborg, The Flash, Green Arrow, Harley Quinn, Hawkgirl, Killer Frost,** and **Raven** strategies. He'd like to give shout outs to his brothers Maximo Figuereo(maxter) and Robin Figuereo(Crazy Dominican), to his friends James Fink(Jamesmk), Michael Mendoza(Yipes), and Kevin Landon(Dieminion) and a big shout out to all his fans, friends and supporters.

BILL MENOUTIS
Bill "Tom Brady" Menoutis has been playing fighting games since the dawn of the competitive fighting game era, starting with *Street Fighter II: World Warrior* in 1991. He has been a top player in several fighting games over the years, most notably in titles such as *Killer Instinct 1 & 2, Tekken 4*, the *Dead or Alive* series, *Mortal Kombat 4, Mortal Kombat: Deadly Alliance, Mortal Kombat vs DC Universe*, and more. Most recently, he won the first *Mortal Kombat 9* tournament held at Power Up 2011, and has placed top in many of the biggest *Mortal Kombat 9* tournaments held to date. Bill handled the **Aquaman, Green Lantern, The Joker, Shazam, Sinestro, Solomon Grundy, Superman,** and **Wonder Woman** strategies. The biggest key to his success has been his support. He would like to thank his family first and foremost, Jop, Eddy Pistons, REO, NetherRealm Studios, MLG, and all his fans along with the MK Community...without them, he would not be here today.

CARL WHITE
Carl "Perfect Legend" White is an accomplished, self-taught player hailing from Toledo, Ohio. Since the age of 3, Carl grew a passion for fighting games starting with *Street Fighter 2* and *Mortal Kombat*. In the year 2005 at the age of 17, his road to competitive play began. That following year, Carl became the first ever World Champion of *Dead or Alive 4*, winning the title in 2006, and currently is the only World Champion of *Mortal Kombat 9*, winning back-to-back World Championships in 2011-12. Known for his high-speed, adaptive, risky, and calculated style of play, Carl chooses aggressive characters that excel at picking the opponent apart in quick fashion. He was responsible for the **Ares, Bane, Batman, Catwoman, Deathstroke, Doomsday, Lex Luthor,** and **Nightwing** strategies. Carl would like to give a shout out to all of his family for believing in him in anything he does. He would also like to shout out to Prima and Major League Gaming for the opportunity, and a big thank you to his fans and supporters.

978-0-804-16116-9 Standard Edition
978-0-804-16123-7 Collector's Edition
Printed in the United States of America.